Praise for *Where the Music Had to Go*

'Exquisitely researched, thrilling and moving. Windolf is extraordinarily attentive to the details of the Beatles' and Dylan's parallel evolutionary tracks, and he is an impressive harvester of their interactions. I felt as if I were listening for the first time to a riveting story, carefully told in cinematic details, about the most interesting people on the planet'
Rosanne Cash, author of *Composed: A Memoir*

'The friendship between Bob Dylan and the Beatles and how they influenced, competed with, and revered each other is meticulously, lovingly told in this delightful history of a magical world in an historic era'
Jann Wenner, co-founder of Rolling Stone

'Dylan's and the Beatles' relations were more than comradely or competitive. They became a call-and-response—a tit for tat—that was an exploration of the consciousness of their generation. Jim Windolf explores this dynamic brilliantly in *Where the Music Had to Go*. It's a book for serious fans and students of the '60s and '70s that's not to be missed'
Toby Thompson, author of *Positively Main Street: Bob Dylan's Minnesota*

'One-part delightful nostalgia, two parts smart analysis and perceptive connections, this book expertly re-explains those magical long-ago years we loved so much'   Lee Child, author of the *Jack Reacher* novels

'Jim Windolf is an American original, and *Where the Music Had to Go* is a great gift – a brilliantly fresh take on Dylan and the Beatles that illuminates connections and crosscurrents between the five immortals that we've never thought of before. Reading this book reignites the giddy thrill that these pop-culture visionaries gave us and each other'
James Kaplan, author of *Frank: The Voice*

'I've always known how important the Beatles and Dylan were to me, but I had no idea how important – even crucial – they were to each other. With backstage tales and critical insights, Jim Windolf connects the dots to paint an astonishing dual portrait'
Susan Morrison, author of *Lorne: The Man Who Invented SNL*

'*Where the Music Had to Go* isn't just a single book. It's at least five: a biography of these great artists, a history of modern music, a meditation on creative influence, a deep dive into the role of politics in art and an analysis of media and fame. The good news: each is wonderful on its own, and together they're absolutely stellar – a joy to read'

A. J. Jacobs, author of *The Know-It-All*

'Windolf has crafted a compelling and knowledgeable narrative chronicling the magnetic push and pull between these two giants of modern music and culture. It's never less than absorbing, even for diehard obsessives like myself'

John Leventhal

'A revelation. The complementary, at times rivalrous, and always influential relationship between Bob Dylan and the Beatles fuelled a musical revolution that transformed popular music into art. With nuance and eagle-eyed research, Jim Windolf offers an unprecedented look at the mechanics of a musical fusion that we're only just beginning to understand. With wisdom and insight, he brings Dylan and the Beatles' story vividly to life'

Kenneth Womack, author of
Living the Beatles Legend: The Untold Story of Mal Evans

'Drawing on a wide range of contemporaneous sources, Jim Windolf's scrupulous account sheds new light on the often rivalrous yet consistently rewarding relationship between the paradigmatic singer-songwriter and paradigmatic rock group. Though the canon of rock biographies contains a multitude of books on these world-changing artists, *Where the Music Had to Go* is the first to examine the full breadth of their interplay and influence on one another'

Jonathan Gould,
author of *Can't Buy Me Love: The Beatles, Britain, and America*

'Tracing the parallel histories of Dylan and the Beatles, Jim Windolf finds creative electricity running between them, an exchange of ideas and influence and mutual admiration. As *Where the Music Had to Go* insightfully shows, that artistic symbiosis – hidden in the details for decades – made a huge impact on popular music in the twentieth century. Elegantly written, magnificently researched, the book is a fascinating and delightful trip, full of unexpected revelations'

Joe Hagan author of *Sticky Fingers:
The Life and Times of Jann Wenner and Rolling Stone Magazine*

WHERE THE MUSIC HAD TO GO

How Bob Dylan and the Beatles Changed Each Other – and the World

Jim Windolf

First published in the United States of America in 2026 by Scribner,
an imprint of Simon & Shuster, LLC
First published in Great Britain in 2026 by White Rabbit,
an imprint of The Orion Publishing Group Ltd
Carmelite House, 50 Victoria Embankment
London EC4Y 0DZ

An Hachette UK Company

The authorised representative in the EEA is Hachette Ireland,
8 Castlecourt Centre, Dublin 15, D15 XTP3, Ireland (email: info@hbgi.ie)

1 3 5 7 9 10 8 6 4 2

Copyright © James Windolf 2026

The moral right of James Windolf to be identified as
the author of this work has been asserted in accordance
with the Copyright, Designs and Patents Act of 1988.

All rights reserved. No part of this publication may be
reproduced, stored in a retrieval system, or transmitted
in any form or by any means, electronic, mechanical,
photocopying, recording, or otherwise, without the
prior permission of both the copyright owner and the
above publisher of this book.

A CIP catalogue record for this book is
available from the British Library.

ISBN (Hardback) 978 1 3996 2784 9
ISBN (Export Trade Paperback) 978 1 3996 2785 6
ISBN (Ebook) 978 1 3996 2787 0
ISBN (Audio) 978 1 3996 3419 9

Printed and bound in Great Britain by Clays Ltd, Elcograf S.p.A.

www.whiterabbitbooks.co.uk
www.orionbooks.co.uk

Dedicated with love to Susan Rushing

In the earliest days we were pretending to be Buddy Holly. Then we were writing like Motown. Then we were writing like Bob Dylan.

—Paul McCartney, 2022

I knew they were pointing the direction of where music had to go. In my head, the Beatles were it.

—Bob Dylan, 1970

■ SIDE ONE

    Introduction xi
1. Pilgrimage 1
2. Disciples of Little Richard 8
3. The Names 19
4. Picture Imperfect 35
5. It'll Never Happen 47
6. Ego Equals 63
7. Beatlemania Here 81
8. Hide Your Love 94
9. The Savoy 111
10. How Does It Feel 130

■ SIDE TWO

11. Number One 151
12. Northern Songs 163
13. Costars 183
14. Retreat 198
15. Penny Lane and Bourbon Street 214
16. Everybody's Song 229
17. Beatles & Co. 251
18. Serve Yourself 272
19. Rolling On 294

    Coda: McCartney on Dylan 311

    Acknowledgments 319
    Notes 323
    Index 351

SIDE ONE

■ Introduction

"What about Bob Dylan?"

That was the question put to Paul McCartney shortly after the Beatles had first come to America in February 1964. The man holding the microphone was Murray Kaufman, a popular New York disc jockey who went by the name Murray the K. He was a resourceful, persistent man who had managed to break through the crowds and police barricades outside the Plaza Hotel and install himself in the Beatles' inner sanctum on the twelfth floor.

"Robert Dylan," Paul replied. "Fantastic. Very good indeed."

He wasn't just being polite. Shortly before their arrival in New York, during a lengthy residency in Paris, McCartney, John Lennon, George Harrison, and Ringo Starr had listened to Dylan's first two albums again and again in their suites at the George V hotel. "Paul got them off whoever they belonged to, and for the rest of our three weeks in Paris we didn't stop playing them," John would later recall. "We all went potty on Dylan."

Murray the K's question to McCartney suggested that, even then, in the early days of Beatlemania, Bob Dylan and the Beatles went together in the public mind, though Dylan had yet to go electric and was regarded as a serious folk music poet, and the Beatles were best known, in the United States, at least, for their unusual hair, their excitable fans, and their energetic hit, "I Want to Hold Your Hand."

After landing a few more exclusive interviews with John, Paul, George, and Ringo, Murray the K started referring to himself on the air as the fifth Beatle. Nobody quite believed that a forty-one-year-old New York deejay in a porkpie hat had much to do with the rise of a group from the north of England, but the notion that there might be some unsung or overlooked Beatle would prove to have real staying power.

For second-generation fans like me, the idea served as a kind of prompt, giving us the premise we needed to trot out the bits of knowledge we had gathered and to put our affection into words. Was George Martin, the producer who was integral to their sound, the fifth Beatle? Or was it their manager, Brian Epstein, who had brought them from Liverpool to the wider world? When I was a kid, that was the kind of thing I talked about with my best friend in the hours we spent by the stereo in the living room of his house, listening to his big sister's worn copies of *Sgt. Pepper's Lonely Hearts Club Band* and the compilation albums *1962–1966* and *1967–1970*.

Dylan didn't have the same presence in our lives, but we knew he was a big deal. For one thing, there he was, on the cover of *Sgt. Pepper*, standing among the personages held in high regard by the Beatles. One day my friend and I went into his sister's quiet bedroom and found something by Dylan in her record stack. It was *Before the Flood*, a live album he had made during the tour he had undertaken with the Band in 1974, after some years away from the concert stage. We gave it a try, only to find it harsh and forbidding, as if it wasn't meant for us. But not long after that, when I was almost twelve, I went to Dylan on my own. What did it for me was "Hurricane," a single he put out toward the end of 1975. It wasn't a big hit, but it was played on the radio now and then—and when I heard it, I was entranced.

At more than eight minutes, it was an epic that brought attention to racist law enforcement practices through Dylan's recounting of the arrest, imprisonment, and trial of the boxer Rubin "Hurricane"

Carter. I was pulled in by the story, which took place in Paterson, New Jersey, a city close to the tranquil suburb where I lived, but I was also drawn to the overall sound. Dylan's supple voice was front and center, floating above a crisp acoustic guitar locked in with a prominent bass. A melancholy violin weaved in an out, as if commenting on the action. Drums and congas came to the fore whenever the band seemed in danger of breaking down.

During the brief appearance of "Hurricane" on the pop charts, I was a regular listener of the syndicated radio show *American Top 40*. I took nerdish pleasure in following the fortunes of hits as they made their way up and down the rankings, and I tended to favor songs that owed much of their appeal to lush arrangements or effects made possible by recording studio technology, a varied parade that included David Bowie's "Fame," Steely Dan's "Rikki Don't Lose That Number," and Barry White's "Can't Get Enough of Your Love, Babe." In this context, "Hurricane" stood out—rough, ramshackle, raw.

After it had left the charts, I fell for something at the other end of the musical spectrum, the glossy, disco-inflected "Silly Love Songs," which would be the biggest selling single of 1976 in the U.S. It was written, arranged, produced, and sung by Paul McCartney (and credited to his band, Wings), with an emphasis on his rubbery bass line and the distinctive vocal harmonies that were so much a part of his post-Beatles work. Its lyrics were as far removed from the world of "Hurricane" as its slick sound, offering a sly defense of the composer's unwavering belief in the love song as a vehicle for serious self-expression. Later that year, I had a new favorite: George Harrison's "Crackerbox Palace," a dreamlike evocation of childhood experience that seemed somehow to match up with my own.

The first albums I bought included Dylan's *Hard Rain*, McCartney's *Band on the Run*, Harrison's *Thirty-Three & ⅓*, and the Lennon compilation *Shaved Fish*, which scrambled my brain as it whipsawed from the gentle utopianism of "Imagine" to the horrors of "Cold Turkey." The years went by, and I did not put those records away. And after

I had been working as a journalist for a while, I thought I saw hints of a story—the long and eventful relationship between Dylan and the Beatles—scattered piecemeal across biographies, out-of-print memoirs, and long-buried articles.

Dylan met the Beatles in the summer of 1964 at the Delmonico Hotel in New York. For many years after that, John, Paul, George, Ringo, and Bob saw one another in various combinations. They got drunk and high together and shared meals at one another's homes. They played advance pressings of their albums for one another, and on those occasions the sense of rivalry bubbling beneath the surface was apparent to others in the room: the Beatles were lukewarm in their initial reaction to Dylan's *Highway 61 Revisited*, a landmark of twentieth-century music, and Bob was at first dismissive of the Beatles' groundbreaking sonic experiments for the album *Revolver*. "Oh, I get it," he told Paul. "You don't want to be cute anymore."

Along with the competitiveness and cutting remarks, there was admiration and respect. At the height of Beatlemania, Bob stood in the wings of the Paramount Theatre in Manhattan to watch the group make its way through twelve songs as waves of screams washed over the stage. Eight months later, the four Beatles sat in a private box at the Royal Albert Hall in London as Dylan, solo in the spotlight, held the audience spellbound. A year after that, when Dylan was getting booed and heckled in venues across America and Europe after having shape-shifted from a man-of-the-people folk singer to a Byronic rock god backed by a four-piece band, the Beatles cheered him once again at the same theater.

In the summer of 1969, as the Beatles were nearing the end, John, George, and Ringo joined the festival crowd at the Isle of Wight to see a milder Dylan give his first full concert in more than three years. Over the following decades, Harrison and Starr attended a great number of Dylan shows, sometimes joining him for a song or two and visiting with him backstage. McCartney has seen Dylan in concert in recent years and described at length his influence on the Beatles in his 2021 book, *The Lyrics*.

They seemed never far from one another's thoughts. During the "Get Back" sessions of January 1969, the Beatles ran through parts of fifteen Dylan songs; and Bob has played Beatles songs—in the studio, during rehearsals, or on the concert stage—in the 1970s, 1980s, 1990s, 2000s, and 2010s. "They took all the music we'd been listening to and showed it to us again," Dylan said in a 1976 interview. "They have everything in their music from Little Richard to the Everly Brothers. They helped give America's pride back to it. There ought to be statues to the Beatles." In the only interview he gave in 2022, Dylan singled out for special praise two songs written chiefly by Paul, "Eleanor Rigby" and "Paperback Writer," and called Ringo "a great musician." "If I'd had him as a drummer, I would've been the Beatles, too," he said. "Maybe."

Dylan wrote songs with Harrison in 1968 and again twenty years later as part of the Traveling Wilburys, the shambling supergroup that put him back in the pop charts after some wayward years. In 1990, during a show in Edmonton, Alberta, Dylan offered a one-off performance of the Beatles' "Nowhere Man," a song written by Lennon under Dylan's influence. In 2004, midway through a show in Boone, North Carolina, for a reason known perhaps only to himself, Dylan sang new lyrics to "Tears of Rage," a song he had cowritten with Richard Manuel of the Band in 1968, to add in mentions of two Liverpool landmarks made famous in Beatles songs.

> *I've never been to Strawberry Fields*
> *I've never been to Penny Lane*
> *But I've been down in the willow garden*
> *And I've ridden the hell-bound trains*

In 2020, he invoked the Beatles once more in "Murder Most Foul," his meditation on the assassination of John F. Kennedy and the popular culture that rose from the tumult of the sixties.

He was especially at ease with Harrison, who had a habit of dropping phrases from Dylan songs into interviews and everyday conversation. "George quoted Bob like people quote scripture," said Tom Petty, a fellow Traveling Wilbury.

Lennon made Dylan laugh, but their relationship was more charged—two lions circling each other. Lennon referred to Dylan by name in songs he recorded in 1968 ("Yer Blues"), 1969 ("Give Peace a Chance"), and 1970 ("God"), and he expressed a desire to work with him a few years later. When John and Bob were living not far from each other in Greenwich Village in the 1970s, Dylan sent a letter to the U.S. government on behalf of Lennon and his wife, Yoko Ono, in support of their efforts to avoid deportation. Four decades later, Dylan wrote "Roll On, John," a tribute to Lennon in which he likens the song's subject to Odysseus and name-checks his first group, the Quarry Men.

Dylan and McCartney grew close in 1971, when Paul was making the album *Ram* in Manhattan and Bob was living with his family in a townhouse in Greenwich Village. "We used to go round to dinner, and he would come up and see us," McCartney said. "We were staying at the Stanhope Hotel, and he would come up and have dinner with us. We'd go down there. So we were really quite intimate."

Of all the Beatles, Bob might have the most in common with Paul, despite their differences in bearing and public image. Both are born entertainers with ever-active creative powers who have proved unable to tear themselves away from studio and stage into their eighties. Both have egos sturdy enough to withstand the adulation and the often-harsh criticism that have followed them through the decades. And both have wide-ranging tastes in music, making them perhaps the only two singers who have rapped on a record (Dylan on "Street Rock," a 1986 duet with Kurtis Blow; McCartney on the 1987 track "Atlantic Ocean") and made albums of standards from the prerock era.

The careers of Dylan and the Beatles followed the same twists and turns. While the similarities resulted, in part, from chronological happenstance and societal tides beyond their control, no one else went through what they went through. They had an outsize effect not only on popular culture but the world at large, an influence that sparked to life when they offered themselves to a populace increasingly shaped by a generation hungry for the messages they conveyed. They came to be seen not so much as entertainment stars in the mold of their two most analogous predecessors, Elvis Presley and Frank Sinatra, but as seers or gurus, a role they sometimes courted with songs of grand pronouncement ("The Times They Are A-Changin'"; "All You Need Is Love") and sometimes dismissed with shows of disdain.

They hit similar heights, but did not move in lockstep. Dylan was the embodiment of the skeptical, often aloof individualist, while the Beatles presented an ideal of unity and friendship. Dylan could be bleak in songs that grappled with injustice and the closer-to-home pains of love and loss, delivering them with a voice-in-the-wilderness anger or the mournful acceptance of Ecclesiastes, while the Beatles tended to glow with an exuberance steeped in a more optimistic worldview bolstered by their love for one another. As Dylan wrote of the Beatles in his 2004 memoir, *Chronicles: Volume One*: "They offered intimacy and companionship like no other group." Throughout much of their evolutions, Dylan and the Beatles worked in a state of mutual awareness, minds in dialogue. Who else could even begin to understand?

This comparative biography starts in the immediate postwar era, when Dylan, Lennon, McCartney, Harrison, and Starr were listening to the same music and adopting similar attitudes, even as they were growing up thousands of miles apart. It goes on to tell the stories of their many interactions, while also, I hope, shedding light on the nature of their respective genius. In these pages I won't go so far as to argue that Dylan was the fifth Beatle, but I will make the case that the relationship was deeper and more consequential than has been noted by earlier writers.

1 Pilgrimage

On a chilly afternoon in 2009, Bob Dylan stepped onto a minibus in Liverpool. At age sixty-seven, he was wearing a hooded sweatshirt, hood up, in an effort to keep himself hidden from the strangers who had been gawking at him for nearly fifty years.

It was May 1. In six hours or so, he would be taking the stage of the Liverpool Echo Arena to play his twenty-ninth show of the year. But right now he was just another tourist who had paid sixteen pounds to visit the childhood homes of John Lennon and Paul McCartney on a tour operated by the National Trust. The minibus wasn't full—it was just Bob, three members of his band, and two women from North Wales.

The driver blasted Beatles songs on the short drive to Woolton Village, a serene, woodsy part of the city where Lennon had spent his childhood days leading a gang of boys in throwing bricks at streetlights, setting fires, and stealing from nearby stores. Sometimes with friends, sometimes alone, John liked to go through the fence to the nicely tended grounds of Strawberry Field, which was then a Salvation Army home for orphans and neglected or abused children.

The bus came to a stop outside a two-story house at 251 Menlove Avenue. From his seat Dylan might have glimpsed the blue plaque above a front window. It was the same type of sign used to designate the homes of Winston Churchill, Lord Byron, Lewis Carroll, and other noted British citizens.

ENGLISH HERITAGE
JOHN LENNON
1940–1980
MUSICIAN
AND SONGWRITER
LIVED HERE
1945–1963

The house, called Mendips, was built in 1933 as part of a middle-class development, the homes given names in the manner of country estates. It belonged to one of John's aunts, the iron-willed Mary Stanley Smith, known as Mimi, and her husband, George Smith, who had been a dairy farmer before he was drafted to fight in World War II. Mendips remained unscathed after bombs rained down close by during the German attacks that destroyed some ten thousand residences and killed more than four thousand people in Liverpool from 1940 to 1942.

John had been born a few miles away, closer to the city center, during a lull in the bombings. His mother, Julia Stanley Lennon, was a freethinking waitress, movie theater usher, and occasional pub singer who accompanied herself on banjo and accordion. His father, Alfred Lennon, known as Alf or Freddie, was a hard-drinking merchant seaman who liked a good laugh and ended up serving two jail stints for petty crimes. With Alf at sea during the war, John spent his first years with his mother and maternal grandfather in a small terrace house near Penny Lane. His first extended stay at Mendips came in the spring of 1945, when he was five. He was sent there because his mother was pregnant by a Welsh soldier she had met at a dance hall.

Julia gave birth and put the baby up for adoption. Then she took John to live in a one-bedroom flat with a new boyfriend in the Gateacre district. Aunt Mimi, horrified by this domestic arrangement, lodged complaints with Liverpool's social services department. Under duress, Julia took her son back to Mendips to be raised by her oldest sister.

John was upset and confused. The trauma of the separation would lend a subtextual charge to the boy-girl songs he would write as a young man. It would also serve as the subject of "Mother," a harrowing ballad cited by Dylan as one of his favorite Lennon songs.

Aunt Mimi, a brisk disciplinarian with no children of her own, was determined to give John a proper British upbringing. Her husband, who had aged quickly after having seen battle in France, did his best to undercut the regime. Always a soft touch, Uncle George recited racy poems for the boy, took him to the movies against his wife's wishes, and secretly delivered buns to his room when Mimi had sent him to bed without supper for some infraction.

On that gray afternoon in 2009, the minibus idled outside Mendips because the earlier tour group was still inside. The driver called the guide, Colin Hall, and told him to hurry up in there because Bob Dylan was among his passengers. Hall laughed, assuming it was a joke.

Moments later, in the tidy front yard, he saw the deeply lined face with its pencil-thin mustache. Dylan was the most famous of the fifty-six thousand people who had come to Mendips since it had been opened to the public in 2003 and the only celebrity who had not bothered to arrange a private visit. A few people were taking his picture as Hall led the new arrivals to the side entrance.

"Welcome to Mendips, the childhood home of John Lennon," he said.

Dylan, the three band members, and the two women from North Wales stepped into the kitchen, a tidy room with a black-and-white tiled floor, a small gas stove, and yellow drapes framing the windows. Like the rest of the house, it had been restored by National Trust curators to its look of crisp postwar respectability. Dylan was heard to remark that the kitchen looked like the one in his own childhood home in Hibbing, Minnesota.

The two women stepped close to the guide and inquired about the man in the hoodie. They knew he was famous, but couldn't place him.

"It's Bob," Hall said. "It's Bob Dylan."

Moments later, Dylan was studying the bookcase in the parlor. Under Aunt Mimi's tutelage, John had been a bookworm from an early age. As Dylan moved through the rooms, he learned about Lennon's early years from Hall, a retired schoolteacher and music journalist.

The enclosed front porch, not much larger than a phone booth, was where John and Paul had started making music together as teenagers. The acoustics brought to mind the distinctive sound of the records made at Sun Studio in Memphis, Tennessee, a place known for its slapback echo effect, where Elvis Presley had created many of the songs that would become staples of their repertoire. John and Paul also played Buddy Holly's "That'll Be the Day," with the more musically adept Paul showing John the chords. It was a song that meant the world to Bob. On January 31, 1959, at age seventeen, he had put himself close to the stage in Duluth, Minnesota, when Holly was the headliner of a show at the Duluth Armory. "He looked me right straight dead in the eye, and he transmitted something," Dylan said in a statement acknowledging his acceptance of the 2016 Nobel Prize in Literature.

The cozy den next to the kitchen was where John and his uncle had paged through the *Liverpool Echo* and the *Daily Express*. Uncle George died in 1955, leaving the fourteen-year-old Lennon deprived of a father figure and ally. He sought out his mother, often skipping school to spend time with her at her home a mile and a half away. Julia took out her banjo and showed John the chords to songs by Presley and Fats Domino, as well as "Maggie Mae," a century-old Liverpool folk song about a thieving prostitute.

Their reunion was short-lived. Julia died in the summer of 1958, when John was seventeen. She had been hit by a car on Menlove Avenue, two hundred yards from Mendips, after having tea with Mimi. An inquest exonerated the driver, an off-duty policeman. John grew bitter and angry. "I lost her twice," he said, "once as a five-year-old, when I was moved in with my auntie, and once again when she physically died."

Dylan and the guide climbed the narrow staircase. Hall noted that student boarders started renting rooms here when Aunt Mimi had to make up for the loss of the money brought in by her late husband, who cleaned trams and worked as a bookie after the war. In other words, although Mendips gave the impression of bourgeois security, its economic foundation was shaky.

Dylan and Hall entered the small front bedroom, its windows overlooking Menlove Avenue. This was where John wrote his first poems, prose sketches, and songs. It was also where he immersed himself in Lewis Carroll's *Alice's Adventures in Wonderland* and *Through the Looking-Glass*, books that would provide inspiration for the dreamily ecstatic songs he would write in 1966 and 1967, when he was frequently dropping acid.

A guitar lay on the narrow bed. The walls were decorated with magazine pictures of two of Bob's own teenage fascinations, Elvis Presley and Brigitte Bardot. At the desk in the corner, John wrote and illustrated his own satirical newspaper, the *Daily Howl*, for the amusement of his friends at the Quarry Bank School, where he was caned by teachers and the headmaster in retaliation for his vulgar jokes and rude imitations of almost anyone in a position of authority. Bob wasn't disruptive in his school days—he once joked that it was too cold in Hibbing for kids to misbehave—but he shared John's penchant for bedroom poetry.

Both boys were discouraged from pursuing a life in the arts. Bob's mother told him, "Don't keep writing poetry, please don't. Go to school and do something constructive." Aunt Mimi made a similar remark that John would relish throwing back in her face: "The guitar is all right as a hobby, but you'll never make a living at it."

Bob noticed a book in John's bedroom, *Just William*, the first in a series of children's novels written by Richmal Crompton about an eleven-year-old suburban scamp named William Brown, the leader of a gang he called the Outlaws. "The nicest moment, for me, was talking to him about *Just William*," Hall, the tour guide, recalled. "He saw the book on the bed and he wanted to know about Just William and the Outlaws. For me, that was totally surreal, talking in John Lennon's bedroom to Bob Dylan, whom I compare to Shakespeare, about John Lennon and *Just William*."

Back outside, Dylan didn't join the others on the minibus that would go on to McCartney's childhood home. After arranging for a private car, he asked the guide the way to Strawberry Field. Hall watched as the hunched figure headed toward the place commemorated in one of the previous century's greatest songs.

Dylan later made his way to the second and final stop of the Beatles' Childhood Homes tour in a brickfront neighborhood of Allerton, a part of Liverpool adjacent to Woolton. In the fading light, he stepped out of the car and stood in front of the anonymous-looking, two-story structure at 20 Forthlin Road. This was where Paul had lived from age fourteen till the start of Beatlemania in 1963.

Unlike Mendips, the McCartney home had no name. It was part of a contiguous housing project built after the war in the effort to replace the residences destroyed by the Germans. And Dylan saw no blue plaque on the facade. To qualify, the honoree must be dead twenty years or have reached age one hundred. But a National Trust sign informed visitors that this had once been the home of Jim McCartney, Mary Mohin McCartney, and their two sons, Paul and Mike.

When the McCartneys moved here in 1955, things were looking up. The place was an improvement over their previous home in the increasingly violent district of Speke, where the Harrisons lived. Paul's father, who had led Jim Mac's Jazz Band in the 1920s, liked to play the upright piano in the front room when he wasn't working as a salesman at the Liverpool Cotton Exchange. But 20 Forthlin Road was also Paul's home when Mary—a nurse, midwife, and the family breadwinner—died of cancer in 1956. Aunts came by to help with the raising of the two boys.

Everybody said Jim was a lovely man, and he was indeed highly sociable and quick with a joke or homespun aphorism. "Put it there," he would say to his boys when they were low, a saying that Paul would make into the title of a song capturing his love for his dad. But in keeping with the child-rearing conventions of that time and place, Jim would strike his sons when they stepped out of line. After a beating that Mike described as "the hiding of our lives," the boys lay side by side in an upstairs bedroom, and Paul started spinning out revenge scenarios. "Some of them sounded like ideas out of a Chinese torture book, only dafter," Mike wrote in an article for a fan magazine soon after his brother had become famous. "Finally, he said: 'If I could, I'd take Dad up to 15,000 feet in a plane, dig a hole, fill it with water, and drop him in!'"

At age sixteen or seventeen, Paul challenged his father outright. "He'd just sort of slap me," he recalled. "We're having an argument, he'd slap me. So I just stood there—and it was like an amazing moment in my life. I said, 'Go ahead, do it again.' And he never did it again." Father and son maintained a strong bond nonetheless, with music at its core. Jim encouraged Paul's efforts, first with the trumpet, then piano, guitar, and drums—but he wasn't enamored with rock 'n' roll and warned his son to stay away from Lennon, who was obviously no good.

During Paul's final year at 20 Forthlin Road, Mike borrowed a copy of Dylan's first album from his first serious girlfriend, Celia Mortimer, a model and art school student. When Paul heard it playing in the front room, he asked, "What's that crap?"

"A bloke called Bob Dylan," Mike said.

"Never 'eard of him," Paul said. "Folk crap."

"It'll grow on you," Mike said.

On that chilly spring day in 2009, Dylan approached the front door of the McCartney home. He waited there, but that was as far as he got. The guide assigned to the property later told a visitor that she had heard someone out front, but hadn't gone to see who it was.

2 Disciples of Little Richard

When they were young, their hometowns were in decline, even as Britain and the United States were headed toward economic recovery. Strict rules of behavior, hammered out and honed decades earlier, held sway in both Liverpool and Hibbing, discouraging those who sought to break from their expected social roles. Beneath the old rigidity, the Cold War had brought to daily life in both places the low hum of existential anxiety. And so it made sense that Dylan and the four future Beatles would find solace, meaning, and joy in rock 'n' roll, the emerging musical genre that laid a challenge to the status quo.

Dylan's hometown, a place of high winds and open skies seventy-five miles northwest of Duluth, had sprung up in the 1890s thanks to Frank Hibbing, a prospector who had divined a rich seam of iron ore. Local entrepreneurs profited from the first flush of activity, only to be outmaneuvered by a pair of tycoons—the oil baron John D. Rockefeller and the steel magnate Andrew Carnegie. When the first mines were nearly spent, town bosses backed by the two billionaires gashed the earth to create an open pit mine three miles long and two miles wide, a monstrosity nicknamed the Grand Canyon of the North. Some days a fine dust of iron oxide suffused the air like mist, which Dylan would evoke in "Under the Red Sky," a 1990 song featuring his friend George Harrison on melancholy slide guitar.

A company controlled by Rockefeller transported the iron by train to Duluth. Carnegie's workers took it by barge across Lake Superior toward the steel mills of Pittsburgh. Hibbing's iron, which helped make the U.S. a military and industrial superpower, fattened the fortunes of the men at the top of the chain and meant steady but hard-earned wages for local laborers, many of them first- or second-generation Americans from Scandinavia and Eastern Europe. With so much money flowing in, no expense was spared in the construction of Hibbing High School, a stone colossus known as the Castle in the Woods. Built from 1920 to 1925 at a cost of nearly $4 million, the equivalent of $60 million today, it housed an auditorium modeled after the Capitol Theatre in New York, with cut-glass chandeliers floating above its two thousand seats. That was where Dylan played some of his first shows.

To accommodate the mining industry's expansion, nearly two hundred of Hibbing's original structures, including a school attended by Dylan's mother, were transported two miles south. The painstaking process began in 1912 and took decades to complete. A hotel didn't survive the move, toppling from logrollers and ending up a pile of kindling in the street. The destruction that went into the making of modern Hibbing didn't sit well with Dylan, who would arrive at a worldview that combined the iconoclasm of a mad prophet and the conservatism of a preservationist. "Bobby's *so* sentimental," his mother, Beatrice Stone Zimmerman, said in a rare interview. "Once, I took him up to Old Hibbing, when the last of the razing was being completed, and showed him where all the old buildings used to be. This was after he was grown and had left home—and he got so upset; he'd look and point and say things like, 'That's where you went to *school*, Mom . . . and it's gone now. Isn't that *sad*?'"

Having fled the pogroms and poverty of the Russian empire, Dylan's ancestors had come to Minnesota when it was beginning to boom. Some settled in Duluth, where Dylan's father, Abraham Zimmerman, was born and raised; others went to Hibbing and the nearby towns, where his mother grew up. The Zimmerman and Stone families belonged to a tiny minority: In those years, 1 percent of Minnesotans were Jews. Abe and Beatty were married at a Duluth synagogue in 1934. Seven years later, their first child, Robert Allen Zimmerman, was born.

Abe worked as an accountant in the Duluth office of Rockefeller's Standard Oil until he contracted polio in 1947. He lost his job after emerging from a hospital stay in pain, with a limp. The family moved to Hibbing, where Abe joined his two brothers at Zimmerman Furniture and Electric. The ethnic mix there wasn't always easy. "In Hibbing, the Finns hated the Bohemians, and the Bohemians hated the Finns," a local teacher said. "Nearly everyone hated the Jews."

The store prospered, and Bobby Zimmerman, as Bob Dylan was known through his first eighteen years, saw movies free of charge at the Lybba and State theaters, which were owned by relatives on his mother's side. By the time he hit high school, it was hard for him to ignore Hibbing's decline, a precursor to the hard times soon to transform much of the industrial Midwest into the Rust Belt. Families left Hibbing amid layoffs and strikes, and some laborers who remained found themselves unable to meet the payments on the goods they had bought on the installment plan from Zimmerman Furniture and Electric.

While working occasionally at the store, Bobby was now and then sent out on the task of taking back radios, TV sets, and sofas. Some people begged in their efforts to avoid losing their prize possessions. In one instance, a man spewed antisemitic insults at Bobby. "He made some pretty smart remarks about Bobby's father and his religion being the cause of things," recalled Benny Orlando, who worked at the store in the 1950s. "Bobby was real quiet after that. He didn't talk to anyone for a long time."

Four thousand miles away, John, Paul, George, and Ringo (born Richard Starkey and known as Rich or Richy) were also growing up in a place whose days of prosperity lay in the past. Liverpool had hit its economic peak in an age when its innovatively designed wet docks hosted vessels from all over the world bearing loads of cotton, tea, coffee, and tobacco. The city was also enriched by its involvement in the slave trade. From 1700 to 1807, local merchants dispatched four thousand slaving voyages to Africa, and for a time Liverpool was Europe's busiest port in the buying and selling of human beings.

The plenitude of jobs attracted immigrants from across the Irish Sea. In the middle of the nineteenth century, after the failure of Ireland's potato crop, millions of men, women, and children arrived as refugees, many of them settling in slums along the River Mersey. Three of the Beatles, all but Ringo, are of Irish ancestry.

The docks bustled anew when the city became the operational center for the British fleet at the start of World War II. Germany countered with two years of aerial attacks. Ringo, the oldest of the Beatles, and John, the second oldest, were born during the raids, known as the Liverpool Blitz; the two infants were spirited to basements and taken beneath kitchen tables amid the explosions. As children, all four future Beatles played at unrepaired bomb sites.

The Liverpool of the Beatles' childhoods was a soot-stained, poverty-stricken, crime-ridden metropolis derided by cultured Londoners as a backwater. The few Liverpudlians to find welcome on the national stage tended to be boxing champions or "northern comedians" whose Scouse cadences were considered part of the act.

■　　■　　■

With bomb sites pocking the streets of Liverpool and bomb-shelter salesmen making the rounds in Minnesota, John, Paul, George, Ringo, and Bob came of age during the shaky peace built on the standoff between the Soviet bloc and the capitalist republics. Young people of that era, the first to know from an early age that humanity was capable of wiping itself out, couldn't help but question the pieties and propaganda of the old order—the stiff-upper-lip stoicism of the British ruling class and the rah-rah conformism of Eisenhower America. Rock 'n' roll, the gleefully defiant genre rooted in Black American culture, seemed to match the speed and tension of the atomic age; and it gave teenagers in its thrall a sense of belonging to a culture distinct from the staid world of their elders. This thrilling music further hinted at a way for John, Paul, George, Ringo, and Bob to escape the monotonous futures that seemed to lie in wait for them.

All five were nonconformists who found themselves transformed, as if experiencing lightning-bolt conversions, by the sounds that would inspire their lifelong devotion. "When I first heard Elvis Presley's voice," Dylan said, "I just knew that I wasn't going to work for anybody, and nobody was going to be my boss. Hearing him for the first time was like busting out of jail." The people closest to him felt the same about Elvis and other rock 'n' rollers. Bobby formed a tight bond with Echo Helstrom, a Hibbing High classmate with an independent streak who would become his first serious girlfriend, partly because of their shared love for Chuck Berry's hard-driving "Maybellene."

In his bedroom with a close friend, John Bucklen, Bobby did a pantomime of Gene Vincent's 1956 hit "Be-Bop-a-Lula." Both boys wore the blue caps that they had bought for the occasion at a Hibbing department store, the better to resemble Vincent's backing group, the Blue Caps. The fun came to a stop when Abe Zimmerman entered the room. The look on the face of this mild, hardworking man suggested not just disapproval but disgust, Bucklen recalled.

Of all the early rock 'n' rollers, Dylan was struck most profoundly by Little Richard, the Black American singer, pianist, and songwriter born Richard Penniman in Macon, Georgia. He called himself, not without justification, the architect of rock 'n' roll. His songs, with an urgent beat that got under your skin, were all about lust and emotional abandon, and he delivered them in the tones of a backwoods preacher.

Bobby did his best Little Richard impression at the start of his apprenticeship, banging away at the piano, his first main instrument, in the key of C and singing his head off as the leader of short-lived groups. The Little Richard hit "Jenny, Jenny" was part of his repertoire, and one of his first original compositions was a rocker titled "Hey Little Richard." Like his role model, Bobby was a wild man onstage, which seemed odd to his fellow students, since he had always been so reserved in class. "Nobody liked their music much, least of all Bob's voice," Echo Helstrom said. "I used to get so upset, for days ahead of time, when I knew he was going to sing in public." During a 1958 show at Hibbing High's grand hall, Bobby broke a pedal on the piano in a particularly unhinged performance. Kids were laughing, and the school principal cut the microphone. "He just got so *crazy*," the principal said.

At around the same time, Bobby and John Bucklen made ten reel-to-reel recordings. On one tape Bobby is heard singing "Hey, Little Richard" while accompanying himself on piano. At another point, he and his friend discuss the man who had inspired the song. The format was a mock broadcast interview, with Bucklen posing the questions.

"What's the best kind of music?"

"Rhythm and blues," Bobby answers.

"State your reason in no less than twenty-five minutes."

"Ah, rhythm and blues, you see, is really something you can't quite explain. When you hear a song—when you hear it's a good rhythm and blues song, chills go up your spine."

After a discussion of whether or not the teenage TV star and singer Ricky Nelson had lifted Presley's sound, Bobby says that Elvis would have been nothing without the Black originators Little Richard and Clyde McPhatter of the Drifters, suggesting an awareness of rock 'n' roll's tangled roots unusual for a white teenager in that time and place.

"Elvis Presley," Bobby says. "Who did he copy? He copied from Clyde McPhatter, he copied from Little Richard."

"Wait a minute, wait a minute!" Bucklen interjects.

"He copied the Drifters."

"Wait a minute. Name four songs that Elvis copied from those little groups."

"He copied all the Little Richard songs."

The next year, in the caption beneath his senior-year portrait in *Hematite*, the Hibbing High yearbook, Bobby stated his aim in life: "To join 'Little Richard.'"

In Liverpool, John and Paul followed the same Presley-to-Penniman path, while also making room (as Bobby had) for Chuck Berry, Buddy

Holly, Gene Vincent, Eddie Cochran, Fats Domino, the Everly Brothers, and Larry Williams, among other innovators. "My whole life changed from then on," John said, describing the moment he first heard Presley in 1956. "I was just completely shaken by it." Paul was equally affected: "It was Elvis who really hooked me on beat music. When I heard 'Heartbreak Hotel,' I thought, *this is it*." From there, John and Paul made the transition from the so-called king of rock 'n' roll to its self-proclaimed architect.

For John, the moment came roughly two weeks after his Presley encounter, when a friend, Michael Hill, told him he had a record by "a singer who's better than Elvis." With Hill and two other friends, John left the Quarry Bank School at lunchtime and biked to Hill's house, stopping at a fish-and-chips shop along the way. In the front room, Hill dropped the needle on the 78 rpm single he had bought in Amsterdam on a school exchange trip. It was a Belgian release of Little Richard's "Long Tall Sally," with "Slippin' and Slidin'" on the flip side, a record not yet available in Britain. The boys shared a Woodbine cigarette as they listened.

"His reaction that day was something that stuck in everybody's memory, because he really was struck dumb by this record," Hill recalled in an interview with the Beatles biographer Mark Lewisohn. "He didn't know what to say, which for John was most unusual, because he was always so quick with an answer, with a bit of repartee." Lennon said, recalling that moment, "When I heard it, it was so great, I couldn't speak. You know how you're torn? I didn't want to leave Elvis. Elvis was bigger than religion in my life. We all looked at each other, but I didn't want to say anything against Elvis, not even in my mind."

Months later, Paul was similarly shaken when he heard the first Little Richard single released in Britain, "Rip It Up," with "Ready Teddy" on the B-side. "Little Richard was this voice from heaven or hell, or both," he recalled. "This screaming voice seemed to come from the top of his head. I tried to do it one day and I found I could. You had to lose every inhibition and do it." He worked out a few Little Richard songs on the piano at Forthlin Road, much to his father's disapproval. On a family trip to a budget resort in Filey, Yorkshire, Paul performed a Little Richard song. "The first song I ever sang solo in public was 'Long Tall Sally' at a Butlin's holiday camp talent contest when I was fourteen," he said. On the last day of a Liverpool Institute school term, he stood on a desk, with guitar, and played "Long Tall Sally" and the song that would become Little Richard's signature, "Tutti Frutti," with its cry of "A-wop-bop-a-loo-mop, a-lop-bam-boom!"

In 1960, the first iteration of the Beatles, with Pete Best on drums and Stuart Sutcliffe on bass, regularly performed five Little Richard songs. On October 12, 1962, three months after the group's lineup had been set—with Sutcliffe having died of cerebral hemmorhage four months earlier at age twenty-one, and Ringo having taken the place of the ousted Best—the Beatles came face-to-face with their hero. The encounter occurred backstage at the Tower Ballroom in New Brighton, seven miles from Liverpool.

Little Richard was the headliner of a twelve-act show that went nearly six hours. It was five years to the day since he had renounced rock 'n' roll in favor of religion. "If you want to live with the Lord, you can't rock and roll, too," he said. "God doesn't like it." From his moment of revelation to his arrival in Britain, he had been playing nothing but gospel music.

The Beatles were the sixth act to appear on the Tower Ballroom stage. There is no documentation of what they played but, according to Little Richard's authorized biography, the Beatles had the courtesy, or good sense, not to attempt any of his songs that night.

When Little Richard took the stage, he tore the place apart. "How do you describe the most fantastically exciting and shatteringly dynamic stage offering you have ever seen?" wrote the reviewer for the British music publication *New Musical Express*. Afterward, the Beatles posed for some pictures with the star of the show. In one photo, Little Richard is seated regally, the group members surrounding him like courtiers. Before the night was out, Lennon asked him to sign the program. "For John," Little Richard wrote. "May God bless You always, Little Richard. 1710 Virginia Rd., Los Angeles, Calif."

His friendliness toward the Beatles was meaningful: In the 1950s, he had been miffed when Pat Boone, a white Tennessean with a cherubic face and a blandly cheerful demeanor, had scored bigger hits with Little Richard songs than Little Richard himself. Boone's versions of "Tutti Frutti," "Good Golly, Miss Molly," and "Long Tall Sally"—polite, polished, stripped of lust—are now largely forgotten; but at his height Boone was second only to Presley in record sales. The upshot was that most white teenagers were more likely to know Boone's version of "Tutti Frutti" than the original. Rare were the fans like Bobby, Echo, and Bucklen, who turned their radio dials late at night to find rhythm and blues programs beamed out of distant cities; or John, Paul, George, and Ringo, who scoured friends' collections and record shop racks in search of sounds deemed unsuitable for the airwaves by the state-run BBC.

"When Pat Boone covered my record, I was mad," Little Richard said in a 1987 interview. "I said, 'I'm going to Nashville to find him.'" It was easier for him to smile on the Beatles, because they were performing far from the cities where rock 'n' roll stars were created and the real money was made—and perhaps because their approach was unlike Boone's. Although they were white men playing a type of music they had taken from Black American culture, they went at it in a way that suggested their love and respect for its power and grit.

Shortly after the Tower Ballroom show, Little Richard, at the time a Seventh-day Adventist, rededicated himself to gospel music. He was a gay man raised on religion who considered his desires sinful and viewed rock 'n' roll as a weapon in Satan's arsenal. Weeks later, he returned to the devil's music when he headlined the Star-Club, the top rock venue in Hamburg, Germany, for a two-week run. The Beatles were second on the bill.

■   ■   ■

The Hamburg residency of November 1962 was the Beatles' third stay in the rough port city, where they had made themselves into a tight and tough musical unit. By then, they had logged more than nine hundred hours of stage time at its gangster-run venues. This time around, they were often in the company of Little Richard, observing him as he complimented his own looks while gazing at himself in the dressing room mirror and watching from the Star-Club floor as he threw himself into a frenzy that usually ended with a partial striptease.

One night George dove under a table to fetch the cuff links he had flung from the stage. And after Little Richard had thrown his shirt to the audience, Paul offered to replace it with a shirt of his own. "A flash shirt, a beautiful shirt," Little Richard recalled, "and he said, 'Take it, Richard.' I said, 'I can't take that,' but he insisted, '*Please* take it.'"

A year after the Star-Club engagement, the Beatles scored what was then the all-time top-selling single in the UK, "She Loves You." Like other early Beatles tracks, it included their adaptation of Little Richard's vocal trademark, the rough falsetto *whooooo*. Three years later, when the Beatles played their final full concert at Candlestick Park in San Francisco, their last song was "Long Tall Sally." Little Richard's influence also informed the post-Beatles music of John and Paul: Lennon's "Whatever Gets You Thru the Night," a No. 1 hit in the U.S., echoed the saxophone-heavy arrangement of "Tutti Frutti"; John also included three Little Richard songs on his album of oldies, *Rock 'n' Roll*.

Little Richard was also a presence when John and Paul played together at a studio in Burbank, California, on March 28, 1974, during Lennon's so-called Lost Weekend period. In a sloppy jam session, which included Stevie Wonder on keyboards, one song they managed to complete was the Little Richard staple "Lucille." Paul, on drums, was the lead singer; John, on guitar, sang harmony. It was the last time Lennon and McCartney are known to have made music together.

In the 1970s, "Lucille" was the song Paul launched into while auditioning musicians. And he recorded "Lucille" for his own tribute to early rock 'n' roll, *CHOBA B CCCP*, a 1987 collection originally released only in the Soviet Union. In 1988, when the Beatles were inducted into the Rock & Roll Hall of Fame, George said in the acceptance speech on behalf of the group: "Thank you very much, especially all the rock 'n' rollers—especially Little Richard. It's all his fault, really."

Once his Hibbing High years were behind him, Dylan didn't attempt his own spin on the Little Richard sound, but he never forgot his debt to his early hero. In 1969, he had one of his biggest hits with "Lay Lady Lay," a country-influenced ballad that borrows a key phrase from "Cherry Red," a track on Little Richard's 1964 album, *Little Richard Is Back.* In the Dylan song, the singer invites a woman to "lay across my big brass bed." In "Cherry Red," Little Richard tells the object of his desire to "throw me in your big brass bed." (Little Richard's "Cherry Red" is a remake of a song written by Pete Johnson and Big Joe Turner first released in 1939; the original doesn't include the phrase "big brass bed.")

In 1985, after Little Richard had survived a nearly fatal car crash, Dylan spent hours at his bedside at Cedars-Sinai Medical Center in Los Angeles. By then, the two had traveled down many of the same paths: Like the idol of his youth, Dylan had gone through a period of refusing to perform the secular songs that had given him his greatest commercial success; he had also filled two albums and much of a third with Christian material. After the hospital visit, Little Richard described Dylan as his "blood brother," saying, "He sat by my bed. He didn't move for hours." Three years later, when Dylan accepted his induction into the Rock & Roll Hall of Fame on the same night as the Beatles, he echoed Harrison in making Little Richard the first person he thanked.

On Little Richard's death in 2020, McCartney wrote on Twitter: "I owe a lot of what I do to Little Richard and his style; and he knew it. He would say, 'I taught Paul everything he knows.'" In a Twitter post of his own, Dylan said: "He was my shining star and guiding light back when I was only a little boy. His was the original spirit that moved me to do everything I would do."

3 The Names

"I know what I'm going to call myself," the teenage Dylan told Echo Helstrom. "I've got this great name—Bob Dillon."

Dillon was the surname of the stoic hero of *Gunsmoke*, the Western series that had been a prime-time fixture on CBS since 1955. It was a name fit for a cowboy, a gunslinger, a loner. Bobby told people, falsely, that it was his mother's maiden name or the name of an uncle.

In the late summer of 1959, when he was shifting his allegiance from rock 'n' roll to traditional folk and blues, he registered at the University of Minnesota under his birth name, but fellow students knew him as Bob or Bobby Dillon; and "Bob Dillon" was how his name appeared on a handbill advertising one of his performances at the Ten O'Clock Scholar, a coffeehouse in Dinkytown, the bohemian neighborhood of Minneapolis.

While Dylan was inching toward the final iteration of the name he would go by for the rest of his life, Lennon dropped "the Quarry Men" in favor of "the Beatles." The idea for an insect-related name was inspired by the Crickets, the foursome out of Lubbock, Texas, led by the bespectacled singer-songwriter Buddy Holly. John had cooked up the name with Stuart Sutcliffe, his group's bass player and a fellow student at the Liverpool College of Art. Stuart, a talented abstract painter with a James Dean look, preferred "Beetles," with two *e*'s. But in a place where rock 'n' roll was called beat music, John, who loved wordplay, decided to go with the pun.

Now that "the Beatles" has become so ingrained as to be almost invisible, it's hard to fathom how attention-grabbing it was back then. The name struck people as ridiculous and vaguely repulsive, and the offensiveness was part of the point, prefiguring a strategy that would be followed by punk and heavy metal bands, from the Germs to Slayer.

"The Beatles" also stood out because it was truly a group name. The usual thing at the time was to have a frontman backed by a band with a name ending in *s*. Top American acts included Bill Haley and His Comets and Frankie Lymon and the Teenagers; Britain's most famous group was Cliff Richard and the Shadows; Liverpool had Gerry and the Pacemakers, Cass and the Cassanovas, and Rory Storm and the Hurricanes (with Ringo on drums, until he decamped for the Beatles in 1962).

John's desire for an all-for-one, one-for-all name was rooted in his love for being part of a gang. He did almost everything with friends—drinking, smoking, shoplifting, setting fires—and he was the instigator. Bonding rituals included group masturbation sessions led by John, some of which took place at Strawberry Field. He would shout out the names of Brigitte Bardot and other screen sirens when he wasn't throwing a wrench in the sexual works with a cry of "Winston Churchill!" One participant, Pete Shotton, an original member of the Quarry Men, described the activity at length in his memoir. McCartney also took part, as he conceded in a 2018 interview. "It was good, harmless fun," he said with his usual matter-of-factness.

Shotton doubted that John would have accomplished much in life without the sense of purpose he derived from running his own little gang. "He was accustomed to being the ringleader and the center of all attention, yet nonetheless required the supportive presence of whoever he felt closest to at the time," Shotton wrote. "It would simply have never occurred to him to organize a band from scratch with a group of strangers."

The first significant meeting between Lennon and McCartney took place on July 6, 1957, during the annual Garden Fete at St. Peter's

Church in Woolton, where John had attended Sunday services, sung in the choir, and received his confirmation. As part of the daylong festivities, the Quarry Men performed in a field next to the church—and Paul was watching. By this time, he had seen John around town and thought of him as a "fairground hero"; he was even more impressed when saw him vigorously strumming his cheap guitar while improvising caustic lyrics to "Come Go with Me," a recent hit by an American doo-wop group, the Del-Vikings.

In the wake of the performance, Paul, age fifteen, made himself known to John, who was sixteen, by borrowing a guitar, turning it upside down (because he was left-handed), and giving his all to Eddie Cochran's "Twenty Flight Rock," an intricate stop-start rocker beyond the guitar skills of anyone in the group. Later that day, Paul installed himself at a piano in the hall where the Quarry Men would perform that evening and did some Little Richard.

It was obvious that Paul was probably the most talented teenage singer and musician in Liverpool, and John knew that if he asked him to join the Quarry Men, he would be putting his own leadership status in jeopardy. He weighed the idea for two weeks before dispatching Pete Shotton to bring him aboard. The group idea had won out again.

The lineup soon went through more changes: Shotton and other original members were out; a school acquaintance of Paul's, George Harrison, joined on guitar, followed by Pete Best (drums) and Stuart Sutcliffe (bass). In 1960, with the "Beatles" name firmly in place, John was at last fully equipped for the work of instilling in others the storm of emotion he found in himself.

■ ■ ■

Dylan was like Lennon in many respects, but he had no need, at least in his teenage years, to surround himself with admiring males. At sixteen, during his stay at Herzl Camp, a sleepaway summer retreat for Jewish kids in the Wisconsin woods, he took his guitar up on a roof and spent hours playing and singing, solo, for the campers and counselors below. "All day long, silhouetted against the sun, Bobby played every rock and blues song anybody had ever heard of and lots that we hadn't," Louie Kemp, a friend from childhood, recalled.

The recitals hinted at Dylan's naysayers-be-damned self-sufficiency that would become even more apparent in later years. And when he led his high school groups, his individualist streak was evident in the way he treated fellow musicians: He would take them into new or unfamiliar songs with little or no rehearsal, a practice he would return to in the mid-1960s, after his phase as a solo performer had come to a close.

Toward the end of 1960, before leaving Minneapolis for New York, he made a crucial adjustment, changing "Dillon" to "Dylan." In assuming an alias, which he would make his legal name at a New York courthouse in 1962, he was following the example of countless writers and entertainers who had found freedom and comfort in the adoption of a persona. One of these was the Broadway star Ethel Merman, a Zimmermann who simply lopped four letters off her surname to arrive at something that looked good on a marquee.

Bob seemed more eager to distance himself from his roots than the more community-minded Beatles, and the name change helped him accomplish that goal. After his arrival in New York at nineteen, he spoke opaquely about his past or told outrageous lies, claiming to have been a member of the Sioux tribe or a runaway who had spent time in carnivals and on the range—anything to blot out the unremarkable fact of his middle-class upbringing. And unlike John and Paul, who sometimes played up their provenance by exaggerating their Scouse accents in early radio and TV interviews (to the chagrin of their status-conscious family members), Bob further camouflaged his origins by speaking in a Dust Bowl dialect more suited to his new role model, the Oklahoma-born folk singer Woody Guthrie, than a college dropout from the Upper Midwest.

Although he had been bar mitzvahed at thirteen, he preferred that the people he encountered not see him as a Jew, and the Dylan name helped him skirt the issue of ethnicity at a time when anti-semitism was all too common. It was the same for one of his early mentors, Ramblin' Jack Elliott, who had crisscrossed the country with Guthrie in the guise of a singing cowboy after having been raised in Brooklyn as Elliott Adnopoz, the son of a prosperous Jewish father, a surgeon, and a conventional Jewish mother. When Bob listened to Ramblin Jack's records during his brief college stint, he took the cowboy persona at face value.

Bob's new name, with its telltale y, had another advantage in that it brought to mind the Welsh poet Dylan Thomas, who had embodied the figure of the hard-living bard before his death at thirty-nine in 1953. The revised spelling did nothing to alter the gunslinger sound Bob had hit upon with "Dillon," while lending the name a look suggestive of a poet's idealistic pursuit of art for art's sake, even at the risk of an early grave. And so the name fell somewhere between nom de guerre and nom de plume: "Bob Dylan" was built to fight, with verse as his weapon of choice.

He has said the name had no direct connection to the famed poet, but Dave Van Ronk, a gruff singer who reigned over Greenwich Village in those years, disagreed. In his memoir, cowritten with the music historian Elijah Wald, Van Ronk said that Dylan confirmed having named himself after Thomas. "I may have rolled my eyes heavenward," Van Ronk recalled. "On the other hand, all of us were reinventing ourselves to some extent, and if this guy wanted to carry it a step or two further, who were we to quibble?" Van Ronk also described the moment when Dylan learned that Ramblin' Jack was Jewish: "We were sitting around shooting the bull . . . and somehow it came up that Jack had grown up in Ocean Parkway and was named Elliott Adnopoz. Bobby literally fell off his chair."

Years after he had gotten to know Dylan, Lennon—who was not above hurling antisemitic insults in his youth, according to Pete Shotton—referred to him as "Zimmerman" in the 1970 song "God." Asked why he hadn't gone with Bob's preferred and legal name, Lennon replied, "Because Dylan is bullshit. Zimmerman is his name." Continuing the rant, he brought up the Welsh singing star Tom Jones, né Thomas Woodward: "You see, I don't believe in Dylan and I don't believe in Tom Jones either in that way. My name isn't John Beatle. It's John Lennon."

But his name might as well have been John Beatle when he was rising to fame. His group presented a united front onstage and in photo shoots, emphasizing the communal ethos hammered home by its name. Even in the Quarry Men days, John and his mates wore matching outfits; as the Beatles, early on, they often went with black leather, bottom and top.

Pete Best contributed to his odd-man-out status when he refused to go along with the hairstyle change instituted by John and Paul, from greasy American quiff to clean Continental moptop, a look that made the Beatles conspicuous and struck many people as foppish and feminine at a time when hair was a key signifier of masculinity. When the Beatles started wearing tailored suits on the advice of Brian Epstein, the polished Liverpool department store magnate who had become their manager, John, ever mindful that the group was the thing, accepted the sartorial makeover without complaint (though he would call the switch to suits a sellout in an angry interview shortly after the Beatles' breakup).

For Dylan and the Beatles, the note-perfect stage names were strokes of marketing genius that served the practical purpose of providing them with the armor that allowed them to thrust themselves unafraid into often hostile territory. How much easier it is to enter the public arena when you are in the guise of a character or a member of a team.

Paul was at ease playing piano and singing in the company of boozy aunts and uncles during the holiday gatherings of his extended family, but he sometimes found himself trembling when he had to face an audience of strangers. The jitteriness struck him during a Liverpool Institute assembly when he accepted an award for an essay he had written, and it hit him anew when he flubbed an attempted guitar solo during a Quarry Men show.

John, beneath the bravado, was rife with insecurities that could be exacerbated *and* exorcised by the public nature of his work. Performance, for him, meant summoning and then slaying his demons.

In the spotlight he was often manic, chewing gum, making mad faces, doing pantomimes as a physically handicapped person or village idiot. Although he would be acclaimed as one of the most distinctive singers of his time, he disliked his voice so much, or so he claimed, that he routinely demanded that the producer George Martin bathe it in effects or double-track it.

Dylan took protective measures of his own. Friends from his Greenwich Village days have spoken of someone who seemed younger than his years and required the close ministrations of his girlfriend Suze Rotolo and other women who watched over him. There was also wine, marijuana, and amphetamines. Like Lennon in those years, he rarely performed sober.

In February 1961, the Beatles made their debut at the Cavern Club, a cellar venue in Liverpool with condensation trickling down the stone walls and the smell of soup, hot dogs, coffee, sewage, disinfectant, and cigarette smoke pervading the musty air. Two months later, Bob started playing at Gerde's Folk City, a cozy Greenwich Village nightspot that had been a homey Italian restaurant not long before his arrival.

The Beatles and Dylan received their first reviews within weeks of each other. In the August 31, 1961, issue of the Liverpool music publication *Mersey Beat*, Bob Wooler noted a paradox at the heart of the Beatles' appeal, a combination of rebelliousness and charm. The group, he wrote, conveyed an "indifference to audience response and yet always saying 'Thank you.'" A month later, Robert Shelton, writing about a Dylan show at Gerde's Folk City for *The New York Times*, pointed out a similar contradiction when he described Dylan as "a cross between a choir boy and a beatnik."

As those early notices suggest, it wasn't just their talent or skill that made them stand out. Suze Rotolo, who became Dylan's girlfriend about six months after his arrival in New York, described his stage presence in her memoir: "When he started out, Bob was playful, a mix of Harpo Marx and Woody Guthrie, with a big dose of himself as a binding ingredient. Onstage he moved around a lot, removing the harmonicas from his pockets and placing them on a nearby stool, fiddling with the capo on his guitar and the corduroy cap on his head.... When he finally began to play, he had the audience's attention and he knew it." Van Ronk compared the Dylan he saw onstage to Charlie Chaplin's "Little Fellow" character. "He would get all of these pseudoclumsy bits of business going, fiddling with his harmonica rack and things like that, and he could put an audience in stitches without saying a word," he recalled.

John Hammond II, a top executive at Columbia Records, the most prestigious U.S. label in those days, knew that Dylan's voice and guitar playing wouldn't impress his colleagues; and he understood that Dylan might not have the undeniable talent of another artist he had brought aboard, Aretha Franklin. Nonetheless, he signed Dylan in 1961. "There was a vice president up there who was so angry with me," Hammond said, "because he *knew* that this was going to louse up CBS's name—the voice was so 'terrible.' But it didn't matter. He was an original."

The Beatles, too, made an impression on audiences and cultural gatekeepers for extra-musical reasons. "They were more than just 'a group singing a few numbers,'" Linda Ness, an early fan, said. "They were true all-round entertainers—no other group had members taking the mickey out of each other during songs. They did silly walks, they larked around, and sent up records in the Top Twenty."

The Beatles created a family atmosphere at the Cavern Club during their lunchtime and evening shows. They smoked and ate onstage. When Paul sang a love ballad, his dark eyes twinkling, John would stand behind him, contorting his face and repeating the song's lines in sarcastic tones. And when the sweat running down the walls caused the electricity to short, silencing the amps and plunging the room into darkness, the Beatles would lead the crowd in sing-alongs of radio hits from the days before the war; or Paul would sit at the upright piano to play an original melody that would eventually become "When I'm Sixty-Four."

George Martin, the gentlemanly producer and head of Parlophone, a record label belonging to the London-based multinational corporation EMI, had the same reaction as the Cavern fans when he met the Beatles in 1962. "I did think they had enormous talent," Martin said, "but it wasn't their music—it was their charisma, the fact that when I was with them they gave me a sense of well-being, of being happy."

In a paradoxical complement to their lovable qualities, Dylan and the Beatles burned to succeed, to move beyond the fans who had taken them in when they were fledglings. And unlike the one-hit wonders who were thrown by success, they had the confidence to accept recognition as their due once it came their way. "Quietly Bob said: This is the beginning of what I have always known," Suze recalled of Dylan's reaction to landing a deal with Columbia Records. "He said it calmly and knowingly, and it was true." Lennon described the pre-fame Beatles as "the biggest bastards on earth" who were confident to the point of arrogance long before they had signed with EMI. "When I was a Beatle, I thought we were the best fucking group in the goddamn world, and believing that is what made us what we were," he said.

People who had never gotten the chance to see Dylan at a coffeehouse or the Beatles in a club were finally able to hear them a year after *The New York Times* and *Mersey Beat* had sung their praises. On October 30, 1962, Dylan received his first British radio airplay when the BBC midday show, *Twelve O'Clock Spin*, broadcast "Freight Train Blues," a song from his debut album, *Bob Dylan*, which he had recorded the year before, with John Hammond producing. The next day, the same BBC program played the Beatles' first single, "Love Me Do," which the group had recorded with George Martin. And now, with their apprenticeships complete, Dylan and the Beatles began moving toward each other.

■ ■ ■

When McCartney formed his poor first impression of Dylan at 20 Forthlin Road, calling his music "folk crap," Philip Saville, a British television director, had very much the opposite reaction.

On a trip to New York in the fall of 1962, Saville stepped into Tony Pastor's Downtown, a cabaret on West Third Street known for its drag shows and gay clientele. The place had been recommended to him by a friend, the British poet W. H. Auden, who lived nearby, and Saville had gone there with no expectations—only to be floored by the night's entertainment, the twenty-one-year-old Bob Dylan.

After his set, Saville offered him the lead role in *Madhouse on Castle Street*, a BBC Television drama scheduled to start filming in December. Dylan said he would have to talk with his manager about it. He had recently agreed to be represented by Albert Grossman, a physically imposing, sharp-tongued impresario out of Chicago who handled the sui generis singer and guitarist Odetta and the smooth-singing trio Peter, Paul and Mary, a group put together by Grossman with the aim of cashing in on the commercial folk boom.

Despite his noncommittal response, Dylan liked the idea of a London trip, partly because it would put him closer to Suze, who had left New York to study in Perugia, Italy. Bob had been miserable in the months since her departure—and he was letting everybody know how he felt. When he sang the British folk song "Barbara Allen," for instance, he left little doubt that he was Sweet William, the swain who dies of love for the "hard-hearted" title character.

Saville's offer appealed to Albert Grossman for a different reason. Like Brian Epstein with the Beatles, he looked upon his charge and saw Elvis Presley potential. In the contract he had worked out with his latest find, Grossman would receive a hefty cut from anything Dylan earned for theatrical, television, and film work.

In those days, Dylan's success beyond Greenwich Village was no sure thing. His first album, a collection of death-haunted folk and blues songs, with two originals mixed in, had sold a mere five thousand copies, and some executives at Columbia Records wanted him gone. But Bob knew he had something in his own compositions, which had been pouring out of him since Suze had left the tiny apartment on West Fourth Street they had been sharing. The batch included "Don't Think Twice, It's All Right," a barbed love song, and "A Hard Rain's A-Gonna Fall," which set Cold War anxieties to the melody and verse pattern of a centuries-old Anglo-Scottish folk ballad, "Lord Randall." He also had in his repertoire "Blowin' in the

Wind," an anthem with a melody that had grown out of the Black American spiritual "No More Auction Block" and words so elemental they might have been etched in stone.

Thus armed in December 1962, Dylan flew to London and checked into the May Fair Hotel, a posh establishment in the affluent Mayfair neighborhood, courtesy of the BBC. He showed himself to be perhaps too well suited to the role he was slated to play in *Madhouse on Castle Street*, that of a young anarchist named Lennie, by strumming his guitar and singing in the lobby, as if it were a busker's street corner, and smoking pot in his room. After he was made to feel unwelcome, he stayed at the home of Philip Saville in Hampstead before stops at other hotels and the couches of friends old and new.

During an early rehearsal of *Madhouse on Castle Street*, it was clear to Saville and the playwright, Evan Jones, that Dylan would not, or could not, learn his lines. "I don't know what I'm doing here," Bob said. "These guys are actors. I can't act!" It is a testament to the mesmerizing effect he must have had on others that the director and the playwright devised a custom role for him, rather than booting him from the production. Instead of Lennie the anarchist, he would play someone even more like himself—a character named Bobby, whom Saville described as "a rather uncommunicative American who's very articulate in song."

Saville was one of the first to recognize the power of "Blowin' in the Wind." He heard Dylan playing it early one morning for the pair of Spanish au pairs who watched over his children. "There he was at the top of the stairs, singing, and these two lovely little girls were like two little robins or starlings looking up at him," Saville said. He persuaded Bob to perform the song, still months away from its official release, in *Madhouse on Castle Street*.

A few people in London had some awareness of Dylan before his arrival—the Irish folk singer Martin Carthy, for one. He had found himself struck by the photo of Bob on the cover of the latest issue of the New York folk music magazine *Sing Out!*, which he had come across at Collet's, a book and record shop with a leftist clientele on Charing Cross Road. On December 21, 1962, shortly after Dylan's arrival, Carthy spotted him in the crowd at the King & Queen, a pub in Fitzrovia where he had often performed with his group, the Thameside Four. "You're Bob Dylan," Carthy said, by way of introducing himself. Later that night, Dylan gave his first performance outside the U.S. "The audience loved him," Carthy recalled.

There were also doubters. "The first time I heard Dylan perform, I thought he was awful," said Karl Dallas, a British journalist, activist, and songwriter. "Everyone appeared to agree. He went to a great many of the clubs, and he learnt a great many songs, and he played some of his own, and he was greeted with derision wherever he went." Another detractor, Nigel Denver, a Scottish folk singer, told Dylan he couldn't sing and couldn't play guitar or harmonica.

Bob soon realized he was walking headlong into an ideological battle when he passed through the doors of certain venues. His chief opponents turned out to be Ewan MacColl, a singer, songwriter, and song collector, and his girlfriend, Peggy Seeger, the half sister to the American folk singer Pete Seeger. They were founding members of the Singers Club, an association of musicians and music aficionados who held in common an idea of what could properly fall under the "folk" banner. In their construction, a folk song must exalt whole groups of people, particularly those who toiled in fields and factories, rather than any individual; and so, to convey a traditional song properly, a performer should deliver it in a neutral or custodial manner, allowing it to reach listeners untainted by personality.

The driving idea was the preservation of cultural artifacts, not the exaltation of the self, and the aim was anti-commercial. MacColl, a member of the Communist Party of Great Britain, had demonstrated his principles by recording an album with his mother, Betsy Miller, who had been born in 1886. Titled *A Garland of Scots Folksong: Betsy Miller and Ewan MacColl*, it included a plain rendition of the ancient Anglo-Scotch ballad "Lord Randall," the song Dylan had used as fodder for "A Hard Rain's A-Gonna Fall." Original compositions were to be created in the same spirit, as MacColl would show with one of his best-known works, "Dirty Old Town," a song (later memorably covered by the Pogues) about young lovers finding solace in their affection for each other against a harsh industrial backdrop.

Those who performed under the aegis of the Singers Club were further discouraged from attempting songs that didn't originate in their own home countries or ethnic groups, a policy intended to prevent them from engaging in the cultural thievery that often yielded music that was cringeworthy (see: Pat Boone) or offensive (see: blackface minstrel singers). On the other hand, this rule, built on a purist's notion of authenticity, promoted the separation of white culture from outside influence in a manner pleasing to the most virulent nationalist, xenophobe, or racist. "Our problem was English, Scots, Irish, and American performers singing songs whose idiom, whose language, they did not understand, hence mishandling the songs," MacColl said.

On December 22, MacColl and Peggy Seeger sat stone-faced as Dylan performed at the Pindar of Wakefield in King's Cross. "Only a completely non-critical audience, nourished on the watery pap of pop music, could have fallen for such tenth-rate drivel," MacColl wrote. Dylan played "Ballad of Hollis Brown," about a South Dakota farmer who kills himself after he is driven by poverty to murder his wife and children. Its melody arose from "Pretty Polly," an Appalachian mutation of a British folk song. Word spread among the hard-liners that this American newcomer was a cribber who didn't have the aims of the movement in mind.

The rules of the Singers Club made little sense to Dylan, who had grown up enthralled with all aspects of show business, from the entertainers passing through Hibbing, which included the wrestler Gorgeous George and the last of the blackface minstrels, to the Technicolor films playing at his uncles' theaters. Unlike MacColl, who had learned the old songs from his parents, Dylan found his calling mainly through the media—the high-watt radio stations that carried gospel, rhythm and blues, country, and rock 'n' roll to his neck of the woods. And when, at the end of his teenage years, he discovered Odetta, Guthrie, and others classified as folk, he was hit just as hard. Music was music, and it was all there for the taking.

In his memoir, Dylan knocks the arbiters he calls "the folk police." Yet he had sympathy for the argument that those belonging to dominant groups might be guilty of artistic theft, as evidenced by his teenage accusation that Presley had stolen from Little Richard. He would grapple with the issue in one of his greatest songs, "Blind Willie McTell," and the late-career album *"Love and Theft"*—but in his early twenties he wasn't about to be slowed by the idea that he might be guilty of something.

■   ■   ■

The Beatles rang in 1963 from the Star-Club stage. It was a rowdy, drunken New Year's Eve engagement, and their final Hamburg club show. In the rough-and-tumble of the St. Pauli district, arguments over cultural appropriation didn't rank high on their list of concerns as they bashed out dozens of songs by Black American artists. Their guiding principle in the early sixties, beyond getting the job done and getting paid, was that they should not play a diluted brand of rock 'n' roll in the manner of the anodyne performers who were staples of the British hit parade.

On January 1, 1963, the Beatles flew from Hamburg to London and checked into the Royal Court, a hotel on Sloane Square. It was a frigid day, part of a deep freeze that would last into the spring. Less than three miles away, Dylan was at the bar of the King & Queen pub with his new pal Martin Carthy. Ale was consumed. "Auld Lang Syne" was sung. Nigel Denver, the Scottish balladeer who had already tangled with Dylan, took the floor and sang a lengthy folk song, a cappella. Dylan heckled him: "What's all this fucking shit?"

The next morning, John, Paul, George, and Ringo woke to a new snowfall and went to London Airport to catch a flight to Scotland for a five-night tour. While they were playing in ballrooms, Dylan flew from London to Rome and met up with Albert Grossman and his client Odetta, who gave two concerts at Teatro Parioli. Bob's hopes of making a side trip to see Suze in Perugia were dashed when he learned she had gone back to New York a few weeks earlier. He drank red wine and wrote a pair of heartsick love songs, "Girl from the North

Country" and "Boots of Spanish Leather," setting the lyrics of both to old British melodies he had heard performed in recent days by Carthy.

Around the time of his return to London, Parlophone released the Beatles' second single, "Please Please Me." On January 12, Dylan and the Beatles played to audiences roughly thirty-six miles apart. Accounts of the two shows provide glimpses of them in the last moments when they still faced the challenge of trying to win over people who had little or no idea who they were.

The Beatles appeared at the Invicta Ballroom, a former vaudeville house in Chatham, Kent. It wasn't much of a room—lately, it had been used as a bingo hall—but it represented some progress in their attempt to conquer their home country in that it was the southernmost venue they had ever played.

While the Beatles still relied on the rock 'n' roll of their heroes, they were now working in what they had picked up from the next wave of American music. In Hamburg, they had gone as long as fifteen minutes playing Ray Charles's "What'd I Say," a song that joined gospel and rhythm and blues with a rumba beat. That rhythm had informed Ringo's lopsided drum pattern on "Please Please Me," setting it apart from the usual rock 'n' roll fare of the previous decade. The Beatles also played chart-toppers and obscurities by American girl groups, including the Ronettes, the Marvelettes, and the Cookies, and added still other flavors with country songs and the rhythm and blues balladry of the Alabama-born singer Arthur Alexander. Additionally, like Dylan, they were working originals into their sets, and audiences seemed to like the Lennon-McCartney songs "Love Me Do," "Please Please Me," and "I Saw Her Standing There" as much as their versions of other artists' hits.

Alan Cackett, who would go on to be a music journalist, was in the audience at the Invicta. "To be brutally honest," he wrote, "the sound that night was awful. It was muddy and far removed from the clear-cut sound of the pop records of the time. But from the opening strains of 'I Saw Her Standing There,' I was mesmerized."

That same night, Dylan played the Troubadour, a pub in Earl's Court. Eric Von Schmidt, an American folk singer who happened to be in town, recalled that Dylan, "outrageously high" on gin and marijuana, gave an arresting performance heavy on antics. "He seemed so wasted that you had a feeling he wouldn't be able to even gain the stage and like he'd fall down or fall off the front," Von Schmidt said.

The audience, he added, was "in near total shock." A man in a traditional Scottish kilt entered the pub and sat close to the stage. He glowered at Dylan and heckled him. Dylan ignored the man, continuing with the slapstick and songs. "At first it horrified me," Von Schmidt said. "And then I started thinking, this is one of the greatest things I have ever seen in my life."

The man in the kilt lit a cigarette and blew smoke at the stage. Dylan was not deterred. Finally, the heckler made his exit. Dylan kept playing.

4 Picture Imperfect

A few days after the Troubadour performance, Dylan, now back in New York, persuaded Suze to come back to the apartment above Bruno's Spaghetti Shop on West Fourth Street. For the rest of January 1963, he didn't play any shows or try to complete the album he had been piecing together in a series of sessions at Columbia Recording Studios in Midtown.

At the same time, the Beatles continued working at their usual frenetic pace. As "Please Please Me," not yet released in the U.S., was climbing the British charts on its way to becoming their first No. 1 single, they kept their Liverpool supporters happy with Cavern Club dates and brought new fans aboard through hit-and-run stops in the hinterlands—Morecambe, Macclesfield, Newcastle upon Tyne. They often played two shows a day, sometimes three. As hard as it was, these were their last days of independence: In early February 1963, they joined the more regimented world of mainstream British show business when they began traveling the country as part of a so-called package tour of seven acts.

At this point in their careers, the Beatles and Dylan needed one more thing to make themselves legible to the wider world: an image that would stick in the mind, an identity easy for the general public to latch onto. They added this element in mid-February, when they posed for album cover portraits that would define them for years to come.

The photographers who got the assignments were well matched to their subjects: Don Hunstein, a Columbia Records staff member who often shot Dylan in those years, had a journalistic approach, preferring to capture his subjects as they were; Angus McBean, a former set designer for the London stage who had photographed a number of British actors, favored elaborate setups and lighting effects that lent his pictures a theatrical touch.

The Beatles' photo shoot came shortly after they had put themselves through a breakneck, ten-hour session at EMI Recording Studios on Abbey Road, during which they recorded ten of the fourteen tracks that would make up their first LP, *Please Please Me*. George Martin's initial idea for the cover was meant to play on the "beetles" pun by having the group pose at the insect house of the London Zoo. Permission was denied, so Martin dispatched Angus McBean to get some suitable shots—and quickly.

McBean was a bearded man in his late fifties with a bohemian flair. When he stepped into the atrium-like lobby of EMI House, a modernist structure on Manchester Square built as the company's headquarters in 1960, he gazed at the ceiling seven stories above. The airy space, with its bright, modern look, struck him as just the right setting for his subjects.

"As I went into the door," McBean recalled, "I was in the staircase well. Someone looked over the banister. I asked if the boys were in the building and the answer was yes. 'Well,' I said, 'get them to look over, and I will take them from here.'" In matching suits, the Beatles appeared and did as the photographer had instructed. "To get the picture I had to lie flat on my back in the entrance," McBean said. "I took some shots and said, 'That'll do.'"

Portraits from the shoot were used not only as the cover of the soon-to-be-released first Beatles album but as the main artwork for *Twist and Shout*, their first four-song extended-play record (known as an EP), as well as the 1973 collection, *1962–1966*. Before the session was over, McBean asked Lennon how long he thought the group would last. "Oh, about six years, I suppose," John said. "Whoever heard of a bald Beatle?" Six years later, McBean returned to the same spot to capture a much-aged but definitely not-bald Beatles, who struck similar poses for a picture that would be used on the cover of the album *1967–1970*.

McBean's approach contrasted sharply with the most recent attempt to come up with the right visual representation of the group. During an October 1962 photo session, the four young men, not always bothering to smile, had posed on a chilly day in Liverpool. The idea was to show them as one with their faded home city, and they had stood near a burnt-out car and then on an empty lot against an abandoned brick warehouse. McBean took an altogether different tack, emphasizing the clean-lined backdrop of EMI House in portraits that depicted the Beatles as creatures of the current moment.

Designed by Gollins Melvin Ward, one of the first architectural firms to bring glass towers to London, EMI House was a novelty in a city of stone edifices. It suggested a stylish new identity for a nation dealing with the loss of its superpower status, the great majority of its former colonies, from Cyprus to Zanzibar, having gained their independence since the war. On the *Please Please Me* cover, the Beatles seem at ease with one another and their sleek surroundings, happy to be posing at a corporate headquarters rather than outside a Liverpool warehouse. Their suits have a relaxed look, more Continental than British, a precursor to the fashions soon to be part of the scene that would go by the name Swinging London. The chic clothes and modern setting were in keeping with the desires of these northerners, who were keen to sample the delights of the capital.

In publicity materials provided to the press in early 1963, John, Paul, George, and Ringo stated frankly that they wanted to make piles of money. They made the same point in a cover of a minor Motown hit that was a highlight of their shows: "Money (That's What I Want)." Lennon shredded his vocal cords as he put across this one, the only song in their repertoire that had nothing to do with romantic love. McBean's rendering of the Beatles captures that same spirit. In other words, while the cover of *Please Please Me* shows off the group's camaraderie, it is beneath the surface a picture of ambition.

The portrait on the cover of *The Freewheelin' Bob Dylan* has a scruffier look but, like McBean's photo, it takes the side of young strivers seeking their rightful place in the world. Don Hunstein, who had photographed Billie Holiday and Miles Davis, showed up at the West Fourth Street apartment on a freezing afternoon. Before his arrival, Bob had selected with care the "rumpled clothes" he wore for the occasion, Suze recalled in her memoir.

Hunstein got some nice shots of Bob and Suze in the cramped rooms, but he found it hard to move around and suggested they continue outside, despite the cold. Bob reached for his suede jacket. "It was an 'image' choice," Suze wrote, "because that jacket was not remotely suited for the weather." The photographer and his subjects walked along West Fourth on that frigid day before turning onto Jones Street, a short stretch of road in the Greenwich Village maze. "Well, I can't tell you why I did it," Hunstein said, "but I said, 'Just walk up and down the street.' There wasn't very much thought to it. It was late afternoon—you can tell that the sun was low behind them. It must have been pretty uncomfortable out there in the slush."

There was no car traffic, so Bob and Suze were able to stroll down the spine of the street, which was lined with small apartment buildings studded with iron fire escapes. Hunstein crouched low and aimed his lens upward, giving the couple the high ground. The portrait that emerged as the choice for the album cover was staged but real, contrived but natural. With its atmosphere of urban grit, it suggested, in the context of its time, a youthful rebellion against an increasingly suburbanized America.

The neighborhood Bob and Suze walked through that day was under threat. Although it was a vibrant part of town, with mom-and-pop shops and a rich street life, it was considered a slum by the people who ran New York City. Chief among them was the backroom political operator Robert Moses, who did more to shape the physical environment of the metropolis than any elected official. In the 1950s, Moses had led the Mayor's Committee on Slum Clearance, which oversaw the demolition of hundreds of homes and small businesses in Greenwich Village to make way for bland housing projects and new buildings for New York University. Since then, Moses had been pushing to eradicate hundreds of other old structures to clear space for the Lower Manhattan Expressway, a highway that would have displaced thousands. He also wanted to extend Fifth Avenue through the neighborhood's prime gathering spot, Washington Square Park. The activist Jane Jacobs led the ultimately victorious fight against those initiatives, a battle that was running hot at the time of Hunstein's photo shoot with Bob and Suze. Dylan had helped the cause by writing a song with Jacobs that was meant to rally the troops, "Listen, Robert Moses."

Aside from its suggestion of a political stance, the cover art of *The Freewheelin' Bob Dylan* is powerful simply because it captures young love. Suze is leaning into Bob with an affectionate familiarity as he steps forward, hands in his pockets, across the caked slush. Because of his downward gaze, his eyes appear half-closed, which puts him at a distance from us, while rendering him the main object of photographic interest. Suze is looking into the lens and smiling. She is one of us, in other words, while he is something else altogether—a youthful poet who has stumbled into a land of bohemian adventure, complete with a muse to guide him.

Suze prized her independence, but didn't quibble with the notion that she was Bob's muse. Their relationship had inspired him to write, among so many other songs, the melancholy "Tomorrow Is a Long Time," one of many Dylan compositions from that time that gave what may be the oldest type of song, the love song, a freshness and credibility. Suze was also Dylan's teacher—and he had sense enough to check with her when his lyrics hit on sociopolitical matters and topical issues, as they did for a number of songs on *The Freewheelin' Bob Dylan*.

At the start of their time together, she was the more wised-up of the two, although she was two and a half years younger. Suze had grown up in a working-class neighborhood of Queens, the daughter of intellectuals. Her mother, born in Italy, was a translator. Her father, an artist whose parents were Italian immigrants, worked a series of factory jobs. Both were active in the American Communist Party, and they provided Suze and her older sister, Carla, with a thorough education in the arts and politics.

At age seventeen, Suze was a budding artist and activist who lived on her own in Greenwich Village and earned money by waiting tables and doing clerical work at the Congress of Racial Equality and the National Committee for a Sane Nuclear Policy. She saw Dylan perform soon after he blew into town, and his unkempt appearance, between waif and rascal, amused her. He thought she was "the most erotic thing I'd ever seen," as he put it in his memoir, and she moved into his place on West Fourth Street when she turned eighteen.

"We got along really well," Suze wrote, "though neither of us had any skin growing over our nerve endings." One of their fights came after a night of drinking, when she noticed the draft card that had slipped out of his wallet: The name printed on it was not the one he had told her was his. He confessed he had been born Robert Zimmerman, but when it came time to explain the discrepancy to Suze's mother, he went into a convoluted tale about how he had been adopted by a wealthy Chicago industrialist, which had led to a mix-up concerning his legal name.

He grew possessive of Suze, though he was sleeping around. They escaped the chaos brought on by Bob's growing fame and sexual straying at the Shack, a cabin owned by Vera Yarrow, the mother of Peter Yarrow, of Peter, Paul and Mary, in Woodstock, New York, a bohemian enclave in the Catskills more than a hundred miles northwest of the city. But that didn't solve much. Suze's mixed feelings about Bob figured in her decision to spend six months in Italy, leaving him to moon about the neighborhood before his London trip. And now that he was back? Well, it wasn't bliss, but they couldn't dismiss the depth of their feelings.

The affection they had for each other is there on the cover of *The Freewheelin' Bob Dylan*. The historian Sean Wilentz, age twelve when the album came out, saw it as "a picture that, with its hip sexiness, was more arousing than anything I'd glimpsed in furtive schoolboy copies of *Playboy*," he wrote in *Bob Dylan in America*. Dylan also understood its power: When he handed out copies to friends, he said, "The cover's the most important part of the album."

■   ■   ■

Not long after the releases of *Please Please Me* and *The Freewheelin' Bob Dylan* in the spring of 1963, cracks began to appear in the attractive public images established by their covers.

As the Dylan album was about to be shipped to record stores, Bob provided fresh evidence for the idea that he was the rightful successor to Woody Guthrie when he withdrew from an appearance on *The Ed Sullivan Show*, the CBS variety program that had made a star of Elvis Presley in 1956.

Dylan had gone to CBS-TV Studio 50, a former Broadway theater in Midtown Manhattan, with the plan of performing "Talkin' John Birch Paranoid Blues," a comic excoriation of the John Birch Society, a group of right-wing extremists. But as showtime approached, the CBS legal department got jittery, and told Dylan he couldn't play it. At considerable risk to his commercial prospects, Bob walked out: The last musician to tangle with *The Ed Sullivan Show* was the rocker Bo Diddley, who had argued with the host after appearing on the program in 1955 and had not been on TV since.

In July, Dylan sang for an audience of Black sharecroppers at a voter registration rally in Greenwood, Mississippi. Later that month he became the darling of the Newport Folk Festival, the annual seaside gathering in Newport, Rhode Island, where he was praised and petted by the old-line leftists, who saw in him someone sure to carry the torch of politically engaged folk music into the future. In August, he sang from the steps of the Lincoln Memorial as part of the largest civil rights march on Washington, during which Martin Luther King Jr. delivered his "I Have a Dream" speech. At the time, Peter, Paul and Mary's version of "Blowin' in the Wind" was a No. 2 hit; and *The Freewheelin' Bob Dylan*, which included Dylan's recording of the song, was rising toward its peak of No. 22 on the album chart.

Bob had allied himself with Joan Baez, a politically minded singer and guitarist who favored traditional material. Four months older than he, she had blazed her way through the folk scene on the strength of her clear soprano voice and made herself into a nationwide star when he was still learning how to carry himself onstage. Theirs was a mutually beneficial relationship: He gave her songs to sing and an image better suited to the changing times, and she gave him access to her considerable fan base. Reporters dubbed them the king and queen of folk in their accounts of the couple's duets at Newport and Washington.

Beneath the acclaim, Bob was sputtering, and Suze felt in danger of losing her identity as someone with artistic aspirations of her own. She also decided she could no longer put up with his infidelities. Dylan was "a lying shit of a guy with women, an adept juggler really," she wrote. She moved out of the place on West Fourth Street, and Bob retreated to the sixty-acre property Albert Grossman had acquired in Bearsville, New York, a hamlet next to Woodstock.

Dylan's interest in Baez went beyond music, and in September he spent a few weeks with her at her modern home in Carmel, California. Staring out at the Pacific, he worked on something new, "Lay Down Your Weary Tune," a song that captured his restlessness. He had filched its enchanting melody from an old Scottish ballad he had come upon in her record collection, but the words that tumbled from his lips urged him to escape the folk scene and its homey but cloying atmosphere.

He went back to New York when he got word that Suze was pregnant. "I was feeling confined, and a child would be even more of a confinement," she wrote in her memoir. "On the other hand, maybe I would like to have a child. Bob was just as confused and very upset at the idea of an illegal—read, dangerous—abortion." She went through with it and fell into a depression.

A few weeks later, *Newsweek* poked holes in Dylan's image. His birth name, the magazine reported, was Robert Allen Zimmerman, and his past was not so intriguing as he had made it out to be. He was "the elder son of a Hibbing, Minn., appliance dealer named Abe

Zimmerman," and he "grew up in a conventional home, and went to conventional schools." *Newsweek* stuck the knife in deeper by noting that he had gotten tickets to his upcoming Carnegie Hall concert for his mother and father right after it quoted him saying: "I don't know my parents. They don't know me. I've lost contact with them for years."

His image took another hit in December 1963, when he was given the Tom Paine Award by the Emergency Civil Liberties Union at its annual dinner at the Americana Hotel in Manhattan. Wearing jeans and a workingman's shirt, and feeling out of place among the city's cultured elite, he drank too much red wine. At the start of his acceptance speech, he laid down the gauntlet by announcing that he was "young." "I'm proud that I'm young," he said. "And I only wish that all you people who are sitting out here today, or tonight, weren't here, and I could see all kinds of faces with hair on their head. Because you people should be at the *beach*."

The crowd laughed, as if this were the young fellow's humorous prelude to an inevitable turn toward grateful sincerity. He kept at it, though, when he described his thoughts on the assassination of President John F. Kennedy, just two weeks after the fact: "I've got to admit that the man who shot President Kennedy, Lee Oswald, I don't know exactly where, what he thought he was doing, but I got to admit, honestly, that I, too, I saw something of myself in him." The audience booed and hissed.

And so, six months after having appeared on the cover of his breakthrough album as the archetypal young bohemian, and a little more than three months after he had been the toast of the Newport Folk Festival, Dylan was revealed to be not just another son of the middle class, but one whose off-kilter political views seemed not to align with those held dear by the people who had propped him up as the new Guthrie. And the *Freewheelin'* portrait of a young couple in the throes of uncomplicated love was now sadly out-of-date.

■   ■   ■

The first crack in the Beatles' image appeared when John made news in Britain because of a violent incident, one that showed him to be at odds with the chipper young man on the cover of *Please Please Me*. The episode was tangentially related to a secret he had been keeping from the public: the fact that he was married.

John and Cynthia Powell had fallen for each other when they were students at the Liverpool College of Art. He was the sharp-tongued bad boy in a leather jacket, and she was the dutiful daughter of a bourgeois family in suburban Hoylake, across the River Mersey. They met not long after the death of John's mother, a time when, as he put it, "I was in a sort of blind rage for two years." Cynthia described herself in those days as "totally under his spell," but also "quite terrified of him for seventy-five percent of the time."

In 1962, they were married at a Liverpool registrar's office. The bride was pregnant. The groom was unenthusiastic. "It was more like a funeral than a wedding," is how Cynthia described the ceremony in her memoir. Afterward, as the Beatles gained fame across Britain, she hid herself away on the advice of Brian Epstein, who, in the tradition of managers before him, held that John had to be seen as available. When *Please Please Me* was in the middle of its twenty-nine-week run as Britain's No. 1 album, there was another secret to keep: John was a father.

Shortly after the birth of Julian Lennon, the Beatles had a rare break. Paul, George, and Ringo vacationed in the Canary Islands; rather than going on a trip with Cynthia, John spent his holiday with Brian in Barcelona, which became the subject of Liverpool gossip.

Brian, who was gay at a time when homosexual acts were illegal in Britain, tried to keep his sexuality secret. But ever since he had become the Beatles' manager in 1962, John had teased him mercilessly about his orientation, as well as the fact that he was a Jew. The two had nonetheless grown close—"almost inseparable," John's friend Pete Shotton wrote in his memoir—as they mapped out the Beatles' plans like a pair of generals in a battlefield tent. Shotton wrote that John confessed to having had some sexual contact with Brian in Barcelona, saying, "I let him toss me off." And in one of his last interviews, Lennon didn't go that far, but said: "Well, it was almost a love affair, but not quite. It was never consummated. But it was a pretty intense relationship."

On June 18, 1963, Paul hosted his twenty-first birthday party at the home of an aunt in Liverpool. He had recently started dating Jane Asher, a seventeen-year-old actress from a cultured London family, and she was present for the celebration. John arrived drunk and looking for a scrap. At some point Bob Wooler, the Cavern Club compere and a friend to the Beatles, needled Lennon about his "Spanish honeymoon." John knocked Wooler to the ground, grabbed a shovel or a stick—witnesses differ on the weapon—and hit him repeatedly in the head. "He'd insinuated that me and Brian had had an affair in Spain," Lennon said years later. "I was off me mind with drink. . . . And obviously I must have been frightened of the fag in me to get so angry. . . . So I was beating the shit out of him, and hitting him with a big stick, too, and it was the first time I thought, 'I can kill this guy.'"

The assault was the basis of the first article on the Beatles to appear in a national newspaper. "Beatle in Brawl Says 'Sorry I Socked You,'" ran the headline in the June 21, 1963, edition of the *Daily Mirror*. The report made no mention of what had set Lennon off; it also included an apology from him crafted by Epstein. But here was evidence that there was more to the Beatles than the good cheer of "Love Me Do" and the *Please Please Me* cover photo.

The mini-scandal was all but forgotten in a rush of concerts and media appearances, including a watershed performance in October 1963 on the popular ITV program *Sunday Night at the London Palladium*. The relentless campaign helped make the group's third single, "She Loves You," the biggest seller of all time in Britain. Mobs filled the streets when the Beatles arrived in this or that town, and police battalions were called in to keep order. The *Daily Mail* broke out a new word, "Beatlemania," to describe what was happening. Soon afterward, the *Daily Mirror* printed the term in an uppercase headline above a photo of a screaming girl.

Word of the phenomenon reached America. A few weeks before *Newsweek* would poke holes in Dylan's image, it ran a short piece on the Beatles, calling their music "high-pitched, loud beyond reason, and stupefyingly repetitive." In a television segment, CBS News noted with amusement the resurgence of a 1950s fad, rock 'n' roll music, in Liverpool, England, of all places. It included footage of the Beatles sprinting from an armored van to a stage door as officers in bobby helmets held back a mob beneath soot-gray skies.

Americans got another glimpse of the Beatles and the hysteria they had inspired on January 3, 1964, when *The Jack Paar Program*, a variety show on NBC, presented snippets of BBC footage capturing the group as it performed "She Loves You" intercut with shots of their fans, mostly girls and young women, screaming, weeping, and dancing. "It's nice to know that England has finally risen to our cultural level," Paar said in a tone of dry mockery.

5 It'll Never Happen

No matter how rocky their relationship, Bob and Suze saw eye to eye on art and culture, sharing a love of Arthur Rimbaud, Bertolt Brecht, Pablo Picasso, and François Truffaut. The only thing they really disagreed on in this regard, from late 1963 into early 1964, was the Beatles.

It's not clear when they first heard the group's music. Suze writes that they listened to rock 'n' roll radio stations in the West Fourth Street apartment; and Murray the K gave some airplay to "She Loves You" on his WINS show in the fall of 1963, when the song came out on a small American label after it had been rejected by Capitol Records, the independently operated U.S. company owned by EMI. But the Beatles didn't start catching on in America until mid-December, when a deejay in Washington, D.C., broadcast an import copy of "I Want to Hold Your Hand." The song took off, and Capitol rushed it into stores.

To help the Beatles catch on, the label plowed $50,000 into newspaper ads, record store displays, and stickers plastered on bus stops, telephone poles, and public bathrooms across the country. Capitol also shipped acrylic "Beatles Hair-do wigs" to its employees, instructing them in a memo to wear the wigs "during the business day" and pass some along to disc jockeys to "start the Beatle Hair-Do Craze that should be sweeping the country soon."

In those weeks of hype, Bob was dismissive when the Beatles came up. He called them "bubblegum" and made fun of the fact that they appealed to "teenyboppers." Suze let him know she disagreed. So did Al Aronowitz, a journalist who had been spending a lot of time with Dylan.

Aronowitz, who had grown up in New Jersey the son of a kosher butcher and a mother who spoke mostly Yiddish, was an unlikely Beatles fan. He was thirty-five years old, for one thing, and he had written extensively on jazz, Beat poetry, and the urban folk music revival. A friend to writers and musicians, and a big-time social connector, he had introduced Dylan to the Beat poet Allen Ginsberg in an apartment above the Eighth Street Bookshop. Bob respected Aronowitz's knowledge and taste, but he wasn't about to go along with his latest enthusiasm. "To me, Bob seemed to be pretty much a folkie purist in those days," Aronowitz wrote in a self-published memoir. "I used to argue with him that today's pop hits are tomorrow's folk music classics. He had no interest in the Beatles."

Sometimes Aronowitz would slip into impresario mode in his talks with Bob, telling him he had to do something to broaden his appeal, so that he wouldn't be stuck with the folk music crowd. "I felt that his message was almost holy and that it was my mission to encourage him to expand his audience," Aronowitz wrote. "I felt it important for him to reach the young. I somehow wanted his lyrics to enlighten the same teenyboppers then trying to claw the clothes off the Beatles. For Bob's part, his attitude was that he didn't want any of his concerts drowned out by teenybopper screeches. 'It'll never happen,' he told me."

In January 1964, Dylan and the Beatles found themselves in a kind of limbo.

Coming off a disorienting year of highs and lows, Bob was telling people he might try his hand as a playwright or novelist. His third album, *The Times They Are A-Changin'*, was coming out on the thirteenth, but he wasn't planning to do anything to promote it till February, when he would appear on a Canadian TV show. After that, he wanted to take a cross-country road trip, seeing America and giving a few concerts along the way.

The Beatles were in Paris, slogging through a three-week engagement at the stately Olympia Theatre before audiences of lukewarm Parisians in evening attire. The mania that had swept through Britain had spread as far as Sweden, as they had discovered on a recent concert tour—but Paris remained standoffish, especially early on.

Past midnight on January 16, after another disappointing show, John, Paul, George, and Ringo returned to their suites at the opulent George V. Their moods lifted when Brian Epstein received a call from New York: "I Want to Hold Your Hand" would appear at No. 1 in the next issue of *Cash Box*, a U.S. music industry publication. This was unimaginable. Even Cliff Richard, England's answer to Elvis Presley, had only gotten as high as No. 30 on any U.S. chart.

Thanks to a prescient deal Epstein had negotiated in November, the Beatles were already scheduled to go to the U.S. for a series of appearances on *The Ed Sullivan Show*. Now they would be able to make the trip with the momentum of a No. 1 hit behind them. And with their planned visit to the birthplace of rock 'n' roll having taken on a new concreteness, the Paris stay began to seem even more pointless.

After an all-night celebration, the Beatles got back to work. They endured the two or three daily sets at the Olympia and tried writing songs for a movie they were scheduled to start filming shortly after the trip to America. They also hit the town in the company of Lido showgirls and the American folk-pop singer Trini Lopez, who was among the acts on the Olympia bill. More consequentially, the Beatles started listening to Dylan.

McCartney was the one who brought Dylan's first two albums back to the suite he was sharing with John, a set of rooms that Brian Epstein had equipped with a stereo and a console piano. Paul had come across *Bob Dylan*, the debut album, as well as the newly available *The Freewheelin' Bob Dylan*, during a visit to a radio station shortly after the Beatles' arrival in Paris. Although he had dismissed

Dylan as "folk crap" about a year earlier, he was interested enough to share the records with his fellow Beatles, who played them over and over again. "Right from that moment," George said, "we recognized some vital energy, a voice crying out somewhere, toiling in the darkness."

John took special notice of the cap Dylan was wearing on the cover of his first album, since it looked so much like his own cap. George taught himself the guitar part for "Talkin' New York," one of the two originals on Dylan's debut, and found himself struck by the sight of Suze Rotolo on the cover of the second LP. All four Beatles knew "Corrina, Corrina," the only track on *The Freewheelin' Bob Dylan* not written by Dylan. It was a country blues first recorded by Bo Carter of the Mississippi Sheiks in 1928, with later versions by Big Joe Turner, Bill Haley, and Ray Peterson, and it had been in the repertoires of the Quarry Men and the Beatles.

One night in Paris, a week after they had learned of their American breakthrough, John and Paul got to work on "One and One Is Two," a song intended for Billy J. Kramer, who belonged to the stable of acts managed by Epstein. The business of writing songs for Kramer, Cilla Black, and other British performers was becoming a lucrative sideline for John and Paul, who took a jobber's pride in their ability to pump them out. The most notable example so far was "I Wanna Be Your Man," a simple rocker that they had finished writing at the request of a friend, the Rolling Stones' manager, Andrew Loog Oldham. John thought of "I Wanna Be Your Man" as a "throwaway," but the Stones' recording hit No. 12 in the UK. The Beatles' version, with Ringo singing, became a highlight of their second album and live shows.

Still in stage makeup after another Olympia performance, John and Paul now found themselves writing a song even more basic than "I Wanna Be Your Man." Paul jotted down the words on hotel stationery.

> *One and one is two*
> *What am I to do*
> *Now that I'm in love with you?*

John, wearing sunglasses, was seated at the small piano. Paul picked up his guitar. Michael Braun, an American journalist who wrote for British newspapers, was watching and taking notes for *Love Me Do: The Beatles' Progress*, the first significant book on the group. At one point, John tugged at his cap and hinted at the anxiety he had about Dylan: "Paul bought a Bob Dylan record," he told Braun, "and he was wearing this exact cap on the cover. He even had the button open, like mine. Everybody will think I copied it from him."

A few nights later, Mike McCartney, the first Dylan fan at 20 Forthlin Road, arrived at the George V—and immediately teased Paul by saying he was surprised to hear a Dylan record playing in the suite. Never one to show weakness, Paul told his little brother that John must have left it on the turntable.

At the end of the month, at Pathé Marconi Studios in Boulogne-Billancourt, the Beatles recorded the basic tracks of a new one by Paul, "Can't Buy Me Love," a blast of joy that would sell more than 2 million copies upon its release in the spring. Unusual for an up-tempo Beatles song in those days, it started with John's acoustic guitar out front, a texture that may have arrived as no accident, given how much they had been listening to Dylan.

In the U.S., *The Times They Are A-Changin'* was now in record stores. The black-and-white cover had the blunt beauty of a propaganda poster, with its portrait of a stern Dylan. The look matched the tone of the album, which was heavy on what Dylan called "finger-pointing songs." Breaks in the mood came in two songs of longing inspired by Suze, "Boots of Spanish Leather" and "One Too Many Mornings."

Al Aronowitz was supposed to have filed a story on Dylan before the album was out—but he had botched the job. "Assigned by *The Saturday Evening Post* to write an article about Bob, I instead had fallen in love with him," he wrote. "To me, no other artist had ever come along with such wit, perception, charm, cleverness, and charisma." At least Aronowitz had a promising new assignment: 3,500 words on the Beatles.

On February 1, 1964, the day "I Want to Hold Your Hand" reached No. 1 in *Billboard*, the leading music trade publication in the U.S., Dylan was in Toronto filming a performance for the CBC program *Quest*. The producer had placed him on a set meant to suggest a bunkhouse in a logging camp. As he strummed and sang, actors in the background, wearing denim and flannel, played cards and puffed on pipes. Bob offered plain renditions of six new songs, including his anthem of generational conflict, "The Times They Are A-Changin'."

The restlessness that had inspired "Lay Down Your Weary Tune" was still with him, however. Here at the height of his social-realist phase, he was questioning whether some of his songs, with their moral certainties, captured the nuances of how he was feeling and what was going on in the world. He also wondered if the critical praise and applause he had received amounted to little more than expressions of support for the political statements in his songs. Writing in pencil on a sheet of Toronto Waldorf-Astoria stationery, he began something not so easy to parse, "Chimes of Freedom."

> *Through the mad mystic hammering of the wild ripping hail*
> *The sky cracked out its poems in (naked) wonder*

Like many of its Guthrie-influenced predecessors, this song took the side of the world's underdogs. But it had none of the Oklahoma locutions Dylan had picked up from his hero—no "a-changin'"—and it struck him as a leap forward from his ballads of poetic reportage. "Chimes of Freedom" was the start of his break from the folk world.

On February 3, back in New York, Bob got in a new sky-blue Ford station wagon provided by Albert Grossman for his cross-country trip, which he had modeled partly after the Beat odysseys fancifully chronicled by Jack Kerouac in *On the Road*. He was joined by three companions: Victor Maymudes, Peter Karman, and Paul Clayton.

Maymudes, who had once given it a shot as a folk singer, had tried to manage Bob until the forceful Grossman took charge. Now, at age twenty-eight, he had taken on the roles of Bob's "mind-guard," chess opponent, roadie, and pal. Tall and thin, he was someone who "had an uncanny ability to keep his mouth shut," as Robert Shelton put it in one of the first Dylan biographies; Suze found him "silent and creepy."

Karman was a former reporter for the *New York Daily Mirror*. Like Suze, he was a so-called red-diaper baby, raised by Queens communists. He had been like a big brother to her when she had left her family home for Greenwich Village, accompanying her to Gerde's Folk City. Karman was also politically engaged, having gone to Cuba in protest of the U.S. travel ban instituted in the wake of the Cuban Missile Crisis, a bit of activism that got him booted from the *Mirror*.

Clayton was a scholarly folk singer who had made more than twenty albums. For one of his best songs, "Who's Gonna Buy Your Ribbons (When I'm Gone)," he had set his own lyrics to the tune of an old folk ballad—and Bob liked it so much that he swiped the melody for "Don't Think Twice, It's All Right." Clayton was thirty-two years old, on the downside of a coffeehouse career, and he got through the days on a combination of pills and pot. Although he had been dating Suze's sister, he was gay, a fact he didn't keep secret. The sniping gossips of Greenwich Village said he was willing to settle for being Dylan's brother-in-law, if that was his best shot at staying close to him.

The station wagon was packed to the brim as it moved down the New Jersey Turnpike—not only with Bob's guitar, typewriter, and the travelers' luggage, but with the clothes and supplies that Suze had gathered for striking coal miners in Hazard, Kentucky, a cause célèbre in their circle. It was dark by the time they reached Charlottesville, Virginia, the college town where Clayton, an alumnus of the University of Virginia, kept a house and a cabin. Bob called Suze from a pay phone before rejoining the others. Clayton pulled out a dulcimer and a stash. Maymudes rolled some joints, and they played Monopoly into the wee hours.

In the morning they stopped in at a record store to see if it had *The Times They Are A-Changin'* in stock. They bought ten copies with the idea of handing them out to strangers on the road. After a customer recognized Bob, a small crowd formed. He slipped out, followed by his little gang, and they motored through West Virginia and into Kentucky. On the way, they gave a ride to a soot-faced miner. In

Hazard, Maymudes went to the post office to pick up a package of marijuana he had mailed to himself, and they dropped off the goods for the striking workers. Bob had the idea of playing for them, but nobody seemed in the mood.

The travelers continued south. In Flat Rock, North Carolina, they showed up uninvited at the 240-acre goat farm belonging to Carl Sandburg, the esteemed poet, biographer of Abraham Lincoln, and folk-song collector born in 1878. Sandburg talked with his visitors for about an hour before saying he had to get back to work.

The next day, February 7, as Dylan and his companions were driving through Georgia, the Beatles boarded Pan Am Flight 101 at London Airport. In addition to the four group members and the people close to them—Cynthia Lennon, George Martin, Brian Epstein, and the tour managers Neil Aspinall and Mal Evans—the flight was packed with journalists and businessmen. Also on board was the young American record producer Phil Spector.

At thirty thousand feet, Paul expressed doubt about how the Beatles would go over in the land of their heroes: "Since America has always had everything, why should we be over there, making money? They've got their own groups."

The plane landed at 1:20 p.m. As it taxied down a runway of the newly renamed Kennedy International Airport (formerly Idlewild) in New York, the Beatles saw crowds on rooftops. They assumed a head of state must have been about to land or take off, having no idea that the big radio stations had heralded their arrival, calling it "B-Day." "The temperature is thirty-two Beatle-degrees!" a WMCA disc jockey shouted into a microphone as three thousand teenagers waited in the cold. There was a roar when the door of the Boeing 707 opened. George stepped onto the landing of the attached staircase, followed by John (in his cap), Paul, and Ringo.

Al Aronowitz was among the two hundred journalists waiting at the international arrivals building. Unlike many old hands in the room, he wasn't out to show that the Beatles were anything but the latest show business gimmick. He made a quick study of the people surrounding them and zeroed in on the sharp-eyed road manager,

Neil Aspinall. "If John was the commanding officer of the Beatles, Neil was his top sergeant," is how Aronowitz described him. He asked Aspinall if there was a place he had dreamed of seeing in New York. "The Apollo!" was his answer. Aronowitz promised to take him to the Harlem theater that night, and he was in.

In the early days of their fame, the Beatles usually found ways to enjoy their face-offs with the press, even when the questions were inane. At Kennedy, they won over their American inquisitors by demonstrating a fluency in the gibes and quips that had long been built into the argot of New York's newsrooms. Asked if they would sing then and there, John said flatly, "No, we need money first." Asked if they planned to get haircuts, George replied, "I had one yesterday." In answer to the question of why their music excited so many people, John said, "If we knew, we'd form another group and be managers."

Thousands of fans, held back by NYPD officers, twenty on horseback, were singing and chanting outside the Plaza Hotel in Manhattan as the Beatles' motorcade pulled in. After settling into their suites on the twelfth floor, John, Paul, George, and Ringo received the Ronettes, the trio from Spanish Harlem whose "Be My Baby," produced by Spector, had been a hit a few months earlier.

Soon the Beatles were on their way to the Peppermint Lounge, a mob-run nightclub that had reached its zenith in the summer of 1962, when it was the unofficial headquarters of a craze ushered in by the Philadelphia rhythm and blues singer Chubby Checker with his wildly popular remake of Hank Ballard and the Midnighters' "The Twist." Ringo, a veteran of Liverpool's dance halls, hit the floor with one of the Peppermint Lounge's twisters-in-chief, Geri Miller. The brothers Albert and David Maysles, a pair of documentary filmmakers based in New York, captured the action with a state-of-the-art lightweight camera and unobtrusive sound equipment; they had reached a deal to chronicle the Beatles' U.S. visit with Granada Television in Britain shortly before the group's arrival.

The next day, February 8, George was in bed with a sore throat and fever as the other three Beatles went through a rehearsal for *The Ed Sullivan Show* at CBS-TV Studio 50 on Broadway, where Dylan had stormed out the year before. From there, Epstein led the group to the Savoy Hilton, a hotel close to the Plaza, where Francis Hall, the owner of the guitar maker Rickenbacker, had filled a suite with his wares. At this point, John had been playing a Rickenbacker 325 with no sponsorship deal. Hoping to capitalize on Lennon's fondness for the brand, Hall had written to Epstein to arrange this meeting. John was fascinated by the Rickenbacker 360/12, one of the first electric twelve-string guitars. "You know, I'd like for George to see this instrument," he said. Later that day, George was heard playing it while giving a radio interview from his sickbed at the Plaza.

Dylan, just then, was nine hundred miles south, making his arrival at Emory University, a center of civil rights activism in Atlanta. As John, Paul, and Ringo dined at the "21" Club in the company of George Martin and Capitol Records executives, Bob played for more than a thousand people at the Glenn Memorial auditorium on the campus. At the reception afterward, he talked with Bernice Johnson Reagon, of the gospel group Sweet Honey in the Rock, and her husband, Cordell Hull Reagon, of the Freedom Singers, both activists who had sung at the Newport Folk Festival and during the recent March on Washington.

The next day, as Bob visited with the Reagons at their home, George emerged from his bed, and the Beatles took the Studio 50 stage to tape a performance that would not be broadcast until after their return to London.

Just after 8 p.m., at the start of the live show, Ed Sullivan threw up his right arm: "Ladies and gentlemen . . . the Beat-les!" The group took care not to alienate the American audience in the three-song set at the top of the program, opening with the cheerful "All My Loving." They followed it with "Till There Was You," a tuneful love ballad by Meredith Willson, the composer of the songs for the long-running Broadway hit *The Music Man*, with catch-in-the-throat singing by Paul and Spanish-style guitar work by George. The Beatles then delivered "She Loves You." Toward the end of the show, they returned with the double shot of "I Saw Her Standing There" and "I Want to Hold Your Hand."

Nielsen reported that more than 73 million viewers had tuned in. The only time more people had been watching TV at the same time had come during the coverage, spread across three networks, of the Kennedy assassination less than three months earlier. Dylan was apparently not among those who saw the show, but many of his friends and fans were riveted. Suze detected an immediate change in the cultural atmosphere, writing that the Beatles "had taken over the airwaves and our lives; folk music wasn't what it used to be." The future music critic and cultural historian Greil Marcus noticed the same thing. After the Beatles' appearance, he wrote, the folk club where he had been hanging out in California started playing the group's first Capitol Records album, *Meet the Beatles*: "The music, snaking through the dark, suddenly spooky room, was like nothing we had ever heard. It was joyous, threatening, absurd, arrogant, determined, innocent, and tough."

Roger McGuinn, a struggling musician who would go on to be a founding member of the Byrds, started playing folk-style arrangements of Beatles songs in the cafés of Greenwich Village. The response was lukewarm. Most people in the crowd didn't see the point of mixing the folk music they loved with the pop music they despised.

As the travelers moved through Alabama on February 11, the taciturn Victor Maymudes at the wheel, Dylan continued working on the opaque verses of "Chimes of Freedom." Unlike Jack Kerouac, who liked to write spontaneously, Dylan was a believer in honing his work until it met the standard he had in mind.

Peter Karman, the former newspaper reporter, got into a debate with Dylan over whether poets were conscious of their themes or if they wrote in a trance. Bob took the pro-trance position. Karman, who preferred the Dylan he saw onstage to the argumentative person he was getting to know in the station wagon, objected to his move away from songs that dealt with social issues. It was selfish, in Karman's view, for someone with Dylan's gifts to indulge the whims of the muse at the expense of making a practical contribution to society.

At the same time, the Beatles were seeing America through the windows of a morning train as it rolled southward out of New York through a snowstorm that would leave six inches along much of the East Coast. They caught glimpses of Newark, Trenton, Philadelphia, and rural Maryland on their way to Washington, D.C., where they had a concert that night. They had decided against a planned flight after George had refused to fly in a "fookin' blizzard."

At the Washington Coliseum, a boxing arena with poor acoustics, the Beatles played their first American show before a sold-out audience of more than eight thousand. Some of the screaming fans pelted them with jelly beans, a tradition that had gotten its start in Britain after John had mentioned in an interview that they were George's favorite candy. To their dismay, the Beatles learned that the jelly beans in the U.S. were harder than the ones in Britain, where they were called jelly babies. After their last bow, they suffered through a formal reception at Britain's U.S. embassy, where someone sneaked up on Ringo and snipped off a lock of his hair. He was unsettled by this invasion of privacy; John was livid.

That same night, Dylan, Maymudes, Karman, and Clayton, having crossed through Louisiana, were drinking and smoking their way through New Orleans, where Mardi Gras was in full swing. On Bourbon Street, Maymudes pointed out a street singer, with guitar, who was in the middle of performing Dylan's "Don't Think Twice, It's All Right."

"You sing that very well," Bob said.

"You aren't Bob Dylan, are you?"

Dylan and Maymudes laughed as they moved away from the young man and into an eventful night. Bob stepped into traffic without checking for cars; boasted that he had read the French author Jean Genet; debated the value of formal education with a high school teacher from Alabama; argued with a white bartender about why he wouldn't serve Black people; argued with a Black bar owner about why he wouldn't serve white people; tripped and fell in the street, twisting an ankle, while chasing two young women; and announced, while limping up a staircase to a fourth-floor party, "We are all just steps."

On the morning of February 12, the Beatles took in the sights of Washington, D.C. Then they boarded a train at Union Station to make the journey back to New York, where they were scheduled for two shows that night at Carnegie Hall. George donned a porter's costume and offered cans of 7Up on a tray to the ever-present journalists; Ringo, having weighed himself down with an equipment bag and several cameras, pretended to be a newshound photographer. "Never mind the music, these boys are as good as the Marx Brothers," a reporter said. Paul sat alone, stone-faced, after three days of American Beatlemania. "I'm not in a laughing mood," he said to the camera operated by Albert Maysles. John spent much of the ride in a compartment with Cynthia, who wore sunglasses and a "Beatles Hair-do wig" to throw off photographers.

More than a thousand fans awaited their arrival at Pennsylvania Station in Manhattan. The police, having determined that the mob was "festive, but potentially dangerous," spirited the Beatles into a freight elevator and led them through underground passageways to a waiting limousine and Yellow Cabs. As John, Paul, George, and Ringo pushed through afternoon traffic, Dylan and his team were moving north on country roads through Louisiana. Seated in the back of the station wagon, Bob was working on something dreamy and mysterious: "Mr. Tambourine Man."

A few hours later, the NYPD tried to control a mob outside Carnegie Hall. It included a contingent of male college students, who carried signs that read "Go back to the English slums where you belong" and "Beatles undermine artistic integrity." Girls charged them.

When the Beatles took the stage, it was hell. Having sold more tickets than there were seats, the organizers had placed 150 spectators in folding chairs on the stage for both shows, at 7:45 and 11:15, and the Beatles couldn't hear themselves over the screams. "It wasn't a rock show; it was just a sort of circus where we were in cages," Lennon said. This was an early creeping in of the doubts that would intensify: Was their purpose to make it big, to be "the toppermost of the poppermost," as John had put it in a half-serious rallying cry when things seemed bleak? Or were they in it for some other reason? If so, what was it?

At 1 a.m., the Beatles were back at the Plaza. A reporter for *Photoplay* magazine had brought along Jill Haworth, an actress on contract with the Hollywood producer Otto Preminger. When Paul entered the suite—one foot in a Chelsea boot, the other in a sock—he locked eyes with her and gave his name, as if she didn't know it. Like the fans who were learning all about the Beatles through the barrage of media coverage, Haworth knew he was in a relationship with Jane Asher. After she had introduced herself, Paul said, "Well, Jill, how about fixing me a drink while I find my other boot? And make one for yourself while you're at it."

After downing a couple of scotch and Cokes, the Beatles' usual drink, she rode in a cab with Paul, John, and Cynthia (in Beatle wig) to the Headliner Club, a Midtown nightspot. As a house band played, Ringo danced the Twist and the Mashed Potato on the parquet floor with Jill and a few other women. A table of hecklers started razzing John. One of them took a swing at him. Cops stepped in to stop the brawl before it began in earnest.

Soon after daybreak, the Beatles were on a flight from New York to Miami. They were en route to the Deauville Hotel, where *The Ed Sullivan Show* was setting up for a special Florida episode. At the same time, the sky-blue station wagon was following a westward course to Dallas. There, Bob and friends inspected Dealey Plaza, the site of the Kennedy assassination, and discussed their theories of what had really happened.

On February 14, as Bob moved north toward Denver, the Beatles went to see the insult comic Don Rickles at the Deauville Hotel's ballroom. Unfamiliar with his act, they were taken aback when he painted a verbal portrait of John, Paul, George, and Ringo lying between satin sheets in their rooms as teenage girls serenaded them with screams from below. The Beatles laughed along with the crowd, but inside they were seething. The next day, they went fishing from a yacht (George caught a red snapper). In Colorado, Bob reached a decision: "Chimes of Freedom" was ready to go. He gave the song its debut in Denver that night.

On the afternoon of February 16, as the Beatles put themselves through their last *Ed Sullivan Show* rehearsal in Miami, Dylan,

Maymudes, Karman, and Clayton were rolling through the Rockies. The Beatles were blasting out of the car radio—and the sound hit Bob with the force of an epiphany, erasing his earlier skepticism.

"Did you hear that? Fuck! Man, that was fucking great. Oh, man—fuck!"

■ ■ ■

He would elaborate on that moment in 1970, speaking with the biographer Anthony Scaduto: "I had heard the Beatles in New York when they first hit. Then, when we were driving through Colorado, we had the radio on and eight of the ten top songs were Beatles songs. In Colorado! 'I Wanna Hold Your Hand,' all those early ones.

"They were doing things nobody was doing. Their chords were outrageous, just outrageous, and their harmonies made it all valid. You could only do that with other musicians. Even if you're playing your own chords you had to have other people playing with you. That was obvious."

Dylan's remarks suggest he could hear what made the Beatles innovative. That set him apart from the critics who said they were merely rehashing a genre that had gone out of style with the death of Buddy Holly, the induction of Elvis Presley into the army, and the religious conversion of Little Richard. As noted, the Beatles had moved beyond that crew, drawing from the musical innovations of the early 1960s, a time maligned by those who would rather make too much of the dull pop of the teen idols Fabian and Frankie Avalon than celebrate the easy joy of Marvin Gaye, the poetry of Smokey Robinson, the catchy sophistication of the Ronettes, and the remarkable fusion of jazz, pop, country, and gospel in the work of Ray Charles.

Underpinning the Beatles' enthusiasm for the latest sounds was their affection for the standards of their pre–rock 'n' roll childhoods, sturdy songs built on finger-stretching guitar chords that George worked seamlessly into their music. The clever weaving of so many threads is what made "I Want to Hold Your Hand" and "She Loves You" leap out of the radio, at once strange and familiar. And an understanding of what the Beatles had packed into their songs might be why Dylan had landed on the word "valid" to describe what they were up to. There was something profound here, despite the simplicity of the lyrics, and in Colorado he was suddenly able to hear it.

"Everybody else thought they were for the teenyboppers, that they were gonna pass right away," he continued. "But it was obvious to me that they had staying power. I knew they were pointing the direction of where music had to go. I was not about to put up with other musicians, but in my head the Beatles were *it*."

After making it to California, Dylan sat in a beach café in Santa Monica, feeding quarters into a jukebox to hear "She Loves You" and "I Want to Hold Your Hand" again and again. Then came one of the biggest shows of his life: the Santa Monica Civic Auditorium on February 29. From the moment he took the stage, his audience was roaring with a new intensity. After the show, fans tried to beat down the dressing room door. Bob felt trapped—he thought he might be crushed if he stepped outside—and he paced like a caged animal.

Finally, he decided to push his way through the mob. In addition to Maymudes, two people helped him make his way forward: Bob Neuwirth, a twenty-four-year-old singer, songwriter, and painter who was becoming part of the entourage; and another friend, Maria D'Amato, a twenty-one-year-old singer who had grown up in Greenwich Village (and who would later have a hit, "Midnight at the Oasis," under her married name, Maria Muldaur).

Bodies swarmed Dylan as he moved toward the station wagon. Once he was inside the vehicle, fans pounded on the hood. Maymudes, at the wheel, inched forward, trying to break free of the crowd without hurting anyone. On the drive away from the auditorium, he saw that other cars were following close behind. Just then, Neuwirth and Muldaur noticed something stirring beneath the tarpaulin in the back. They pulled it aside to reveal two teenage girls.

Dylan had said it would never happen, but it seemed he was becoming a pop star.

6 Ego Equals

Al Aronowitz loved the Beatles—but not so much that he couldn't complete his assignment for *The Saturday Evening Post*. His profile of the group was the cover story of the March 21, 1964, issue, which sold more copies than any other edition of the magazine since its founding in 1821. In the piece, Aronowitz chronicled the U.S. visit, contrasting the manic reaction of the fans and media hordes with vignettes that captured the grind of the Beatles' working lives. He described Lennon as the group's leader and reported that he had lately been listening to Ray Charles, the Chiffons, the Marvelettes, Marvin Gaye, and Bob Dylan.

John was "as much stricken by the photograph on the album cover as he was by the emotional power of Dylan's words, music, and voice," Aronowitz wrote. As in his interview with Michael Braun in Paris, Lennon seemed concerned that people might think he had stolen something from Dylan—namely, the cap. "I've got a photograph of myself at home which looks just like him," he told Aronowitz. "It surprised me, you know. With the cap pulled down and unbuttoned. Do you wear them that way in America, too?" Aronowitz was the first writer to note similarities between the two. If Lennon had been born in the U.S., he wrote, he would have ended up in Greenwich

Village, "where he and Dylan might have met like two mirrors at the opposite ends of a hall."

Lennon and Dylan were also alike in that they shared literary ambitions, something almost unheard of in those days for anyone who had a song in the pop charts. Years before his arrival in New York, Dylan's interest in the written word had been stoked by his love for John Steinbeck's *The Grapes of Wrath* and the classical authors he had read at Hibbing High. During his college stint, he became enamored of Woody Guthrie's autobiography, *Bound for Glory*, and Keroauc's *On the Road*. In one of his first big interviews, with Studs Terkel in 1962, he said he was thinking of writing an autobiography. He wouldn't come through with anything in that vein until 2004, with *Chronicles: Volume One*, but he regularly wrote poems and prose sketches that didn't lend themselves to music. In the fall of 1963, he met with the Beat poet and publisher Lawrence Ferlinghetti to discuss writing a book for City Lights, the company behind Allen Ginsberg's *Howl and Other Poems* in 1956.

The issue of *The Saturday Evening Post* with the Beatles on the cover included an excerpt of Lennon's forthcoming book, *In His Own Write*, a collection of poems, prose pieces, and drawings. It ran across three pages beneath a précis that read "Original fiction and poetry by the brainiest Beatle of them all." And so a large-circulation magazine with a heartland audience was treating its readers to such literary grotesqueries as "Randolf's Party," the tale of a lonesome guy—based on the former Beatles drummer Pete Best, whose given first name was Randolph—who is murdered by his closest friends.

Lennon had reached a deal with the London publisher Jonathan Cape in the fall of 1963. He added the finishing touches to his manuscript during the Beatles' stay in Paris, and the book was published in Britain on March 23, 1964. Across its seventy-eight pages, *In His Own Write* brimmed with puns, spoonerisms, malapropisms, and grammatical absurdities—a style that drew from the author's love of Lewis Carroll, as well as Peter Sellers, Spike Milligan, and Harry Secombe, the creators and stars of the BBC radio comedy *The Goon Show*.

The cover photograph showed Lennon wearing the much-discussed cap, with the snap undone, à la Dylan.

The reviews were not only good but ecstatic. Critics compared the twenty-three-year-old author to Carroll, Edward Lear, James Joyce, and Geoffrey Chaucer. The line between high culture and low culture was beginning to blur as the intellectual establishment grappled with the seeming paradox that the co-composer of "She Loves You" was capable of producing the stuff of literature. And perhaps the Beatles' music was not so mindless after all: In an essay for *The Times* of London, the critic William Mann called Lennon and McCartney "the outstanding composers of 1963." He had special praise for "the Aeolian cadence at the end of 'Not a Second Time,'" noting that it had the same "chord progression which ends Mahler's *Song of the Earth*."

Among those trying to uphold the old standards was Paul Johnson, a thirty-five-year-old Oxford-educated journalist who wrote an essay denouncing the Beatles and the new youth culture. Published under "The Menace of Beatlism" in *The New Statesman*, a journal of the British intelligentsia, the piece doubled as an attack on Black American art. In the years before the Beatles, Johnson wrote, jazz was the battleground for British intellectuals, with some finding it profound and others dismissing it as junk. Much to Johnson's dismay, the pro-jazz side had won that fight. "Nowadays," he wrote, "if you confess that you don't know the difference between Dizzy Gillespie and Fats Waller (and, what is more, don't care) you are liable to be accused of being a fascist." But Johnson had hope: The teenagers who liked the Beatles, he asserted, were not representative of British youth. "Those who flock around the Beatles, who scream themselves into hysteria, whose vacant faces flicker over the TV screen, are the least fortunate of their generation, the dull, the idle, the failures," he wrote.

Lennon seemed halfway inclined to agree with those who saw his songs as disposable. The introduction of Dylan into the Beatles' bloodstream was part of what would inspire him and his songwriting partner to take a more ambitious approach, a shift they would put into practice not long after John had a talk with the BBC journalist Kenneth Allsop on the day *In His Own Write* was published.

By the time of his interview with Lennon, Allsop had written ten books, including a critical study of the Angry Young Men, a group of working-class writers known for their rude naturalism. Allsop didn't consider the Beatles the next step in that movement, but he saw value in *In His Own Write*. And while John had been liberated from the drabness of mid-century England by Little Richard, he was enough of a budding man of letters to have doubts about an ideology built on "A-wop-bop-a-loo-mop, a-lop-bam-boom." In an off-microphone chat, Allsop appealed to John's literary side, asking why he didn't infuse his lyrics with the darkness of vision and flights of linguistic fancy that had given the book such charm and power.

The question stayed with John, reinforcing what he had felt while immersing himself in Dylan. He was attracted to Dylan's sound and image—but he believed the lyrics set his work apart, and he rebuked himself for writing words that seemed to fit a formula. "I'd have a separate songwriting John Lennon who wrote songs for the meat market," he said, "and I didn't consider them, the lyrics or anything, to have any depth at all." Dylan nudged him toward a new mode: "Instead of projecting myself into a situation, I would try to express what I felt about myself. . . . I think it was Dylan who helped me realize that—not by any discussion or anything, but by hearing his work."

Lennon didn't give himself credit for the innovations of "Please Please Me," "I Want to Hold Your Hand," and "She Loves You," which sounded like nothing else on the radio because of their absorption of so many musical strands. And he may not have realized that he had already strayed from the usual pop lyrics in "There's a Place," a track on the Beatles' debut LP. The "place" of the song is the self—if it can be made inviolable, the outside world will cease to matter. It was a theme Lennon would return to again and again.

For *A Hard Day's Night*, the album the Beatles were recording at the time of the book's publication (while also filming a movie of the same title), John had come up with another one at odds with his earlier work. It was "I'll Cry Instead," and it cut deeper than the usual heartbreak song, because its narrator is not sad and lonely in the sympathetic manner of his counterparts in laments by Johnnie Ray, Roy Orbison, or Elvis Presley; he is, instead, a man who vows to exact revenge on an ex by purposely breaking other women's hearts. Al Aronowitz considered "I'll Cry Instead" the first Lennon composition to bear the stamp of Dylan.

■   ■   ■

Although he was taking steps away from what he had come to see as the restrictions of pop songwriting, John was flummoxed in the first days of his literary success by the disparity between the establishment's sudden approval of his work and his perception of himself as a rocker. So it came as a bit of a shock on the afternoon of April 23, 1964, when he found himself the guest of honor at the Foyle's Literary Luncheon, a monthly gathering hosted since 1930 by the family-run book franchise with a grand flagship store on Charing Cross Road.

The night before the event, John and Cynthia had gone to the recently opened Ad Lib Club in Soho. "Totally ignorant of what was to be our fate the following day," Cynthia wrote, "we drank, danced, and enjoyed ourselves with gay abandon until the very early hours of the morning. After about four hours' sleep and a great deal of grunting and groaning, we fell out of bed, heads banging, eyes bloodshot, and hands trembling." As they stepped from a chauffeured car toward the entrance of the Dorchester Hotel, an art deco palace overlooking Hyde Park, they consoled themselves with the thought that "it was only a luncheon and would soon be over," Cynthia recalled. Once inside, they were overwhelmed: "Reporters surrounded us firing questions like ammunition."

Among the white-tied gents and jeweled dowagers in the formal dining room, John saw a few familiar faces, including the comic actor Wilfrid Brambell, who played the foil to the Beatles in the film *A Hard Day's Night*. The majority of guests, however, belonged to the class that he had long purported to despise, leaving him as ill at ease as Dylan had been among Manhattan's intellectual establishment four months earlier at the Americana Hotel.

Lennon refrained from lobbing insults at the audience, but he didn't exactly endear himself to those feting him. In their accounts of the luncheon, Cynthia and Brian Epstein recalled that John had no idea that Foyle's honorees were expected to deliver a speech. The moment of truth arrived when the guests raised their glasses in a toast. "The silence was deafening," Cynthia wrote, "and the lone, terrified, crumpled figure of John stood up slowly and nervously, his face white and twitching in the glaring lights."

"Uh, thank you all very much," Lennon said. With a mock military salute, he added: "God bless you." He sat back down, turned to an aged gentlemen seated to his left, and made a crack that was picked up by a microphone: "You've got a lucky face." Cynthia noted "the disappointment and disgust of all who were gathered there." Sir Alan Herbert, a novelist and member of Parliament, was aghast. "A shameful affair," he said to Epstein. Four days later, *In His Own Write* was published in the U.S. The copies disappeared from bookstores.

On or about that date, at Albert Grossman's house in rural Bearsville, New York, Dylan is said to have tried a potent hallucinogenic, lysergic acid diethylamide 25, with a group of friends. "Everybody had a lot of fun," said Paul Rothchild, who would later distinguish himself as the producer for the Paul Butterfield Blues Band, the Doors, and Janis Joplin. "And if you ask me, that was the beginning of the mystical Sixties right there." Maymudes, in his memoir, recalled that, when the LSD kicked in, Dylan did what he did so often—sat down at his typewriter and "wrote several pages."

Dylan has given conflicting accounts of his drug use over the years, but strongly implied in a 1966 interview that he had taken acid: "LSD is medicine—a different kind of medicine," he said. "It makes you aware of the universe, so to speak; you realize how foolish *objects* are. But LSD is not for groovy people; it's for mad, hateful people who want revenge."

Around this time, Dylan wrote a letter to Lawrence Ferlinghetti, saying he still intended to come up with a book for City Lights. In later years, he would often say that his decision to write a full-length work—*Tarantula*, which would not be published until 1971—was inspired by Lennon's *In His Own Write*.

■   ■   ■

The Beatles finished up the filming of *A Hard Day's Night* and went on holiday. John and Cynthia spent much of May in Tahiti with George and his girlfriend, Pattie Boyd, a model who would soon appear wearing a nightgown in a *British Vogue* feature headlined "Things That Go Wham in the Night." Paul and Ringo jetted off to the Bahamas in the company of Jane Asher and Ringo's girlfriend, Maureen Cox, a former Liverpool hairdresser who had been a Cavern Club regular.

In the hull of a yacht, Paul worked on "Things We Said Today," a song more ambitious in its lyrics than anything he had attempted before, suggesting he was as ready as his songwriting partner to move beyond the pat scenarios of the early Lennon-McCartney hits. Like "Bob Dylan's Dream," a track from *The Freewheelin' Bob Dylan*, Paul's new one was a melancholy song suffused with memory and longing.

In the Dylan composition, the narrator drifts off to sleep on a train and falls into a dream of the days he had spent laughing and talking with "the first few friends I had." The dream leaves him yearning for those times. In the McCartney composition, the narrator imagines a future version of himself who yearns for what he is going through in the current moment. This notion of looking back on the present—"future nostalgia," Paul would call it—leaves him wistful in advance. The Beatles recorded "Things We Said Today" a few weeks after it was written, during the last session for *A Hard Day's Night*; Dylan would end up recording his own version of the song for a McCartney tribute disc in 2014.

While John, Paul, George, and Ringo were on vacation, Bob arrived in London, ready to give his first major concert outside the U.S. If the Beatles had won over America by selling their take on American music to Americans, Dylan was about to attempt something similar by offering British audiences his own adaptations of songs he had borrowed from England, Ireland, and Scotland.

Before his performance at the Royal Festival Hall, he sat for an interview with Maureen Cleave, of the *Evening Standard*, who had been deftly chronicling the Beatles for more than a year. Although Dylan had been exposed as a teller of tall tales, he didn't hesitate to fill Cleave's notebook with wild stories of his wayward youth, telling her, "I ran away with motorcycle gangs, carnivals, traveling druggists." After mentioning that he was writing two books of poetry and a novel, he said he found the Beatles to be more sensitive than most folk singers.

He took the stage just after 3 p.m. on May 17 before a sold-out audience of nearly three thousand. Seated in the crowd was his old Hibbing pal John Bucklen, who had pantomimed "Be Bop a-Lula" with Bob several years earlier and was now a U.S. Air Force officer stationed in East Anglia. Dylan started with "The Times They Are A-Changin'," a song with a tune he had soldered together from a pair of ballads in the Scottish-Irish songbook, "Come All Ye Bold Highwaymen" and "Come All Ye Tender-Hearted Maidens." Next came "Girl from the North Country," which had a melody adapted from the traditional British standby "Scarborough Fair." Later in the show, he played "The Lonesome Death of Hattie Carroll," which he had built on the tune of "Mary Hamilton," a sixteenth-century Scottish ballad.

If the melodies were old, the lyrics were startlingly new, by turns plainspoken and ornate, and of the moment in their concerns. "The Lonesome Death of Hattie Carroll," for instance, was based on the true story of a Black housemaid who was killed in 1963 by her rich white employer, William Zanzinger. In this song, Dylan ventures into surprising lyrical territory when he follows his stark account of the murder by instructing his listeners:

> *Take the rag away from your face*
> *Now ain't the time for your tears*

In his grim view of human nature, forged in the years after the Holocaust and the atomic bombing of Japan, a horrible murder is simply to be expected. The truly sickening thing is the judicial system's refusal to condemn such an act. And so Dylan allows that his listeners' tears are justified only after he notes the fact that the judge gave Zanzinger "a six-month sentence."

> *Oh, but you who philosophize disgrace and criticize all fears*
> *Bury the rag deep in your face*
> *For now's the time for your tears*

During the intermission of his big London debut, he was handed something backstage: a telegram signed by John Lennon. This is the first known contact between Dylan and the Beatles. It said that the Beatles had hoped to attend the show, but were unable to make it.

Dylan showed the telegram to his old Hibbing pal. "Oh, man, that's pretty neat," John Bucklen said.

After intermission, Dylan played more songs with roots in the English, Scottish, and Irish folk traditions, including "With God on Our Side," "Ballad of Hollis Brown," "A Hard Rain's A-Gonna Fall," and "Don't Think Twice, It's All Right." He also hinted at the less easily classifiable artist he would become, giving "Mr. Tambourine Man" its concert debut. Bucklen was amazed that his childhood friend had been able to pull off such a show. He had even seen a man weeping in the audience.

After the performance, even here, so far from home, a throng descended on the dressing room, and fans pounded on the taxi that took Dylan away. "I think the people in the crowd just wanted to touch him," said Kenneth Pitt, a Columbia Records publicist who escorted Dylan that day. In the taxi, Bob pointedly asked his old Minnesota friend what he thought of him now. Bucklen replied only that he seemed a little thinner, a little strung out. The answer did not please Dylan, who, in the wake of the ovations he had received, seemed suddenly out of sorts.

Back at the May Fair Hotel, Dylan indulged in a bit of a star tantrum, arguing with staff members who objected to his attempt to take a young woman to his room. When Bucklen told him to let it go, he lit into his friend, ending the diatribe with: "Mind your own damn business!" Bucklen walked out of the lobby in anger. The two wouldn't see each other again until 1989, when they reunited backstage at the Dane County Memorial Coliseum in Madison, Wisconsin. Dylan apologized for his behavior at the May Fair, as if it had happened a week or two earlier.

On the evening of June 7, 1964, shortly after his return to New York, Dylan arrived at Columbia's Studio A in Midtown. He was accompanied by Al Aronowitz and Ramblin' Jack Elliott, and he had brought with him two bottles of Beaujolais. He planned to make his next album that very night, in one go. In a session that went from about 8 p.m. to 1:30 a.m., he favored spontaneity over polish in songs that presented him as flawed, intemperate, lustful, hectoring, and sometimes just plain unpleasant—in short, no longer on the side of the angels. Although he was performing solo, accompanying himself on guitar, harmonica, and piano, he further distanced himself from folk with a musical attack straight out of rock 'n' roll.

The session included "Ballad in Plain D," a confessional song in which Dylan recounted the final breakup with Suze, which had taken place recently at the apartment of her sister, Carla, on Avenue B in the East Village. During the argument, Suze had grabbed a knife, threatened to kill herself, and collapsed to the kitchen floor. She didn't harm herself, but was mumbling in gibberish as she lay there. "I was a mess of whirling, wordless, and no longer containable sounds," she wrote in her memoir. Carla and Bob shoved each other. "The two of us were really going at each other as if our lives depended on it," Carla recalled. In "Ballad in Plain D," Dylan describes the Suze character as an innocent and castigates her "parasite sister." Suze would write of the song: "He sure knew how to maul me." And Bob would say of "Ballad in Plain D": "That one, I look back at and I say, 'I must have been a real schmuck to write that.'" It took up more than eight minutes of the album, which Columbia Records titled *Another Side of Bob Dylan* against Dylan's wishes and much to his annoyance.

On the night of his recording session, the Beatles were playing two shows at the Princess Theater in Kowloon, Hong Kong. From there they bounced through severe storms on a flight to Australia.

Thousands greeted them at the Mascot International Airport. Thousands more lined the roads as they were paraded through a cold rain on the back of a flatbed truck. Nothing like this had been seen in Australia since the royal tour of Queen Elizabeth II a decade earlier. Britain's reputation, now that it was more of a cultural than military power, lay with these four young men from Liverpool.

As the tour continued, the crowds became almost unfathomable. In Adelaide, an estimated 200,000 people watched the Beatles ride from the airport to the city center; another 30,000 were packed outside the city hall. In Darwin, a reported 100,000 people filled the streets; in Melbourne, it was 250,000.

Increasingly, the Beatles were viewed as healers. A woman tried to give her handicapped six-year-old son to Paul in hope of a cure. The fans also expressed their ardent feelings in a kind of unconscious hostility, continuing to fire jelly babies. "Many times we come off the stage and it looks like we've gone through a war zone," Lennon remarked at the time. The Beatles learned they were in more serious danger when the authorities informed them that a bomb threat had been made before one of their shows. There were also bacchanals that went unmentioned in the reporters' dispatches. Years afterward, one of the journalists noted that "with the amount of Beatle screwing that went on, I just can't believe there wasn't an explosion of little Beatles all over Australia."

The group returned to London on July 2, four days before the film release of *A Hard Day's Night*, a comedy that owed much of its sensibility to *The Goon Show* and the anti-Hollywood ethos of cinema verité and the French New Wave. Despite the unpolished quality that set it apart from the usual fare, it still presented a rosy view of Beatlemania and the group's life on the road by skipping over the sex, death threats, and cultish adulation. At the premiere, a crowd estimated at twelve thousand brought Piccadilly Circus to a standstill, with fans waiting for the group's arrival at the London Pavilion theater.

Chronicling the Beatles on this day, once again, was Al Aronowitz, who had flown to London after watching Dylan record *Another Side of Bob Dylan*. Once the film had played, he accompanied the four

Beatles to a party at the Dorchester Hotel. There, he saw John and Paul congratulate Brian Jones and Keith Richards of the Rolling Stones on the No. 1 success of their new single, "It's All Over Now." At the next stop, the Ad Lib, Aronowitz drank with John, Paul, Richards, Jones, and Pete Hamill, an American journalist working as the European correspondent for *The Saturday Evening Post*. As the night wore on, Aronowitz kept singing Dylan's praises—irritating John, who was deep in scotch and Coke.

"To hell with Dylan," Lennon said.

"No, John, listen to him," Aronowitz said. "He's rock 'n' roll, too."

"Dylan. Dylan. Give me Chuck Berry. Give me Little Richard. Don't give me fancy crap. Crap. American folky intellectual crap. It's crap."

Months after he had been honored by the literary establishment and challenged by Kenneth Allsop to go deeper in his lyrics, the mercurial John was a rocker once more. Wasn't the overall sound the main thing? Wasn't "A-wop-bop-a-loo-mop, a-lop-bam-boom" as profound as anything produced by poets who had the blessing of highbrow critics? This argument would rattle around in Lennon's head for years to come, never to be resolved.

After his outburst, he complained about the "Yanks" at the Ad Lib, saying they should "get the hell out of here."

"Ach, come off it, John," Paul said.

John's next target was Pete Hamill, a Brooklyn-bred, street-tough son of Irish immigrants who had gone into journalism after having served in the U.S. Navy.

"Why don't you fuck off?" Lennon told him.

"Why don't you make me?" Hamill replied.

"Hey, come on," Aronowitz said, "let's just try to have a good time."

Lennon and Hamill held each other's glares. Aronowitz detected something in the eyes of both men that prevented them from coming to blows—"a fear each one had of the other."

From London, the Beatles flew to Liverpool for the northern UK debut of their movie. An estimated two hundred thousand people clogged the familiar streets as they arrived by motorcade. John,

Paul, George, and Ringo felt embarrassed to be receiving a heroes' welcome in their bedraggled home city. Aronowitz was with them once again. At some point, he told Lennon he should really get to know Dylan, adding that he could arrange a meeting himself.

"John kept saying he wanted to wait until he was Dylan's 'ego equal,'" Aronowitz wrote. "'Yes, I wanna meet 'im,' Lennon told me, 'but on me own terms.'" The journalist also kept singing the praises of marijuana, telling John it was better than the "purple hearts" and other pills the Beatles had ingested since their Hamburg days. "Finally, John said he would try some if I brought it to him," Aronowitz recalled.

A few weeks later, Dylan was at the Newport Folk Festival, presenting a new version of himself to many of the same fans who had taken him into their hearts the previous summer. This was not the night he famously "went electric," but a step along the way. At the topical-song workshop on the afternoon of July 24, he showed his independence, or recalcitrance, by performing the decidedly non-topical "It Ain't Me, Babe" and "Mr. Tambourine Man." Two nights later, he stepped onto the main stage dressed in tight jeans, pointed boots, and a suede jacket. "He no longer looks like a gaunt Okie bard; he looks like a cheery Beatle," the music historian Elijah Wald wrote of his appearance.

Strumming his acoustic guitar, Dylan performed his new songs ("All I Really Want to Do," "To Ramona," "Mr. Tambourine Man," "Chimes of Freedom"), each of them miles distant from the overtly political material of *The Times They Are A-Changin'*. Robert Shelton, the author of the *New York Times* review that had helped make Dylan's career, omitted any mention of Dylan's set from his Newport write-up. Other critics welcomed the new incarnation, however, and the audience demanded two encores. Bob seemed in high spirits, uncharacteristically telling the crowd, "I love you."

He left the festival grounds with Ramblin' Jack Elliott. In the Ford station wagon, the two of them heard something on the radio that immediately seized their attention: the age-old folk song "The House of the Rising Sun," which they had both performed, in a radically new version by the British rock band the Animals. According to Ramblin' Jack's perhaps overly polished account, he and Dylan pointed at the car radio and cried out simultaneously: "That's *my* version!"

The details of Dylan's reaction aside, he was indeed struck by the Animals' treatment of "The House of the Rising Sun," a song he had recorded for his debut album in an arrangement that closely followed the version by Dave Von Ronk. The Animals had built their rendition on Dylan's while serving as an opening act for Chuck Berry on a recent UK tour. By the time Dylan and Ramblin' Jack heard the song, it had already hit No. 1 in the UK. Considered alongside Dylan's Colorado epiphany, the Animals' reworking of an old folk ballad would prove one more factor in his musical evolution.

■   ■   ■

Al Aronowitz's second feature on the Beatles was the cover story of the August 8, 1964, issue of *The Saturday Evening Post*. He ended it with a soliloquy from Derek Taylor, a onetime reporter who had grown up near Liverpool and was now the Beatles' press liaison. "Here are these four boys from Liverpool," Taylor said. "They're rude, they're profane, they're vulgar, and they've taken over the world. It's as if they'd founded a new religion. They're completely anti-Christ. I mean, I'm anti-Christ, as well, but they're so anti-Christ they shock me, which isn't an easy thing. But I'm obsessed with them. Isn't everybody? I'm obsessed with their honesty. And the people who like them most are the people who should be outraged most. In Australia, for example, each time we'd arrive at an airport, it was as if de Gaulle had landed or, better yet, the Messiah. The routes were lined solid, cripples threw away their sticks, sick people rushed up to the car as if a touch from one of the boys would make them well again."

When the issue hit the newsstands, *Another Side of Bob Dylan* was in the record stores, and Dylan invited Joan Baez to stay with him at Grossman's compound in Bearsville. "Most of the month or so we were there, Bob stood at the typewriter in the corner of his room, drinking red wine and smoking and tapping away relentlessly for hours," Baez wrote in her memoir.

On August 8, Joan and Bob went down to New York City for a concert of hers at Forest Hills Tennis Stadium in Queens, where she entertained a sold-out crowd of nearly sixteen thousand with traditional songs including "I Once Loved a Lass" and "Pilgrim of Sorrow." *The New York Times* praised the show, adding that it was almost ruined when Dylan joined her for three songs and annoyed the crowd with his "raucously grating singing."

Four days after that, nine thousand screaming fans greeted the Beatles at San Francisco International Airport. They were at the start of their first lengthy tour of North America, a west-to-east excursion of twenty-five shows. Amid the cheers and adulation, there were daily annoyances and nightmarish moments. At the Cow Palace just outside San Francisco, fifty fans were injured. The next day, between the group's 4 p.m. and 9 p.m. performances at the Las Vegas Convention Center, the police evacuated the hall because of a bomb threat. Finding no explosive devices on the premises, the authorities allowed the nighttime show to go on.

In Seattle, the Beatles had a lovely view of Elliott Bay from their rooms at the Edgewater Inn, but they were virtual prisoners. Police boats patrolled the waters, and the hotel property was blocked off by a plywood fence topped with barbed wire. The next stop was Vancouver, where they played to their largest audience yet, a crowd of more than twenty thousand at Empire Stadium. Thousands rushed the stage, bringing the show to a temporary halt, and dozens of girls suffered broken ribs in the crush.

The atmosphere was different when the Beatles made their debut at the Hollywood Bowl. It was a pleasantly cool night at the sold-out amphitheater, with nearly nineteen thousand fans in the seats. For a change, they didn't have to fight a losing battle against the screams, thanks to the venue's state-of-the-art sound system. "The Hollywood Bowl was marvelous," Lennon recalled.

The sonic clarity allowed the Beatles to take one of their gentler songs, "Things We Said Today," and make it into something dynamic.

Working as a tight unit, they built dramatic tension by playing softly through the first verse, which is in the melancholy key of A minor. Then came the joyous release of the bridge, which is in the hopeful key of A major. In this portion, the Beatles played with abandon. Then, all at once, they reined themselves in, playing softly as they reentered the minor key, with Ringo propelling the music with a calmly loping drum pattern and George adding delicate guitar accents on the offbeats. Before the next shift into major, Paul threw back his head and gave a shout. That set off a siren-like surge from the rafters, a chorus of wails that filled the night air. He was making the crowd into a fifth musical instrument.

Two days after that show, as the Beatles were preparing to fly from Los Angeles to Denver, a reporter asked Lennon: "What about folk music, Joan Baez and that type of thing?"

"Well, we all like Joan Baez, but we love Bob Dylan."

"Joan's boyfriend, there," the reporter said.

"Oh, is *that* what it is?" John said. "Well, well, Bob, you've got to watch the image, you know."

■   ■   ■

Toward the end of her summertime stay in Bearsville, Joan described her relationship with Bob in a letter to her mother: "We understand each other's need for freedom, and there are no chains, just good feelings and giggles and a lot of love. And I enjoy his genius." In the next paragraph, she noted that she had made plans to see the group that had sent the nation into such a frenzy: "I'm gonna meet the Beatles in Denver. I just adore them."

As part of her light concert calendar that summer, Joan had agreed to perform at Red Rocks Amphitheatre, a nine-thousand-seat venue in Morrison, Colorado. The Beatles were scheduled to play there on August 26. That show was briefly in jeopardy because of a letter sent to the local police by a man who signed himself "Beatle Hater." "If you know what's good for you, cancel Denver engagement," he wrote. "I'll be in the audience and I'm going to throw a hand grenade instead of Jelly Babies."

After an investigation, the authorities gave the all clear. George Martin and Brian Epstein watched the stage with concern as the Beatles raced through their set. "We looked down at the boys below during the performance," Martin said, "and the amphitheater is such that you could have a sniper on the hill who could pick off any of the fellows at any time, no problem. I was very aware of this, and so was Brian, and so were the boys."

Baez attended the show in the company of a folk music purist she had dragged along, Harry Tuft, the founder of the Denver Folklore Center. Shortly after the final bows, she hung out with the Beatles at the Brown Palace Hotel in Denver, where she was also staying. She was charmed by the fact that the Beatles were thrilled that they could get bottles of Coke free of charge from the hotel's soda machine, simply by pressing a button. At some point, the topic turned to Baez's onstage and offstage partner—"All she could talk about, really, was Dylan," Tuft recalled—and she encouraged John, Paul, George, and Ringo to meet him during their stopover in New York.

Two days later, at 3 a.m., the Beatles touched down at Kennedy Airport. Even at this hour, an estimated two thousand fans, confined by police to a roof deck, were waiting to greet them. One man in the crowd was found to be carrying a rifle. The weapon was confiscated by police. To the din of screams, the Beatles sprinted from the jet to a waiting limousine.

At the Delmonico Hotel, on the corner of Park Avenue and East Fifty-Ninth Street in Manhattan, they had to break through a mob at the entrance. A girl snatched Ringo's St. Christopher medal, a gift from an aunt that he wore for luck, while trying to kiss him. A trio of more enterprising fans, the Brandstatter sisters of Queens—Lynn, age twenty-one; Penny, sixteen; and Debbie, five—were already staying in a $48-a-night room at the Delmonico in hopes of meeting their heroes.

As the Beatles made their way to their sixth-floor suite, the police warned them not to go near the windows. At daybreak, there were thousands of people below.

The Brandstatter sisters tried to breach the sixth floor, only to be turned away by security guards. During a noontime press conference in the Delmonico's Crystal Ballroom, the Beatles showed some weariness with the questions they had fielded a thousand times before. Back in the suite, Lennon placed a phone call to Al Aronowitz. He got right to the point.

"Where is he?"

"Who?"

"Dylan!"

"Oh, he's up in Woodstock, but I can get him to come down."

"Do it!"

It seemed that now—after hundreds of thousands of people had filled the streets to see the Beatles in Australia, Europe, and North America; after *A Hard Day's Night*, the movie, had been acclaimed by critics, and *A Hard Day's Night*, the album, had gone to No. 1 around the world; after five of their songs had appeared in the U.S. Top 10 at the same time; after *In His Own Write* had been praised as something akin to Joyce and Chaucer—now, finally, Lennon saw himself as Dylan's "ego-equal."

7   Beatlemania Here

A light rain was falling in Bearsville on August 28, 1964. Toward evening, Victor Maymudes was at the wheel of the station wagon, rolling down the dirt road through the woods of Grossman's property. Dylan sat next to him, smoking a Marlboro. He was dressed for the occasion in a dark suede jacket over a dark turtleneck. Maymudes, also in a turtleneck, lit a joint as he followed country roads to the southbound lanes of the New York State Thruway.

On the car radio, it was Beatles, Beatles, Beatles. Earlier that month, "A Hard Day's Night" had become the fifth of the seven No. 1 hits the Beatles would have in the U.S. that year. It was a catchy song with a complex arrangement—blues-based, but with sophisticated chord voicings—and it put on full display the advantages of the group's collaborative mindset. The title came from a playful phrase, coined by Ringo, that Lennon had already seized upon for a prose sketch in *In His Own Write*. John was the main writer of "A Hard Day's Night," but the melody for the bridge lay beyond his vocal range—so Paul took that part, giving the song some textural variety and a kick of energy.

> *When I'm home, everything seems to be right*
> *When I'm home, feeling you holding me tight, yeah!*

The most prominent instrument was the recently acquired twelve-string Rickenbacker electric guitar played by George, which provided a novel jangling sound. Other innovations of "A Hard Day's Night" included the dissonant chord at the start, a mysterious blend of notes that would be reverse engineered by guitar geeks for years to come, and a dreamlike fade-out heavy on the twelve-string's chiming tones.

"Bob could feel the magic in their music," Maymudes recalled. "As we listened to their songs on the drive, we focused on the architecture of their sentences." He further noted that Dylan understood why the Beatles had "crossed over into mainstream culture," adding: "It was a boundary he very much wanted to cross."

Al Aronowitz was nervous with anticipation as he waited for Dylan at his home in Berkeley Heights, a commuter suburb in New Jersey. Although he counted himself a friend to such paragons of hip as Miles Davis, Allen Ginsberg, and Jack Kerouac, he wasn't always able to play it cool, and he knew it. Aronowitz was an excitable person given to bouts of self-loathing, and he often found himself racked with the worry that he would say or do the wrong thing in the company of people he admired. Tonight the stakes were high.

He had been working toward this moment for nine months—starting in the weeks before the Beatles' arrival in America, when he had tried to persuade Dylan of the group's genius, and continuing through his reporting trips to England, when he had tried to sell a hot-and-cold Lennon on the possibility of a meeting. In Aronowitz's mind, tonight's get-together would be not just a gathering of show business luminaries, but a major event "in the overall history of culture." Dylan and the Beatles were "fated to meet," he wrote, and he saw himself as "fate's helper."

Marijuana was very much on the night's menu. To Aronowitz, who had become a pot smoker in the 1950s under the tutelage of Ginsberg and Kerouac, cannabis wasn't just a relaxant or social lubricant, but a "wonder drug." Like many Beat writers and the hippies soon to arrive on the cultural scene, he considered it a gateway to enlightenment. He was also well aware that, in the days when the mandatory minimum federal prison sentence for possession was two years, his plan came with risks for everyone involved. Still, he had seen to it that Maymudes would bring along a stash to the planned summit at the Delmonico Hotel.

As the station wagon approached Aronowitz's house in the fading late-summer light, the Beatles were en route to the Forest Hills Tennis Stadium by helicopter. Thirteen months after their last show at the homey Cavern Club, they would now be separated from an audience of more than sixteen thousand by a phalanx of policemen. A chain-link fence topped with barbed wire kept out the overflow crowd. There had been nothing like this when Joan Baez, with Dylan as her mid-show guest, had played the same venue two weeks earlier.

The Beatles finally took the stage at 9:50 p.m., after four opening acts. The strict security measures didn't deter Mary Smith, a seventeen-year-old from Connecticut, who had told her parents she was babysitting that night. Before the show, she had sneaked her way into the VIP section. When the Beatles were onstage, she simply climbed the stairs. "I'm not sure George saw me coming," she recalled, "so when I put my arms around him, he was at once surprised, terrified, and seemed to be screaming." Dozens of other fans, some crying uncontrollably, others nearly comatose, were treated in a Red Cross tent on the grounds.

The Beatles survived their half-hour set—which included "A Hard Day's Night" and Little Richard's "Long Tall Sally"—before the quick helicopter ride back to Manhattan. They entered the Delmonico through a service entrance and rode the elevator to the sixth floor. Ringo was the first to step into the hallway. Someone was there to greet him.

"Good evening, Mr. Starr."

The voice belonged to a little girl in a pink dress: Debbie Brandstatter of Queens, the five-year-old who was staying at the hotel with her two Beatlemaniac sisters.

"What a clean little girl. Would you like to come to our room for a little while?"

Ringo, whose ease with children had been captured by the Maysles brothers in their documentary of the Beatles' first visit to the U.S., took her by the hand. In the inner sanctum, Debbie shook hands with John, Paul, and George and mentioned that her sister Penny was out in the hall, hoping to say hello. Ringo said they'd love to meet her sometime, but right now they just wanted to relax. After a few minutes, George left for a side room, and Ringo showed Debbie to the door.

Waiters streamed in and out of the suite. As the Beatles settled in for a late-night room-service dinner, Maymudes was driving across Manhattan in the Ford station wagon, with Dylan riding shotgun. The bearded Aronowitz, wearing a dark blazer and a necktie, sat in the back.

Maymudes parked on a side street a few blocks from the Delmonico. At this hour, the neighborhood was serene. Aronowitz popped out of the car, saying he would see what was going on. For Bob and Victor, the journey from the Catskills to Manhattan by way of suburban New Jersey had taken more than five hours. Now they had to bide their time in the parked station wagon as Al made the final arrangements.

■   ■   ■

Nearly an hour later, Aronowitz returned. The three men began walking the quiet blocks toward the Delmonico. "As we got closer," Maymudes recalled, "we started to hear what sounded like an ocean. Like white noise from a television. We turned a corner onto Park Avenue and there was this huge crowd. We couldn't believe it. It was like a crisis had happened. There were people behind barricades on both sides of the street and cops on horses walking up and down Park Avenue."

None of the fans seemed to recognize Dylan, something Maymudes attributed to his shape-shifting ability: "Bob can walk and look unlike Bob. He hunches over, he softens his body, curls his shoulders and walks so innocuously that you don't pay attention to him." His chameleon routine fooled Henry Grossman, a *Life* magazine photographer who had made the Beatles one of his specialties.

He didn't recognize Dylan, even when he aimed his lens at him. Grossman had decided to take a picture only because he recognized someone at his side, Neil Aspinall, the Beatles' road manager. It wasn't until forty years later that Grossman realized, while looking through old contact sheets, that Dylan was in the photo he had snapped that night. In a suede jacket, his unkempt hair falling over his ears, he struck a figure much different from the Depression-era proletarian he had embodied on the cover of *The Times They Are A-Changin'* at the start of the year.

The visitors spun through a revolving door. In the lobby, Maymudes felt a hand gripping his shoulder—and was thrown. He landed on his back, on the sidewalk out front, "in the middle of the braying masses." "It happened in an instant," he wrote. "I was thinking, Oh, fuck! I'm going to get arrested; I'm holding all the pot!" Aspinall came to his rescue, crying out, "He's with me!" Maymudes got to his feet. He checked his pocket. The stash was still there.

Dylan, Aronowitz, and Maymudes rode the elevator to the sixth floor. They saw before them a smaller version of the carnival they had witnessed outside—reporters, photographers, and various others hoping for an audience with the Beatles, with twenty cops watching over them. The throng included Peter, Paul and Mary, and the cleancut folk group the Kingston Trio. The inevitable Murray the K had also made the scene.

Dylan, Aronowitz, and Maymudes were ushered past the courtiers and into the suite. This was the eye of the storm. They saw a dining table laden with the remnants of the room-service dinner and bottles of scotch and champagne. There was also a glass coffee table with four chairs set around it. Through the closed windows they could hear the crowd chanting and singing Beatles songs. Aronowitz felt like "a proud and happy *shadchen*, a Jewish matchmaker, dancing at the princely wedding I'd arranged." As the go-between, he was the one to make the formal introductions—and when he did so, it was "with an awkwardness for which I will always hate myself," he wrote.

Maymudes recalled that Dylan extended "his traditional limp handshake" to the four Beatles, "and each shook it in turn." John lit a cigarette and offered smokes all around. Aronowitz mentioned that Maymudes had nearly gotten trampled on the sidewalk below. "They were very kind to me," Maymudes wrote, "asking if I was feeling all right. I checked again to make sure the pot was still in my pocket and told them I was fine."

Brian Epstein offered refreshments. Dylan asked for his usual—cheap red wine. "I'm afraid we only have champagne," Epstein said. There was some talk of procuring some Chianti. This was a job for Mal Evans, a big friendly giant of a man in thick-frame glasses who had worked for the Beatles as a road manager and jack-of-all-trades since the Cavern Club days. But the mission was called off when Dylan helped himself to scotch. His choice of beverage caused some concern for Aronowitz, who had often seen Bob passed out or vomiting after drinking even small amounts of hard liquor.

An awkward hush fell over the room.

"At first Bob said very little," Maymudes wrote. "He cannot talk to a group of people, except from the stage, and that's hardly a conversation. It's a monologue. John Lennon was the same way." Aronowitz made a similar observation: "For two of the greatest communicators of their time, Dylan and Lennon both certainly seemed to give the appearance of being tongue-tied every now and then." Lennon concurred: "When I met Dylan, I was quite dumbfounded."

After some shoptalk about guitars, the Beatles offered the Dylan camp some pills from their supply. Starting in the Hamburg days, one of Lennon's favorite ways of getting to know someone was to hand over a Preludin and then sit back and listen to them speed-talk. Aronowitz and Maymudes, who disapproved of synthetic drugs, said they had brought along some pot.

"We've never smoked marijuana before," Epstein said.

This was true for Epstein, but not for everyone else in the suite. Harrison would say in later interviews that the Beatles had tried marijuana in Liverpool around 1960 and again in Hamburg, apparently to no great effect. But it seems that no one present mentioned those experiences, given that a number of participants would mention the following exchange:

"But what about your song?" Bob asked. "The one about getting high?"

"Which song?" John asked.

"You know . . ." And Dylan sang a snatch of "I Want to Hold Your Hand": "'I get high! I get high! I get high!'"

"Those aren't the words," John said. "The words are, 'I can't hide, I can't hide, I can't hide.'"

Despite his years of experience, Aronowitz couldn't roll a proper joint. He asked Dylan to do the honors, though he wasn't much good at it, either, and he seemed to be showing the effects of the scotch, scattering leaves everywhere. The result of his handiwork was a skinny, ill-formed joint.

Because there was the possibility of waiters barging in, not to mention the cops outside the door, the group retreated to a bedroom. Dylan handed the joint to Lennon, who passed it on to Ringo, saying he was his royal taster. Ringo lit up. "Take a deep breath of air together with smoke and hold it in your lungs for as long as you can," Aronowitz said.

Unacquainted with the custom of passing a joint to the next person, Ringo took hit after hit. Rather than explaining the niceties of marijuana etiquette, Aronowitz asked Maymudes to roll a few more. John, Paul, George, and Brian were soon equipped with joints that rivaled factory-made cigarettes in their neatness and firmness.

Derek Taylor, the Beatles' press liaison, was in a separate room, charged with keeping outsiders away from the action. He spent much of the night babysitting cops, journalists, the Kingston Trio, Peter, Paul and Mary, and Murray the K.

"We all had a puff," McCartney recalled, "and for about five minutes we went, 'This isn't doing anything,' so we kept having more." Ringo was the first to crack. He claimed the ceiling was coming down and started giggling—which set off the others. "His laughing looked so funny," Aronowitz wrote in his account of the night, "that the rest of us started laughing hysterically at the way Ringo was laughing hysterically. Soon, Ringo pointed at the way Brian Epstein was laughing, and we all started laughing hysterically at the way Brian was laughing."

"I'm so high, I'm on the ceiling!" Epstein kept saying.

The Delmonico would report that its switchboard fielded more than two hundred thousand calls during the Beatles' two-night stay, and the phone rang nonstop as the party went on. Dylan picked up, saying: "This is Beatlemania here."

In Hamburg, Paul had been the most prudent of the Beatles when it came to the amphetamines that had powered them through their onstage marathons. Now, as he began to feel the effects of the marijuana, he believed he was truly thinking for the first time. "I suddenly felt like a reporter, on behalf of my local newspaper in Liverpool," he said. "I wanted to tell my people what it was. I was the great discoverer, on this sea of pot, in New York."

He asked the trusty Mal Evans to find a pencil and paper. By this time, Mal was high, too, so it took him quite a while to carry out the task. Piece of paper finally in hand, Paul wrote "The Message of the Universe" at the top. Then he asked Mal to follow him from room to room and write down every word he said.

George asked Bob about the woman on the cover of *The Freewheelin' Bob Dylan*. Dylan said she wasn't far and suggested that George give her a call and ask her to come by.

These days Suze Rotolo was living on Avenue B, in the same narrow apartment where, five months earlier, she and Dylan had gone through the fight that had given rise to the song he would come to regret, "Ballad in Plain D." Now that apartment had a Beatles poster on the wall.

When her phone rang on this mild August night, the place was crowded with people. Someone held the receiver out, saying there was an Englishman on the line claiming to be George Harrison. Suze grabbed it and heard George saying he was at the Delmonico with Dylan. She should come by, along with "some girls." He'd leave her name at the front desk.

Since the breakup with Bob, Suze had thrown herself into protest. Her main issue was the U.S. ban on travel to Cuba, which had gone into effect after the Cuban Missile Crisis in late 1962. In the spring of 1964, she had led a group of activists to Havana in an effort to test the ban's constitutionality. They stayed two months and met with Fidel Castro, his brother Raúl, and Che Guevara. Upon their return to America, their passports were invalidated. At the time of George's call, many of the activists in Suze's apartment had a new concern: the Gulf of Tonkin resolution recently passed by Congress, which allowed the U.S. to conduct military operations in Vietnam without a declaration of war.

Although the Beatles seemed to have little in common with politically engaged singers like Joan Baez, Phil Ochs, and Dylan, Suze and her friends, like many other leftists, looked upon them as kindred spirits. Once Suze mentioned George's invitation to her guests, she had a hard time keeping them from joining her trip uptown. "Everybody wanted to come with me—even the politicos," she wrote.

She left the East Village with a group that included Albert Maher, a radical from Texas who had studied at Harvard College under the LSD proselytizers Timothy Leary and Richard Alpert. In Midtown, they found the Delmonico "impenetrable" because of the fans, cops, and security men clogging the sidewalks and streets. "I finally convinced a guard to at least go to the desk and check for my name," Suze recalled. "The crowd pressed close, hungry and eager. The guard returned shaking his head. Oh well, nice try—if he even bothered to check."

Maher led Suze to a nearby pay phone and called the hotel switchboard. Speaking, for some reason, in an Irish brogue, he spooled out a sob story about a wife in the hospital. The tale persuaded the operator to put the call through. Maher said hello to Dylan—and handed the phone to Suze, who could tell right away that her ex-boyfriend was not pleased. "Bob was annoyed that I had brought other people with me," she recalled. "We both got testy, and I told him: Oh, never mind. Or maybe he was the one who said it. Either way, the implication was clear. We weren't ready to deal with each other easily quite yet. Beatles be damned: I hung up the phone and went home."

Up in the suite, the party was in full swing. "We smoked and laughed all night," John said. "I don't remember much of what we talked about. We were smoking dope, drinking wine, and generally being rock 'n' rollers and having a laugh, you know, and surrealism."

After the initial bashfulness, Dylan and Lennon were able to talk. "We fell into conversation so easily it surprised us all," John said. "Beatlemania is something Dylan can understand and relate to. His experiences have been the same, but very different. He tried to explain what his fans were like, how they acted. Then we talked about music, especially about writing lyrics, how he got started with a new song, how the ideas came."

Paul and George sat on the bed, where Epstein lay on his back. It struck them as hilarious that their manager, usually so correct in his appearance, was holding between his lips the stub end of a joint, giving him the look of an old-time tramp.

His inhibitions having melted away, Brian looked in a mirror and brought up something he didn't mention in the presence of John, Paul, George, and Ringo: "Brian was pointing at himself and going, 'Jew!'" Paul said. "And it was hilarious! . . . It may not seem the least bit significant to anyone else, but in our circle, it was very liberating."

After the long car ride, the pot, the scotch, and the conversation with Suze, Dylan was beat. And now the Beatles saw that he was out cold. The sight of this crumpled figure on the carpet triggered more laughs. "By this time," Maymudes reported, "Paul was laughing so hard that tears were streaming out of his eyes. This was their very first encounter and Bob passed out!"

In the morning, Paul hugged Maymudes, saying, "It's all your fault, because I love this pot!"

Mal Evans approached McCartney: "Hey, Paul, do you want to see that bit of paper?"

Paul read the words he had dictated the night before. Amid the mystical gibberish, one line stood out: *There are seven levels*. "And we pissed ourselves laughing," Paul said. "I mean, 'What the fuck's that? What the fuck are seven levels?'"

There was still a huge crowd below. Maymudes went to the window. When he was close enough to be seen by the mob, a roar went up. For a while after that, Dylan and the Beatles amused themselves by taking turns going to the window. "We could control the level of noise; it was like we were making a song," Maymudes recalled.

After playing their second show at Forest Hills Tennis Stadium that night, the Beatles went by helicopter to their next stop, Atlantic City, New Jersey, where John and Paul wrote "Every Little Thing" and "What You're Doing" in a hotel room. Then came a blur of shows—Philadelphia, Indianapolis, Cleveland, St. Louis, Dallas, Kansas City—as Dylan spent more time in the quiet of Bearsville.

The Beatles flew back to New York on September 20 for the final show of the tour, a benefit for the United Cerebral Palsy of New York City and Retarded Infants Services. Dylan and Maymudes met them in the dressing room of the Paramount Theater on Broadway and West Forty-Third Street shortly before they took the stage.

The Paramount show was an anomaly: It was the only charity concert of the tour, and the Beatles played for a smaller audience than usual, a crowd of roughly three thousand, seven hundred. Dylan and Maymudes, along with Aronowitz and Albert Grossman, had a close-up view, watching from the wings. At one point Dylan stood on a chair to get a better look.

What he witnessed was an assault on the senses. Maymudes reported that "the audience was so loud, you could not hear the band"; and it was hard to see what was going on because of the "billions of flashbulbs." In a remark to Aronowitz, Dylan noted with pride the difference between the pandemonium of the show and his own concerts, during which audiences showed their appreciation only after a song was done. Standing nearby was the thirty-year-old journalist Gloria Steinem, who was years away from becoming known as the foremost feminist in the U.S.

After a late-night dinner, the Beatles and their new friends made their way to the Riviera Motor Inn, close to Kennedy Airport in Queens. There, they smoked more pot. This time around, Epstein had a less-than-happy reaction, withdrawing to a corner.

At 4 a.m., Steinem, who was on assignment for *Cosmopolitan* magazine, found herself in a room with Lennon, Ringo, Dylan, and an unidentified young woman. Unlike the male reporters, who were happy to keep the Beatles' road secrets, Steinem included in her article the fact that a girl who had spent time with McCartney in Philadelphia was hoping to see him again on this night—only to find that he had shut himself in his room, refusing to see her.

"She's rather upset," Derek Taylor said. "After all, Paul did make a big thing of her and now he won't even say goodbye."

"Paul is Paul and nothing's going to change him," Lennon said.

Steinem paid little attention to the famous non-Beatle in the room. "I knew nothing about Dylan," she recalled. "He seemed very distant." She asked Lennon if he had really been influenced by the great authors cited in the reviews of *In His Own Write*. "I mean to read Joyce but I never have," he said. "I got a laugh from all those intellectuals saying I was like him." She also asked him if success had changed him. He replied, "Yes, it's made me richer." Dylan was still in the room when Steinem made her exit at 5 a.m.

The Beatles flew back to London and threw themselves into almost nightly concerts across England, with recording sessions at EMI Studios squeezed in between dates. In these weeks after their gatherings with Dylan, Mal Evans was given a new job: supplying John, Paul, George, and Ringo with neatly rolled joints.

On October 18, the Beatles recorded their next single, "I Feel Fine," a song written by Lennon. It began with something innovative, a squall of feedback. From there, rather than going on the attack in the manner of their previous rockers, the Beatles just cruised along, creating something light, easy, and fresh, with optimistic lyrics to match, and the richest vocal harmonies on any of their recordings yet.

It was the first in a batch of songs that John and Paul would write, together or separately, based on a guitar riff. For this one, Lennon went with a variation on the recurring figure of "Watch Your Step," a minor 1961 hit for the American rhythm and blues singer Bobby Parker. "I Feel Fine" would reach No. 1 on both sides of the Atlantic—but John had a quibble related to his desire to measure up to Dylan as a lyricist. In one verse, he had settled for the phrase "diamond rings," a cliché that had previously made its way into "Can't Buy Me Love." "It's gear," Lennon said on the day the song was recorded, using a slang term for "cool," "except for one thing: we've got the phrase 'diamond rings' in again."

In America, Dylan played more than twenty concerts between stays in Bearsville. In November, he wrote to Tony Glover, a musician and writer whom he had befriended during his time in Minneapolis. It was a typewritten stream-of-consciousness letter filled with his impressions of his life in the Catskills. In the middle of it, he mentioned his newfound friends.

i am outside an somewhat free / long for nothing. john lennon groovy also ringo.

8 Hide Your Love

Folk fans grappled with Dylan's changing identity in the pages of *Sing Out!*, a magazine that served as a community hub for those who embraced traditional music and leftist politics. The editor, Irwin Silber, a onetime Communist Party member, let his feelings be known in "An Open Letter to Bob Dylan," a reprimand that formed the centerpiece of the November 1964 issue.

Silber started off by assuring Dylan that he had his best interests at heart. And then he really let him have it: "Your new songs seem to be all inner-directed now, innerprobing, self-conscious—maybe even a little maudlin or a little cruel on occasion," he wrote. "And it's happening on stage, too. You seem to be relating to a handful of cronies behind the scenes now—rather than to the rest of us out front.

"Now, that's all okay—if that's the way you want it, Bob. But then you're a different Bob Dylan from the one we knew. The old one never wasted our precious time."

In the same issue, one of the magazine's readers, Eileen Strong, pointed out similarities between Dylan and "another current idol—John Lennon" in a letter to the editor. Among her bits of evidence, she noted that both men played guitar and harmonica; both wore "Huck Finn" caps; both "express a disdain for worldly things"; both had a "Chaplinesque sense of humor"; and both wrote poetry. "The similarities between the two," she concluded, "are so striking as to suggest Lennon and Dylan may be one and the same person."

Ralph J. Gleason, a music writer for the *San Francisco Chronicle*, used Strong's letter as the starting point for a column headlined "Who REALLY Is Bob Dylan?" It was illustrated with side-by-side, postage-stamp-size photos of Dylan and Lennon, each wearing the distinctive cap, with the snap undone. The caption was this: "Folksinger and Beatle—are they the same person?" In the body of the piece, Gleason laid out a jocular description of the "historic theory" he had discovered in the letters pages of *Sing Out!* In a touch of his own, he added: "Do we know of any published photos of Dylan and Lennon together?"

Gleason wrote that column for a laugh, but there was something to it: The Beatles and Dylan were indeed becoming more alike. As we've seen, Dylan's embrace of the Beatles had coincided with his desire to break away from the folk scene. At the same time, Lennon had started mulling his failure to put more of himself into his songs, discounting the fact that recent Lennon-McCartney compositions had demonstrated a shift away from the hormonal enthusiasm of "I Want to Hold Your Hand" to the airy brightness of "I Feel Fine" and the wistfulness of "Things We Said Today," "And I Love Her," and "If I Fell." Following up on Gleason's half-serious column, a reporter asked Lennon: "John, is it true that you and Bob Dylan are the same person?" "I didn't read that article," John replied, "but I think it's quite funny. No, we're not. Mind you, we could be."

By the end of 1964, the Beatles no longer had to stomp their feet to command the attention of the crowd. The context had changed. With screaming girls serving as their shock troops, and journalists taking the role of their communications operation, they had achieved real cultural power. The question now was, What would they do with it?

Beatles for Sale, the album they put out in December 1964 in the UK, hinted at their new aims. The best of its eight Lennon-McCartney originals promised that, rather than repeat the stratagems that had gotten them to the top, they would move away from moptop fun toward songs with more varied musical textures and more reflective lyrics. The second track, "I'm a Loser," startled listeners with its opening cry, in Lennon's pained voice, of its main self-damning statement. The bluntness here, along with the singer's admission of something so raw, showed an affinity with *Another Side of Bob Dylan*.

Beatles for Sale also contained the first hint of death to appear on a Beatles album. It came in "Baby's in Black," a waltz-time lament sung by John and Paul in Everly Brothers–style harmony. In the lyric, the narrator expresses the desire that a woman in mourning give up her old love and accept him in the dead man's place. "Rather different from what we expect of the boys," wrote a critic for the *New Musical Express*.

The scenario of "Baby's in Black" would have fit neatly onto any Dylan album. Like the romantic poets and the anonymous composers of the ancient folk ballads, he seemed to take pleasure in contemplating the grave. Lennon and McCartney, on the other hand, had avoided such stuff until *Beatles for Sale*, sticking to the ups and downs of romantic love—though they had more firsthand experience with death than Dylan, who might have emphasized dark material to make up for his baby face and comfortable upbringing.

Unlike earlier Lennon-McCartney compositions, and very much like the Dylan songs "Boots of Spanish Leather" and "Ballad in Plain D," "Baby's in Black" was also noteworthy in that it seems to have sprung from personal experience. John and Paul, who consistently described the song as a fifty-fifty collaboration, never stated that it was based on true events or that its titular character wore black because she was in mourning; but it's reasonable to infer that it was inspired by a friend of theirs from their Hamburg days, Astrid Kirchherr, a talented photographer who had helped transform the Beatles from leather-clad scruffs into long-haired bohemians.

Astrid, who had been engaged to the group's former bass player, Stuart Sutcliffe, at the time of his death, wore black even before his passing and would continue to dress that way for the rest of her life. She was hip, thoughtful, and attractive, and she reunited with the four Beatles in the spring of 1964, when she visited England to photograph them on assignment for the German magazine *Stern*. Shortly after her departure, John and Paul, in one of their eyeball-to-eyeball sessions, came up with "Baby's in Black."

Another track on the album was rooted in real life: "I Don't Want to Spoil the Party." In that one, the heartbroken protagonist decides to make an early exit from a social gathering because he knows his presence will only bring the other guests down. Lennon wrote it in Los Angeles on August 24, when he hadn't felt up to attending a party hosted by the movie star Burt Lancaster. While "I Don't Want to Spoil the Party" wasn't so revealing as many of the songs he would write in years to come, it's significant in that it shows him creating something out of what he was experiencing in the moment.

The new strain in the Beatles' music didn't go unnoticed, and not everyone liked it. "One might hope that John Lennon soon ceases to be so influenced by Bob Dylan," Maureen Cleave wrote in her *Evening Standard* review of *Beatles for Sale*.

A few weeks after the album's release, Lennon and Harrison declared their enthusiasm for Dylan in an interview with Ray Coleman of *Melody Maker*. Under the headline "Beatles Say—Dylan Shows the Way," the article informed readers that all four group members had listened to Dylan almost nonstop during their stay in Paris a year earlier and had spent time with the man himself during their North American tour. Lennon revealed that Dylan had inspired him to write "I'm a Loser." "Anyone who is one of the best in his field, as Dylan is, is bound to influence people," he said. "I wouldn't be surprised if we influenced him in some way."

John also mentioned that an older song, "A Hard Day's Night," had been in the Dylan vein before the group had "Beatle-fied" it. In the same interview, Harrison noted that the Beatles' high regard for Dylan might strike some people as strange. "After all," George said, "there must be a lot of staunch folk fans who like Dylan but who don't like the Beatles. I do know he likes our work, and that knocks us out."

The Dylan-Beatles relationship was part of a larger development, a newly vibrant British-American cultural exchange. Seven movies made in the UK or with British actors in lead roles were among the ten highest-grossing films of 1964 in the U.S. The top moneymaker was *Mary Poppins*, followed by another London-set musical, *My Fair Lady*; two James Bond films (*Goldfinger*, *From Russia with Love*), made the list, as did a pair of Inspector Clouseau comedies (*A Shot in the Dark*, *The Pink Panther*) starring the *Goon Show* alumnus Peter Sellers. *A Hard Day's Night* was at No. 7.

The same thing was afoot in music. Disc jockeys across the U.S. played a string of British singles including the Kinks' "You Really Got Me," the Dave Clark Five's "Glad All Over," and the Rolling Stones' "Time Is on My Side." At the same time, several American artists managed to make strong showings in the UK hit parade, which included three Motown hits—"My Guy" by Mary Wells, as well as "Baby Love" and "Where Did Our Love Go" by the Supremes—alongside Roy Orbison's "Oh, Pretty Woman."

▪ ▪ ▪

Harrison was onto something when he said some people might find the Beatles-Dylan alliance strange. To this day, some Dylan fans see the Beatles as pop lightweights who benefited from a social contagion. They find their match in the Beatles fans who consider Dylan an abrasive singer whose poetic gifts have been overrated.

Starting in the mid-1960s, however, there were plenty of people, aside from Dylan and the Beatles themselves, who were attuned to both frequencies. Their ranks included musicians and producers on both sides of the Atlantic who sought to mix the two strains, thereby creating the fusion that would go by "pop folk," "folk pop," or "Dylan beat," until "folk rock" emerged as the catchall term. It began, more or less, with a group out of Los Angeles, the Byrds. "The Byrds took the best of Dylan and the best of the Beatles and synthesized it," said Derek Taylor, who represented the group after leaving his Beatles post. Even its name was a blend of Dylan (the telltale y) and the Beatles (a sort of animal pun).

The Byrds' origin can be traced to the moment when Roger McGuinn, a skilled folk musician from Chicago, found himself knocked out by the Beatles in early 1964. After playing Lennon-McCartney songs in the basket houses of Greenwich Village, he moved west and did the same at the Troubadour in Los Angeles. And when he saw *A Hard Day's Night* in a post-midnight showing at the Pix Theater on Hollywood Boulevard, he was thunderstruck once more. McGuinn enjoyed the depiction of the Beatles' everyday existence, with its screaming girls and authority figures who prove no match for the lads' wit; but he was more affected by the tones Harrison produced with his newly acquired electric guitar, the Rickenbacker twelve-string, especially how he made it jangle in the fade-out of the title song. "Roger went, 'That's it!'" recalled a friend, the singer-songwriter Barry McGuire, who would soon join the folk rock brigade himself.

McGuinn teamed up with Gene Clark, a fellow folk musician who had become a Beatles convert, and they recruited the like-minded David Crosby. Calling themselves the Jet Set, they started working with the producer Jim Dickson, who had free-of-charge, off-hours access to World Pacific Studios on West Third Street, the site of influential recordings by the Indian sitarist Ravi Shankar and the West Coast jazz players Gerry Mulligan and Chet Baker.

McGuinn, Clark, and Crosby threw themselves into rehearsals, speeding their development by listening critically to playbacks of their demo recordings, a luxury for a fledgling band in the days when studio time was expensive and home recording was rare. Jac Holzman, the founder of Elektra Records, a folk label now veering into pop, signed the Jet Set for a single, with one stipulation: The group would have to call itself the Beefeaters, after the royal guard, to capitalize on the American craze for all things British.

The single did nothing upon its release, but the musicians kept at it, adding Chris Hillman and Michael Clarke as members and adopting the name the Byrds. Along the way, Jim Dickson acquired an acetate of "Mr. Tambourine Man." It was the version Dylan had made at the session back in June, with Ramblin' Jack Elliott singing harmony, a recording deemed unworthy of inclusion on *Another Side of Bob Dylan*. Dickson believed it had the makings of a hit for the group he was molding, though he knew he would have to do something about its length, which, at nearly seven minutes in this incarnation, wasn't fit for radio. He would also have to do something about McGuinn and Crosby, who found Dylan's voice so grating that they couldn't hear the beauty of the song.

Dickson persisted, and the Byrds worked up an arrangement that swapped out the march-like 2/4 time signature of the original for the 4/4 meter typical of rock 'n' roll. They also lopped off three of the four verses and added a heavenly haze of vocal harmonies that complemented the sound McGuinn was wringing from his recently purchased Rickenbacker twelve-string. And when he sang the song, as he would later say, he pitched his voice halfway between Lennon and Dylan.

The Byrds became Dylan's labelmates when Columbia Records signed the group in November 1964, and Dylan stopped in at the studio while on a visit to California a few weeks later. Accompanied by his lieutenants Victor Maymudes and Bob Neuwirth, he listened as the Byrds jingle-jangled their way through "Mr. Tambourine Man."

"Wow," Dylan said. "You can dance to it."

■   ■   ■

Dylan would shock much of his audience by "going electric" at the Newport Folk Festival in the summer of 1965. But he had been moving toward rock 'n' roll for some time. There was, as mentioned, the one-off session during which he had recorded "Corrina, Corrina" and other songs backed by studio pros. That was followed by his flight from the public-spirited anthems cherished by the *Sing Out!* crowd. Then came his shift of opinion concerning the Beatles; his admiration of what the Animals had done with "The House of the Rising Sun"; and, now, his presence at a session where an unknown group was changing one of his most complex compositions into something catchy.

His decision to go electric was also helped along by Tom Wilson, a Columbia Records staff member who had produced *The Times They Are A-Changin'* and *Another Side of Bob Dylan*. A Black intellectual from Waco, Texas, with a Harvard degree in economics, Wilson had also produced the jazz musicians Sun Ra and Cecil Taylor. He was tall and sure of himself, and his training in jazz meant that, unlike George Martin or Jim Dickson, he ran recording sessions in a hands-off manner, leaving the music to the musicians. Dylan impressed him with his lyrics more than anything else. "I thought folk music was for dumb guys," Wilson said. "This guy played like the dumb guys, but then these words came out. I was flabbergasted."

In the lore of rock 'n' roll, there is the story that Sam Phillips, the proprietor of the Sun Records label in Memphis, Tennessee, had been on the lookout for a white singer able to put across rhythm and blues as persuasively as its Black originators before he stumbled onto Elvis Presley. Something similar occurred to Tom Wilson when he observed an early Dylan session in the company of the singer's manager: "I said to Albert Grossman, 'If you put some background on this, you might have a white Ray Charles with a message,'" he recalled. "But it wasn't until a year later that everyone agreed that we should put a band behind him." In his impatience to capture the blend of folk and rock that he heard in his head, Wilson took the liberty of hiring musicians to provide an electric backing to Dylan's solo recording of "House of the Rising Sun," a sonic experiment that wouldn't leave the Columbia vaults for decades.

Now Dylan himself decided the time had come. On January 14, 1965, the second day of sessions for his fifth album, in the high-ceilinged Studio A of Columbia Recording Studios in Midtown Manhattan, he led four musicians through "Subterranean Homesick Blues," a rocker in which he grafted four Beat-inspired verses replete with jokes, aphorisms, and social commentary onto the bones of "Too Much Monkey Business," a Chuck Berry single from eight years earlier.

In keeping with his usual practice, Wilson didn't tell the musicians what to do. And in keeping with how he had run the Golden Chords, the Shadow Blasters, and the Rock Boppers in his Hibbing High days, Dylan started playing without a rehearsal. As "Subterranean Homesick Blues" roared to life, he was at last acting on his Colorado epiphany, having concluded that rock 'n' roll was no longer something he had to leave in his teenage past, but could transform into a medium for what he needed to say right now.

It wasn't all sunshine for Dylan and the Beatles as they moved into each other's musical territories. In the *Melody Maker* interview,

Lennon had taken a swipe at the man who had inspired him, saying that, as a singer, Dylan was a "neigher." John also predicted that, while Dylan might attain a measure of popularity in Britain, there would be no "Dylan-mania" in his home country. For his part, Dylan made mocking reference to the Fab Four, as the Beatles had been nicknamed, when he cried out, "Fab!" in a line referencing an Englishman in the shaggy-dog rock song "Bob Dylan's 115th Dream," which he recorded the same day he committed "Subterranean Homesick Blues" to tape.

Dylan would also draw a line in the sand by calling the album he was working on *Bringing It All Back Home*. This title, the first that he himself (rather than someone at Columbia Records) had given to one of his LPs, was a reminder that rock 'n' roll was an American invention. It was also a bit of a boast, with its beneath-the-surface suggestion that Dylan was better equipped to play this brand of music than any outsider, that he was the one who would reclaim the crown from the pretenders of the British Invasion.

Recorded over a mere three days, *Bringing It All Back Home* was electric on one side, acoustic on the other. In addition to "Mr. Tambourine Man," its non-amplified songs included "It's Alright, Ma (I'm Only Bleeding)," a critique of American conformism and materialism that picked up where Allen Ginsberg's "Howl" had left off, and "It's All Over Now, Baby Blue," a tender ballad that made apt allusion to Gene Vincent's "Baby Blue," while serving as a bittersweet kiss-off to the earnest coffeehouse culture knocked into irrelevance by the Beatles.

The album's cover portrait, shot by the photographer Daniel Kramer in the parlor of the renovated Bearsville farmhouse owned by Albert Grossman, helped convey the idea of Dylan's break with the folk community, presenting him as a hip dandy in a dark blazer and lavender cuff links. Lounging in the background is Sally Grossman, a twenty-five-year-old music lover and former Greenwich Village waitress who had married Albert the year before. Perfectly composed in a red jumpsuit, cigarette in one hand, she portrays a woman of mystery.

Less than a week after Dylan had completed recording the album, the Byrds entered Columbia Studios on Sunset Boulevard in Los

Angeles. After months of practice, they were finally ready to record "Mr. Tambourine Man" properly. But before the session could begin in earnest, the producer, Terry Melcher, insisted on installing top-flight studio musicians in place of the band members, with the exception of McGuinn on the Rickenbaker. The keeper take, with Hal Blaine on drums and Larry Knechtel on bass, was more polished than the run-throughs Dylan had witnessed at World Pacific Studios. With its aural sheen and metronomic beat, it belonged to the careful and considered school of record-making that was developing far from the gritty, feel-first style of the laissez-faire Tom Wilson and the devil-may-care Dylan in New York. The Byrds went on to record three more Dylan songs for their debut album: "Chimes of Freedom," "Spanish Harlem Incident," and "All I Really Want to Do." As with "Mr. Tambourine Man," the group treated "All I Really Want to Do" as raw material for a radio-ready version.

Dylan's original consisted of six musically identical verses, each taking aim at the pitfalls of conventional romantic relationships before giving way to a punch line of sorts, when the narrator tells the woman he simply wants to be friends with her. The repetitiveness is broken only by Dylan's laughter and a swoop into falsetto; and that very repetitiveness hammers home what made the song innovative—the fact that, like a companion piece of the same vintage, "It Ain't Me, Babe," it was an anti-romance song.

The Byrds, who valued sound over sense, music over words, took the final verse of "All I Really Want to Do" and refashioned it as a minor-key bridge placed midway through their sprightly version. By adding this bit of structural variety, along with their sunny harmonies and a jangling guitar, the Byrds can be said to have truly "Beatle-fied" the song: Nearly every Lennon-McCartney composition up to this point had included a bridge (or a B section, in the case of the many Beatles songs written in the AABA format typical of standards); John and Paul referred to this part as a "middle eight," even if it was shorter or longer than the usual eight bars.

The idea of marrying Dylan and the Beatles was too good not to be picked up on by rival acts. And there in the crowd at the nightclub

Ciro's Le Disc on the Sunset Strip, where the Byrds were building a following in the months before Columbia put out their debut, Sonny Bono was watching and listening. He had put in a hard apprenticeship under the tyrannical Phil Spector at Gold Star Studios in Hollywood. Now he wanted something that would allow him to establish himself as a producer while putting his much younger live-in romantic partner, Cherilyn Sarkisian, on the pop music map.

Cher had already been part of a scheme to cash in on Beatlemania. Days after the group's arrival in the U.S., she had recorded the novelty single "Ringo, I Love You (Yeah, Yeah, Yeah)" and released it under the name Bonnie Jo Mason. Cowritten and produced by Spector, it failed to catch on. "My voice was so deep that a lot of people thought I was a gay guy singing a love song to Ringo," Cher recalled, "and the deejays weren't about to play a homosexual love song." A year later, with her partner running the session and a stronger piece of material at her disposal, she had the makings of a hit. Sonny's arrangement of "All I Really Want to Do" didn't mimic the Byrds' trick of making a verse into a bridge, but it did include a chiming guitar that pushed it closer to their Beatle-fied version than Dylan's original.

■   ■   ■

A songwriter who departs from the typical pop song vocabulary is taking a risk—especially if that songwriter happens to be world-famous; is married with a child; and has slept with scores of people around the world while also having more involved affairs. That was the problem Lennon faced when, following Dylan's lead, he resolved to be more personal as a lyricist.

He began writing more revealingly in the summer of 1964, a season of change for him and his family. John and Cynthia had grown weary of the fans camped outside their London home, a modest flat above the apartment of a couple they knew well: Robert Freeman, the photographer who had captured defining images of the Beatles, and his wife, Sonny, a fashion model born in Germany. And so, after Brian Epstein had seen to the financial details, John, Cynthia, and their fifteen-month-old son, Julian, moved to a twenty-two room, mock-Tudor mansion called Kenwood, in Weybridge, Surrey, about twenty miles from the city. The place went nicely with another of John's recent acquisitions, a Rolls-Royce Phantom V.

Not long after they settled in, the Lennons had visitors—their old neighbors, Bob and Sonny Freeman. John answered the door, his wife close behind. In Cynthia's telling, Bob was "furious" and Sonny "was in tears." John led the distraught couple toward the living room, where they had a long talk, just the three of them. Once Bob and Sonny were gone, Cynthia asked what was going on; John shrugged and trudged upstairs. "I couldn't escape the conclusion that she'd had an affair with John," she recalled, "although I never had any proof."

Cynthia also had her suspicions about Alma Cogan, a British singer eight years older than her husband. Alma had hit the peak of her fame in the 1950s with "Sugartime," "Mama, Teach Me to Dance," and that seasonal favorite, later covered by Dylan, "Must Be Santa." Known as "the girl with the giggle in her voice," she was someone whom John had mocked from afar in his student days, screeching out her songs to the delight of his pals. But he was charmed when he met her backstage in 1964, before the Beatles' second appearance on the TV show *Sunday Night at the London Palladium*, and he found he could talk with her about almost anything.

John and Paul became regulars at the apartment Alma shared with her sister and widowed mother. It was a homey but glamorous flat in Kensington that served as a salon for theater people and celebrities, including Princess Margaret and Sammy Davis Jr. One night at Alma's, Paul played something he had been working on, an incomplete song with dummy lyrics that he was calling "Scrambled Eggs." The melody, which had come to him in a dream, was as pure and distinctive as that of the ancient ballad "Greensleeves" or one of the great standards. Paul was hoping that Alma—"a bit of a song buff," as he described her—might help him figure out whether or not he had unconsciously stolen it. She told him she had never heard the tune, adding that she found it beautiful.

John's relationship with Alma went beyond shoptalk. Her sister, the singer Sandra Caron, said in a 2006 interview that the two had carried on a long-term affair, often meeting in disguise and checking into West End hotels as "Mr. and Mrs. Winston," after John's middle name. If that account is accurate, John and Alma managed to keep their relationship secret—but only just. "Alma Cogan was one of the women I suspected he was having an affair with," Cynthia wrote. "I could see the sexual tension between them and how outrageously she flirted with him."

At Kenwood, John lay for hours in the sunroom, immersing himself in newspapers and magazines, the *Just William* series he had loved as a boy, and books by George Orwell and Oscar Wilde. Other pastimes included watching endless hours of TV and sleeping. When he needed solitude, he got it in the rooms on the third floor that he had equipped with a toy car racing track, a dozen or so guitars, a Vox organ, and recording gear. Far from the din of Beatlemania and domestic life, he helped himself to the Quality Street tin box where he kept his stash.

He was also writing songs, some on his own, others with Paul, who would drive out to Kenwood from London, where he was leading the life of a cultured and energetic man about town, even as he was living with his longtime girlfriend, Jane Asher, at the Asher family's townhouse in Marylebone. One of the first Lennon-McCartney collaborations written at Kenwood was "Eight Days a Week," a slick piece of pop product considerably less ambitious than Paul's burgeoning "Scrambled Eggs" or the songs John was piecing together upstairs.

At the end of January 1965, John and Cynthia went on a ski trip to St. Moritz, Switzerland, with George Martin and his longtime girlfriend, Judy Lockhart-Smith. John, who had never been skiing, didn't want to look foolish in the Beatles' second film, which was about to start production and included scenes on the slopes. The couples took suites close to each other at Badrutt's Palace Hotel, a resort formerly patronized by Greta Garbo and Charlie Chaplin.

John and Cynthia made quick progress during private lessons, graduating within a few days to runs that began at the summit. On an après-ski evening a week into the trip, Cynthia heard peals of laughter coming from the suite shared by the other couple. When she looked in, she saw the distinguished George Martin, in long underwear and socks, attempting a series of girlish ballet moves, with flurrying feet. June and Cynthia screamed with laughter—which died all at once when George banged a foot, breaking a toe.

A bit later, John appeared, guitar in hand, and shared his most intimate song yet. It wasn't quite finished—Paul would help him bring it home later in the year—but it made a strong impression. "It had a slightly sick lyric, which was very apt to me nursing my injured toe," Martin recalled. "The song was 'Norwegian Wood.'"

Its easy-to-strum chords came straight out of folk music. Its structure was equally simple: in contrast with the majority of Beatles songs, and very much like the ones Dylan had written so far, it had no bridge. On that sturdy foundation lay a hypnotic tune. The classical composer Ned Rorem would call that melody "unique and memorable, rather than merely original."

The lyrics were something new for John, belonging to the adult realm of after-hours regret. In the verses, the first-person narrator tells of a visit to a woman's apartment. They talk until 2 a.m., when she says she must go to work in the morning—meaning he's not welcome to join her in bed. Our disappointed hero retreats to the bathroom and sleeps in the tub.

Two references to "Norwegian wood" provide the song with its enigmatic title. Some commentators have noted that the phrase was shorthand for a kind of decor then popular in London's bohemian circles; others have viewed it as a sly nod to Sonny Freeman, who often told people she had come from Norway, rather than Germany, out of concern for the lingering ill feelings toward her former home country. "'Norwegian Wood' was about an affair I was having," Lennon said. "I was very careful and paranoid, because I didn't want my wife, Cyn, to know that there really was something going on outside the household. . . . I was trying to be sophisticated in writing about an affair, but in such a smokescreen way that you couldn't tell. I can't remember any specific woman it had to do with."

Another person cited as a model for the character in the song—by Lennon's pal Pete Shotton, among others—was Maureen Cleave of the *Evening Standard*, one of the first journalists to take the British pop music explosion seriously. John paid her a compliment when he said her prose style reminded him of that of Richmal Crompton, the author of the *Just William* books. And the two were close enough that she felt free to make fun of him for using so many one-syllable words in his songs. Couldn't he do better than that? Cleave would deny that their relationship went beyond a collegial friendship—and a careful listen to "Norwegian Wood" reveals that the song is not really "about an affair I was having," as Lennon put it; instead, it describes an attempt to woo someone who remains aloof.

John debuted another nearly completed song at the Swiss hotel, "Ticket to Ride." It was a catchy rocker—"I liked it straightaway," George Martin said—but it contained an unusual lyrical sentiment. Differing from the usual first-person breakup song, which prizes the narrator's wounded feelings, "Ticket to Ride" focuses on the sense of relief, even glee, experienced by a woman who leaves a man who has been "bringing her down, yeah."

■   ■   ■

While Dylan could work more or less on his own schedule, with no pressure from Columbia, the Beatles perpetually owed another single, album, four-song extended-play record (EP), or movie, thanks to their contractual obligations with EMI and United Artists. In February, two months after the release of *Beatles for Sale*, John, Paul, George, and Ringo entered the modest white building on Abbey Road to record a new single, as well as songs for the film then called Beatles Production 2 or *Eight Arms to Hold You*.

Perhaps feeling extra motivation because of "You Really Got Me," a Kinks hit with the heaviest guitar sound yet, the Beatles rocked hard in their first effort, "Ticket to Ride." Paul had helped John finish writing the song—and then he asserted himself in the studio, contributing not only his usual bass lines and harmony vocals but electric guitar, which meant he had thrust himself into the sonic domain of

John and George. He also moved in on Ringo's turf by dictating the song's syncopated drum part, an off-kilter offshoot of the pattern played by Hal Blaine on "Be My Baby," the big Ronettes hit produced by Phil Spector. The inventive ending of "Ticket to Ride," with a distinct melodic figure that seemed to come out of nowhere, also suggests the hand of McCartney: Codas would increasingly become a part of Beatles songs written mainly by Paul, not to mention his own compositions in the decades to come.

George Martin made a big contribution by allowing for more overdubs than ever, an innovation that the Beatles and their producer would continue to take forward as they broke down the barriers that had separated songwriting, arrangement, and production. More and more, the studio was a composition tool; more and more, the recording *was* the song.

A few days later, Lennon showed up with his most Dylan-esque creation yet, "You've Got to Hide Your Love Away." Similar in mood and structure to the song he had unveiled at the Alpine hotel, it comprised two eight-line verses, each followed by a simple refrain, with no bridge. The lyrics, like many of Dylan's, were open-ended enough to invite interpretation—perhaps because, as with "Norwegian Wood (This Bird Has Flown)," John was describing something he wanted to keep secret.

The first two lines of "You've Got to Hide Your Love Away" show that he was not bothering to conceal his new influence: "head in hand" echoes "my head in my hand" on "Honey, Just Allow Me One More Chance" from *The Freewheelin' Bob Dylan*; "face to the wall" is a close match for "facing the wall" in "I Don't Believe You (She Acts Like We Never Have Met)," a favorite track of John's from *Another Side of Bob Dylan*.

Although the session took less than two hours, "You've Got to Hide Your Love Away" includes grace notes that wouldn't have been part of a recording made by the songwriter who had inspired it. As EMI's studio logs show, John's voice and twelve-string acoustic guitar appear on separate tracks, meaning he sang the melody after the main instrumental backing had been committed to tape, a manner of recording that Dylan didn't bother with. Other overdubs included Paul on maracas; Ringo on tambourine; George on a second twelve-string; and, for the first time, the contribution of an outside musician whom Martin had brought in to add something that lay beyond the capabilities of any Beatle. This was the classical player John Scott, whose tenor flute and alto flute in the final passage seem to echo the harmonica runs that close out many Dylan tracks.

It wasn't lost on the others, what John was up to on "You've Got to Hide Your Love Away." "I asked him not to sound too much like Dylan," George Martin said. "He wasn't doing it deliberately; it was subconscious more than anything." McCartney heard the same thing. Noting that Dylan's music had "hit a chord with John," Paul said: "It was as if John felt, That should have been me. And to that end, John on this one track did a Dylan impression."

Lennon had drawn from Motown's great in-house songwriter Smokey Robinson to write "Not a Second Time." But now he was going to Dylan as a source of inspiration for at least a fourth time. What would Bob think when he heard this batch of songs? Would he be flattered? Annoyed? John was so musically smitten that he didn't care, at least in the moment. "Indeed," Pete Shotton wrote, "Dylan's initial impact on John was almost comparable to that of Elvis Presley a decade earlier."

Paradoxically, by assuming the Dylan guise, John felt free—free enough to write on a subject he had not dared to approach in his earlier songs; and free enough to allow himself to sing in a voice unadorned, without asking Martin to double-track it or having Paul or George provide supportive harmonies, as he had for nearly every previous Beatles recording. So while Lennon might have been doing a Dylan impression on "You've Got to Hide Your Love Away," he was also, for once, nakedly himself.

9 The Savoy

The Beatles escaped the drab English winter of 1965 to spend two weeks in the Bahamas and roughly the same amount of time in the Alps. In both locations they filmed scenes for their second movie, a musical comedy that wasn't exactly shaping up to be a worthy successor to *A Hard Day's Night*. McCartney said they didn't bother learning their lines because the script was so weak; Lennon said the Beatles were "smoking marijuana for breakfast."

While they were miming "Another Girl" among models in bikinis on a rocky shore of New Providence island, or taking part in slapstick chase scenes on the pistes of Obertauern, Austria, Dylan was singing his old political anthems and new impressionistic songs to hushed crowds across the U.S. on a double bill with his sometime romantic and musical partner Joan Baez. Away from the stage, he made preparations for his planned springtime tour of England.

At the Cedar Tavern in Greenwich Village, with his new right-hand man Bob Neuwirth at his side, Dylan met with the documentary filmmaker D. A. Pennebaker. Like Albert and David Maysles, who had chronicled the Beatles' first visit to America, Pennebaker used the latest handheld cameras and portable sound equipment to achieve something fresh in nonfiction cinema—the illusion of unmediated, fly-on-the-wall observation. Pennebaker knew the Maysles brothers, too, having worked with them at Drew Associates, a production company often hired by the media giant Time-Life to make documentaries.

In 1965, Pennebaker and the Maysles were following their muses as much as they could. On March 20, for instance, the Maysles made a documentary short that was little seen in its day, but would have lasting value. Filmed at the Carnegie Recital Hall in New York, it captured an unsettling performance by Yoko Ono, a conceptual artist raised in wartime Tokyo who had made a name for herself in Manhattan's avant-garde circles. As Albert Maysles operated the camera and David Maysles recorded the sound, Ono instructed audience members to cut off her clothing bit by bit with a large pair of scissors. She sat stoic on the stage as people did her bidding with varying degrees of enthusiasm and embarrassment. Ono called the performance *Cut Piece* and would reprise it in London the next year.

Pennebaker credited Sara Lownds, a young Drew Associates employee, for bringing Dylan to his attention. Born Shirley Noznisky in Wilmington, Delaware, the daughter of a scrap-metal dealer, Sara met Bob around the time she was splitting from her husband, Hans Lownds, a magazine photographer. As Bob and Sara got to know each other, they kept their relationship secret. In March 1965, as if making their love official, they posed for Daniel Kramer at the Shack, the cabin in Woodstock where Dylan had once stayed with Suze Rotolo. Kramer's portraits hinted at the couple's future as householders: Bob and Sara would marry by year's end.

Once Pennebaker had signed on to make the film that would become *Dont Look Back*, Dylan got the word out in a mock Q&A he concocted with a friend, the writer J. R. Goddard.

"Tell us about your movie."

"It's gonna be in black and white."

"Who's writing it?"

"Allen Ginsberg. I'm going to rewrite it."

"What about your friends, the Beatles?"

"John Lennon and I came down to the Village early one morning. They wouldn't let us in the Figaro or the Hip Bagel or the Feenjon. This time I'm going to England. This April. I'll see 'em if they're there."

The faux interview ran in *The Village Voice* shortly before the release of Dylan's rock 'n' roll single, "Subterranean Homesick Blues." Promotional copies sent to radio stations played up his connection to the Beatles by including a reprint of the *Melody Maker* article headlined "Beatles Say—Dylan Shows the Way" on the back cover. Despite the earlier hand-wringing in *Sing Out!*, there was no outcry about Dylan's use of electric instrumentation and drums. *Cash Box* treated it like any other disc in an early review: "Dylan could hit the pop charts once again with this rockin' country folk blueser with a solid beat and catchy lyrics."

The Baez-Dylan tour hit California. At Ciro's in Hollywood on March 26, Dylan made his onstage postadolescent rock 'n' roll debut when he appeared as a guest of the Byrds, who were waiting impatiently for Columbia to put out their version of "Mr. Tambourine Man." The next day, in an interview with the *Los Angeles Free Press*, Dylan spoke of having lost interest in his old style: "Hey, I'd rather listen to Jimmy Reed or Howlin' Wolf, man, or the Beatles, or Françoise Hardy, than I would listen to any protest-song singers."

One evening around this time, after a day of shooting at Twickenham Film Studios outside London, Lennon arrived at Kenwood with Ray Coleman, the writer of the *Melody Maker* story on the Beatles' endorsement of Dylan. As Cynthia made dinner, John played "Subterranean Homesick Blues" (which had yet to be released in the UK) on the living room stereo. "Great—very Chuck Berry-ish," is how Lennon described it. Then he played it again, trying to suss out what Dylan was singing in the pileup of words. "Hope we get the chance to get together when he comes over," John said. "I'll have him out to the house if he'll come."

Next, he brought up Britain's music star of the moment: Donovan, a nineteen-year-old singer from Scotland whose debut single, "Catch the Wind," was climbing the UK charts. It sounded like a Dylan song, if Dylan's voice and outlook were sweeter, and Lennon was one of many who had pegged the newcomer as nothing more than an imitator. "First time I saw Donovan on TV, I fell off my chair," he said. "I couldn't believe it. We'd got back from Austria and I thought: 'Good God, Dylan's in Britain.' I still can't believe it."

The British hit parade's move toward folk sounds struck Lennon as a hilarious and somewhat irritating development. Never mind that he had written songs for the last two Beatles albums that bore the Dylan influence; or that he had just recorded his most Dylan-inspired song of all, "You've Got to Hide Your Love Away."

After dinner, John, Cynthia, and Coleman rode in the Rolls-Royce Phantom V toward a movie theater in Leicester Square, where they were going to see *The Ipcress File*, a new thriller starring Michael Caine, with the other Beatles and their wives and girlfriends. As they cruised along, "I'll Follow the Sun," a gentle track from *Beatles for Sale* written by McCartney, came on the car radio, sending Lennon into a rant: "I suppose they think *that's* folk, so they might as well plug it. Paul wrote it when he was *ten*—so how could it be folk?" He was exaggerating a little: McCartney had written an early version of the song when he was sixteen.

■   ■   ■

George Harrison, the youngest Beatle, had written only one song, "Don't Bother Me," that had been deemed worthy of inclusion on a Beatles album. Now two of his compositions, "I Need You" and "You Like Me Too Much," were headed to the next one.

As he started coming into his own, he was developing an interest in Indian music. It started on April 5, 1965, at Twickenham Film Studios, when a few Indian musicians were background players in a scene shot on the set of a curry restaurant. Soon afterward, George bought a sitar at a specialty shop, Indiacraft, on Oxford Street.

He was also growing closer to Lennon, who had considered him something of a pest back in Liverpool, when the teenage George sometimes tagged along with John and Cynthia on their dates. Now, after having gone through so much together, they were on a more equal footing.

It helped that George was living nearby. Shortly after the Lennons' move to Kenwood, he had bought a ranch-style house, called Kinfauns, in Esher, about five miles away; his girlfriend, Pattie Boyd, joined him there. As the two Beatles got the hang of the country squire life, they began seeing more of each other apart from Paul and Ringo. One of their favorite activities was to race through the hills of Surrey in their new sports cars. John, a clumsy driver, tended to grind the gears of his Ferrari as George flew smoothly along in his Aston Martin. They also saw each other socially—most notably at a dinner party where they had their first acid experience.

It came about in the spring of 1965 thanks to Harrison's friendship with a dentist, John Riley, a likable fellow whose other celebrity clients included the actor Dudley Moore. Riley, a regular at London's hip nightspots, invited George, Pattie, John, and Cynthia to join him and his girlfriend, Cyndy Bury, at his place near Hyde Park. In preparation for the evening, unbeknown to the four guests, he had procured some LSD made by a chemist in Wales.

After the meal, John and George said they really had to be going. An old friend from their Hamburg days, Klaus Voormann, was about to perform at the Pickwick Club as part of a new trio, Paddy, Klaus & Gibson, and they didn't want to miss it. "You haven't had any coffee yet," Cyndy Bury said. "I've made it—and it's delicious." The hosts and guests repaired to the living room. Once they had finished, the dentist confessed that he had dropped sugar cubes laced with acid into their cups. "How dare you fucking do this to us?" said John.

The guests made a hurried exit and piled into Pattie's bright orange Mini Cooper. As they drove toward the Pickwick, Pattie noticed the car was shrinking. At the club, John saw that a table was lengthening. "And I thought, 'Fuck, it's happening,'" he recalled. George took things more in stride: "I felt in love, not with anything or anybody in particular, but with everything." John soon came around. "It was just terrifying," he said, "but it was fantastic." After taking in the set by Paddy, Klaus & Gibson, they moved on to the Ad Lib, where the elevator was on fire (it was just a glowing red light). From there, they rolled along, very slowly, for nearly twenty miles, with George at the wheel of the tiny orange car, to Kinfauns.

Pattie called the overall experience "frightening"; Cynthia said it was "horrific." George thought it had provided him with a glimpse of a higher consciousness, and John believed it had given him insight into the universe. "God isn't in a pill," he said, "but LSD explained the mystery of life. It was a religious experience."

The trip further lessened the distance between the two Beatles, at least from George's point of view. "After taking acid together," he said, "John and I had a very interesting relationship. That I was younger or I was smaller was no longer any kind of embarrassment with John." Observing John and George from the outside, however, Pete Shotton, a friend to both men, detected a condescension in Lennon's treatment of Harrison that would continue through the Beatles' last days: "In John's eyes," Shotton wrote, "George was still the little kid who tagged along: who happened to play the guitar and had thereby gained entry into the band, but essentially remained (like Ringo) a second-class Beatle."

The Beatles continued work on their film, now called *Help!* Richard Lester, the director, asked Lennon and McCartney for a title track. Although it had begun as an assignment, "Help!" turned out to be a song Lennon would regard as one of his most revealing.

The journalist Maureen Cleave was having tea with Cynthia at Kenwood when Paul arrived on April 11. On the third floor, the two collaborators started with a Lennon song fragment. Paul came up with the pretty countermelody lines that anticipate and echo the narrator's pleas. John was responsible for the no-nonsense lyric. "I meant it," he said. "It's real! It's just me singing 'Help!' and I meant it." Mindful of Cleave's having teased him about his penchant for one-syllable words, he tossed in one of the four-syllable variety.

> *And now my life has changed in oh so many ways*
> *My independence seems to vanish in the haze*

■　　■　　■

Dylan was chief among the the singers and groups working in the folk style now having hits in the UK. In April 1965, eighteen months after its release, *The Freewheelin' Bob Dylan* stood at No. 1 on the British album chart, having taken the place of *Beatles for Sale*. And though it was more than a year old, "The Times They Are A-Changin'," the song, was rising on the singles chart; and *The Times They Are A-Changin'*, the LP, held the fourth position on the album chart. Not far behind, at No. 13, was *Another Side of Bob Dylan*. In the weeks ahead, his new album, the half-electric, half-acoustic *Bringing It All Back Home*, would shoot to No. 1 in the UK.

After the last show of the Dylan-Baez tour, Bob and company boarded a flight out of Seattle-Tacoma International Airport. Moments after landing at London Airport on the night of April 26, Dylan saw that he was a much bigger star there than he had been on his last visit: Dozens of fans, teenage girls and bespectacled young men, were waiting in the terminal, and when they spotted Dylan, a roar went up, with a few tentative screams mixed in. Suitcases "went flying," according to a *Melody Maker* report, resulting in a smashed window. Officers in bobby helmets stepped into the fray, separating Dylan from the people tearing at his hair and clothes. While the number of airport greeters didn't match Beatle levels, it seemed that Lennon's prediction—that there would be no Dylan-mania in the UK—had been off the mark.

In addition to Joan Baez, who assumed she would continue sharing the stage with Dylan during this run of eight shows in seven English cities, the entourage included: Albert Grossman; his wife, Sally; the producer Tom Wilson; the filmmaker D. A. Pennebaker; the cameraman Howard Alk; the sound engineer Jones Alk (Howard's wife); and Bob Neuwirth. Walking briskly at a distance from the fans, Dylan found an industrial-size lightbulb in a trash can. He was carrying it when he faced a scrum of reporters outside the customs hall. A little more than a year after the Beatles had charmed American journalists at Kennedy's international arrivals building, Dylan seemed more inclined to turn his own airport press encounter into a piece of absurdist theater.

"What's the lightbulb for?"

"I thought you would ask me that. No, I usually carry a lightbulb."

"Are the Beatles on the way out?"

Dylan seemed to take offense: "They will *never* be on the way out—you know that."

"Have you ever heard of Donovan?"

"No. Who?"

"What is your real message?"

"My real message? Keep a good head and always carry a lightbulb."

"Have you ever written anything about Vietnam?"

"No, I don't write *about* anything."

"How much do you think the Beatles contributed to your wide success here?"

"I find it very hard to understand the meaning of the word success. . . . I like the Beatles—I think they are the best. I don't know what they said about me, or anything."

The Dylan crew set up camp at the Savoy, an expensive hotel overlooking the Thames, near Covent Garden. Not long after waking up in his suite, Dylan met with reporters once again. One of the first questions concerned Donovan. "Who is this Donovan?" Dylan said. "I'd never heard of him until yesterday."

He soon gravitated toward Bill Harry, a journalist from Liverpool who knew the Beatles well. In addition to having founded the music paper *Mersey Beat* with his wife, Virginia, he had introduced Lennon to Stuart Sutcliffe back when all three were students at the Liverpool College of Art; he had also published Lennon's prose sketches in his publication. "Dylan and I became involved in a long chat," Harry recalled, "and I took him to a phone booth in the hotel and got John Lennon on the phone and arranged for Dylan to visit him at his home." On a sheet of paper embossed with "The Savoy" at the top, Dylan jotted down the main phone number ("WR45028") and the second number ("WR4659") of Kenwood. Then he drew an arrow pointing to the second one and added the words "John Lennon bed."

Dana Gillespie, a sixteen-year-old singer signed to Pye Records, the label of the Kinks and Manfred Mann, liked being in the middle of the action, and there she was at the Savoy. Before going into music, she had attained minor fame as Britain's junior waterskiing champion, which gave London's tabloids a pretext for running photos of her in a bathing suit. Once Dylan was done with the journalists, she chatted with him. "There was definitely some sort of spark between us," she recalled in her memoir.

The daughter of bohemian parents, Dana lived in the basement of a townhouse on Thurloe Square. At one point, the home's other inhabitants included her mother, her father, and her father's girlfriend. Her first boyfriend, David Jones (soon to call himself David Bowie), had often spent the night with her when she was fourteen and he was seventeen, and she would remain lifelong friends with him. She was also a regular at the Troubadour, the Marquee, and other London clubs, and her flat became a gathering spot for musicians.

She ended up spending a lot of time with Dylan during his stay, a fact the British music papers noted in passing. "I can't remember now what excuse I gave my parents when I finally got home," she recalled. "I doubt I told them I'd been keeping Bob Dylan's bed warm." Like her friendship with Bowie, her relationship with Dylan would last. They would reunite the next year and reconnect decades later, when, at his request, she was the opening act on his 1997 UK tour. In the film *Dont Look Back*, Gillespie appears as a very occasional background figure, but pops up frequently in the many hours of outtake footage.

Early in his time at the Savoy, Dylan entertained John, Paul, George, and Ringo in his suite. "I think the Beatles are a little confused by Bobby," Joan Baez wrote in a letter to her younger sister, Mimi. "He got so drunk and they all had to be ha ha funny, so I made friends with John's wife & Paul's girl." Pennebaker didn't film the visit, but a *Record Mirror* reporter noted it in a dispatch.

Once again away from the cameras, Dylan had dinner with John and Cynthia at Kenwood. "We played a few records and talked," Lennon said. "He's an interesting bloke with some good ideas." In a 1985 interview, Dylan recalled writing a song with Lennon that night. "I don't remember what it was, though," he said. "We played some stuff into a tape recorder but I don't know what happened to it. I can remember playing it and the recorder was on. I don't remember anything about the song." Soon after his visit to Kenwood, in an interview with Ray Coleman, he praised his host: "I dig John, as a writer, a singer, and a Beatle. There are very few people I dig every time I meet them, but him I dig. He doesn't take things so seriously as so many guys do. I like that."

While the Beatles were busy making *Help!* at Twickenham on April 30, Dylan traveled to Sheffield for the first show of his UK tour. Before taking the stage, as the film crew captured what was going on, he lounged in a hotel room with Albert Grossman, Tom Wilson, and the twenty-three-year-old Alan Price, who was in his last days as the Animals' keyboardist. On the TV, the Everly Brothers were performing "The Price of Love." Dylan watched them with laser focus as Price spoke of his fondness for an early Everly Brothers hit, "Wake Up Little Susie."

"They were great then," Grossman said. "Much better than they are now."

"Naaah, man," Dylan shot back. "They're better *now*, man."

Alan Price, whose head seemed to be bursting with theories and opinions, brought up a charged topic: "There's been a big argument in this country on—can a white man sing the blues? Can Englishmen sing about Chicago?"

"It's interesting," Grossman said, "because, in the States, the Beatles have pretty much ended that for most Americans."

Price looked puzzled, perhaps because in London the Beatles weren't seen as having anything to do with the blues revivalists that included the Rolling Stones and the Bluesbreakers. "They sing about things which appeal to little girls," he said, "and even the parents accept them, because there's nothing in the lyrics that's suggestive."

"I don't think it's a question of the lyrics," Grossman said. "I think it's a question of just accepting the Negro blues feeling, and I think the Beatles have been accepted in that kind of way."

After Price said that American music fans didn't appreciate the blues sufficiently, Tom Wilson, the only Black person in the room, fixed him with a look and asked: "What do you call a cat like Ray Charles? Here, what do they call him?" Price hemmed and hawed and said he thought of Charles as a gospel artist, mainly. "That's *blues*, man!" Wilson said. "That's the blues that the Negroes sing." As Grossman, Wilson, and Price debated the relationship between gospel and the blues, Dylan sat silent, seemingly uninterested in any talk of genre distinctions.

The next night, he played the Odeon Theatre in Liverpool, where a fifteen-year-old Paul McCartney had seen Bill Haley perform "Rock Around the Clock" eight years earlier. After the show, Dylan went back to his room at the Adelphi Hotel with Bill and Virginia Harry of *Mersey Beat*. They talked about Liverpool's Beat-influenced poetry scene and two of its main players, Roger McGough and Paul's little brother, Mike. Dylan said he'd like to meet them. Then he walked with the Harrys to the Blue Angel, a pub for writers, musicians, and artists. "I said, 'What would you like to drink?'" Bill Harry recalled. "And he said, 'Beaujolais.' But the Blue Angel only sold spirits and beer. So he said, 'Oh, no, let's go back then.'"

The return to the Adelphi was forestalled when Dylan met the Poppies, a trio from Liverpool modeled after American girl groups that was soon to make its debut at the Cavern Club. As he chatted with the young women, in walked Roger McGough and Mike McCartney, who had just seen his concert. The Poppies vouched for them, saying they were "great."

"If the girls like you," Dylan said, "*I* like you."

They all went back to the hotel suite and helped themselves to the crate of Beaujolais provided by Grossman. As the hour grew late, the Poppies announced they would sing something. The small audience sat quietly as they launched into what Mike McCartney described as a not-quite-on-pitch version of "Da Doo Ron Ron," a hit for the Crystals in the days before Beatlemania. At the end of the Poppies' performance, Dylan roared with laughter and led the others in a round of applause.

When he got back to London, he found that the Savoy was very much the place to be. In his suite late one night, Donovan was in the crowd of revelers. Seated in a chair was a man with a weathered face who looked out of place among the scenesters and students. It was the the thirty-nine-year-old singer and banjo player Derroll Adams, a hard-traveling expatriate American troubadour. Dylan told him, with a fan's enthusiasm, that he liked *The Rambling Boys*, a 1958 album Adams had made with Ramblin' Jack Elliott. Adams, who had lately become a mentor to Donovan, accepted the compliment with a nod and a smile, revealing a missing tooth. Then he looked on with pride as his young charge sang for everyone in the room.

Donovan was a sure-handed, inventive guitarist, and Bob Neuwirth complimented his technique. But the mood sank when he started playing a song with the very same melody as "Mr. Tambourine Man." Donovan sang the first line—"Oh my darling tangerine eyes, sing a song for me"—and Neuwirth burst out laughing. Dylan watched with a half smile . . . until he couldn't take it anymore and interrupted the performance to say the song was actually one he had written. A sheepish Donovan said he thought the tune had come from an old folk song.

"It's not an old folk song *yet*," Dylan said.

At the Savoy, Dylan also played host to Marianne Faithfull, an eighteen-year-old daughter of a baroness. Described as a "raving beauty" in a story by Maureen Cleave, Faithfull had been a student at a convent school before scoring a hit with "As Tears Go By," a delicate piece of chamber pop written by Mick Jagger and Keith Richards of the Rolling Stones. Her follow-up, a tepid "Blowin' in the Wind," had been a flop.

The idea of meeting Dylan didn't come without its moral complications for Faithfull, who had recently agreed to marry her boyfriend, John Dunbar, a Cambridge student with artistic leanings, after learning she was pregnant. "Dylan was, at that moment in time, nothing less than the hippest person on earth," she wrote in her memoir. "The zeitgeist streamed through him like electricity. He was my Existential hero, the gangling Rimbaud of rock, and I wanted to meet him more than any other living being." When she stepped into Room 208, she saw "swallow-tailed waiters, folkers, Fleet Street hacks, managers, blondes, and beatniks." Joan Baez was there, too, along with the film crew. Most intimidating of all was Dylan himself: "I was completely overwhelmed by this very cool guy on lots of methedrine." As he clattered away on a typewriter, Baez took out her guitar and asked Faithfull what key she had used for "As Tears Go By." Told that it was in A, Joan found the chords and delivered a strong harmony part—she knew all the words—as Faithfull sang the melody line in a tentative voice.

Dylan went next. He strummed the guitar and sang, "I'm a rolling stone, all alone and lost." This was the start of "Lost Highway," a country standard written by Leon Payne that had been a signature piece for Hank Williams. When the song was done, Bob, with a welcoming look, invited Joan to sing along with him on a Scottish folk standard with a bewitching melody, "Young but Daily Growing." Their voices achieved an ideal blend in what turned out to be the last moment they would sing happily together for many years.

The songfest came to a halt after Joan offered up two recent hits: "Here Comes the Night," by Them, featuring Van Morrison, and "Go Now," by the Moody Blues. "Dylan moaned as she sang," Faithfull recalled. "Her voice had become the banner for a genteel folksinging movement that he had, by this time, developed a loathing for. At one point he held up a bottle as she sang a high note, and drawled, 'Break that.' She just laughed."

Joan was in the limo the next day with Dylan, the film crew, and John Mayall, the leader of the Bluesbreakers. Wearing an outback hat and eating a banana, she launched into a parody of Dylan's "It's All Over Now, Baby Blue": "Yonder stands your orphan with his gun," she sang, "crying like a banana in the sun." Dylan maintained a neutral expression.

In Birmingham that night, he once again didn't invite her to the stage. The next day, Joan wrote to her sister Mimi: "We're leaving Bobby's entourage. He has become so unbelievably unmanageable that I can't stand to be around him. Everyone traveling with him is going mad—He walks around in new clothes with a cane—Has tantrums, orders fish, gets drunk, plays his records, phones up America, asks if his concert tonight is sold out—stops all three limousines every morning to buy all the newspapers that might have his name in them. He won't invite me to sing with him even when the kids yell out my name. . . . Last night I was so incredibly battered by the whole thing that I cried through his entire concert (which was, by the way, a magnificent performance)." From the Savoy, Joan went to the Lennons' house in Weybridge. Then she left England altogether to spend some time with her parents, who were living in Paris for a time.

Allen Ginsberg blew in from Prague, effectively replacing her in the entourage. At thirty-eight, he was "a kind of cultural hero and sometimes a true prophet," as *The New York Times* described him that year; and yet he was besotted with Dylan and even looked up to him.

In Prague, Ginsberg had somehow gotten himself elected Kral Majales, the king of the May Day festival, by students looking to tweak the Soviet-controlled Czech government. The elevation of this merry rabble-rouser led to a rowdy street celebration. The authorities duly uncrowned Ginsberg and ejected him from the country. The newspaper *Mladá Fronta* reported that he was an undesirable person, a homosexual corrupter of youth.

In London, he studied the manuscripts of the romantic poet William Blake at the British Library. He also spent time at the Savoy, where he helped with the job of scrawling words and phrases from "Subterranean Homesick Blues" onto sixty-four placards. In an alley next to the hotel, as Ginsberg, Neuwirth, and Wilson stood nearby, Dylan tossed away the cards in time to the song for Pennebaker's film crew. The sequence, which would be used as the opening of *Dont Look Back*, was completed shortly before the highlight of Dylan's stay: his two-night engagement at the Royal Albert Hall. For the first show, on Sunday, May 9, Brian Epstein had reserved Box 12 for the Beatles.

■   ■   ■

Sundays were quiet in the London of 1965, and the Beatles took advantage of the lack of foot and car traffic to shoot a scene for *Help!*

outside the Dolphin Restaurant in Marylebone. The facade had been changed to show that it was an Indian restaurant. During a break in the filming, the Beatles sat with an American radio host, Sandy Lesberg, of WOR-AM in New York. Word was out that they were about to play the biggest concert ever, and Lesberg wanted details.

"When are you going to be at Shea Stadium in New York?" he asked.

"I don't know," John said.

"Mr. Shenson is just getting his piece of paper out," Ringo said, referring to the producer Walter Shenson, who was standing nearby. "He'll tell us."

"You still call Mr. Shenson 'Mr. Shenson'?"

"Either that or 'Soft Wally,'" John said. "Depends how we're feeling."

That same afternoon, Dylan was riding with Neuwirth and his UK tour manager, Fred Perry, in a limo to the Albert Hall. When Dylan stepped inside, aided by a gentleman's cane, he was struck by the grandeur of the place, which had been opened by Queen Victoria in 1871 and had more than five thousand seats. "Wow, this must be a very old theater, huh?" he said. He moved toward the lone figure perched on one of the chairs onstage: Dana Gillespie. Dylan said hello before going to the dressing room area.

He had some nerves to kill before showtime. First, there was the suddenly pressing matter of a briefcase left behind at the Savoy. At Dylan's request, Fred Perry phoned Grossman and asked: "Would you do me a great favor and bring it along for me? It's a brown one."

While Perry listened to Grossman's reply, Bob got his attention: "Oh, also? Could you bring John Lennon's telephone number? Which is on—"

"Bob says—*Bob Dylan* says—could you bring John Lennon's telephone number?"

A large man in a suit appeared. In a plummy voice, he said, "I saw Paul McCartney this afternoon. He was making a film in the next street to me."

Dylan looked uninterested . . . but then something clicked: "Paul McCartney was *where*?"

"In the next street to where I live," the man said. "He was making a film. They'd taken over an old restaurant and put up a new facade. There was a big mob of people."

"I talked to John last night," Dylan said. "He said they had a box—but they were gonna come in and go out in a very secret way."

Time inched along. Horace Judson, a London correspondent for *Time*, who had previously written on the Beatles, met with Dylan for an interview. After a routine back-and-forth, things got testy. Dana Gillespie looked on like someone watching a tennis match.

"Do you *care* about what you sing?" the reporter asked.

"How could I answer that if you've got the nerve to ask me?" Dylan replied.

"Well, then, you, how could you—"

"I mean, you've got a lot of *nerve*, asking me a question like that."

"I *have* to ask that."

"Do you ask the Beatles that?"

Around 5 p.m., Dylan sat at an upright piano in the backstage area and started playing and singing "Slow Down," a song by the pioneering rock 'n' roller Larry Williams. Williams was also a favorite of the Beatles: They had released their own version of "Slow Down" the year before; and the very next day, at EMI Studios on Abbey Road, the Beatles would record two more of his songs, "Dizzy Miss Lizzy" and "Bad Boy."

At 7 p.m. the audience started filing into the Albert Hall. Marianne Faithfull went in through a back entrance. Although she notes in her memoir that she had turned down an advance by Dylan at the Savoy, he was apparently concerned that someone close to him might suspect he was involved with her. "I had to have an escort, because Sara had arrived," Faithfull wrote, referring to Sara Lownds, "so Dylan set it up so that I'd go with Allen Ginsberg."

Minutes before showtime, Dylan was pacing.

"Hey, the Beatles are here," Neuwirth said.

The hall was now filled to capacity. Fans were flipping through a program instructing them that a Bob Dylan concert was not something merely to be enjoyed: "Dylan is a committed voice, committed to the dignity of man, committed to the exposure of injustice wherever he sees it by his poetry and his grasp of the folk song idiom. An evening with Bob Dylan is an unforgettable experience."

He took the stage and opened with "The Times They Are A-Changin'." Faithfull thought he seemed "especially tightly wound," but Max Jones of *Melody Maker* reported that he "quickly and quietly took over the vast, respectful audience with his weirdly compelling songs."

In the postshow crush, Neuwirth escorted Dana Gillespie to the getaway car. At the Savoy, she found herself in Grossman's suite. Sitting with the star of the night were John and Cynthia; Paul and Jane; Ringo and the former Maureen Cox, who had recently married; George and Pattie Boyd; Marianne Faithfull; and Alma Cogan, the singer whom Cynthia suspected of sleeping with her husband.

Lennon offered a casual compliment: "Lovely gig, man."

"They didn't dig 'It's Alright, Ma,'" Dylan said, referring to "It's Alright, Ma (I'm Only Bleeding)," a torrential song from his new album.

"Maybe they didn't get it," John said. "It's the price of being ahead of your time."

"Maybe, but I'm only twenty minutes ahead, so I won't get far."

The room fell silent when Ginsberg made his entrance and "plonked himself down on the armrest of Dylan's chair," Faithfull recalled in her memoir.

"Why don't you sit a bit closer, then, dearie?" Lennon said.

"The insinuation—that Allen had a crush on Dylan—was intended to demolish Allen, but since it wasn't far from the truth anyway, Allen took it very lightly," Faithfull wrote. "The joke was on them, really. He burst out laughing, fell off the arm and onto the lap of Lennon, who was on the couch with his wife, Cynthia. Allen looked up at him and said, 'Have you ever read William Blake, young man?'"

"Never heard of the man!" John said.

"Oh, John, stop lying!" said Cynthia.

The mood was light after that. "Everyone got very high on wine, which is the only thing Dylan ever drinks," Gillespie said. "He seemed to get on very well with John Lennon—they both share the same sense of humor. At one point all the boys got up and went into the bedroom for a chat. We were told it was a 'staff party' in there and girls were not admitted."

※ ※ ※

Dylan was still plotting his move away from solo folkdom, despite the applause he had received at the Albert Hall. Which meant he would need a group.

At around 8 p.m. on May 12, he entered Levy's Sound Studios on New Bond Street for a recording session with the Bluesbreakers. In addition to its leader, John Mayall, the group consisted of Eric Clapton on guitar, John McVie (soon to be the "Mac" of Fleetwood Mac) on bass, and Hughie Flint on drums. Perhaps in an effort to add a touch of Liverpool magic, Dylan had arranged for the Poppies, the girl group he had met at the Blue Angel, to be there, too.

Tom Wilson was producing. The goal was to get an electric version of "If You Gotta Go, Go Now (Or Else You Got to Stay All Night)," a lusty song that got a terrific response when Dylan played it onstage, and release it as the follow-up single to "Subterranean Homesick Blues." But the mood was sour. As he had during the making of *Another Side of Bob Dylan*, Bob was hitting the Beaujolais. Clapton was not yet a Dylan convert; and his willingness to give his all may have been dampened when Neuwirth told him, "You're playin' too much blues, man. He needs to be more country." They kept at it till ten thirty before calling it a night.

Soon after the failed session, Bob left with Sara to spend a week in Portugal. After their return to London, he was in such bad shape that two private nurses were dispatched to care for him at the Savoy. His spokesman put out the line that he had picked up a virus; his most prolific biographer, Clinton Heylin, has suggested that Dylan was laid low by bad acid.

Joan Baez was back in England and getting ready to make her own Albert Hall debut. On May 23, she couldn't help herself from going to Dylan's suite, taking along a shirt she had bought for him as a get-well gift. "I went unannounced and uninvited to his door," she wrote. "It was answered by Sara, whom I'd never seen before."

That night, a crowd of more than five thousand cheered Baez. "It was a sold-out success, but I was too sick to enjoy it," she recalled.

Three days later, still ailing, Dylan checked into St. Mary's Hospital in Paddington. After his stay, he continued his recovery at the Savoy. On May 29, Joan was back in the suite, along with Donovan, trying to persuade Dylan to join her in a protest march against the Vietnam War. Like so many others in the growing antiwar movement, she was alarmed by the recent escalation: In addition to its deployment of ground troops, the U.S. had begun dropping napalm bombs under the operation name Rolling Thunder. Dylan was unmoved by her pleas. Off Joan went, Donovan in tow. Hours later, she stood in a red raincoat before a big crowd in Trafalgar Square to sing "We Shall Overcome" and Dylan's "With God on Our Side."

One night at the very end of Dylan's stay in London, Donovan made one last visit to the Savoy. He was a little stoned. "Hey, Don," said Neuwirth, leading him into the suite, which was illuminated only by the gray light of a TV set that glowed with the 1965 Horlicks and Rediffusion World and British Professional Skating Championships.

"Hey, Don," Dylan said. "Come in, siddown."

As Donovan's eyes adjusted, he noticed shadowy figures on the sofas and chairs. Then he heard the unmistakable voice of Lennon: "Hullo, Donovan, how-are-ya?"

He sat down and watched the rest of the ice-skating, feeling like "a younger brother" to Dylan and the Beatles in the room. When the broadcast was over, he took the back stairs with John, George, and Ringo to the lobby. Outside the hotel entrance, he saw Mini Coopers, one for each Beatle, parked on the cobblestone.

"See ya, Donovan," John said. "Let's get together and play a few songs."

George drove him home. With sympathy for a fellow underdog, he said: "You felt out of your depth, but you weren't, you know."

10 How Does It Feel

Far from the scene at the Savoy, in sunny Portugal, the twenty-two-year-old Paul McCartney and the nineteen-year-old Jane Asher rode in the back of a chauffeured car for nearly two hundred miles—"a long, hot, dusty drive," as Paul would describe it—from Lisbon Airport to Albufeira, a fishing village in the south, close to Faro. Jane slept much of the way. Paul sat wide-awake, his mind occupied with the melody that had been stubbornly resisting his attempts to equip it with anything but placeholder lyrics.

Scrambled eggs
Oh my baby how I love your legs

Suddenly, he had the title: "Yesterday." Then came some lines on the theme of lost love. He was careful to match each syllable to the meter of his wide-ranging tune. When Albufeira came into view, the song was far from complete, but he knew he had the right idea. He worked on it for the next two weeks. His idyll was cut short when Brian Epstein called him back to London because the Beatles were to be named Members of the Order of the British Empire.

The wide appeal of the Beatles had never been more apparent than it was on June 11, 1965, the day the MBE news made front-page headlines. Even as they were held up as most distinguished citizens by the crown, the Beatles were praised by the antiestablishment figure Allen Ginsberg during a night of poetry at the sold-out Albert Hall.

Called the International Poetry Incarnation, the event featured bards from around the world. One of the organizers was Dan Richter, an actor and mime from Connecticut who had become friends with Yoko Ono while studying Noh and Kabuki theater in Tokyo the year before. As he looked out at the crowd, Richter was amazed to see so many young women in loose cotton dresses or miniskirts and casually dressed men with long hair. The word "counterculture" wasn't yet in common usage, but that's what he saw before him, an early gathering of a fast-growing tribe.

Ginsberg, half-drunk on wine, closed the show, raving and gesticulating through some wild verses. A highlight of his performance was "Who to Be Kind To," a poem he had written for the occasion. It mentioned the Dylan song "Gates of Eden" and included a tribute to the Beatles and the venue that had given them their start.

> *the boom bom that bounces in the joyful*
> *bowels as the Liverpool Minstrels of*
> *Cavernsink*
> *raise up their joyful voices and guitars*
> *in electric Afric hurrah*
> *for Jerusalem*

The next morning, Lennon was still in bed at Kenwood as the other Beatles, along with an anxious Epstein, waited at Twickenham to meet with a pack of journalists who wanted their comments on the MBE news. When the press conference was finally underway, John explained his tardiness: "I set the alarm for eight o'clock, and then I just laid there. I thought, 'Well, if anyone wants me they'll phone me.' The phone went lots of times, but that's the one I never answer. My own phone didn't go at all, so I just laid there."

Two days later, at EMI Studios, Paul ran through "Yesterday" for John, George, and Ringo, who said they couldn't think of anything to add; it seemed fully realized as it was, with Paul solo on acoustic guitar. That raised a knotty question: Was a Beatles record still a Beatles record if it had only one Beatle on it?

It proved a banner recording session for McCartney, one that showcased his talent, versatility, and ascending status within the group—while also hinting at the limits of the all-for-one, one-for-all spirit that had animated the Beatles and made them so loved. The first song they tackled was Paul's skiffle-style "I've Just Seen a Face." Then came "I'm Down," a rocker he had written in the manner of Little Richard. The nighttime hours were given over to the gentle "Yesterday." Perched on a stool, McCartney sang while accompanying himself on acoustic guitar.

Aside from being the first Beatle to record a song at EMI Studios with no musical contributions from his bandmates, something else set Paul apart: He had just bought a house around the corner from Abbey Road, on Cavendish Avenue, meaning he wouldn't be joining his fellow Beatles in Surrey, where Mr. and Mrs. Starkey would soon be moving into Sunny Heights, a mansion not far from John's Kenwood and George's Kinfauns. McCartney's decision to remain in London, apart from the gang, left Lennon "taken aback," according to Pete Shotton.

As for "Yesterday," which would go on to be among the most covered songs of all time and the one played more than any other on the radio in decades to come, Paul sometimes wondered if he deserved praise for it, given that the melody had come to him in a dream. He decided that his alertness allowed him to take credit: "Now, the difference is, I remembered it," he said. "I think a lot of people hear beautiful music in their dream but don't necessarily remember them."

A big reason for the song achieving the status of a standard lies in its words. While McCartney may have thought he was creating a scenario in which the narrator bemoans the loss of romantic love, the words are flexible enough, ambiguous enough, to suggest he is mourning the death of someone close to him. That same subtext was at play in one of his first songs, "I Lost My Little Girl." "I wrote it when

I was fourteen, just after I'd lost my mother," Paul said. "I don't think the song was about that, but of course any psychiatrist getting hold of those two bits of information would say it was. It's fairly obvious with a title like 'I Lost My Little Girl.'" "Yesterday" could have been its sequel, a song that ostensibly tells a tale of heartbreak, but may describe a more devastating experience.

Around 10 p.m., George Martin said that this unadorned recording could use something more. Acting on the precedent he had set during the making of "You've Got to Hide Your Love Away," when he had brought in a classical flutist, he suggested strings. Paul flinched: "I said, 'Are you kidding? This is a rock group!'" By the next day, he had come around enough to join Martin in composing the arrangement for a string quartet.

Not only was "Yesterday" effectively a McCartney solo work, but the presence of classical players on the finished track took the Beatles further from their original rock 'n' roll mission than any of their previous ballads. Lennon would never be able to bring himself to praise the song without hedging, as when he said: "That's Paul's song, and Paul's baby. Well done. Beautiful—and I never wished I'd written it." Dylan, as we will see, would also express mixed feelings about "Yesterday" before deciding to record it himself.

The musicologist Walter Everett has cited "Yesterday" as the start of a movement that would send songwriters and producers away from the rhythm and blues that had been their main wellspring toward the more formally composed works of previous centuries: "The Beatles' arrangement is probably responsible for the late-1960s explosion of interest in classical instrumentation in pop music," Everett wrote. "Take these sorts of instrumentations, add the psychedelia of 1967 Beatles, and you have the roots of British progressive rock."

Paul knew he might have been going against the group ethos long evident in the uniform hairstyles and unison onstage bows, so he raised no objection when the Beatles decided against releasing "Yesterday" as a single in the UK, despite its commercial appeal. "That would have been getting above yourself," he said. "We were always watching each other for any signs of that."

Lennon, though, had already set himself apart with the publication of *In His Own Write*. The media regularly characterized him as the brainy Beatle partly on the strength of it, while Paul had to endure the indignity of being tagged the cute one. The same week that "Yesterday" was recorded, John burnished his reputation as the group's resident intellectual when he appeared on two BBC programs to promote his follow-up book, *A Spaniard in the Works*.

■   ■   ■

While McCartney was bringing "Yesterday" to fruition, Dylan was also working on a song that would stand the test of time and challenge genre conventions: "Like a Rolling Stone." It came pouring out of him, "very vomitific in its structure," he said. He was writing it while staying with Sara at the same cabin in Woodstock where they had posed for portraits in March. As he moved between typewriter and piano, he might have had in mind a song he had sung in his suite at the Savoy, "Lost Highway," with the opening line "I'm a rolling stone, alone and lost." Whatever the origins of his new creation, he wasn't quite sure what it was at first.

"It was ten pages long," he said a year after writing it. "It wasn't called anything, just a rhythm thing on paper all about my steady hatred directed at some point that was honest. In the end it wasn't hatred, it was telling someone something they didn't know, telling them they were lucky. Revenge, that's a better word. I had never thought of it as a song, until one day I was at the piano, and on the paper it was singing, 'How does it feel?' in a slow motion pace." Like McCartney with "Yesterday," he didn't know what to make of his own role in the creation of "Like a Rolling Stone." "It's like a ghost is writing a song like that," he said. "It gives you the song and it goes away."

The melody came to him atop the sturdy chord sequence Ritchie Valens had used in 1958 for his hit adaptation of the Mexican folk song "La Bamba." "It was just a riff, really," Dylan said. "It was like the, you know, the 'La Bamba' riff." That same progression—a Latin inversion of the I-IV-V pattern that was a building block of so much blues and rock 'n' roll—had also served as the foundation of "Twist and Shout," a rave-up cowritten by Bert Berns, a songwriter and producer who had a boundless love for Valens's version of "La Bamba" and often brought a south-of-the-border touch to his own work. Like almost anyone with a radio back then, Dylan was also deeply familiar with "Twist and Shout," which had been a hit for the Isley Brothers in 1962 and a bigger hit two years later for the Beatles; he had even seen the Beatles open with it at the Paramount Theatre eight months earlier.

Dylan invited Mike Bloomfield, the lead guitarist of the Paul Butterfield Blues Band, a Chicago group that was about to record its first album, to Woodstock. When Bloomfield played along with "Like a Rolling Stone," bending the strings in his best bluesman style, Dylan told him he didn't want "that B.B. King shit"; he was aiming to capture a blues feel without relying on tropes that were becoming shopworn.

The day after McCartney recorded "Yesterday," Dylan stepped out of the rain and into Studio A in Midtown Manhattan. Bloomfield was by his side. In addition to his chosen guitarist, there were a few musicians in the room who had played on "Subterranean Homesick Blues." Although Dylan was relatively new to recording with others, he comported himself like someone in charge. And why not? After Dylan-mania had swept the UK, American radio stations were constantly playing the Byrds' version of "Mr. Tambourine Man," which was now at No. 2 on the *Billboard* chart.

Seated at the piano, Dylan led the musicians through several takes of "Like a Rolling Stone," but failed to capture what he was hearing in his head. Unlike the Beatles, who welcomed the expert assistance of George Martin, he worked up arrangements without input from Tom Wilson.

When Dylan attempted the song the next day, he was playing a Fender Stratocaster. Al Kooper, a songwriter and session guitarist from Queens, whom Wilson had invited to the studio as an observer, took the liberty of placing himself at an unoccupied Hammond B3 organ. "Hey," the producer said, "you don't even play the organ." Kooper stayed put. Bluffing his way through the song, he found a playful hook that would help make it a hit. The sound realized by the band was rich and full, more resonant than the spiky tone of "Subterranean Homesick Blues." And at six minutes, "Like a Rolling Stone" had the weight of an epic.

During playback, Dylan said, "Turn the organ up."

"Hey, man," Wilson replied, "that cat's not an organ player."

"Hey, now don't tell me who's an organ player and who's not. Just turn the organ up."

After the session, Wilson never worked with Dylan again.

For decades after its release, whenever "Like a Rolling Stone" was named the best or one of the best rock songs of all time in this or that poll, Dylan fans would speculate on the identity of the character at its heart, a person called "Miss Lonely," who has broken from a bourgeois or upper-class background only to end up in the streets. Joan Baez thought Miss Lonely might be Bob Neuwirth. Others pointed at Baez herself, the daughter of a diplomat. Still others suggested Edie Sedgwick, a tragically glamorous figure of Dylan's acquaintance in the Andy Warhol orbit.

Another possible "Miss Lonely" is Dylan himself. He's the one, after all, who had roughed it after having grown up in pleasant circumstances. And now, four years into his New York phase, after so many people in the Village had given him shelter, encouragement, and wine, he was turning his back on many of his most ardent supporters. So how does it feel?

"Like a Rolling Stone" provides a stark contrast with the romantic vision of bohemian life shown on the cover of *The Freewheelin' Bob Dylan*. By now the rube from the provinces has tasted the delights of the city, and they are turning to ashes in his mouth. There is some hope, though, in this song of (self-)condemnation. It comes in the group sound, which weighs against the protagonist's isolation. The drums, bass, guitars, piano, and cheerful circus organ tell the listener that our hero, or antihero, is not so alone as he might make himself out to be. "Like a Rolling Stone" is also saved from bleakness by the universality of its theme: Everybody grows up and leaves home and ends up disappointed.

In recent years Dylan has encouraged the interpretation of the song as a self-portrait: Two key phrases from the chorus, "no direction home" and "a complete unknown," have been used as the titles of Dylan-sanctioned films about his life and legend. And unlike the singers who profess disdain for their biggest hits, he has never run away from this one, playing it more than two thousand times in concert, second only to a later song, "All Along the Watchtower."

Dylan intended "Like a Rolling Stone" as his next single, which put Columbia in a bind, given that it was more than twice the length of the typical hit. Company executives ordered up an edited version that chopped the song in two, the second part relegated to the B-side of the 45 rpm disc, just as Atlantic Records had done six years earlier with Ray Charles's "What'd I Say." Dylan balked at the result, and the release fell into limbo.

During the standoff between corporation and artist, Shaun Considine, a Columbia publicist who loved Dylan's new sound, took an acetate copy of the song to Arthur, a discotheque on East Fifty-Fourth Street that had attracted Truman Capote, Liza Minnelli, and Rudolf Nureyev to its opening night weeks earlier and had been packed every night since. The club got its name from a quip spoken by George Harrison in *A Hard Day's Night*, when a reporter asks him what he calls his hairstyle. "Arthur" is George's deadpan reply.

When the disc jockey dropped the needle on "Like a Rolling Stone" at around eleven o'clock on a Sunday night, the reaction was immediate. "People jumped to their feet and took to the floor, dancing the entire six minutes," Considine recalled. "'Who is it?' the DJ yelled at one point, running toward me. 'Bob Dylan!' I shouted back. The name spread through the room, which only encouraged the skeptics to insist that it be played again, straight through. Sometime past midnight, as the grooves on the temporary dub wore out, the needle began to skip." The clubgoers' response, in other words, was a lot like Dylan's when he first heard what the Byrds had done with "Mr. Tambourine Man": "Wow, you can dance to it."

A radio host and a music programmer at two of New York's biggest pop stations witnessed the scene at Arthur. The next day, they called their contacts at Columbia. The executives took the record off the back burner and sent it to stations across the country in time for Dylan's scheduled appearance at the Newport Folk Festival.

Up in Woodstock, Dylan waved friends and acquaintances into the Café Espresso to play for them his advance copy of "Like a Rolling Stone." He also wrote new songs in preparation for the sessions that would yield his next album. One of these, "Ballad of a Thin Man," a dirgelike denunciation of a status-obsessed square, included a structural element that had long been a staple of Lennon-McCartney compositions, but was brand-new for Dylan: a bridge. He placed it midway through the song, breaking it up nicely.

He was also shopping for a house. He decided on an eleven-bedroom Arts and Crafts mansion in Byrdcliffe Colony, a former utopian community in Bearsville, a mile from the Woodstock town center. He paid $12,000 for it, thinking it would be the perfect place for himself, Sara, Sara's daughter from her first marriage, and the child they were expecting. The inspiration was Lennon's home in Weybridge. "I dug his situation where he lived," Dylan said. "It was a twenty-two-room house. You know what I did when I got back from England, man? I bought me a thirty-one-room house. Can you imagine that? Mine!" And just like Kenwood, Dylan's mansion had a name: Hi Lo Ha.

On July 25, 1965, he made his famous final break with the folk community at the Newport Folk Festival. He was backed by Bloomfield on electric guitar, Kooper on organ, Barry Goldberg on piano, Jerome Arnold on bass, and Sam Lay on drums. Dylan, who wore a leather jacket beneath his Stratocaster, opened with "Maggie's Farm," the lament of a laborer who's sick of the abuse he has suffered at the hands of his bosses. It was just the song to use as a weapon against the traditionalists: "Maggie's Farm" was an update of "Down on Penny's Farm," a song recorded by the Bentley Boys in 1929 that had appeared on *Anthology of American Folk Music*, a collection beloved by the folk crowd. If the Newport audience didn't like the song, it could only be because of their fogyish objection to the way he was putting it across.

The backbone of this new arrangement of "Maggie's Farm," which hit harder than the version on *Bringing It All Back Home*, was Bloomfield's guitar riff. It was closely related to the one that had driven Bobby Parker's "Watch Your Step" in 1961—the same riff Lennon had modified for the recent Beatles hit "I Feel Fine." Amid the cheers and boos that night, at least one heckler made reference to the Beatles, who were seen by folk diehards as purveyors of crass commercialism: "Go back to the Sullivan show!" That line sent derisive laughter rippling through the crowd. Dylan followed "Maggie's Farm" with "Like a Rolling Stone." Then came the third and final song of his brief electric set, "Phantom Engineer," which would become "It Takes a Lot to Laugh, It Takes a Train to Cry" upon further revision.

When Dylan left the stage, he was shaken, even despondent. "After it was over, I said, 'Bob, how do you think we did?'" Bloomfield recalled. "And he said, 'They were booing. Didn't you hear it?' I said, 'No, man. I thought it was cheers.'" Many of the festival's organizers believed Dylan had destroyed the event and the community that had been gathering at Newport each summer. They weren't wrong—although, as Suze Rotolo, Greil Marcus, Roger McGuinn, and others have pointed out, the arrival of the Beatles had already made the folk scene seem stodgy to many of its young acolytes.

Joe Boyd, a future record producer who was working backstage at Newport, loved what he saw and heard in the moment. In hindsight, though, he came to think that, paradoxically enough, Dylan might have dealt a crushing blow that night not only to folk music but to another genre: rock 'n' roll. "This was the birth of Rock," Boyd wrote in his memoir. "So many taste crimes have been committed in rock's name since then that it might be questionable to count this moment as a triumph, but it certainly felt like one in July 1965."

From here on out, in other words, songs created in the old rock 'n' roll spirit—as a soundtrack for dancing, courtship, or just having fun—were no longer the thing. To be sure, the pop charts of 1965 included a number of infectious records made in that style, including "Wooly Bully" by the Sam the Sham and the Pharaohs and "Hang On Sloopy" by the McCoys; but the catchy escapism of those hits marked them out as passé to music fans who now wanted something more—something you could listen to in the privacy of your room, perhaps with headphones clamped to your ears; something that would make you think.

Shortly after his last studio session with Dylan, Tom Wilson turned his thoughts to "The Sounds of Silence," an acoustic ballad on *Wednesday Morning, 3 AM*, the debut album by Simon and Garfunkel, a duo with a college-student sensibility from Queens, New York.

Wilson was the producer of that LP, which hadn't sold much. Now, a year after its release, "The Sounds of Silence" was receiving some airplay thanks to enterprising disc jockeys in Boston and other cities. The track's surprise popularity gave Wilson an idea: What if he assembled some studio musicians and spruced up the original recording with overdubs of electric guitar, bass, and drums? This he did without bothering to inform the song's composer, Paul Simon, who was now making a steady living, sans Art Garfunkel, on the London folk scene.

From late June, when the Byrds' version of "Mr. Tambourine Man" reached No. 1 in the U.S., to September, when the souped-up "The Sounds of Silence" was released (under the title "The Sound of Silence"), the blending of the Dylan sensibility and the Beatles sound was all the rage: Cher's rendition of Dylan's "All I Really Want to Do" made the Top 10, with the Byrds' take on the same song close behind; the Turtles, a Los Angeles group that had previously spelled its name "Tyrtles," scored with a remake of Dylan's "It Ain't Me, Babe"; and Manfred Mann had a UK hit with the one that had gotten away from him, "If You Gotta Go, Go Now."

Other artists who put out their own versions of Dylan songs in 1965 included Johnny Cash, the Four Seasons, Duane Eddy, and Gerry Mulligan. Dylan's reach had extended so far beyond the folk crowd that he was even popping up in fan magazines. *Fabulous 208*, a British publication, included a shot of Dylan as one of its "king-size full-colour pin-ups"; *TeenSet*, an American publication, ran side-by-side pictures of Dylan and Lennon on its cover.

Singers and groups who weren't putting out Dylan remakes had hits with songs influenced by him. Sonny Bono swiped the "babe" from "It Ain't Me, Babe," as well as Dylan's anti-authority attitude and vocal intonations, for "I Got You Babe," a big hit for Sonny and Cher. With "(I Can't Get No) Satisfaction," the Rolling Stones combined Keith Richards's infectious guitar riff with lyrics by Mick Jagger that amounted to a Dylanesque critique of consumerism.

"Eve of Destruction," a roll call of societal ills set to a thumping beat, verged on parody. Composed by the versatile Los Angeles songwriter P. F. Sloan and sung by the rough-voiced Barry McGuire, it climbed steadily up the *Billboard* charts all summer until it reached No. 1. In *The New York Times*, the early Dylan booster Robert Shelton cited it as a prime example of "the trend of meaningful rock 'n' roll lyrics." Others, including Dylan himself, found it heavy-handed. McCartney was also a detractor. "The one thing I can't understand is the protest songs like 'Eve of Destruction,'" Paul said. "That was absolute rubbish."

In a pop culture landscape that had changed so much since the days of "She Loves You," Beatlemania was alive and well. Ten thousand fans clogged Piccadilly Circus on July 29 to see John, Paul, George, and Ringo arrive at the London Pavilion for the premiere of *Help!* The people in the theater that night caught the first glimpse of Lennon strumming an acoustic while singing "You've Got to Hide Your Love Away." Shortly afterward, the Beatles' new single, "Help!," replaced the Byrds' "Mr. Tambourine Man" at the top of the UK chart.

In the U.S., "Like a Rolling Stone" was getting significant airplay. Some disc jockeys even cobbled together the A-side and the B-side of the promo-only 45 rpm disc so that they could air the full version in all its six-minute glory. An uncredited writer for the Los Angeles music publication *KRLA Beat* observed that Dylan had "bridged the gap between the folk world and the rock world and has bound together the tastes of adolescence and maturity."

Ralph J. Gleason weighed in with a column for the *San Francisco Chronicle* headlined "Rock and Roll: The Folk Music of the Day." "The twin themes, it strikes me, are exemplified by the Beatles and Bob Dylan," he wrote. "The Beatles are, when all is said and done, a roaring, raging, riotous protest in favor of life and love and laughter and the thrill of living and against pretense and pomposity and falsehood. Dylan wears more than one hat but the two which have had the biggest effect on popular music are his teen-age protest songs such as 'Subterranean Homesick Blues,' which, basically, says that society will blame the kids no matter what really happened, and his lyric songs of alienation with their great poetic imagery."

Dylan went back to the studio to complete his sixth album, which he would call *Highway 61 Revisited*. He was working with a new producer, Bob Johnston, an affable white man from Texas who usually recorded in Nashville and wanted Dylan to try his luck there. When Dylan was dissatisfied with an early take of "Desolation Row," one of his most ambitious songs, Johnston enlisted a young Nashville player, Charlie McCoy, to decorate it with flamenco guitar. "Now see how easy that was?" Johnston said. "That's how it would be in Nashville." Dylan then got to work on his next single, a put-down song with electric backing, "Positively 4th Street."

As he was further committing himself to rock, the Beatles were continuing their move toward acoustic sounds. At a studio in Central London on August 9, Lennon and McCartney oversaw a session by the Silkie, a British folk foursome that Brian Epstein had signed to a management contract. The song the group recorded that day—with John in the control room, Paul on guitar, and George on tambourine—was "You've Got to Hide Your Love Away." "It was really Paul's arrangement of John's song," Mike Ramsden, a member of the Silkie, said.

At the end of the session, an exultant Lennon called Epstein: "Listen, Brian, we've just made a No. 1!" He wasn't that far off: The Silkie's "You've Got to Hide Your Love Away" would reach No. 9 in the U.S. and make the Top 40 in the UK. As if putting an exclamation point on this moment of Beatles-Dylan crossovers, the Silkie would soon return to the studio to record its debut album: *The Silkie Sing the Songs of Bob Dylan.*

■   ■   ■

Insured by Lloyd's of London for more than $5 million apiece, John, Paul, George, and Ringo left Britain on August 13 for their second major North American tour. This time, they would be playing stadiums and arenas in a coast-to-coast sprint—sixteen shows in ten cities, including what would be the largest rock concert at Shea Stadium in Queens.

They landed in New York at 2:30 p.m. The TWA jet taxied to a distant part of the Kennedy Airport runway, two miles from the area where the police had enclosed hundreds of fans. The Beatles stepped off the plane and into the kind of reception they weren't used to—a scattering of indifferent cops and ground crew workers. Limos ferried them to the Warwick Hotel, a thirty-six-story structure in Midtown Manhattan just a few blocks from the studio where Dylan had made his albums. The NYPD had barred automobiles from the area, and thousands of people filled the streets, cheering, singing, pressing up against the barricades. "So the Americans still like us, after all," George said.

In a public room of the hotel, Capitol executives presented John, Paul, George, and Ringo with a gold record of their latest U.S. album, *Beatles VI*, which had been No. 1 all summer. Like other American versions of their LPs, it was slapdash in comparison with the Beatles-sanctioned Parlophone releases. The cover photo, originally shot for a fan magazine, was a bland image lacking the moody depths of the portraits taken by Robert Freeman for their British sleeves. And the songs on *Beatles VI* had been plucked seemingly at random from the EMI vault. Capitol went even further in its handling of the *Help!* album, which came out on this day. The U.S. version included five instrumentals from the movie soundtrack written or arranged by the British TV and film composer Ken Thorne. None of those tracks appeared on the superior British edition.

After making nice with the executives, the Beatles met with 250 reporters in a fifth-floor reception room. The questions were idiotic—how many times could they be asked about their hair? When a reporter asked them what they *didn't* like about America, Lennon shot him a look and said: "You." Once they were done with the press, the Beatles repaired to the thirty-third floor. They settled in and waited for the arrival of their friend Bob.

Al Aronowitz had been charged with the task of picking him up downtown. As usual, Dylan was with Bob Neuwirth, whose penchant for barbed wisecracks always made Aronowitz uneasy. As he piloted his station wagon toward the Warwick, he was perhaps even more of a nervous wreck than he had been a year earlier, when he had arranged the first Dylan-Beatles get-together at the Delmonico.

At this point in his career, Aronowitz was hoping to escape journalism and make some real money as a manager. He started by representing the Myddle Class, a promising group from suburban New Jersey; and in the coming months, Aronowitz would start booking gigs for a band that had recently formed in Lower Manhattan, the Velvet Underground.

His attempt to make himself into the next Albert Grossman gave Neuwirth a fresh line of attack. He needled Aronowitz by saying he was misguided if he thought he could work as a journalist while profiting from the business he covered. Neuwirth also mocked his association with the husband-and-wife songwriting team Carole King and Gerry Goffin, friends of Aronowitz's who were providing the Myddle Class with material.

The Beatles loved Goffin and King and had performed or recorded a few of the duo's songs, including "Chains" and "Take Good Care of My Baby." But over the last two years, the couple had been losing confidence: King worried that the style of her melodies had been knocked into obsolescence by the arrival of the Beatles; Goffin, a lyricist, was so awed by Dylan's poetic powers that he had sunk into despair. By writing for the Myddle Class, they were hoping to make a return to cultural relevance. To Neuwirth, who foolishly considered Goffin and King hacks, the enterprise seemed like nothing but a cynical cash grab, and he wasn't shy about telling Aronowitz how he felt.

Another source of tension during the ride to the Warwick was the presence of Scott Ross, whom Aronowitz had invited against his own better judgment. Ross, a good-looking, confident young man who was dating Nedra Talley of the Ronettes, hosted a show at a Long Island radio station. Aronowitz needed the goodwill of any disc jockey who might promote the Myddle Class, and so he was taking Ross to meet the Beatles as part of a schmooze campaign.

He parked close to the hotel. Then he walked with Ross, Neuwirth, and Dylan into the sea of people, many of whom were chanting and singing, aiming their voices at the stately Warwick. The Beatles were stuck in there, having been advised not to leave the premises by the police, who feared the crowd would riot if they set foot outside.

Was this level of fame worth it? Dylan didn't think so. Even as "Like a Rolling Stone" was making its way up the charts and dozens of artists were recording his songs or ripping off his style, he had been telling Aronowitz that he wouldn't want to trade places with the Beatles, wouldn't want to be suffocated by his fans.

Scott Ross mentioned having seen similar crowds when he had hung out with the Rolling Stones, who were in New York at the time. That bit of name-dropping made Aronowitz wince. The thing to do, when you were with Dylan and Neuwirth, was to play it cool. Ross's comment also annoyed Aronowitz because it was an exaggeration. He himself had been spending time with the Stones and he had seen nothing like Beatlemania-level crowds in their vicinity. Making things worse, Ross mentioned that some of his own "radio fans" had asked for his autograph when they saw him outside the Stones' hotel. That remark drew a "look of disgust" from Neuwirth, Aronowitz wrote.

On the thirty-third floor, the visitors were greeted by John, Paul, George, and Ringo, along with Brian Epstein and the two road managers, the sharp-eyed Neil Aspinall and the bearlike Mal Evans. Aronowitz detected a "relaxed stiffness" at the moment of reunion, with handshakes instead of hugs. As he stepped into the suite, he was inwardly berating himself for having brought Ross into the Beatles' inner circle without having asked first.

The Beatles had been expecting Dylan, and so they had plenty of Beaujolais on hand. They were "their usual charming selves," according to Aronowitz, but they displayed a "psychic solidarity" that kept them at a slight remove. Dylan and Neuwirth tried "probing the Beatles' defenses," to no avail, he wrote. This wasn't the Kettle of Fish, the Greenwich Village tavern where the two Bobs regularly held court, raking over the music scene and laying into anyone foolish enough to risk their wrath. A thought passed through Aronowitz's mind: "If this is going to turn into a shootout, the Beatles have Bob outgunned."

They lit up joints, and Dylan mentioned that he had brought along a pressing of his soon-to-be-released album, *Highway 61 Revisited*. After a pause that struck Aronowitz as unduly long, John said, "Well, let's hear it." Dylan handed it to Aronowitz, saying, "Here, Al, you play disc jockey." As Al carried the acetate disc to the hi-fi, he brought up Dylan's recent Newport misadventure, recounting for the Beatles how he had been booed for the crime of going electric.

"That's not what happened!" Dylan said.

"Yeah, that's wrong, man!" Neuwirth said. "That ain't the way it was!"

Aronowitz felt he had put his foot in his mouth—but he was puzzled. The reaction to the concert had made national news, after all, and people were still talking about it all these weeks later. And he certainly hadn't meant what he had said as a criticism. In his view, Dylan had done the right thing by effectively telling the folk crowd to go to hell. It seemed that Dylan, with his denial, didn't want to risk showing even a hint of weakness in this setting.

The music started—"at maximum volume," Mal Evans wrote in his diary. The opening track, "Like a Rolling Stone," was known to everyone in the room. Weeks before it had become a hit, John and Paul had listened to an advance copy at Kenwood. "It seemed to go on and on forever," McCartney said of his first impression. "It was just beautiful." The next eight songs expanded on its themes of alienation and hard living. The title track included a police whistle and

God commanding Abraham to "kill me a son" on Highway 61. That one derived much of its power from two facts probably unknown to the Beatles: Dylan's father was named Abraham, and Highway 61 was the road he had followed out of Minnesota and into the wider world.

This was a rock album, more so than *Bringing It All Back Home*, but Dylan had carried over something from traditional music by allowing his songs to go on for as long as they needed to, giving no thought to the time limits that recording technology and radio programmers had imposed on pop since the 1920s. Each track the Beatles heard that night was longer than the longest one they had put out so far, "Ticket to Ride," which clocked in at just over three minutes.

The finale was "Desolation Row," in which Dylan weaves together characters from literature and lore, an assemblage that includes Cinderella, Romeo, Ophelia, Cain, Abel, Robin Hood, and the Hunchback of Notre Dame. When it was over, after more than eleven minutes, the reaction of John, Paul, George, and Ringo struck Aronowitz as lukewarm: "The collective consciousness of the single, larger Beatles organism seemed to be saying, 'Yeah, it's okay,'" he wrote.

Scott Ross appeared to be feeling the effects of all he had ingested that night. He rushed across the room and grabbed the knob of the bathroom door, only to find it locked. Then he vomited on the carpet. A moment later, Paul emerged from the bathroom, and Aronowitz saw a zippered Chelsea boot sidestepping the mess.

Ross continued barfing, his head over the vacated toilet bowl. Once he was through, Neil Aspinall ejected him from the suite, along with the man who had brought him. With a parting glance at Ross, Neuwirth landed one last jab: "Hey, man, if any of those *kids* down there ask you for your *autograph* on the way out, don't forget to tell 'em you're with the Rolling Stones!"

The Stones had positioned themselves as down-and-dirty foils to the Beatles, thanks largely to a marketing strategy concocted by their savvy manager, Andrew Loog Oldham. But the relationship between the two camps had been mostly friendly since their first get-together in the spring of 1963.

Two nights after the Dylan-Beatles hangout at the Warwick, Mick Jagger and Keith Richards joined John, Paul, George, and Ringo in the dugout on the third-base side of the Shea Stadium field. It was moments before the Beatles were to play before 55,600 fans. The place was thrumming.

"It's the famous Stones," John said when he saw his supposed rivals.

The dugout was as crowded as a rush-hour subway car. The police were annoyed.

"Who *are* these people?" a cop asked, gesturing toward Mick and Keith.

"They're the same as Beatles," John said.

Ed Sullivan did the introduction from the stage, which was set on the middle of the baseball diamond, and the Beatles hurried across the field. The constituency that had given them so much of their power—teenage girls—unleashed a torrent of screams. The sound was otherworldly. "Deafening," said Keith. "Frightening," said Mick. The din continued as the Beatles launched into "Twist and Shout." The sound system, paltry by today's standards, had no chance. "You couldn't hear what the boys were doing unless you happened to be sitting right next to one of the big amplifiers," Mal Evans recalled.

The only person who wasn't a pro athlete to have appeared before such a crowd in recent memory was the Southern Baptist minister Billy Graham, who had preached to one hundred thousand people at Yankee Stadium in 1957. Graham appealed to those who looked askance at rock music and the societal changes that went with it. Scores of millions strong, these people were lying low during the sea-change moment when the Beatles and Dylan were ascendant and President Lyndon B. Johnson was winning support for the liberal policy initiatives of his Great Society plan, even as he ramped up U.S. military involvement in Vietnam.

Shea Stadium provided John, Paul, George, and Ringo with some of the last enjoyable moments they would have onstage. They laughed throughout their twelve-song set and were jubilant afterward, celebrating till 5 a.m. at the Warwick with Mick and Keith, Andrew Loog Oldham, and the Supremes, who were in the middle of a residency at the Copacabana a few blocks away. The next night, the Beatles said no to an invitation to dine with Frank Sinatra in favor of reprising the festivities with the Supremes, the American singer Del Shannon, and, once again, Dylan.

SIDE TWO

11 Number One

The Shea Stadium concert was an unprecedented triumph of spectacle and commerce. For a half hour's labor, the Beatles earned $160,000, the equivalent of $1.6 million today, from box-office receipts alone. And there was more to be made from the television documentary that would be assembled from the footage shot by fourteen cameras.

But they suspected they were slipping as a live band—and an early cut confirmed for them how far they had fallen since their onstage peak two or three years earlier. The TV special, *The Beatles at Shea Stadium*, wouldn't be deemed fit for broadcast until they had put in considerable work with George Martin to improve the sound by patching in overdubs and recording all-new, faux-live versions of two songs, "Help!" and "I Feel Fine."

Much of the shoddiness can be attributed to the screams, but it also came about because the Beatles rarely rehearsed these days, a sign that they regarded live performance as less important than their increasingly ambitious songwriting efforts and studio sessions.

The only real risk they took on the 1965 tour was to play "Baby's in Black," the morbid ballad that hadn't been released as a single, midway through shows loaded with hits. In contrast with Dylan, whose brief Newport set had triggered a furious reaction not seen since the debut of Stravinsky's *The Rite of Spring* in Paris more than fifty years earlier, the Beatles aimed to please the crowd, survive the night, and get paid. The idea of using a concert to make an artistic statement seems not to have occurred to them.

One thing working against them was the fact that they still had a foot in a show business world that smacked of vaudeville. The 1965 tour, like those before and after it, was a so-called "package tour," with the Beatles one of six acts on the bill. Each show started with the Discotheque Dancers, a troupe consisting of five young women wearing sparkly tops, tights, and go-go boots led by a smiling young man in a V-neck sweater. As the saxophone great King Curtis led his band through Tom Jones's "It's Not Unusual" and the Beatles' "Can't Buy Me Love," the dancers did the Watusi, the Swim, the Frug, and other steps that, even then, were passing out of fashion. Such revue-style shenanigans would have no place in the realm Dylan began carving out when he undertook his first tour with a backing band later that same summer. He would lead his audience through lengthy shows that had heft and dramatic shape, thereby setting the template for modern-day rock and pop concerts.

But it might be ungenerous to fault the Beatles for putting their ambitions on hold when they played live. They had to be constantly on their guard against the irrational behavior of their devotees, who, in addition to the harmless screaming, continued their habit of throwing things from their seats and rushing the stage with no regard for their own or their idols' safety.

The phenomenon that had made for such amusing scenes in *A Hard Day's Night*—fans chasing; Beatles running—was no longer so innocent. When the group landed at the William P. Hobby Airport in Houston, Texas, around 2 a.m. on August 19, hundreds of Beatlemaniacs broke free from the police and charged the plane as it rolled down the runway, ignoring the steel propeller blades whirring not far above the ground. A quick-thinking pilot prevented bloodshed by cutting the engines before the mob swarmed the aircraft. Many of the crazed young people climbed the tires, giving one another boosts.

In a flash they were on the wings. They pounded on the fuselage and pressed their faces against the porthole-size windows.

The passengers were stuck inside the plane for forty minutes. Flight attendants shouted when they saw fans lighting cigarettes near the fuel tank. Unable to contain the mob, the cops and ground crew workers decided to extract the Beatles with the help of a hydraulic lift attached to a small truck, rather than risk the usual practice of placing a portable staircase at the main door. Once the equipment was in position beside a rear exit hatch, John, Paul, George, and Ringo, along with members of their team, stepped onto a flatbed surface nine feet above the concrete. Fans took the opportunity to throw things at them—magazines, shoes, lipstick cases—in a peculiar attempt to make contact with their heroes. The hurled objects included a heavy lighter that hit the assistant road manager Alf Bicknell in the face. The surprise blow caused him to lose his footing. Paul caught him before he went over the side.

A break in the madness came later that month, when the Beatles spent six days in the Beverly Hills mansion belonging to the socialite-actress Zsa Zsa Gabor and her fourth husband, the investment banker Herbert Hutner. It turned out to be not quite the sanctuary they had hoped for. Newspapers published the address, radio jocks spread the word, and fans massed at the wooden fencing that walled off the property. Still, they had more privacy than usual; and with no immediate commitments, John and George decided the time was right for their second LSD experience.

They pressured Paul to join them to no avail. Ringo said yes with no hesitation. Neil Aspinall also took part, along with three people who had stopped by, the actor Peter Fonda and two members of the Byrds, Roger McGuinn and David Crosby.

George felt the same all-encompassing ecstasy he had experienced the first time around, especially when he slipped into Zsa Zsa's swimming pool. "The water felt good," he said. Then things took a turn—he felt certain he was about to die. Fonda told the panicked George to relax, saying, "I know what it's like to be dead," as if it were no big thing, before describing a childhood accident when he had shot himself in the stomach. That upset John, who told Fonda to quit talking about death.

Joan Baez, who had come down from Carmel at Lennon's invitation, was a bit put off to see all the young women who sat for hours in the living room. "These poor girls," she said, "just waiting to see whether they're gonna be picked by somebody—they don't talk, they don't even knit." But during her stay she grew closer to Lennon, who offered her his bed, since the house had only four bedrooms. "It had a bed in it the size of a small swimming pool," Baez recalled. "I said, 'Well, John, don't worry. You just come in and use the other side of the bed when you're tired.' So I went to sleep, and he came in, in the middle of the night. And I think he felt compelled—'Well, I've asked her, and she *is* a star, oh, dear'—and he started coming on to me, very unenthusiastically. I said, 'John, you know, I'm probably as tired as you are, and I don't want you to feel you have to perform on my behalf.' And he says, 'What a relief! Because, you see, well, you might say I've already been fooked downstairs.'"

George and Paul left the house to visit Columbia Recording Studios on Sunset Boulevard on the day when the Byrds were hoping to record their next single. As the two Beatles looked on, McGuinn and company struggled to nail a satisfactory take. The song they had chosen, Dylan's sermonic "The Times They Are A-Changin'," just wouldn't give itself over to the folk-rock treatment so easily as "Mr. Tambourine Man."

■   ■   ■

As the Beatles neared the end of their Beverly Hills respite, Dylan was hustling four musicians through rehearsals in preparation for his first concert appearance after Newport. In addition to Al Kooper on organ and Harvey Brooks on bass, both of whom had played on *Highway 61 Revisited*, the group included Levon Helm on drums and Robbie Robertson on guitar.

Helm and Robertson were members of the Hawks, a big attraction in Toronto. Mary Martin, a music enthusiast from that city who was working as a secretary in Albert Grossman's office, had often seen the Hawks in the clubs along Yonge Street and recommended them highly. They had gotten their start as the backing group for the Arkansas-born rock 'n' roller Ronnie Hawkins, who had made a reputation for himself in his home state before finding greater success north of the U.S. border.

Helm, the son of Arkansas cotton farmers, had quit high school to join Hawkins a few years before the move to Canada. Robertson, who had grown up in Toronto, came aboard after watching Rompin' Ronnie (as the frontman was billed) at Le Coq d'Or. Hawkins shaped the musicians into a crackling unit able to get crowds going with anything from honky-tonk to rhythm and blues, but he was a taskmaster who paid haphazardly. In 1963, the band broke away from him to try their luck under the names the Canadian Squires, the Levon Helm Sextet, and Levon and the Hawks.

Dylan told Helm, Robertson, Kooper, and Brooks to be ready for anything when they played Forest Hills Tennis Stadium on August 28—and he was right to warn them. Boos greeted the emcee, Murray the K, when he did the introductions on that unseasonably chilly evening. The very sight of this deejay, who sounded like a salesman whether he was talking up the latest Beatles single or Kent cigarettes, couldn't help but incite the New Yorkers who saw him as the embodiment of the hype-happy culture they so despised.

When Dylan made his entrance with his acoustic guitar, the fans were calm; and they sat rapt as he played solo renditions of "Mr. Tambourine Man" and six other songs. The jeers erupted when the musicians joined him for his first full-length rock set as a professional. *The Village Voice* reported that the crowd "booed their former culture hero savagely." *Newsday* noted a heckle—"Where's Ringo?"—that demonstrated the contempt folk fans had for the Beatles. Robert Shelton of *The New York Times* praised Dylan and his "excellent rock 'n' roll quartet," reserving his brickbats for the crowd: "Nothing so dramatized the childishness of the audience's reaction to folk rock than when it ceased to boo and started to sing along with the popular song, 'Like a Rolling Stone.'"

Dylan kept his cool even when a young man crashed the stage and knocked Al Kooper off his stool. "I was on my ass and not the least pleased about the situation," Kooper recalled. When the show was over, the musicians were upset, but Dylan was happy. "It was fantastic," he said at the postshow party. "A real carnival, and fantastic." He had hit upon something rare—an interaction between artist and audience that went beyond the usual ho-hum cycle of song-applause-song-applause and into a contentious give-and-take. It was as if he had finally become the carnie he had pretended to be in the tall-tale interviews he had given earlier in his career.

The next day, at the Capitol Records Tower in Los Angeles, the Beatles sat for another press conference. For a change, the questions weren't so vacuous. One reporter, addressing Lennon and McCartney, said he understood they were Dylan fans.

"We all are," Paul said. "All of us are."

Another reporter said he had noticed that the U.S. versions of the Beatles' albums were different from the British editions—especially *Help!*, with all those tracks from the film score.

"It's a drag," Paul said. "We make an album to be like an album, to be a complete thing."

"We plan it," John said, "and they wreck it."

That evening, they returned to what seemed to be their favorite American venue, the Hollywood Bowl, for the first of two concerts, during which they were able to hear themselves more clearly than usual. From there they made their way north, back to the Cow Palace, the site of so much chaos the year before, for the last stop of the tour.

They played two shows there. During the matinee, fans threw shoes at the stage. Between performances, the Beatles had a moment's peace while hanging out with Joan Baez and another famous visitor, Johnny Cash. At the evening show, fans threw bottles and chairs. Then they charged, overwhelming the 120 police officers and 90 security officers. Thirty people were injured, most of them teenage girls. In the crush of bodies, the Beatles' folk-singer pal showed real courage. "Baez behaved in an extraordinary way," said the reporter Larry Kane, "braving the onrush to pick the injured children out of the crowd one at a time." Tony Barrow, a Beatles press attaché, seconded that observation: "Joan Baez was doing a kind of Florence Nightingale, and sort of holding kids up to safety and bringing them around the back, laying them out on the floor."

On September 2, the day the Beatles made it back to London, Dylan and his group arrived in California. There would be plenty of booing in the nights to come, but not during their appearance at the Hollywood Bowl before an audience that included the Byrds, the Beach Boys, and Sonny and Cher. In a review for the *Los Angeles Times*, the critic Charles Champlin contrasted the show with the pair of Beatles concerts he had seen the week before: "The monumental difference was that this vast audience paid folksinger Bob Dylan the vast compliment of pin-drop silence while he was performing. His rewards thereafter were thunderous applause, a scattering of whistles but no screams, which is interesting because there was at least a partial overlap between his audience and the Beatles'."

Despite the welcoming reaction, Al Kooper begged off the rest of the tour. He was wary of going onstage in Texas, where Dylan was scheduled to play two shows toward the end of the month. He reasoned that Dylan might be a target in the state where a president had been gunned down in broad daylight.

Once again in need of musicians, Dylan talked things over with Levon Helm and Robbie Robertson, who said they would continue with him only if he agreed to take on the other members of the Hawks. They traveled to the band's home base, Toronto, to give it a try. Dylan quickly realized that this was a road-tested ensemble well-versed in the music he loved. Garth Hudson was a classically trained pianist and organist who happened to play a nice saxophone; Rick Danko and Richard Manuel were also skilled multi-instrumentalists; and three members (Helm, Manuel, and Danko) were terrific singers.

For Dylan, meeting the Hawks was a stroke of luck. They were confident, better on any given night than the Beatles or the Beach Boys, in Helm's view, and they had the kind of chemistry that develops only after thousands of hours onstage. None of them had emerged as a songwriter of note—the group's two singles had flopped—which meant they had no pressing obligations, leaving them free to join the tour mapped out by Albert Grossman, one that would take them across North America and Australia before a final leg in Europe.

■   ■   ■

As the summer of 1965 waned, the pop charts reflected the primacy of Dylan and the Beatles at a time when their still-fresh influence on each other was making itself known to the wider world. On September 4, *Billboard* listed "Help!" at No. 1 and "Like a Rolling Stone" at No. 3. That same week, *Cash Box*, which many record-industry people viewed as having the more accurate chart, had "Help!" at No. 1 and "Like a Rolling Stone" at No. 2. The following week, the Beatles still held the No. 1 slots at *Billboard* and *Cash Box*, with Dylan at No. 2 in both rankings. On September 18, there was parity: "Help!" was *Billboard*'s top single, and "Like a Rolling Stone" was No. 1 at *Cash Box*.

Dylan had done it. Nine months after having led some plugged-in session musicians through "Subterranean Homesick Blues," he had outflanked the British Invasion bands and outrun his own imitators to make himself the top challenger to the world's biggest group. And he had pulled it off on his terms, by serving up an untamed and sometimes harsh brand of rock 'n' roll that had none of the sweet harmonies or careful arrangements of the Beatles or the Byrds.

Phil Ochs, a politically minded folk singer roughly the same age as Dylan, observed his rise from afar with an almost scientific interest. Although he had an uneasy relationship with his more famous friend, Ochs was rooting for Dylan to become even more popular. In the weeks when "Like a Rolling Stone" was receiving so much airplay, he believed Dylan would indeed take that leap into that next echelon of stardom. "I thought then that he could become Elvis Presley," Ochs said. "Essentially, he could physically represent rural America, all of America, and put out fifteen gold records in a row. Meaning fifteen grandly produced, musically exciting hit singles, with all the great lyrics, and thereby revolutionize the music business."

Ochs's hopes sank a little when he heard "Positively 4th Street," the single Dylan put out as the follow-up to "Like a Rolling Stone."

It was a fine record, and catchy, too, thanks to an amusing organ riff by Kooper. But its venomous verses, in which a pitiless Dylan portrays one of his detractors as a hypocrite, made it seem small in comparison with its predecessor. Even so, "Positively 4th Street" was a sizable hit, reaching No. 7 in the U.S. and No. 8 in the UK.

For its initial release, Columbia Records had mistakenly placed "Can You Please Crawl Out Your Window?" on the B-side. That song, a rocker Dylan had made with studio musicians back in July, had been left off *Highway 61 Revisited* so that he could rerecord it from scratch. George Harrison was one of the few people who had obtained a copy of this accidental release before a replacement version of "Positively 4th Street" was put out with a different song on the flip side—and he loved what he heard. In an interview with *Record Mirror*, George listed "Can You Please Crawl Out Your Window?" among his favorite songs of 1965. "This is a collector's item," he said with a fan's pride while showing off this rarity at his home in Esher.

To Ochs, the decision to release a song as angry as "Positively 4th Street" as the sequel to "Like a Rolling Stone" was tantamount to sabotage. "My first reaction when 'Positively 4th Street' came out was the thought, 'Oh, no, that's not a hit single at all. What are they trying to do? They're gonna blow it,'" he said. "It was a hit anyway, but I thought it was a disastrous thing to do." Its commercial success demonstrated the depth of Dylan's appeal in that moment. No one else had managed to get something so acidic into the Top 10.

In late September, Dylan traveled to Texas to play his first shows with the Hawks as his backing band. At a press conference in Austin, he was asked if the Beatles had influenced his work. "Well," he said, "they haven't influenced the songs or the sound. I don't know what other kind of influence they might have had." That night, at the Municipal Auditorium, Dylan and the Hawks received a fair reception, with only scattered boos and a few walkouts. The show in Dallas was much the same. At Carnegie Hall in New York a few days later, the thunderous applause during the first part of the show gave way to boos in the second half.

The next week, Dylan, with the Hawks in tow, entered Columbia Studios in Manhattan. Despite his statement that his work hadn't been influenced by the Beatles, his main task that day was to record "I Wanna Be Your Lover," a rocker he had modeled after "I Wanna Be Your Man," the Lennon-McCartney song that had been a hit for the Rolling Stones and a showcase for Ringo on the 1963 album *With the Beatles*. With this one, Dylan was harking back to a type of record that had been especially popular in the previous decade: the answer song.

Woody Guthrie's signature composition, "This Land Is Your Land," a plainspoken anthem for everyday Americans, was an answer song. He wrote it in 1940 in direct response to the hand-on-heart patriotism of Irving Berlin's "God Bless America." Another noteworthy example of this subgenre is "Bear Cat," a minor 1953 hit for the Memphis singer Rufus Thomas. It was written by the Sun Records impresario Sam Phillips in reply to "Hound Dog," a hit on the rhythm and blues charts that had been composed for the Alabama-born singer Big Mama Thornton by the Los Angeles duo Jerry Leiber and Mike Stoller. (Later in the decade, it would be a much bigger hit for Elvis Presley.) The original version is filled with a woman's complaints about a no-good man, the "hound dog" of the title. To write "Bear Cat," Phillips took the melody from Leiber and Stoller, but turned the tables on them lyrically by allowing the man to have his say against his accuser.

Dylan was working in that tradition when he wrote "I Wanna Be Your Lover." While echoing the melody, structure, and title phrase of "I Wanna Be Your Man," he took aim at its simplistic lyrics by strewing his verses with the surrealistic characters (including a "rainman" in a "wolfman's disguise") that were fast becoming staples of his work. Dylan's answer song thus represented a more sophisticated version of what Sam Phillips had attempted in "Bear Cat." With "I Wanna Be Your Lover," Dylan was trying to one-up his rivals artistically by providing a catchy rock 'n' roll song with lyrics that had unexpected poetic depths. And so this exchange between Dylan and Lennon-McCartney can be seen as the songwriter's version of the cutting contests that had long been a pastime of jazz and blues players—spirited competitions in which the participants would try to blow away their counterparts with ever more inventive feats of instrumental soloing, either onstage or during more casual woodshedding sessions.

But if Bob had hoped to convey to John and Paul (and music fans at large) the message that a pop song didn't have to be limited by unimaginative lyrics, his plans were scuttled when Columbia shelved "I Wanna Be Your Lover." The song ended up not coming out until 1985, when it was included as a curio on the archival box set *Biograph*. "I always thought it was a good track," Dylan said, "but it just never made it onto an album." "I Wanna Be Your Lover" turned out to be the first of many compositions in which Dylan and the Beatles would engage in a not-always-friendly musical dialogue over what a pop song could or should be.

In that same October session, Dylan and the Hawks recorded an instrumental listed in the studio logs as "Number One," a title suggestive of its composer's focus on the charts. Another song captured that day, the revamped "Can You Please Crawl Out Your Window?," would be released at year's end as the follow-up single to "Positively 4th Street." Phil Ochs thought this one was a notch below Dylan's usual standards; furthermore, he believed it didn't sound like much of a hit. He was right. "Can You Please Crawl Out Your Window?" reached only No. 58 in the U.S. and No. 17 in the UK.

"I think he definitely could have pulled it off," Ochs said of Dylan's bid for superstardom. "I have no idea what short-circuited it. If he would ever talk about it, he might say it wasn't important to him—he didn't want that, it didn't occur to him. My feeling at the time was that he *did* want that. There was that one flash, that one moment he could have done something on a whole higher level." Dylan's onetime mentor Dave Van Ronk agreed: "The big thing to keep in mind is that Bobby wanted to be a superstar," he said. "When he discovered the reality of being a superstar, he freaked out."

While Dylan incurred diminishing returns with his follow-ups to "Like a Rolling Stone," the Beatles immediately capitalized on the chart success of "Help!"—though not in the way they would have planned it, if they had been in charge of how their music was sold to the American public. In yet another instance of Capitol packaging their material with no regard for the Beatles-approved British releases, "Yesterday" was the group's next U.S. single.

Through the fall of 1965, it was at the top of the charts as audiences continued giving rude receptions to Dylan and the Hawks across North America. "Everywhere we went they booed us," Robertson said. The carnival atmosphere, once so amusing to Dylan, was starting to rattle him. The jeers also caused Levon Helm to exit the tour. "It's a hell of a sound," he said of the booing. "At the time it cut me all the way to the bone." He even quit music altogether for a time and took a less stressful job—working on an oil rig in the Gulf of Mexico.

Kristin White, a music lover who worked for the musical instrument manufacturer Hohner, couldn't see what all the fuss was about. If Beatles fans could embrace the frilly "Yesterday," why should Dylan's audiences be offended by electric guitars? She summed up her thoughts in a bit of verse published in the letters section of *Sing Out!*:

> *McCartney sings, backed up by celli,*
> *And no one gets a pain in the belly.*
> *Why do folkies, then, get cramps*
> *On hearing Dylan play with amps?*

12 Northern Songs

It was now a little more difficult for John and Paul to write as naturally, as unthinkingly, as they had in the days when their main goal was to pump out hits. Even so, they entered a particular sweet spot of their collaboration in the weeks after their return from their North American tour.

Lennon would refer to this period as the end of the Beatles' "childish, tribal" phase and the start of their "self-conscious" period. The group had moved from innocence to experience, and John and Paul could no longer create songs untainted by their own awareness of themselves as artists expected to go beyond pop clichés and infuse their work with real significance. At the same time, they had to come up with a lot of new material right away: The Beatles were due back at EMI Studios on October 12, 1965, to record fourteen songs for their next album and two more for a stand-alone single.

At Kenwood, John racked his brain. "I'd spent *five* hours that morning trying to write a song that was meaningful and good and I finally gave up and lay down," he said. "Then 'Nowhere Man' came, words and music, the *whole* damn thing, as I lay down." He was still sleeping when Paul arrived, eager to get down to work as usual. Soon after rousing himself, John took out his guitar and ran through his latest. It would be the first Beatles song that had nothing to do with romance. In this regard, he was catching up with Dylan, who had written and recorded dozens of songs on subjects other than love.

"Nowhere Man" had a lot in common with "Ballad of a Thin Man," one of the *Highway 61 Revisited* tracks John had heard at the Warwick Hotel. The two are so closely related that "Nowhere Man" qualifies as another answer song in the Dylan-Beatles back-and-forth, though Lennon didn't write it as a conscious reply, as Dylan had done with "I Wanna Be Your Lover."

"Nowhere Man" and "Ballad of a Thin Man" have the same subject: a conventional man who's ill-equipped to understand the changing world around him. Dylan sings, "Something is happening here, but you don't know what it is, do you, Mr. Jones?"; Lennon hits on the same thing with the line "Nowhere Man, you don't know what you're missing."

While the two protagonists are close cousins, the narrators' attitudes toward them couldn't be more unalike. Dylan treats Mr. Jones as the butt of the joke, a dolt who is perplexed by the "one-eyed midget" and the other sideshow types he encounters in a bleak fantasyland. The world has gone surreal, in keeping with a larger shift from the tameness of Eisenhower America to the wilder cultural atmosphere of the 1960s, and Mr. Jones is lost. Lennon takes his own clueless protagonist and, in lyrics that favor concision over Dylan's expansiveness, makes him something other than a mere villain or straw man by offering him compassion.

He begins the song by establishing the character's isolation and ignorance. Then he moves into a melodic B section (or middle eight, as he would have called it), in which he shifts from third person to second person. Now addressing the Nowhere Man directly, he tells him that, if he would only listen, he would know that "the world is at your command." From there, rather than placing the Nowhere Man on the wrong side of an us-versus-them divide that would separate hip people from conformist squares, Lennon sings, "Isn't he a bit like you and me?"

Paul added the finishing touches to "Nowhere Man" before joining John in composing the second Beatles song that had nothing to do with romantic love, "The Word." Despite their discomfort with having been treated as healers by some deluded fans, they were taking it upon themselves to deliver a sermon, one that promoted selfless love as a unifying force. "This could be a Salvation Army song," is how Paul described it in an interview at the time of its release. "The word is 'love,' but it could be 'Jesus.' It isn't, mind you, but it could be."

A touch of grandiosity sets "The Word" apart from the usual Sunday homily. It comes when Lennon assumes the role of messianic instructor: "I'm here to show everybody the light," he sings. Because of the musical setting, an Abbey Road attempt at a James Brown groove, the Beatles were able to put it across as less obviously a statement song than, say, Dylan's "The Times They Are A-Changin'," leaving casual listeners free to enjoy the beats, hooks, and vocal harmonies in the assumption that it was just another feel-good rocker.

As the productive writing days continued, Paul helped polish "Norwegian Wood," the Dylan-style ballad that John had debuted in Switzerland for George Martin and his broken toe. McCartney has taken credit for the ending, in which the first-person narrator concludes his night of sexual frustration by lighting a fire in the apartment. While good-hearted commentators have assumed he is warming himself beside the hearth, shrewd listeners have concluded that he is burning down the woman's home as repayment for having been denied a place in her bed—an interpretation endorsed by McCartney and Lennon themselves.

Days after the writing session, John crowed about the song in a call with his journalist friend Maureen Cleave: "Wait till you hear it, it's great. It's about this fellow who gets in with a girl and then he leaves her and *sets fire to her flat*." That ending lends a dark irony to the narrator's final statement: "Isn't it good, Norwegian wood?" It also ties up the narrative very neatly, pushing it further away from Dylan's fragmented story-songs. The Beatles made "Norwegian Wood" even less Dylan-ish when John asked George to replicate the main guitar figure on his sitar at EMI Studios.

The fresh batch of Lennon-McCartney compositions also included "Drive My Car." Paul based it on Otis Redding's "Respect," a single that had been close behind "Help!" and "Like a Rolling Stone" in the charts. He began by transforming the bass line, played by Donald "Duck" Dunn, into a stinging guitar riff. That spawned a vocal melody that bore little relationship to the top line of the Redding song, thus concealing the theft. The only problem was, he couldn't come up with any decent words for it. All he had was some doggerel that rhymed "rings" with "things," a pairing that John and Paul had used, to their embarrassment, in "Can't Buy Me Love" and "I Feel Fine." In a zeitgeist marked by the ascendancy of Dylan, that kind of thing wasn't going to cut it anymore. John and Paul were finally able to raise "Drive My Car" to their new standard when they hit upon a scenario unusual for a pop song: A confident woman with dreams of becoming a movie star flirts with a man by offering him a job as her chauffeur. Never mind that she doesn't yet own a car.

Like several other compositions written solely or mainly by McCartney in the mid-1960s, "Drive My Car" sounded nothing like a Dylan song; but as he wrote the words, he was following general principles exemplified by Dylan's work—namely, that a lyric must avoid cliché in its overall scheme and, whenever possible, in its individual lines; and that it must have enough complexity, mystery, or beauty to reward repeated listening.

In terms of coming up with dazzling turns of phrase, he thought he couldn't compete. "Dylan is a fantastic composer," Paul said in an interview soon after the writing of "Drive My Car." "At first I didn't understand. I used to lose his songs in the middle but then I realized it didn't matter. You can get hung up on just two words of a Dylan lyric. 'Jealous monk' or 'magic swirling ship' are examples of the fantastic word combinations he uses. I could never write like that and I envy him. He is a poet." But as a lyricist McCartney had something that wasn't a usual part of Lennon's or Dylan's songwriting kit—the ability to come up with fictional scenarios.

Paul has mentioned that the idea for "Drive My Car" was rooted in the blues, without citing anything specific. His main inspiration was probably "Me and My Chauffeur Blues," a 1941 song by the

Mississippi-born singer and guitarist Memphis Minnie that had a second wave of popularity in the mid-1960s, thanks to cover versions by Big Mama Thornton and the San Francisco group Jefferson Airplane. In that song, the narrator lauds the sexual potency of her male driver, tossing in suggestive lines to make her meaning all the more clear. "Drive My Car" might also have been rooted in another song that goes into the same terrain, "Automobile Blues," a 1961 track by the Texas troubadour Lightnin' Hopkins.

After Paul and John had fleshed out the verses, they considered "Drive My Car" a comedy number—but it was more than that. Unusual for a song by a male-dominated group then or now, it is partly narrated by a woman; rarer still, the woman is the sexual aggressor, and the man is the subservient object of her desire.

The Beatles' new lyrical sophistication was also apparent in "Girl," a song written by John with some help from Paul. What might have been a straightforward paean to a young woman is rendered more interesting by the fact that the dream girl of the song seems to enjoy insulting the narrator in front of his friends, a habit that only endears her to him. Lennon took the lyric further from convention by imbuing it with an idea inspired by the hairshirt tendency in Christianity—which, in his view, had its secular match in sexual masochism.

> *Was she told when she was young*
> *That pain would lead to pleasure?*

McCartney added to the Beatles' newly ambiguous depictions of romantic relationships with "You Won't See Me," "I'm Looking Through You," and (in collaboration with Lennon) "We Can Work It Out," a trio of thematically related pieces in which he avoids the two big moments at the heart of the typical love song—the rush of emotion that comes early on and the heartbreak at the end. Instead of rehashing that kind of thing, Paul delved into the troubles that arise for couples who've been together for quite some time, like himself and Jane Asher. Two years into their relationship, they were getting into heated arguments over her desire to pursue a serious stage career and his insistence that she focus a bit more on, well, him.

On a cool autumn day, when the new songs were just about ready for release, John, Paul, George, and Ringo went into the woods of Surrey with Robert Freeman, who was still the Beatles' main portraitist despite his having jealously confronted Lennon at Kenwood the year before. With their long, thick hair, statuesque bearing, and faces etched with experiences known to very few, they looked more wizened than most guys in their mid-twenties. After the photo shoot, during a meeting with the Beatles in a darkened room, Freeman projected his results onto a piece of white cardboard the size of an album cover. At one point, the cardboard tipped back slightly, making the image appear stretched. The Beatles liked this distorted effect and asked if it could be printed that way, and that's what Freeman ended up doing.

Rubber Soul was released December 3, 1965, the same day the Beatles put out a stand-alone single with "Day Tripper" on one side and "We Can Work It Out" on the other. The album earned raves, even from *The New York Times* and *Newsweek*, which had savaged the Beatles in the early days of Beatlemania. But while *Rubber Soul* was a critical and commercial triumph, it disappointed many of the group's longtime supporters. "They have tried to do too much," Maureen Cleave wrote in a review for the *Evening Standard*. A fan who signed her name "Annabel Lee" lamented the appearance of John, Paul, George, and Ringo on the *Rubber Soul* cover in a poem published in the fan magazine *Beatles Book Monthly*.

> *I tried to Work It Out but could not*
> *Why such a very photogenic lot*
> *Should want to see yourselves portrayed as freaks;*
> *You look as if you'd all been dead for weeks*

For the first time, the group's name didn't appear on the cover. The only things record buyers had to go on were the gloomy portrait and the words "Rubber Soul" in a groovy typeface. For the British audience, "rubber" meant *ersatz*, as "plastic" did for Americans at the time. Cooked up by McCartney, the title signaled that the Beatles were well aware that their brand of rhythm and blues wasn't quite the real thing. More specifically, the phrase applied to the beat-driven sound of the first track on the UK edition, "Drive My Car." But "rubber soul" made very little sense as the title of the very different American edition, which emphasized the Beatles' acoustic side by starting with "I've Just Seen a Face" and dropping "Drive My Car" altogether, changes that put the LP squarely within the folk-rock trend.

On both the American and British versions, "Norwegian Wood" was the second track. When Dylan heard it, he felt things had gone too far. He would have to respond.

■   ■   ■

He was moving in two directions at once. Just as he was turning himself into a rock star, and indulging in the behaviors that went along with that role, he was becoming a family man. In November 1965, Bob and Sara were married in a small ceremony on Long Island, and he would soon become the father to her three-year-old daughter from her first marriage. Shortly after the wedding, he returned to the job of facing the still-hostile audiences in city after city. In January 1966, during a break in the action, Sara gave birth to a boy.

At the end of the month, Dylan showed he was once again thinking along the same lines as the Beatles during a nighttime session in Manhattan. Backed by Robbie Robertson, Rick Danko, Al Kooper, and a pair of studio musicians, he recorded the bluesy "Leopard-Skin Pill-Box Hat," a newly written song that drew upon the likely inspirations for "Drive My Car."

> *Well, can I be your chauffeur, honey, can I be your chauffeur*
> *Well, you can ride with me, honey, I'll be your chauffeur*

Those lines wouldn't make it into the released version of "Leopard-Skin Pill-Box Hat," but in all its incarnations Dylan would echo the structure of Lightnin' Hopkins's "Automobile Blues" and the suggestiveness of Memphis Minnie's "Me and My Chauffeur Blues."

After the session, he went across town to the studio of the FM radio station WBAI during the broadcast of *Radio Unnameable*, an all-night show hosted by Bob Fass, a free-form disc jockey who was the antithesis of Murray the K. Dylan took calls from listeners, one of whom asked him why he hadn't protested America's involvement in Vietnam. "It's a *war*," Dylan said. "Hey, wars have been around a long time. What makes you think it's anything special now?" Moments later, he asked Fass to play Lightnin' Hopkins's "Automobile Blues." Interestingly, he referred to it as "Drive My Car," a phrase that doesn't appear in that song.

Feeling less than satisfied with his recent studio outings, Dylan decided to heed the advice of his producer, Bob Johnston, and decamp to Nashville to continue recording tracks for what would turn out to be his most ambitious full-length work yet, the double album *Blonde on Blonde*. On a frigid afternoon before he left New York, he posed for the photographer Jerry Schatzberg outside a squat building just below the Meatpacking District in the hopes of capturing a cover image. When they looked through the prints afterward, Dylan said he liked the blurred picture that showed him against the bricks. In addition to featuring a distorted portrait, the cover of *Blonde on Blonde*, like that of *Rubber Soul*, would include no mention of the artist's name, a first for a Dylan album; and Bob would do the Beatles one better by leaving off the title, having it appear only in tiny type along the spine.

A few weeks after the photo shoot, Dylan and his fellow long-haired northerners Al Kooper and Robbie Robertson arrived in Tennessee, a culturally conservative state where the laws limiting the rights of Black people had been overturned only recently, thanks to the Civil Rights Act of 1964 and the Voting Rights Act of 1965. Kooper writes of being chased by Nashville locals who thought he looked like a freak. It was a reminder that the country was filled with Mr. Joneses. The backlash was also apparent in the popularity of "The Ballad of the Green Berets," a patriotic spoken-word song, with military-band backing, by Staff Sergeant Barry Sadler, a former combat medic with the U.S. Special Forces in Vietnam. While Dylan was recording his surrealist love songs at Columbia Studio A on Music Row, Sadler's tribute to the troops was zooming up the charts on its way to becoming America's top-selling single of 1966.

In terms of sound, Dylan's goal in Nashville was to capture the excitement of live performance, with the musicians playing as one. That was easier for him to pull off than it was for almost any other artist, given his new standing as not only a critical favorite but a potent commercial force. He now had the budget to hire some of the city's ace session players to work alongside Robertson and Kooper; and unlike most singers, who were expected to knock out a finished track in two or three hours, Dylan could take as long as he wanted. So while he didn't use the recording studio as a compositional tool in the manner of the Beatles, who increasingly took advantage of overdubs and audio effects, he did spend however many hours it took to hit upon the pristine takes that would have been out of reach for less coddled recording artists. In other words, Dylan was capturing the illusion of spontaneity, rather than the real thing.

He even had the luxury of using expensive studio time to write songs while his hired guns smoked cigarettes and played Ping-Pong to fill the empty hours. That's how it was on February 14, 1966, his first workday in Music City, when the musicians earned the highest union wage for doing not much of anything as Dylan worked on his reply to the Beatles' "Norwegian Wood."

"Johnston came to us and said, 'Hey, if you want to go to dinner, go on and come back,'" the guitarist Charlie McCoy recalled. "'He's not finished writing a lyric, so go and do your dinner and get on back, because I don't know when he's gonna be ready.' So we all left and came back—and then sat around for eternity."

Dylan's new answer song, which he completed that night, writing in pen on a yellow legal pad, was "Fourth Time Around." Like "Norwegian Wood," it tells the story of a man who goes to the home of a woman who seems not to be his main romantic partner; and, as in the Beatles song, the visit ends badly. For the music, Dylan borrowed

Lennon's melody for "Norwegian Wood," following a method he had employed before, as when he had hung his own lyrics onto the bones of "Lord Randall" to write "A Hard Rain's A-Gonna Fall." "Dylan was quite blatant with the virtual wholesale lifting of Lennon's tune, which he then set his own words to," wrote Derek Barker, the founder of the Dylan-centric publication *Isis*.

Al Kooper noticed the likeness when Dylan unveiled the song for the gathered musicians. "I thought it was very ballsy of Dylan to do 'Fourth Time Around,'" Kooper said. "I asked him about it. I said, 'It sounds so much like "Norwegian Wood."' And he said, 'Well, actually, "Norwegian Wood" sounds a lot like *this*. I'm afraid they took it from me, and I feel that I have to, you know, record it.'" With that koan-like statement, Dylan seems to have been saying that the Beatles song was so much like one of his own that he felt he must reclaim it. He led the musicians through twenty takes before landing on the version that pleased him.

The phrase "Fourth Time Around" doesn't appear in the lyrics. It seems he meant this cryptic title to signal that "Norwegian Wood" was the *fourth* instance of Lennon's having filched from the Dylan songbook. Note that in his January 1965 interview with *Melody Maker* Lennon had said that "I'm a Loser" and "A Hard Day's Night" were influenced by Dylan. Then came the release of "You've Got to Hide Your Love Away." And now, with the release of *Rubber Soul*, there was a fourth song in the same vein, "Norwegian Wood."

George Harrison addressed the relationship between the two songs in a 1992 interview, saying, "There's a funny thing that I don't think anybody else has noticed, and that is when John wrote 'Norwegian Wood,' it was obviously a very Bob Dylan song, and right after that Bob's album came out, and it had a song called 'Fourth Time Around.' You want to check out the tune of that—it's the same song, going round and round."

Every answer song is a critique of the one that inspired it: "Bear Cat" gives the man's side of the story laid out by the female narrator of "Hound Dog"; "Nowhere Man" offers a forgiving view of the conventional type who's treated harshly in "Ballad of a Thin Man."

With "Fourth Time Around," Dylan was sending Lennon a warning, while also setting him straight on how to depict a late-night romantic call gone awry.

In "Norwegian Wood," the narrative is crystal clear, and the man and the woman at the center of the action behave like characters in a drawing room comedy. In "Fourth Time Around," the storytelling is fractured, and the couple take part in a wild scene, with the woman screaming and falling to the floor before the man goes through her things. Another point of contrast is the fact that the two characters of "Norwegian Wood" end up sleeping apart, while their opposites in the Dylan song are deep in postcoital conversation at the start of the first verse. The endings are also quite different from each other. Thanks to the closing lines supplied by McCartney, the Beatles song comes to a firm resolution, while "Fourth Time Around" departs from its storyline in its last verse, with Dylan removing his narrative mask to address Lennon directly.

> *And I, I never took much*
> *I never asked for your crutch*
> *Now don't ask for mine*

■   ■   ■

Just as Lennon and McCartney were turning away from their old subject matter in "Nowhere Man" and "The Word," Dylan was focusing his creative energies on romantic relationships. So now, in addition to working in the same musical style, as they had been doing for more than a year, Dylan and the Beatles were moving toward each other in the substance of their lyrics.

The titles of the songs that Dylan wrote in the first months of 1966 made his new direction clear: "I Want You," "Just Like a Woman," "One of Us Must Know (Sooner or Later)," "Absolutely Sweet Marie." He also continued the Lennon-McCartney practice he had begun the year before with "Ballad of a Thin Man"—coming up with bridges for his songs. Five tracks on *Blonde on Blonde* would have middle eights.

At the same time, Lennon and McCartney continued on their new course while writing the songs for their next single and the album *Revolver*. With "Paperback Writer," Paul told the tale, in epistolary form, no less, of a workaday *Daily Mail* reporter who dreams of cashing in with a bestseller. It was the first song he had written on his own that had nothing do with love. Its immediate inspiration was a Liverpool aunt who challenged him to come up with something other than his usual boy-girl stuff.

He followed it with another one of his fictional songs, "Eleanor Rigby." As with "Yesterday," Paul settled on a melody before embarking on a search for the right words. He made it into a tale of existential loneliness as bleak as anything in the Dylan oeuvre: The heroine dies alone and unmourned; the secondary character, Father McKenzie, gives sermons "no one will hear"; and the song's key line is as blunt as a hammer blow—"No one was saved."

To flesh out the verses, Paul didn't sit with John for one of their intimate writing sessions. Rather, he solicited contributions from George Harrison, Mal Evans, Neil Aspinall, and Pete Shotton when they were all lounging by the pool at Kenwood. "That's the kind of insensitivity he would have, which upset me in later years," Lennon said. George elevated the song from a depiction of two isolated individuals to something that applied to everyone by kicking in the refrain (for which he received no writing credit): "Ah, look at all the lonely people." Shotton came up with the idea for the last verse, in which Father McKenzie officiates Eleanor Rigby's burial service. Lennon fumed for years afterward that Paul hadn't asked for his help on the song, which would be held up by critics as the Beatles' weightiest and most poetic creation.

After the completion of "Eleanor Rigby," Paul came up with something more in keeping with his usual outlook, "Good Day Sunshine," a ditty that captured the joy of strolling about in lovely weather before it veered into love-song territory. He went on to write other love songs for *Revolver*, the stark "For No One," the lovely "Here, There and Everywhere" and the rhythm-and-blues-inspired "Got to Get

Bob Dylan at Gerde's Folk City in Greenwich Village, 1961. A *New York Times* critic described him at the time as "a cross between a choir boy and a beatnik." *(Michael Ochs Archives / Getty Images)*

The Beatles at the Cavern Club in Liverpool in 1962, about a year after they started playing there. A writer for Mersey Beat noted in a 1961 review that the group conveyed "an indifference to audience response" while being sure to thank the crowd after each song. *(Michael Ochs Archives / Getty Images)*

Young strivers in the city: The cover portraits for the albums *The Freewheelin' Bob Dylan* and *Please Please Me,* both taken in February 1963, helped establish the public images of Dylan and the Beatles. *(Dylan: Records/Alamy; Beatles: Vinyls/Alamy)*

Little Richard was a key influence on Dylan and the Beatles. In a 1964 appearance on *American Bandstand,* he shows the host, Dick Clark, a 1962 photo of himself with the group backstage at the Tower Ballroom in New Brighton, England. *(ABC Photo Archives / Getty Images)*

Dylan arrives at the Delmonico Hotel in Manhattan on August 28, 1964, the night he met the Beatles in their sixth-floor suite. From left to right: Victor Maymudes, Neil Aspinall, Al Aronowitz, an unidentified fan, and Dylan. *(Henry Grossman / Mirrorpix / Getty Images)*

In the mid-sixties, Dylan rivaled the Beatles as a commercial force. It is now all but forgotten that he was also something of a teen idol, appearing in magazines aimed at young fans. Here he is, alongside Lennon, on the cover of the November 1966 issue of TeenSet. *(Courtesy of Allison Bumsted and Scholastic Inc.)*

Dylan famously "went electric" at the Newport Folk Festival on July 25, 1965. He alienated many of his old fans, but expanded his audience considerably. Three weeks after his Newport performance, the Beatles played to more than fifty-six thousand fans at Shea Stadium in New York, earning $160,000 (about $1.6 million in today's dollars) for their half-hour set. *(Dylan: Alice Ochs / Getty Images; Beatles: Michael Ochs Archives / Getty Images)*

Two days before the Shea concert, John Lennon, left, and Paul McCartney, right, head to the entrance of the Warwick Hotel in Manhattan. The Beatles spent time with Dylan on two nights of their four-night stay. *(New York Daily News Archive / Getty Images)*

At the Isle of Wight Festival on August 31, 1969, a cheerful Dylan plays to a crowd of more than 150,000. Three Beatles and their wives are seated close to the stage. George Harrison and Pattie Boyd Harrison can be seen to the left, with John Lennon and Yoko Ono (partially obscured) one row back, while Maureen Cox Starkey and Ringo Starr sit toward the front. *(Dylan: Terence Spencer / Popperfoto / Getty Images; Beatles: Daily Mail/Shutterstock)*

In 1969, the Beatles briefly discussed the possibility of adding two members to the group—Billy Preston and Bob Dylan—under the name Beatles & Co. They came close to realizing that lineup during the Concert for Bangladesh at Madison Square Garden in August 1971. From left to right: Ringo, George, Bob, and Leon Russell. *(TK / Getty Images)*

McCartney and Dylan became especially close in 1971, when Paul was recording the album Ram in New York City, and they often crossed paths in the years afterward. Here they are, with Gregg Allman of the Allman Brothers Band, at a party in Los Angeles in 1975. *(Fairchild Archives / Getty Images)*

The Traveling Wilburys, 1988. From left to right: Roy Orbison, Jeff Lynne, Dylan, Tom Petty, and Harrison. George started this casual supergroup to record a B-side for a single. The Wilburys ended up making a multiplatinum album, which put Dylan in the pop charts after he'd begun to feel he'd entered "the bottomless pit of cultural oblivion," as he put it in his memoir. *(Pictorial Press / Alamy)*

Harrison and Dylan lead an all-star band through "All Along the Watchtower" at the Rock & Roll Hall of Fame ceremony in New York on January 20, 1988, the night that the Beatles and Dylan were inducted. Both men made Little Richard the first person they thanked in their acceptance speeches. *(Ron Galella / Getty Images)*

Mendips, the home in Woolton, Liverpool, where John Lennon lived from 1945, when he was five, until the early days of Beatlemania. Dylan visited the house on the afternoon of May 1, 2009. Hours later, he played Harrison's "Something" during a concert at the Liverpool Echo Arena. *(John Lennon's Childhood House / Alamy)*

Paul (McCartney)

6th May 2009

Dear Bob,

    Just had the pleasure of listening to your Theme Time radio show, "Friends and Neighbours", and enjoyed it so much that I had to write and tell you. The music you played was fabulous and the chat in between was both edifying and amusing. Thanks for an hour of listening pleasure.

    Hope all is well with you.

    All the best you lovely boy,

        Cheers,

        Paul

A week after Dylan's stop in Liverpool, McCartney sent a letter to Bob expressing his appreciation for an episode of his satellite radio show, *Theme Time Radio Hour*. *(Courtesy of the Bob Dylan Center and Paul McCartney)*

You into My Life." That last one should come with an asterisk, given that Paul has said it was his ode to pot in the guise of a love song. Lennon agreed it was a drug song, but said it had nothing to do with cannabis: "It actually describes his experiences taking acid," he said. Indeed, McCartney wrote it after finally trying LSD in the company of Viv Prince, the drummer for the Pretty Things, and Tara Browne, a young heir to the Guinness beer fortune.

Now that the Dylan influence had been fully absorbed into Lennon-McCartney songcraft, John reveled in the freedom to write about almost anything. In "Tomorrow Never Knows," he offered an introduction to mysticism cum guide to acid-tripping, building the lyrics on lines from *The Psychedelic Experience: A Manual Based on the Tibetan Book of the Dead*, a 1964 treatise by the LSD proselytizers Timothy Leary, Richard Alpert, and Ralph Metzner. He also wrote "She Said She Said," an account of his Beverly Hills acid trip.

With "Rain," John used weather as a metaphor to explore the idea he had put forth in "There's a Place," that personal perception shapes or even trumps reality. He withdrew further into solipsism with "I'm Only Sleeping," a bleary-eyed tribute to indolence. Harrison contributed to the Beatles' new lyrical direction with "Taxman," a rant against the British tax system, and "I Want to Tell You," in which he grappled with the difficulty of speaking one's mind.

While the Beatles were preparing this material for the *Revolver* sessions at EMI Studios, the musicians at Studio A in Nashville couldn't help but notice that Dylan kept a Bible close at hand while writing songs for *Blonde on Blonde*. He was looking for phrases that would lend his lyrics a timeless quality, as the author Daryl Sanders notes in his study of the album. The book of Ezekiel informed Dylan's "Sad Eyed Lady of the Lowlands," an epic tribute to Sara. And a punishment that figures in the book of Acts—stoning—inspired "Rainy Day Women #12 & 35," a satirical number with the double-meaning refrain "Everybody must get stoned!" For that song's title, Dylan seems to have plucked words from a line in Proverbs: "A continual dropping in a very rainy day and a contentious woman are all alike."

When he ran through it at the piano, his producer said it sounded like something for a ragtag Salvation Army band. Dylan liked that idea. Charlie McCoy called in a trombone player and grabbed a trumpet himself. Dylan then led a merry one-take recording, complete with whooping, hollering, and laughing. Released as a single weeks before *Blonde on Blonde* was in stores, "Rainy Day Women" climbed the charts while Dylan and his road band continued pitting themselves against unruly crowds.

■   ■   ■

In March, high above the Great Plains during a flight from Lincoln, Nebraska, to Denver, Colorado, Dylan glanced at the galley proofs of his book, *Tarantula*, which was scheduled for release later in the year by the New York publishing house Macmillan. Then he turned his attention to the man seated next to him, the writer Robert Shelton. This was no ordinary interview. Shelton was planning a biography of Dylan, who had agreed to cooperate on the condition that the book capture him as he really was. It was past midnight as the two fell into intimate conversation.

"It takes a lot of medicine to keep up this pace," Dylan said, making a not-so-veiled reference to the amphetamines that were fueling him. "It's very hard, man. A concert tour like this has almost killed me." He spoke frankly about Suze Rotolo and Joan Baez, and admitted to having had suicidal thoughts. He also said that, early in his time in New York, he had developed a $25-a-day heroin habit. Shelton ended up leaving that detail out of his book.

As Dylan smoked and tugged at his collar, he mused that he was never going to be accepted by polite society. "I would like to be accepted by them people," he said. "But I don't think I'm ever going to be. Whereas the Beatles have been." Shelton asked if he wanted the Beatles' kind of acceptance. "No, no, no," Dylan replied. "I'm not saying that. I'm just saying the Beatles have arrived, right? . . . The Beatles are accepted, and you've got to accept them for what they do. They play songs like 'Michelle' and 'Yesterday.' A lot of smoothness there."

"Michelle," a track on *Rubber Soul*, was a melodically sophisticated ballad composed mainly by McCartney. Although it had not been released as a single, it would come to rival "Yesterday" as a contemporary standard, generating hundreds of covers by a range of artists including Chet Atkins, Count Basie, Booker T. & the MG's, and the Supremes.

Shelton mentioned that Baez planned to record "Yesterday" for her next album. "Yeah, it's the thing to do," Dylan said, "to tell all the teenyboppers, 'I dig the Beatles,' and you sing a song like 'Yesterday' or 'Michelle.' Hey, God knows, it's such a cop-out, man, both of those songs. If you go into the Library of Congress, you can find a lot better than that. There are millions of songs like 'Michelle' and 'Yesterday' written in Tin Pan Alley."

In Honolulu, the Dylan troupe took on two new members: the cheerful but hard-hitting Mickey Jones as the drummer, and the expert sound engineer Richard Alderson, who had worked with the pop-folk singer Harry Belafonte and the jazz artist nonpareil Nina Simone. From Hawaii, they flew on to Australia, where Dylan and the musicians began to jell while playing seven shows in nine nights. Interviewed in Melbourne, Dylan was drawn into the media-fueled rivalry between the Beatles and the Stones.

"What do you think of Jagger-Richards as songwriters?"

"I don't think I like them," Dylan said.

"Why is that?"

"They say things—try to kid you. No, I don't like the Rolling Stones."

"What about the material of Lennon-McCartney?"

"Great! They started it all in England. They are honest, sincere, in their own way."

The Australian leg reached its end in Perth, where Dylan sat for a press conference. Asked to give his opinion of the war in Vietnam, he said, "Nothing. It's Australia's war."

"But the Americans are there," a reporter said.

"They're just helping the Australians," Dylan said.

He stayed up all night with Robbie Robertson after the Perth show and they slept through much of a marathon flight, with refueling stops along the way, that took them to Stockholm. Facing members of the Swedish press, Dylan was asked: "What's your opinion of the Green Berets, the U.S. special forces in Vietnam?"

"I was thinking of joining them, if they want me," he answered.

Three more people joined the Dylan crew that day: the filmmaker D. A. Pennebaker, the cameraman Howard Alk, and the sound engineer Jones Alk, the team behind *Dont Look Back*. They would end up shooting seventy thousand feet of film in the weeks to come for a planned ABC television special. Perhaps naively, Bob thought he could slip an unconventional documentary into prime time, though Grossman had gotten the network to pay $100,000 for the rights.

The brigade arrived in London on May 2. Given his previous experience with British audiences, Dylan expected there would be no more booing during the run of shows that would finish up at the site of one of his former triumphs, the Albert Hall.

■   ■   ■

The Beatles' road manager Neil Aspinall called May 1966 "Dylan Month" in the column he wrote for the *Beatles Book Monthly* shortly after Bob's arrival. He gave it that name because of the many occasions John, Paul, George, and Ringo would spend with Bob in the coming days. "Just like last year," Aspinall noted, "the Beatles booked seats for the Bob Dylan concert at London's Royal Albert Hall."

Dylan checked into the May Fair Hotel and played host to a gaggle of journalists in his suite. Pennebaker was wearing a top hat as he filmed the goings-on. Dylan, looking bored, posed for the photographers before the farcical press conference was underway.

"Does the term 'folk rock' mean anything to you?"

"Folk rot?"

"How many people are there in your backing group?"

"Oh, fourteen, fifteen."

"Who's the guy with the top hat?"

"I don't know. I thought he was with you."

That night, Dylan went to Dolly's, a nightclub on Jermyn Street, where he met up with McCartney, as well as Keith Richards and Brian Jones of the Rolling Stones, according to Aspinall's report in *Beatles Book Monthly*. The Beatles' associate Tony Bramwell indicated that Lennon was there, too—and "quite jealous" of Bob's suede Levi's jacket. On Dylan's second night in London, he went with McCartney to see John Lee Hooker perform at Blaises, a basement club in Kensington. Dana Gillespie, who had just turned seventeen, joined them.

Dylan mostly avoided reporters during this London stay, and so there are few contemporaneously published reports of his activities there. Still, a clear picture of the time he spent with the Beatles has emerged, thanks to the reminiscences of those who were present, though they don't always agree on the particulars.

There are many accounts of the five of them getting together at his May Fair suite. The Beatles arrived with acetates of songs from their ongoing *Revolver* sessions, and Dylan was armed with tapes of the tracks from *Blonde on Blonde*, which wouldn't come out for another month. In a sign of Dylan's stature, the Beatles found themselves in the role of supplicants. "It was a bit like an Audience With Dylan in those days," McCartney said. "You went round to the May Fair Hotel and waited in an outer room while Bob was, you know, in the other room, in the bedroom, and we were getting ushered in one by one." Robbie Robertson noted the "good humor and high spirits" of Mal Evans when the Beatles arrived one night early in Dylan's stay. There was also some ribbing, as when Dylan mentioned the "screaming girls" in the Beatles' audience and asked them if that was still "going well."

"We're waiting until all this blows over," John replied. "What about you, Bobby? The girls still screaming for you?"

"Oh, yeah, the girls and the boys are still screaming at what we're doing, but not in the same way as for you."

Gillespie recalled that Dylan and the Beatles ended up "listening to music, drinking, and smoking joints until the early hours." When the sounds of *Revolver* filled the suite, Robertson listened closely.

"What caught my ear immediately was the use of the recording studio as a musical instrument—incredible experimentation with sounds and effects, quite the opposite of a Bob Dylan record," he wrote.

Paul was keen to drop the needle on "Tomorrow Never Knows," which defied convention by staying mainly on one chord in the manner of Indian ragas or the proto-funk of Bo Diddley as its lyrics dispensed with rhyme to capture the death of the ego experienced by an acidhead or solitary monk. The track was also the Beatles' most adventuresome studio production yet. In a late-night session, George Martin had recorded Lennon's voice through a rotating speaker after John had requested that he sound like "the Dalai Lama singing from the highest mountaintop." The drone of a tamboura, a stringed Indian instrument played by Harrison, provided a hypnotic effect; and there was a newly heavy drum sound achieved by the twenty-year-old engineer Geoff Emerick, who placed microphones up against Ringo's kit. The Beatles completed it by overdubbing sounds from the tape loops they had assembled on their own reel-to-reel machines. McCartney was the one most interested in constructing these bizarre audio snippets, and he had led the effort in bringing this element to "Tomorrow Never Knows."

"It was very far ahead of its time," Marianne Faithfull recalled, "and Paul was obviously proud of it." But the track didn't do much for Dylan. "Oh, I get it," Bob said, as McCartney remembered it. "You don't want to be cute anymore." Faithfull, in her account, reported that Bob "just walked out of the room." "The expression on Paul's face was priceless," she wrote.

Robertson agreed that Dylan was skeptical of "Tomorrow Never Knows," but he made no mention of a sudden walkout. In his telling, Dylan asked, "What's that supposed to be?"

"Something new, Bobby," John replied. "Gotta give the folks something new."

When it was Dylan's turn to play disc jockey, he unveiled his "Norwegian Wood" soundalike, "Fourth Time Around." John felt ill at ease to hear his own melody coming back at him. "That ought to be in Northern Songs," he said in an aside to Paul. And they laughed.

"What's Northern Songs?" Dylan asked.

Lennon didn't bother to explain that it was the company founded by John, Paul, Brian Epstein, and the veteran music publisher Dick James to house Lennon-McCartney compositions.

As "Fourth Time Around" reached its final verse, the Beatles heard Dylan singing that he had "never asked for your crutch." That line struck John with force. Was Dylan talking to *him*? Was this song a personal attack in the guise of a lilting ballad?

"What do you think?" Bob asked.

"I don't like it," said John.

That was as far as the conversation went. For now, Dylan was content to allow the song to speak on his behalf—though, as we'll see, he wouldn't be able to resist returning to this sore subject before his departure from London.

John would have a topsy-turvy relationship with "Fourth Time Around." He would eventually tell himself he had no reason to take offense—that if he *did* feel wounded, it was only because he was being neurotic. In a 1968 interview, he expanded on how the song had struck him: "I didn't like it and I was very paranoid. Just didn't like what I felt I was feeling. I thought it was an out and out *skit*, you know, but it wasn't. It was great. I mean, he wasn't playing any tricks on me."

Dylan left London to play shows in Dublin and Belfast. During his time away from the capital, someone showed up at Epstein's office with a gift for Lennon: the suede Levi's jacket that Dylan had been wearing at Dolly's. John made it a regular part of his wardrobe until he decided it was too small and passed it on to Tony Bramwell.

In Ireland, the naysayers made their presence felt in the shows' second halves with slow claps and heckles. At a hotel in Dublin, seated on the edge of a sofa as a camera filmed him, Dylan teetered back and forth while talking with a promoter, who was apparently trying to persuade him to extend his tour into Italy.

"I want to go home," Bob said in a soft voice. "You know what home is? I don't want to go to Italy no more. I don't want to go nowhere no more. You end up crashing in a private airplane in the mountains of Tennessee. Or Sicily."

On May 13, Dylan arrived in Liverpool. He planned to see much more of the Beatles' home city than he had the year before.

13 Costars

Liverpool went from medieval fishing village to global trade center thanks to the innovative "wet docks" built along the River Mersey starting in the 1700s. Picture vast swimming pools, enclosed in stone, each large enough to provide a berth for a great sailing ship. They were designed to be unaffected by the tides, so that the vessels would stay level while laborers loaded or unloaded heavy sacks of tea, tobacco, and cotton. Few cities could boast of a port equal to that of Liverpool, and the Mersey was thick with ships for nearly three centuries.

In 1830, Clarence Dock, a wet dock built to accommodate steamships, opened two miles north of the city center. Over the next several years, immense warehouses sprang up nearby. The largest of these, Clarence Warehouse, was completed around 1844. Dockers packed it with casks of rum and sacks of tea and corn, until it was time to hump them aboard outbound ships or onto the narrow boats headed to the interior via the UK's extensive canal system.

The waterfront hummed with the shouts of dockers and merchants until the combination of new shipping technologies and German bombs doomed the city's main industry. Clarence Dock was filled in with cement. Clarence Warehouse fell into decay. Vandals smashed the windows. Birds nested inside. People left junk at the foundation.

On a chilly October day in 1962, the Beatles posed for pictures on the vacant lot close to the old Clarence Dock, between Dublin Street and Saltney Street. At their backs was Clarence Warehouse, with the words "Bonded Tea Warehouse" emblazoned in faded paint across the bricks. The reason for the shoot was the fact that Ringo had recently replaced Pete Best as the group's drummer, and Brian Epstein wanted some good publicity shots of the new lineup.

Despite the Continental flair of their narrow suits, the Beatles seemed at one with the desolate cityscape. The hardness of their appearance was enhanced by George's black eye. He liked to say he had suffered the injury while sticking up for Ringo against an aggressive Pete Best loyalist; others said the blow was delivered by one Dennis Peter Flynn, a street tough. "He was notorious in Liverpool as a hard case," said a Cavern Club regular, Dave Spain.

As they were posing, the Beatles didn't know they were standing steps away from the site where, a hundred years earlier, Lennon's ancestors had lived in cramped quarters among other refugees after having fled Ireland during the Great Famine. Epstein used the photo in programs and press handouts during the months when the Beatles rose from popular local act to nationwide sensation, and it helped shape the group's image before the moptop idea took hold.

On May 14, 1966, a few hours before his concert at the Odeon Theatre in Liverpool, Dylan made a special trip to the vacant lot where John, Paul, George, and Ringo had stood. With the abandoned warehouse at his back, he posed for a photo shoot of his own, as if claiming for himself a symbolic piece of turf left unguarded by the enemy.

■   ■   ■

Dylan had arrived in Liverpool the day before, riding in the back of an Austin Princess limousine piloted by Tom Keylock, a World War II veteran from South London who often worked as a chauffeur and fixer for the Rolling Stones. Keylock's duties now included keeping Dylan and his team supplied with drugs, according to the soundman Richard Alderson, but he wasn't picky about it. "We'd send him out for hash and he'd come back with kif, and we'd send him for kif, he'd come back with heroin," Alderson said. "He always came back with something, but he never came back with the right thing."

Dylan checked into the Adelphi Hotel and met up with two Liverpudlians he had gotten to know the year before, Bill and Virginia Harry of *Mersey Beat*. They took him on a tour of Beatles sites, including the Cavern Club on Mathew Street, which had just gone out of business. Dylan also met, and was photographed with, Dennis Peter Flynn, the man suspected of having given George the shiner back in 1962.

Bob set aside part of his second day in town for his excursion to the area near the Clarence Dock. This was not a part of Liverpool that a tourist would stumble upon. It lay two miles from the Adelphi Hotel, and there was nothing to it but the decaying warehouses and a few bedraggled shops, garages, and pubs. Dylan was accompanied not only by the still photographer Barry Feinstein but by the film cameraman Howard Alk, the sound engineer Jones Alk, and his aide-de-camp Bob Neuwirth. As Feinstein snapped pictures, the Alks chronicled the photo shoot for possible inclusion in the planned TV special.

Dylan was dressed for the occasion in narrow-cut jeans over black boots, a blouse with a harlequin design, a dark four-button jacket, and his customary sunglasses. With the hulking Clarence Warehouse as a backdrop, he moved athletically through the lot, picking up rocks and tossing them. At one point he held his arms wide apart, as if preparing to fly. "Bob felt great in Liverpool," Feinstein said. While John, Paul, George, and Ringo had maintained stoic expressions in the Beatles portraits taken at this spot, Bob was smiling as he put on a joyful one-man version (perhaps a parody) of *A Hard Day's Night*.

On the cobblestones of Dublin Street, he encountered nine boys and two girls who ranged in age from about three to nine. They had the appearance of Victorian-era urchins. Dylan sassed them: "I think you're all American." Addressing one child in particular, he said, "You said you're from Pittsburgh, didn't you?" Instead of answering, the boy offered a deadpan expression. Dylan then made a sudden wardrobe change, trading his dark jacket for the striped purple one worn by Bob Neuwirth. Once Dylan had it on, a boy remarked, "That doesn't suit him."

"The professor says that jacket doesn't suit you," Neuwirth said.

Dylan laughed and led the children to an alcove surrounding one of the warehouse's sheet-metal doors. He sat on a stone step and crossed his arms. The kids clustered all around him. The youngest, in short pants, took a seat on a lower step. "Everybody's gotta look right into the camera," Dylan said. Feinstein asked for smiles, and he got them. Except for one boy, who wouldn't drop his tough-guy expression. "He's the heavy," Dylan said.

At the end of the photo shoot, Dylan told the kids he would see them again next year, saying, "Same time, same place." Then he broke into a run, sprinting toward the van on the far side of the empty expanse. The scamps gave chase, laughing and screaming. The littlest one, unable to keep pace, let out a wail.

An Englishman in the entourage ran back to fetch him, with Dylan close behind. The man picked up the toddler, saying, "There, there, love." Dylan partly removed the striped purple jacket, as if throwing off his rock star guise, and took the boy in his arms. Now moving at a measured pace, he carried the child across the lot. "He loved those kids," Feinstein said.

That night, Spencer Leigh, a twenty-one-year-old fan who would go on to write more than twenty books on pop music figures, including Dylan and the Beatles, was in the crowd at Liverpool's Odeon Theatre. When Dylan took the stage, Leigh could see that he was stoned. "Really stoned," he wrote in a later reminiscence. Dylan played the first song, "She Belongs to Me," at an especially slow tempo. Same with the second, "Fourth Time Around," which Leigh had never heard before. The tune, though, was oddly familiar. "Wasn't it 'Norwegian Wood'?" Leigh wrote, describing what was going through his mind in the moment.

Like everyone else in the hall, Leigh could see the drums and amplifiers on the stage. And yet many in the audience expressed shock at the start of the second half, when Dylan and the band barreled through "Tell Me, Momma." The anger that had greeted him ten months earlier at Newport had still not abated. Hecklers let loose between songs.

"Traitor!"

"Go home!"

"What happened to your conscience?"

Dylan replied to that last heckle: "Oh, there's a fellow up there looking for the savior."

The jeers continued. About a third of the crowd walked out, in Leigh's estimation.

The next day, Dylan, Albert Grossman, the musicians, and the film crew were killing time in a hotel room in Leicester before a show at De Montfort Hall when a clerk popped in to announce that a man had "phoned in to the front of the house" to say he was going to shoot Dylan dead. Bob seemed staggered before quickly regaining his poise. "I don't mind being shot, man," he said, "but I don't dig being *told* about it." Then he sat down and pretended to read a magazine.

The next night, in Sheffield, the show was delayed because of a bomb threat. The night after that, at the Free Trade Hall in Manchester, Dylan played a concert that would become as much a part of rock lore as his electric debut at Newport. During a between-songs stillness in the second half, a heckler shouted, "Judas!" Dylan replied, "I don't believe you." Then: "You're a liar!" He led his band into a ferocious "Like a Rolling Stone." Dozens fled the theater. A few shared their thoughts with the documentary crew in the lobby.

"Dylan was shit."

"He needs shooting."

"It was worse than the Beatles."

The next stop was Glasgow. In a room at the North British Station Hotel, Dylan found some relief when he took out his guitar and lost himself in three lovely songs—"What Kind of Friend Is This," "I Can't Leave Her Behind," "On a Rainy Afternoon"—that he would never get around to recording in a studio. He sang in a gentle voice, almost a croon, much different from the sandpaper timbre of his recent solo sets or the barbed-wire tone he used for the rock portions of his shows. He was entering a musical territory he would go into more deeply when he got back home, an exploration that would last several years.

At the end of the concert in Glasgow, a young woman climbed the stage as the musicians were stepping toward the wings. If Dylan had taken her for a well-meaning fan, he quickly learned how wrong he was. "She came right up and punched the shit out of my face," he said.

Back at the hotel, a uniformed waiter entered the suite. Instead of simply delivering the room-service order, he hurled abuse at Dylan, calling him a "fucking traitor." Then he made an aggressive move. Tom Keylock, who was handy with his fists, grabbed the waiter and escorted him to the outer hallway. "He pulls a knife on me," Keylock recalled. "I've still got the scar to prove it. So I gave him a good kicking."

A few nights later, while performing at the Olympia in Paris on his twenty-fifth birthday, Dylan tested everyone's patience in the acoustic portion of the show by endlessly and inebriatedly tuning his guitar, with occasional locomotive blasts of his harmonica. When the crowd grew restive, he said, "Oh, don't be so bored. It's fun—just watch me tune it," to scattered laughs and the briefest applause. Then he added: "Hey, I wanna get out of here as fast as you wanna get out of here." In the second half, he seemed to taunt his fans by playing against the backdrop of a huge American flag. "Bob Dylan, Go Home," ran a headline in the next day's *Paris Jour*.

He flew back to London. After having been called "traitor," "Judas," and "shit" by people who had paid to see him, after having endured a death threat, a bomb threat, a sucker punch, and a potential knife attack, he was as big as ever: "Rainy Day Women," which had just reached No. 2 in America, entered the British Top 10 on the day he checked back into the May Fair.

He returned to work the next evening, playing the first of his two shows at the Albert Hall. Even there, before an audience that included members of the Rolling Stones, he was subjected to the wrath of zealots. Robertson noted in his memoir that he could feel "the hostility" that "truly spewed toward the stage." Dana Gillespie, who was watching from the wings, noticed that Dylan and the band reacted by rocking harder.

That same night, three miles away, in the calm of EMI Studios on Abbey Road, the Beatles were recording yet another new Lennon-McCartney song that had nothing to do with romance. It had started with John. The earliest versions were so sad, so despairing, that they were almost unbearable to listen to. In a pained voice thick with those strange Lennon overtones that sometimes made it seem as if he were hitting three notes at once, he sang:

In the place where I was born
No one cared, no one cared

After singing mantra-like variations on those words, he was unable to muscle what he had into a finished song. The enterprising McCartney, in search of something for Ringo to sing on *Revolver*, seized on this delicate fragment as the foundation for a nautical tale that had popped into his brain one night when he was drifting off to sleep. With assistance from John, Paul transformed it into "Yellow Submarine," a cheerful children's sing-along about a band of adventurers who find bliss at sea. The arrangement, which would include background revelers and a sample of ragtag marching-band horns, gave it a sound unlike anything else on the radio, with the exception of a sing-along now rising on the British charts: "Rainy Day Women."

The Beatles knocked off at 1 a.m. Lennon left the studio, along with the trusty Mal Evans, and paid a visit to Dylan at the May Fair. Before the sun was up, John had agreed to do something all the Beatles had avoided up till then: He would be filmed by Pennebaker's camera. But it's not like he said yes to Dylan's invitation without qualms: "He said, 'I want you to be in this film,'" John recalled. "And I thought: Why? What? He's going to put me down!"

■   ■   ■

Only a brief portion of the scene filmed that day would make its way into the documentary that Dylan and Howard Alk would eventually carve out of the footage, but the complete take, at roughly twenty minutes, circulated for many years on bootleg videos and now surfaces online. A pristinely restored version is in the archive of the Bob Dylan Center in Tulsa, Oklahoma. Over the years, it has become one of those cult artifacts, an interesting disaster that holds a grim fascination for certain music fans, like the studio outtakes of the blues singer Sonny Boy Williamson chewing out his producer during the recording of the song "Little Village" or the secretly made tapes of the big band drummer and bandleader Buddy Rich going on vicious tirades against his fellow musicians.

At the start of the scene, it is 7 a.m. Seated on the leather back seat of the Austin Princess, which is rolling through sparse London traffic, Dylan and Lennon are separated by about three feet of space. They are dressed sharp for their debut as costars—John in a blazer over a turtleneck, Bob in a dark four-button jacket and a stiff-collared shirt—and they are wearing sunglasses. Tom Keylock is at the wheel. Bob Neuwirth is perched on a jump seat across from Lennon. Pennebaker is filming from the front passenger seat.

Speaking of that morning in an interview a few years later, Lennon said that he and Dylan were "on junk"—slang for heroin. That contradicts other statements made by John, who would admit to using heroin, but said he didn't start till 1968. It also goes against what we see in the footage: Lennon seems sober, or close to it; Dylan, on the other hand, appears under the influence of something, sometimes slurring his words and eventually becoming nauseated.

It seems that Dylan has gone into the scene with a goal in mind: As he flits from topic to topic, he is wending his rhetorical way, like a prosecutor out of an old courtroom drama, toward wrangling an on-camera statement from Lennon concerning his view of "Fourth Time Around." If he can get John to say he feels it's a rip-off of "Norwegian Wood," Bob will have the opening he needs to mention the many Lennon-McCartney compositions that motivated him to write his pointed answer song.

Once the camera is rolling, Dylan starts off with some chitchat. "There's the mighty Thames," he says. "That's what held Hitler back. Winston Churchill said that. Tom, ain't that right?"

"Yup," the chauffeur replies.

Dylan now rattles off a litany of famous names—including the blues singers Sleepy John Estes, Robert Johnson, and Peetie Wheatstraw—which leads to Lennon's chiming in with: "Johnny Cash, all the rest of them."

"I have Johnny Cash in my film," Dylan says. He's referring to a scene in which Cash paid him a backstage visit before his recent concert in Cardiff, Wales. "You'll *shit*, man."

"Oh, really?" John says.

"You're gonna *shit* when you see—you won't believe it."

John affects the voice of a television announcer for a children's program: "Hear that, kids? John's gonna shit again."

Dylan laughs and says: "You know what he looks like, right, Johnny Cash? Have you spent much time around him?"

"No," Lennon replies, without mentioning that he had met Cash at the Cow Palace.

"He moves great," Dylan continues. "Like all good people. Like prizefighters."

"Good ol' Johnny," Lennon says. In a rich baritone, he breaks into a Johnny Cash song: "Big River! Big River!"

"Yeah," Dylan says, "he's on film. He's quite a—"

"He's quite a guy, huh?" Lennon says in a parody of an American accent.

"Quite a guy, John," Dylan says.

After Pennebaker mentions something about the filming process, Dylan says, referring to Lennon: "I'm gonna show him the whole flick, when we get it."

"*Nobody's* ever gonna see this whole flick," Pennebaker says, perhaps thinking of the endless reams of footage . . . or a scene shot earlier on the tour that shows Dylan snorting an unknown substance off the top of a piano.

There is a lapse in the footage. When Dylan reappears, he is addressing Lennon: "You asshole. You had a— *That's* the thing I was pissed off about. I wasn't pissed off about— It ain't about the flick." He turns sideways so that he is facing Lennon as he prepares to hit him with the thing that has been on his mind.

It goes back to that night at the May Fair a few weeks earlier, when Bob, the Beatles, Robbie Robertson, and assorted others were listening to tracks from *Revolver* and *Blonde on Blonde*. The big moment, for Dylan, occurred when "Fourth Time Around" was playing and John turned to Paul and made a cryptic remark. The words he spoke in that moment—"That ought to be in Northern Songs"—had stuck in Bob's craw.

"Do you remember what you said to me when I played you those tapes?" Dylan asks. Then he seems to have second thoughts, perhaps thinking this isn't a conversation that should go on film. "I'll say it later," he says.

Lennon realizes something is up. "Say it now," he says firmly.

"Do you remember what you said to me? I played you this song, and you said something about, this has gotta be in—I didn't realize it at the time; Robbie told me—you said, This has gotta be in your song publishing company. What's the name of it?"

"Oh, the *song* publishing company," Lennon says. His tone suggests that Dylan has gone cuckoo and must be humored: All this buildup, all this hemming and hawing, has led only to a question about an inconsequential business detail.

But Dylan isn't kidding. "Yeah," he says. "What is the name of it?"

"Dick James," Lennon replies in the muted voice of a schoolboy in trouble.

"No, no. *That* wasn't the name I heard."

"Northern Songs?" Lennon offers.

"*Right*," Dylan says. "That was it. 'That ought to be in Northern Songs.' And I said, 'What's Northern Songs?' And then I was never *told*, man. I had to go out and *find out*."

"Didn't we tell you?" John asks mildly.

"No, man, you *didn't* tell me. You said, 'This ought to be in Northern Songs.' And everybody—and you *laughed*. And Paul McCartney looked the other way, talking to Ringo."

John tries to wriggle out of this suddenly uncomfortable exchange by turning the story of the night at the May Fair into an absurd show business anecdote. He adopts the sure tone of a narrator to spin a tale featuring the Rolling Stones' lead singer and the Scottish folk hero Robert Roy MacGregor: "And Mick Jagger looked down," Lennon says, "and a *balloon* dropped out of his face! And Rob Roy leapt into the room with a big kilt on and he said, 'Hey, Bobby! Have you heard *this* one?'"

Lennon's embellishment draws cackles from everyone in the limo. He has broken the tension. Dylan's laugh, a kind of goose honk, is the loudest of all. Bob signals further that he's done with the touchy topic by telling John, "You oughta live in Texas, man."

Lennon changes the subject to Barry McGuire, the singer of the heavy-handed protest song "Eve of Destruction." "Barry McGuire's a great war hero," he says, conflating him with another hitmaker, Staff Sergeant Barry Sadler, the man behind "The Ballad of the Green Berets."

Bob picks up the thread with the idea of debating who deserves more blame for McGuire's success—himself or the Beatles.

"Barry McGuire?" Bob says. "He's a great friend of *yours*, John, I understand."

"He met me through *you*, Bob. Remember that? You said, 'Here's a great buddy, Sergeant Barry.'"

Dylan bursts out laughing. "Yes, yes, yes, John, I remember."

Moments later, while pretending to be the director of a scripted film, John asks Bob to redo the dialogue on McGuire.

"All right," Dylan says. "Uh—Barry McGuire tells me he's a good friend of yours."

"Well, I hate to say this about Barry, Bob—or 'Bobby'?—but I don't know him at all, personally, at all. But I *did* have a letter from his manager saying he was very, very close to you, being on the bosom of the current folk-a rock-a boom."

Bob returns the jab by mentioning another act that owed its success to Dylan and the Beatles: the Silkie. It seems he's well aware that Lennon had produced the group's hit remake of "You've Got to Hide Your Love Away," which led to the album *The Silkie Sing the Songs of Bob Dylan.*

"So tell me about the Silkies," Bob says.

"No!" John replies. "I'm not telling you about *them*!"

"Tell me about— Oh, I got a pain in my side. Tell me about this pain in my side and also the Silkies while you're at it."

"No. If we're gonna keep— Why don't you take some for yourself?"

"Hey, I've taken—I've taken a few milligrams of Silkie once," Bob says.

He looks stricken, as if whatever substance he ingested has fully kicked in. A mournful tone replaces the joking irony that had characterized his speech moments earlier. He sounds suddenly like the deeply homesick person who was unburdening himself to the concert promoter a few weeks earlier in Dublin.

"I wanna go back home, man," Dylan says. "Where I come from, we got baseball games. Baseball games. We got all-night TV. I come from the land of paradise, man."

The other passengers have gone silent. It is a Friday, about thirteen hours before Dylan will once again mount the stage of the Albert Hall for the final show of his punishing tour, and on the other side of the limo's windows, office employees are clomping down the sidewalks.

"Well, I'm getting, I, I, uh, I don't understand," Dylan says, slurring his words. "Hey, you know, I'm getting very *sick*, man. I'm glad it's over, 'cause I am getting very *sick* here."

"With the tremors?" John says, none too helpfully.

Dylan's head falls onto his right palm. He's scowling. He's miserable.

"How far are we from the hotel, Tom?" he says.

"Five minutes."

"Permission to land, Tom?" Lennon says.

"I don't wanna get sick in the— What if I vomit into the camera?" Dylan says.

That gets Pennebaker's attention: "What?!" he cries.

"I've done just about everything else into that camera, man. Except vomit into it."

Lennon breaks the next silence by speaking in the voice of a British commercial pitchman: "Do you suffer from sore eyes, groovy forehead, or curly hair? Take Zimdon." There are laughs from Neuwirth and Pennebaker. Sunglasses off, Dylan covers his face with both hands. And now Lennon strikes the tone of an energetic British film producer doing his best to buck up his ailing star: "Come, come, boy—it's only a film! Come, come! Pull yourself together. Have a few dollars, eh? That'll get your head up. Come on, come on, money, money!"

In spite of himself, Dylan is reduced to soft honking laughter. Then he goes back to rubbing his face, saying, "Please go back to the hotel." He's using his fists to support his head. Pennebaker turns the camera on Lennon, who offers a wooden smile.

What happened once the limo arrived at the May Fair was not recorded on film. Pennebaker would later recall that he and Lennon hauled Dylan up to his suite.

"John kept looking at me," Pennebaker said, "and I could see that his instinct was to bolt, because he didn't want to be around if something happened. He didn't want to get caught up in it. But he stuck with us. And John was a very good friend of Dylan's. John just loved him. And vice versa. They adored each other. . . .

"We laid him down on his bed," he continued, "and he looked really weird. We sat on his bed and just looked at him. He looked dead. We went downstairs and back outside, and John said, 'Well, I think we just said goodbye to old Bob.'"

Somehow it wasn't goodbye. That evening, the Beatles were at the Albert Hall to see Dylan attempt to go out there one more time.

Once the audience was seated, Robbie Robertson said, "You got one more show left in you?" "Oh, yeah," Bob replied. "I'm just getting warmed up." The *New Musical Express* reporter Tony Tyler, who was backstage, begged to differ: "His eyes were rolled up inside his head. He was in no fit state to perform."

Dylan stepped onstage and started with "She Belongs to Me." Then he played the song at the center of his friction with John, "Fourth Time Around." In a review for *Record Mirror*, Norman Jopling wrote: "If any of the Beatles were in the audience they may have been embarrassed—or flattered—by Bob's version of 'Norwegian Wood.'"

After the mid-show break, Robertson, Richard Manuel, Rick Danko, Garth Hudson, and Mickey Jones entered to a mix of boos, applause, and catcalls, and threw themselves into "Tell Me, Momma." "The tempo and attitude were aggressive," Robertson recalled. "We had nothing left to give back but a cold shoulder. It struck me as odd, playing in front of all these famous musicians from the British Isles—our peers, our brethren—*Bet you guys have never been through anything like this*, I thought."

Between songs, some people in the crowd exercised their lungs.

"Go home!"

"Drop dead, Dylan!"

"Rubbish!"

The heckles triggered an impassioned reaction from the Beatles: "Shut up! Leave him alone!" they shouted, according to the music journalist Ray Coleman, who was seated one row ahead of their box.

Jopling reported that 25 percent of the audience headed for the exits. "The people who walked out must have been idiots," Harrison said, "and they couldn't have known the real Dylan. It was all still pure Dylan." McCartney agreed: "It was really good. We didn't agree with the folkies who were complaining that he was playing with an electric band."

In the car after the concert, according to Robertson, Dylan received a message from the Beatles: "The booing didn't matter, the music did." "Bob nodded his head slowly, tiredly, taking in the encouragement," Robertson recalled.

Back at the hotel, the band members were winding down when Grossman placed a call to the room shared by Robertson and Rick Danko. He told Robbie to come to Dylan's suite—"quickly, please."

When Robbie got there, he found that "Bob had fainted or was deliriously exhausted."

Grossman and Robertson thought Dylan might come around if he had a bath. Robbie cranked the knobs and was about to help with the job of taking off Dylan's clothes when he heard a knock at the main door to the suite. "It was the Beatles," Robertson recalled, "with some friends and family." He stalled them by saying Bob was "freshening up."

Back in the bedroom, he and Grossman lifted Dylan into the tub. Robbie stayed close by while the manager entertained the guests; but when Bob spoke, he "sounded delirious, muttering about some stuff back home."

Robbie made a quick trip to the living room. "Bob's just pulling himself together," he told the Beatles. Back in the bathroom, he found that Dylan had slipped beneath the water. "My heart stopped for a moment," he wrote in his memoir. He brought Bob's head above the surface. Moments later, Grossman stood outside the bathroom door, asking for an update. Robbie told him to inform the guests that Bob was too tired to see anyone.

Once the Beatles were gone, Robbie and Grossman put Bob to bed. "So strange," Robertson recalled, "but now I saw a slight smile of contentment on his face."

Dylan had reason to be happy. His labors were done.

Unless you counted the Bob Dylan TV special he had to deliver to ABC. Or the Bob Dylan book, *Tarantula*, which was supposed to be in stores in time for the holiday season.

There was also another tour in the works. An early highlight was planned for August 13, when Dylan was scheduled to become only the second headlining rock act to play Shea Stadium.

14 Retreat

When Lennon wasn't working on *Revolver*, dropping acid, or listening to the records he kept in his home jukebox (which in 1966 included Little Richard's "Ooh! My Soul," the Miracles' "Shop Around," and Dylan's "Positively 4th Street"), he was reading, reading, reading. He read the London papers. He read Aldous Huxley, Jonathan Swift, and the Bible. And he read with special interest one of the biggest bestsellers of the mid-1960s, *The Passover Plot*, by Hugh J. Schonfield, a contrarian biblical scholar.

Schonfield was born a Jew in London in 1901 and considered himself a Jew until his death in 1988—but, as he argued in his many published works, he believed Jesus was the messiah. That would seem to make him a Christian, but he held that Jesus was not divine. The notion of Jesus as a god was just part of the legend concocted by his wrongheaded followers, Schonfield argued. In *The Passover Plot*, he presents what he believed was a more accurate account of the messiah's life story, one that shunned supernatural elements. Writing with the pacing of a thriller, the author claimed that Jesus didn't die on the cross, but plotted with a few close disciples to give the impression of his death. His actual demise occurred, in Schonfield's account, after he had come down from the cross, when he was pierced by a Roman spear.

This radical revision of the narrative at the heart of the New Testament offended devout Jews and Christians alike, even as it enthralled millions of readers. The book rang a bell with Lennon partly because of its depiction of the hothouse atmosphere of the ancient world. He couldn't help but see similarities between the ecstatic movements of the first century and the explosions of Beatlemania that had upended his own life. Here was Jesus, an exceptional man, but just a man, who was misrepresented as a god by fantasists. Hadn't a similarly delusional mindset created the fanatics who had swarmed the Beatles in London, New York, and Sydney?

The Passover Plot was fresh in his mind on the February day he spent with Maureen Cleave, the amiable but sharp-quilled journalist who planned to write profiles of John, Paul, George, and Ringo under the series title "How Does a Beatle Live?" Lennon was her first subject, and he welcomed the chance to talk with someone who took him seriously.

He led her through Kenwood, showing off a suit of armor called Sidney, an enormous old Bible, and a gorilla costume he had worn only twice. He also shared a brainstorm: "Christianity will go. It will vanish and shrink. I needn't argue about that; I'm right and I will be proved right. We're more popular than Jesus now; I don't know which will go first—rock 'n' roll or Christianity." With that, he was echoing an argument of *The Passover Plot*, that Christianity's emphasis on Jesus's divinity would cause an upswing in atheism in the increasingly scientific twentieth century. Lennon also served up a Schonfield-inspired view of Christ: "Jesus was all right, but his disciples were thick and ordinary. It's them twisting it that ruins it for me." (In Schonfield's telling, the apostles are "loyal in their own way, but of limited intelligence.")

Cleave's profile ran across two pages in the March 4, 1966, edition of the *Evening Standard*. No one took special notice of it in Britain, where adult followers of the Beatles had come to regard Lennon as a common-enough type, the caustic pub-room philosopher. And they got a laugh from Cleave's description of him as "probably the laziest person in England."

On the day after the article was published, Tony Barrow, now the top publicist in Epstein's office, sent a letter to Arthur Unger, the editor of *Datebook*, an influential American teen magazine run out of an office in Greenwich Village. "I think you might be more than interested in a series of 'in-depth' pieces which Maureen Cleave is doing on each Beatle for the *London Evening Standard*," Barrow wrote. Unger soon agreed to publish edited versions of Cleave's profiles of John and Paul in his September issue. In a separate deal, *The New York Times Magazine* acquired the rights to the story on Lennon. It appeared in that publication, to no outcry from *Times* readers, on July 3.

That same day, the Beatles landed in the Philippines, which had recently elected a new president, Ferdinand E. Marcos. Marcos was not yet the repressive autocrat he would turn out to be, but the Beatles and their entourage encountered hostility from the moment of their arrival.

Even before things began to go very wrong, they had serious doubts about this tour. Their last trip to North America had drained them of their remaining enthusiasm for playing live—and yet they had signed on for another run of stadium and arena shows in the U.S. and Canada scheduled to start soon after the Philippines concerts. Like Dylan a month earlier, John, Paul, George, and Ringo were fast approaching a breaking point.

■   ■   ■

The Beatles had started their 1966 tour in June, with six shows in West Germany, where they were reminded of a pitfall of their lives on the road when George received a letter containing a creepily specific death threat: "You won't live beyond the next month." From Hamburg, they flew across the globe to face the challenge of being the first entertainers to perform at the Nippon Budokan in Tokyo, an arena then considered a sacred space for martial arts.

Japan was split into three camps when it came to the Beatles. There were the young fans, who welcomed their arrival at Tokyo International Airport with cheers and screams; the traditionalists, who took to the streets in civil protest; and the hard-liners, who sent death threats, which Epstein kept secret from John, Paul, George, and Ringo.

Once again, the Beatles were hotel room prisoners. Merchants arrived at the Presidential Suite of the Tokyo Hilton, hoping to interest them in Nikon cameras and other wares. Reporters stopped by to quiz them on their romantic lives and Vietnam. Unlike Dylan, who had repeatedly expressed no opinion on U.S. involvement in the war, Lennon said, "Well, we think about it every day, and we don't agree with it, and we think it's wrong."

At each of the five Budokan concerts, three thousand policemen, on the lookout for snipers, stood among the nine thousand fans, which made for a strangely quiet hall. Such was the price of being the first outside musicians to play a venue that would in the coming years host shows by Led Zeppelin, Frank Sinatra, the Bay City Rollers, Queen, Kiss, Diana Ross, and Dylan.

From Japan, the Beatles flew to Manila, where they were met by thousands of teens, hundreds of cops, and scores of military troops. There were also "thugs in short-sleeved shirts over their trousers, and they all had guns," Neil Aspinall recalled. John, Paul, George, and Ringo were escorted to a yacht in Manila Bay and informed that this would be their quarters. They were much relieved when Brian came aboard a few hours later. After a screaming match, he persuaded the authorities to move the group to the Manila Hotel.

That day's edition of *The Manila Sunday Times* contained Marcos's marching orders to the Beatles in the guise of a news article: They were to pay "a courtesy call" to President Marcos, the first lady, Imelda Marcos, and their three children at eleven o'clock the next morning, a few hours before the first of their two shows at Rizal Memorial Stadium. Epstein had already turned down a 3 p.m. palace visit, and this suddenly announced morning appointment came as news to him. It had been his practice to say no to such requests, since Ringo had lost a lock of hair at the British embassy in Washington two and a half years earlier.

Paul was the only Beatle who woke up early the next day. He and Neil Aspinall sneaked past the guards and explored Manila's financial district, where flimsy shantytowns all but leaned up against the glassy skyscrapers. The two escapees shared a joint in some isolated sand dunes before returning to the hotel, where they found a charged atmosphere: Officials had come to collect the Beatles for the 11 a.m. palace visit and Epstein was refusing to comply.

In a fourth-floor suite, uniformed colonels pressed President Marcos's case directly to John, Paul, George, and Ringo. The chargé d'affaires from the British embassy joined the effort, telling the Beatles that any refusal of hospitality would be taken as a grave insult. The Beatles were unmoved.

It was now past eleven. The TV in the room was showing the palace gathering—the ruling family and three hundred sons and daughters of the local gentry, all in a state of high anxiety as they awaited the guests of honor. After an hour or so, the Marcos children were seen ripping up their concert tickets.

The Beatles played late that afternoon in heavy Pacific heat to assorted screams from the estimated thirty thousand fans. It was a lifeless show, according to Nick Joaquin, a Manila-born novelist, poet, and journalist. "Alas, they performed like any local combo, only not so spiritedly," he wrote in the *Philippines Free Press*. "There was no style, no verve, no poetry to their performance. . . . Even the periodic squealing of girls seemed mechanical." In the hours before the nighttime show, Epstein kept seeing the faces of the jilted Marcos children and their little friends on the TV news. Realizing that the perceived slight was rising to the level of international incident, he filmed an apology at the studio of the government-run Channel 5. When it was shown that night, the sound went out, uncoincidentally.

The Beatles woke the next day as public enemies. "Imelda Stood Up: First Family Waits in Vain for Mopheads," ran a front-page headline. The hotel switchboard lit up with death threats. No cars came to take them and their equipment to the airport. Soldiers menaced the Beatles and their retinue as they tried to make their escape. At the terminal, John and Paul hid behind a group of nuns after their road managers, Mal Evans and Alf Bicknell, were roughed up. "I was petrified," Lennon said. Finally, they boarded a Cathay Pacific jet. As it built up speed on the runway, Epstein looked ill.

The flight took them to Delhi, India, for a two-day stopover. This side trip had been requested by George, who had met Ravi Shankar before the start of the tour and was increasingly enthusiastic about all things Indian. Shankar had been friendly during that first encounter, but he was blunt about George's sitar work on "Norwegian Wood," saying it reminded him of the "frightful" music on radio commercials for soap powder in his home country.

Even here in Delhi, the Beatles encountered mobs shouting, "Beatles! Beatles!" While strolling through a village among so many who lived in poverty, George felt sheepish to be carrying a brand-new Nikon camera that was "worth more than they could earn in their entire lives," he recalled.

At the Oberoi Intercontinental, with the ailing Epstein confined to his room, the Beatles discussed their future with Neil Aspinall, who told them that an extensive run of concerts for 1967 was in the works. "No more for me," John said. The Beatles informed their manager that, once they had completed their obligations in the U.S. and Canada, they would no longer tour.

At London Airport, they recounted their Manila misadventure to a group of reporters. "We're going to have a couple of weeks to recuperate before we go and get beaten up by the Americans," George said. He thought he was joking.

■   ■   ■

Although Dylan had longed for the serenity of home during the low points of his world tour, he seemed unable to shake the habits of the road upon his return to New York in early June 1966. Instead of nestling into family life in the Catskills, he took up residence in that famously shabby headquarters of Manhattan bohemian life, the Chelsea Hotel on West Twenty-Third Street. At a party there one night, the painter Brice Marden found Dylan "comatose" in the middle of the room. And when Albert Grossman arranged for his star client to meet with one of his latest signings, the promising singer Carly Simon, Dylan arrived at his manager's office in no state to provide mentorship. Simon recalled that he "seemed like he was very high on speed—very wasted and talking incoherently, saying a lot about God and Jesus."

He finally escaped the city for Bearsville—but found himself unable to find much peace and quiet at Hi Lo Ha. Macmillan, the book publisher, wanted to get *Tarantula* into stores, but when he read over the galleys he found that he was no longer confident in what he had written. He also had to tame all that film footage into a TV special. And there was the not-insignificant matter of his main job. On August 6, he was scheduled to travel with his band to New Haven, Connecticut, to perform at the Yale Bowl, a stadium with more than seventy thousand seats. A week after that—Shea Stadium.

Blonde on Blonde came out to high praise from a new generation of critics who wrote about rock music in underground publications and small-circulation weeklies with an earnestness that distinguished them from the cheekier pop music journalists whom they would displace. In *The Village Voice*, Richard Goldstein, age twenty-two, wrote that *Blonde on Blonde* represented "a major step" in Dylan's "development as an entertainer and folk poet." He had special praise for the combination of complexity and straightforwardness in "I Want You," which came out as the follow-up single to "Rainy Day Women" and soon made the Top 40.

At the same time, Dylan was a darling of the mainstream press. On newsstands and in doctors' waiting rooms all across the country, he could be seen posing moodily, in profile, with a white scarf and cigarette, on the cover of *The Saturday Evening Post*. The accompanying article summed up the general view: "This year Bob Dylan is the king of rock 'n' roll, and he is the least likely king popular music has ever seen." Written by Jules Siegel, the piece ended with a quote from its subject—"I'll die first before I decay"—that burnished his image as a tragically romantic figure in the mold of Rimbaud and James Dean.

After the upcoming dates at the Yale Bowl and Shea Stadium, Grossman's itinerary had Dylan playing around the world. There was even talk of a concert in Moscow. But before Bob could even think of all that, he had to edit the footage. The amphetamines that had fueled him on the road now gave him the energy he needed to sit in a room at Hi Lo Ha with Howard Alk, Bob Neuwirth, and D. A. Pennebaker and try to make sense of it.

That scene he had shot with Lennon in the limo in London—Dylan made notes about how it should appear. He listed five categories at the top of the page: "Home; Chase; Film; Lennon looking into camera; (intersection) stopped." Below those headings, he jotted down words meant to guide the exact sequencing of images:

> *baseball*
> *me with head down*
> *"come now, it's only a film"*
> *head down*
> *"well"*
> *Need shot of me getting into car*

Elsewhere in the papers housed at the Dylan archive in Tulsa, there are notes that seemingly pertain to a lost scene (or scenes) featuring Dylan and Lennon:

> *me, hitchhiking*
> *Hitch-hiking with Richard, Lennon comes along*
> *Lennon slow (looking into camera)*
> *Lennon drives off*
> *looks back out of window*
> *car changes from Barry into Lennon*
> *Lennon slow + follows bus*
> *Lennon needling me after "makes you feel at home"*

Bob told his journalist friend Al Aronowitz that, with the aid of speed, he had stayed up three days straight while editing the footage. Immediately after that, on July 29, he decided to take his Triumph motorcycle from Grossman's property to a repair garage in

Woodstock. It was a warm, breezy morning when he set out for Striebel Road. Sara, at the wheel of the sky-blue Ford station wagon, was not far behind as she followed her husband down the long dirt driveway. She planned to take him back home after he had dropped off the bike.

As Bob and Sara were driving off, Sally Grossman was watching them from inside the house. She was standing in the first-floor hall, talking on the phone with her husband, who was at his office in Manhattan. She was steps away from the parlor where she had posed with Dylan for the cover of *Bringing It All Back Home*, in which she looked so languid and he looked so intense. That was back when Bob was bristling with ambition . . . but also when almost no one figured he would end up with a run of Top 10 hits and a booking at Shea Stadium. Now, a year and a half later, Sally was here for the moment that would put an end to his first bout of stardom. A few minutes into the call with her husband, she saw the station wagon pulling back into the driveway.

"Hold on," she said into the phone.

Dylan emerged from the car. He was "kind of moaning and groaning," Sally recalled in an interview with the biographer Howard Sounes. He made it onto the porch—and then he just lay there. Sally told her husband what was happening before hanging up and stepping outside.

"Keep away from him!" Sara said.

There were no signs of obvious injury, but it seemed that Bob had taken a spill. Neither Sara nor Sally called an ambulance. Sara just bundled him back into the station wagon and took him away—not to a hospital, but to the home of Edward Thaler, a physician in Middletown, New York. It was more than an hour drive, about fifty miles south of Bearsville.

Bob had gotten to know Dr. Thaler and his wife, Selma, two or three years earlier, while spending pleasant days with the couple at their summer cabin on nearby Yankee Lake. Dr. Thaler, who went by Eddie, was a Brooklyn-born music lover, civil rights activist, and a friend to Odetta. He had been in private practice since 1960, while also serving as the chief staff internist at Horton Medical Center, the hospital in Middletown. In the summer of 1966, Eddie and Selma were in their mid-thirties, with three children. Unlike so many others in Dylan's orbit, they didn't seem impressed by his fame and didn't want anything from him.

According to Selma, Bob was "very upset" when Sara brought him into the family's old-fashioned home on Highland Avenue. "He didn't want to go to the hospital, so we said, 'You can stay here,'" she recalled. Bob moved into a spare room on the third floor. A few days later, a two-sentence news brief appeared in *The New York Times*.

> **DYLAN HURT IN CYCLE MISHAP**
> Bob Dylan, the folk singer and song writer, is under a doctor's care for injuries suffered in a motorcycle accident last Friday. A representative of Mr. Dylan said the injuries have forced the cancellation of a concert scheduled for Saturday night at the Yale Bowl in New Haven.

The Shea Stadium concert and other shows were also scratched. *Tarantula* was put on hold. The TV special was shelved. Dylan was off the hook.

■　　■　　■

On the morning of the apparent motorcycle accident, Al Benn, a journalist in Birmingham, Alabama, was driving along, listening to the pop station WAQY. The morning show hosts, Tommy Charles and Doug Layton, were getting very worked up as they discussed statements made by John Lennon in a recent interview—that the Beatles were more popular than Jesus and that Christianity would vanish.

"That is it for me," Charles said. "I'm not going to play the Beatles anymore."

Calls poured into the station. Almost every one was in favor of barring the Beatles from the airwaves. Which was all very interesting—but Al Benn knew for certain he had a story only when the deejays spoke of burning Beatles records in a great bonfire.

Shortly after he reached his office, he started typing up what he had. Anything he wrote had the potential to reach millions of readers, given that he worked for the United Press International (UPI), a news agency whose articles were carried by more than five thousand newspapers around the world.

Charles and Layton had come upon Lennon's statements in *Datebook*'s reprint of Maureen Cleave's profile. Art Unger, the editor, had sent advance copies of his September issue to people in the media across the South in hopes of stirring up a controversy that might generate publicity for his publication and perhaps lead to positive social change. Unlike the usual teen magazine, *Datebook* had a political agenda: Beneath the celebrity coverage, it promoted views in favor of the civil rights movement and against the war in Vietnam.

Unger billed the September edition as the "Shout-Out Issue" because it contained so many controversial statements. In addition to Cleave's story on Lennon, it included her profile of McCartney, in which he bluntly expressed his views on race relations in the U.S. That was the article Unger figured would spark a reaction in the South. On the cover, next to a close-up photo of Paul, he stacked some attention-grabbing quotations from the issue, with exclamation points tossed in for tabloid-style emphasis.

PAUL MCCARTNEY: "It's a lousy country where anyone black is a dirty nigger!"
JOHN LENNON: "I don't know which will go first—rocknroll or Christianity!"
BOB DYLAN: "Message songs are a drag!"
TIM LEARY: "Turn on, tune in, drop out!"
TEENS: "Vietnam must go!" "Long hair must stay!" "LSD is for creeps!"

The two Alabama deejays had flipped past Paul to focus their wrath on John. And on July 31, newspapers across the U.S. ran Benn's UPI article on the planned Beatles bonfire.

Ticket sales for the upcoming shows went slack. In an ABC News segment, Tommy Charles was seen urging WAQY listeners "to take your Beatle records, pictures, and souvenirs to the pick-up points about to be named, and on the night of the Beatles' appearance in Memphis, August 19, they will be destroyed in a huge public bonfire at a place to be named soon."

Unger had gotten much more than he had bargained for. He called Epstein, who was still recovering from the illness that had struck him in Manila. "This is getting out of hand here," the *Datebook* editor said. The Beatles' manager couldn't fathom that a spasm of anti-Beatles sentiment in the Deep South amounted to anything serious. "Arthur," Brian replied, "if they burn Beatles records, they've got to buy them first." But there were more headlines in the days to come: "'Ban the Beatles' Campaign Growing"; "Beatles Flying into Religious Storm."

It was no surprise when radio stations in the South barred the group's music; but the anti-Beatles movement became impossible to ignore when outlets across the nation followed suit. Concert promoters and a Capitol executive called Epstein to express concern over ticket sales. They also fretted that they wouldn't be able to keep the group safe from physical harm.

A week before the Beatles' arrival in the U.S., Epstein faced the news media at the Americana Hotel in Manhattan, hoping to quell the furor. It was early in the era of celebrity pillorying, so he can be forgiven for trying the "taken out of context" gambit. The lukewarm apology he offered—"In the circumstances, John is deeply concerned, and regrets that people with certain religious beliefs should have been offended in any way whatsoever"—did nothing to douse the flames.

Beneath the squall of controversy, *Revolver* was released in Britain. *Melody Maker* called it "a brilliant album" that had "broken the bounds of what we used to call pop" but noted uneasily that its complex instrumentation and production effects meant its songs could not be reproduced onstage. *Disc and Music Echo* handed the job of reviewing the album to Ray Davies, the leader of the Kinks, who called "Yellow Submarine" "a load of rubbish" and opined that "Eleanor Rigby" sounded as if it were meant "to please music teachers in primary schools." American critics embraced it. Richard Goldstein, who had heaped praise on *Blonde on Blonde*, called *Revolver* "a revolutionary record." Another pro-Dylan critic, Ralph J. Gleason of the *San Francisco Chronicle*, called it "the most outstanding pop album in years, possibly the best of all time."

On August 11, costumed Ku Klux Klan members in Chester, South Carolina, tossed Beatles albums onto a flaming wooden cross as news photographers captured the scene. The next day, John, Paul, George, and Ringo arrived in Chicago, the first stop of the North American tour. On the twenty-seventh floor of the Astor Tower Hotel, they endured a press conference that didn't include questions about their hair. Major outlets, including the three national television networks, had sent journalists with hard-news experience to give Lennon a thorough going-over.

"I'm not saying that we're better, or greater, or comparing us with Jesus Christ as a person or God as a thing or whatever it is, you know," he said. "I just said what I said, and it was wrong, or it was taken wrong. And now it's all this." Asked if he was regretful, he said: "I am. Yes, you know. Even though I never meant what people think I meant by it, I'm still sorry I opened my mouth." Later that day, he was asked if he would say sorry to Tommy Charles of WAQY. "I apologize to him," Lennon said. "I'm sorry I said it and for the mess it's made."

The two shows at the thirteen-thousand-seat International Amphitheatre were sell-outs, according to the *Chicago Sun-Times*, but the reporter noted that the fans seemed less excited than those who had screamed their lungs out a year earlier at White Sox Park.

There were empty seats at the pair of shows they played at Olympia Stadium in Detroit. Backstage, George told a reporter, "The George of the Beatles isn't me." That same night, a thousand miles away, in Longview, Texas, two thousand teenagers gathered outside the radio station KLUE for a Beatles bonfire. In the darkness, they watched their records go up in smoke.

In Cleveland, Ohio, Reverend Thurman H. Babbs of the New Haven Baptist Church told his parishioners they would be expelled from the congregation if they attended that night's Beatles concert. Only twenty-five thousand people showed up for the 7:30 p.m. show at the Cleveland Municipal Stadium, which held more than seventy-three thousand. Asked how the tour was going, Lennon said, "Well, it's dwindling."

The Cleveland crowd made up for its size during the fourth song, "Day Tripper," which McCartney had mistakenly introduced as the final number. Two thousand fans rushed the stage. The local emcee, Jack Armstrong, stepped up to a microphone: "Back up!" A girl grabbed Paul and ripped his jacket. The Beatles made their exit and returned a half hour later, over Amstrong's objections, to finish the show. If there was any consolation, it came with some surprising news out of Texas: A bolt of lightning had struck KLUE, the station that had sponsored the bonfire the night before, knocking out the news director (who recovered) and damaging the equipment.

In Washington, the Beatles were surprised to find they didn't have the usual police escort to take them from the airport to the hotel; they were perhaps more surprised to see they didn't need it—only twelve fans stood outside the lobby to greet them. Later that day, five Ku Klux Klan members protested outside D.C. Stadium. When the Beatles took the stage, they saw eighteen thousand empty seats. A reporter asked Paul if they might break up. "We can't go on forever," he replied.

In Memphis, six Ku Klux Klan members picketed the Mid-South Coliseum, where the Beatles were scheduled to play two shows. One Klan member told a reporter there would be "surprises" during the performance. At the nearby Memphis Union Mission, Reverend Jimmy Stroud staged an anti-Beatles rally attended by eight thousand.

A bomb threat delayed the 4 p.m. concert. Early in the nighttime show, the Beatles were playing "If I Needed Someone" when they heard a loud bang. "Somebody let off a firecracker," Lennon said, "and every one of us looked at each other because each thought the other had been shot." The culprits were two teenagers, a boy and a girl, who had lobbed a cherry bomb from the balcony; three young fans were injured in the blast.

The misery continued into the next night, when fifteen thousand people braved a heavy rain, hoping to see the Beatles at Crosley Field in Cincinnati. The show was canceled after Mal Evans sustained a full-body shock while trying to set up the electrical equipment on the wet stage. Nat Weiss, a New York lawyer who worked with Epstein, noticed that the group's hardiest trouper was in a bad state afterward. "The strain had obviously been too much for Paul," he said. "When I got back to the hotel, Paul was already there. He was throwing up with all this tension."

From Cincinnati the Beatles flew to St. Louis, where they performed in the rain at Busch Memorial Stadium in front of twenty-three thousand fans and seventeen thousand empty seats. Paul called that show "the worst little gig we ever played, even before we'd started as a band." The soaked Beatles left the stage and piled into an armored car. "We were sliding around, trying to hold on to something and, at that moment, everyone said, 'This bloody touring lark—I've had it up to here, man,'" Paul recalled. "But finally I agreed with them."

Next stop, New York. "This is to all of you," a reporter said during the press conference at the Warwick Hotel. "You seem to be doing a Bob Dylan in reverse. That is, you became popular playing rock 'n' roll and now you seem to be doing a lot more folk rock."

"It's not folk rock," McCartney said. "Honest."

"Songs like 'Eleanor Rigby' and . . ."

"No," Paul said. "The thing is that—the thing about Bob Dylan is probably right, in reverse, because we're getting more interested now in the content of the songs, whereas Bob Dylan is getting more interested in rock 'n' roll. It's just, we're both going toward the same thing, I think."

Just as Dylan's shift from folk to rock had alienated many of his fans, the Beatles' move from rock 'n' roll toward something less easily classifiable had contributed to a quieter reaction from their audience. *Revolver* was selling briskly—it would soon hit No. 1 in the U.S. and the UK—but the group's return to Shea Stadium proved yet another disappointment. Ten days after Dylan was supposed to have played there, the Beatles performed to an audience of forty-five thousand, more than ten thousand shy of a sellout.

The tour concluded on August 29 at Candlestick Park in San Francisco. The Beatles reached the stadium entrance in a bus, only to find the gate locked. Fans swarmed the vehicle, and the driver took off, leading the mob in an absurd chase around the parking lot as evening fell.

Only 25,000 tickets had been sold for the 45,000-seat stadium. A ten-foot steel livestock fence enclosed the stage, penning in the Beatles on that foggy, chilly night. Ralph J. Gleason, who witnessed the show with Joan Baez and her sister Mimi, was disappointed. "As a spectacle, it is not without sociological interest, of course," he wrote in the *San Francisco Chronicle*. "As a performance it is, like John Lennon says, a puppet show. It can hardly continue to be attractive to four such rational, intelligent, and talented human beings."

It ended as it had begun on the day when John and Paul met in 1957—with a Little Richard song. After the final crash of "Long Tall Sally," the Beatles left their cage, walked across the soggy baseball field, and climbed into an armored truck. On the flight out of San Francisco, George said, "That's it then. I'm not a Beatle anymore."

15 Penny Lane and Bourbon Street

And so the Beatles and Bob Dylan had arrived at the same place at the same time. There was no longer any need to subject themselves to mobs, to be trapped in hotel rooms as maniacs phoned in death threats. All they had to do was . . . well, the pathway wasn't entirely clear . . . but they sensed that, before they could rededicate themselves to their art, they would have to dismantle the mythic identities that had grown around them and now threatened to suffocate them.

Dylan spent several weeks at the Thalers' home in Middletown. Sometimes Sara came to see him, as did a few friends. Selma Thaler posited that her orderly household was comforting to Bob because it was "reminiscent of his childhood." He read a lot in the calm of his third-floor bedroom. The windows were open to the cool summer breezes, and at regular intervals he heard the chimes of the bells from the Methodist church down the street.

The leaves were starting to turn when he went back to Hi Lo Ha. One night, he found himself under a full moon, looking out at the woods. "Something's gotta change," he said. He began to make a habit of waking up early and reading the enormous old Bible on the lectern in the study. He tended to the baby. He put aside the clothes he had worn on tour, the four-button jacket, the pointed boots, and he was just himself again as he walked his daughter to the school-bus stop. While he was living in this simple way, rumors were spreading through the outside world, as if to fill the void created by the lack of detail in the *New York Times* report on his accident. People said he was dead. Disfigured. In a vegetative state.

Lennon, at the same time, was in Celle, Germany. He had gone there, just a week after that chilly night at Candlestick Park, to play a World War II soldier, Private Gripweed, in *How I Won the War*, an anti-war comedy directed by Richard Lester. To look the part, John sat for a military-style haircut in the breakfast room of the Hotel Heide Kröpke. The director watched with amusement as some of the world's most famous locks fell to the floor.

The barber left a few inches on top, but it was still a dramatic change. A pair of eyeglasses, steel-framed and round-lensed, completed the new look. "Now John loved his National Health glasses, ugly as they were," Cynthia Lennon recalled. He put in a couple weeks of filming before moving on with the crew from Germany to southern Spain. A reporter caught up with him there, and almost the first thing he said was: "You look a little like Bob Dylan this way. Have you noticed it? Anybody else say that?" Lennon replied: "About two people have said it. It's because me hair's standing on end."

The role wasn't too taxing, giving him a break from the frenzied days and nights of his recent past. He showed up on the set even when he wasn't scheduled to go on camera, and the other cast members were pleased to see he didn't ask for star treatment. But it wasn't as if he had suddenly rid himself of all trappings of wealth and fame. For one thing, he had his chauffeur come down with his Rolls-Royce Phantom V, which had been rigged with a microphone, a stereo system, and a loudspeaker. One day the Beatles road manager Neil Aspinall was a passenger in the Rolls when John decided to play a Dylan album. "We were going down the road with Dylan blaring out all over the place," Aspinall said. In a different mood, off by himself, John thought of the childhood days he had spent in a tree at Strawberry Field, the paradise in Woolton that gave him a retreat from his traumatic family life. Here in remote, dusty Spain, he could slip into a dreamy state that reminded him of what he had felt back then.

With a nylon-stringed Spanish guitar, he sat on El Zapillo beach, or else he holed up in his bedroom at the villa where he was staying, and he worked up a melody and some words. "I heard him playing the same bar over and over again, until he had the right sequence," said Michael Crawford, a castmate. John recorded his efforts onto cassette tapes. At one point in the song's development, he may have followed the example of the songwriter who had inspired him before, as when he tried a fingerpicking pattern described by the musicologist Walter Everett as "highly reminiscent of Dylan's 'Boots of Spanish Leather.'" For six weeks, John honed what he had. He was careful to keep the words conversational, unpolished, the better to convey the unsettled mental state he sought to describe.

If he no longer wanted much of what went with being a Beatle, he couldn't deny that creating something like this—rather than, say, acting in a movie, which he would never do again—was the main thing in his life. The work was interrupted only toward the end of his time in Spain, when he learned of the death of Alma Cogan, the British singing star of the 1950s whom Lennon had mocked when he was a teenager, but had grown to love. She had died, at thirty-four, of ovarian cancer in a London hospital. Cynthia, who had long suspected an affair between Alma and her husband, described him as "inconsolable."

Shortly after his return to England, John made the acquaintance of an artist recently arrived in London, Yoko Ono. She had performed her unsettling *Cut Piece* at the Africa Center and was now preparing an exhibition, *Unfinished Paintings*, at the Indica Gallery. "He met Yoko when he needed to, just a fortnight into his grief," Cynthia said.

John went back to work on his song in the upstairs rooms of Kenwood. Like Paul's "Yesterday" and Dylan's "Like a Rolling Stone," this new composition required a lot of time, a lot of revision, before it would find its final form. It was "Strawberry Fields Forever," a spooky evocation of youth, an attempt to put into words and music his ambivalent sense of self, the feeling that he was always apart from others and yet might not know who he really was.

McCartney in this same period was also shedding the persona that had gone with his fame. First he busied himself with a commission, composing music for the film *The Family Way*, a quick bit of labor at the piano that would earn him a prestigious Ivor Novello Award. Then he glued on a mustache from Wig Creations, a shop for theater people in London, and slicked back his hair. To render himself even less like Beatle Paul, he put on a pair of round eyeglasses, draped himself in an overcoat, and called himself Hunt Hanson.

In Lydd, Kent, he boarded a Silver City Airways flight to Le Touquet in northern France. The plane was built to carry three automobiles and twenty passengers, and Paul's Aston Martin went with him. From Le Touquet, he set out on a road trip in his disguise. He fancied himself an observer, a poet, a novelist, a man apart, as he watched café patrons and passersby through the veil of anonymity. He was studying people, inventing scenarios, just as he had done in the writing of "Eleanor Rigby." Perhaps that was a way forward.

He arranged a rendezvous with the Beatles' faithful road manager, Mal Evans, and the two of them rode from Bordeaux to Spain with the idea of finding John on the film set. They laughed along the way, and the weather went cold and wet, and they stopped in at a souvenir shop. Paul bought a postcard and dashed off a note to the Starkeys, not forgetting to include the names of the baby and the three dogs in his salutation.

> Dear Ringo, Maureen, Zack, Tiger, Donovan, and Daisy,
>   We're going through Spain for a bit, not understanding a word but having fun. Lousy weather, but lovely indoors.
>   Paul & Mal
>   Available for social functions.

They changed course after receiving word that the film shoot was done and John had gone home. Someone in Epstein's office was dispatched to fetch the Aston Martin, and the two travelers flew to

Nairobi. Paul sang for some children in the street before he and Mal went on a safari. By this time a real mustache had crept into the bit of territory formerly occupied by the fake one.

On the flight back to London, Paul was struck by an idea inspired by his recent playacting: What if the Beatles were no longer the Beatles? What if they were to adopt alter egos? Wouldn't they be able to write and record free of expectations and old habits? He and Mal hit upon the name for the group they could pretend to be: Sgt. Pepper's Lonely Hearts Club Band. Paul pictured the uniformed brass bands that had once been a staple of municipal life in seemingly every British town of the industrial north. A few of them had still been around when he was a kid. There was, for instance, the Salvation Army band that John had loved to see at the annual fete on the grounds of Strawberry Field. It could be something like that, but modern. Old-fashioned brass and distorted electric guitar, together.

By the time McCartney had come up with the Sgt. Pepper idea, George Harrison had moved well past his old identity. A few days after declaring he was no longer a Beatle, he cut off his hair, started growing a mustache, and adopted an alias, Sam Wells. That was the name he used when he and Pattie checked into the Taj Mahal Palace hotel in Mumbai. He had made the trip to India at the invitation of Ravi Shankar, who had agreed to give him serious instruction.

George was determined not to be a dilettante. Alongside other students, he practiced the sitar several hours a day under the tutelage of Shankar or his leading pupil, Shambhu Das. He sat in the recommended manner, the half lotus position, the gourd placed against the ball of his left foot. "My legs were in terrible pain," he recalled. With the help of yoga, he got the hang of it, and now the sitar seemed almost to balance itself, leaving his left hand free to roam the frets as his right hand, holding the pick called the misra, struck the strings in an upward or downward motion (or sometimes both, in rapid succession, in the manner of a surf guitarist). He was delighted to find an infinity of notes in the cracks between the twelve tones of the Western scale.

He read *Raja-Yoga* by Swami Vivekananda; he read the *Yoga Sutras*; he read the *Bhagavad Gita*. A through line of those texts was the divinity in all things, which matched the insights he had gained, the sensations he had experienced, while tripping. From Mumbai, George and Pattie traveled north, more than a thousand miles, in the company of Shankar. They saw funeral pyres along the Ganges. They mixed with crowds at the religious festival Ramlila in Shankar's home city, Benares, Uttar Pradesh. In a stony area where the Jamuna river had once flowed, they met an old man who led them through ancient temples. Before a predawn religious service, they slept a few hours in his home. It was "the deepest sleep I ever had in my life," George recalled, "and all through the sleep I could hear choirs singing."

Unlike the other Beatles, Ringo didn't change much. Although he was the only Beatle with a stage name, he could never be anyone but himself. That's why the fans had a special affection for him. That's why the critics singled him out for praise in their reviews of *A Hard Day's Night*. Perhaps he had already found whatever it was that John, Paul, and George were seeking as they sloughed off their old identities. At Sunny Heights, his estate in Surrey, he rarely practiced the drums. It wasn't any fun to play alone. Worried that John might feel lonesome celebrating his twenty-sixth birthday at such a distance from home and his fellow Beatles, he went with Maureen to Almería. Then it was back to England. When a reporter asked what he had been up to, Ringo said, "Me? I'm just having a good time."

Toward the end of November, the Associated Press reported that the Beatles were back at EMI Studios on Abbey Road. "So lovely," Lennon said when asked how it felt to be reunited with his bandmates. On the first day, he sang "Strawberry Fields Forever" for George Martin. "It was absolutely lovely," the producer recalled. But the song would prove difficult to translate into a record without losing the haunted quality that made it special. Twenty-five takes and three weeks later, Martin decided to enhance it. In keeping with Paul's notion of the Beatles as a municipal band from the Edwardian era, he wrote parts for four trumpets and three cellos. John approved the result, only to request that Martin somehow join the starker original recording to this more elaborate take. With the help of the young engineer Geoff Emerick, Martin managed to splice them together, despite the variations in pitch and tempo of the two versions.

While the Beatles were working on John's song, Paul presented "When I'm Sixty-Four," the first of the many musical character studies he would write in the days to come. This one was an affectionately satirical depiction of a humble British householder imagining his later years in the company of his beloved. Paul built it on the old-fashioned melody he had composed as a teenager and performed on piano during blackouts at the Cavern. The details in the verses—man and wife consider renting a cottage on the Isle of Wight "if it's not too dear"—suggested the delight its composer took when writing in a voice not his own. Martin completed the portrait by adding three 1920s-style clarinets and placing them high in the mix.

The decision to go with an antiquated sound was influenced by an unlikely hit of late 1966, "Winchester Cathedral," a thoroughly English novelty number by the New Vaudeville Band. So much of pop music had jumped forward in recent years, increasingly electric, increasingly American, and "Winchester Cathedral" brought back the supposedly simpler days before miniskirts and marijuana. As it made its way up the charts on both sides of the Atlantic, a new group, Pink Floyd, which Paul had seen at the underground club UFO, was entrancing London scenesters with ethereal songs steeped in childhood, pastoral life, and folklore. A similar nostalgic longing had taken hold of the hippies in the U.S., who dreamed of an Eden unspoiled by violence, bourgeois notions of respectability, and the individualism that made capitalism go.

After recording "When I'm Sixty-Four," the Beatles got to work on "Penny Lane," Paul's complement to "Strawberry Fields Forever." In it, he conjured a surreal, child's-eye view of the bustling Liverpool street and neighborhood just south of the city center. As with the first two songs recorded during the *Sgt. Pepper* sessions, the ideal version lay beyond what the Beatles themselves could play. The final recording overflowed with flutes, oboes, cor anglais, and trumpets, including the B-flat piccolo trumpet that helped make the song so memorable.

The studio was packed a month and a half into 1967, when the Beatles enlisted forty orchestral players to fill out twenty-four bars of what was perhaps the greatest Lennon-McCartney collaboration, "A Day in the Life." The musicians were directed to start with the lowest note of their instruments and slide little by little to the highest, thereby creating what Lennon described as "a musical orgasm."

The song had begun with John, who was inspired by a newspaper story on the death of the twenty-one-year-old Beatles acquaintance and Guinness heir Tara Browne in a car crash. Paul contributed the refrain, "I'd love to turn you on," with its ghostly oscillations during the stretched-out word "on," as well as the bouncy middle eight, which details the rushed morning routine of a student or office employee. The verses are shot through with the names of institutions and places—Blackburn, Lancashire; the Albert Hall; the House of Lords—that made it of a piece with "Strawberry Fields Forever," "Penny Lane," and "When I'm Sixty-Four." In sound and sense, the album was shaping up to be a depiction of British life past and present.

■   ■   ■

By the end of 1966, journalists had not gotten far in their attempts to solve the biggest mystery in rock music. "Few of Bob Dylan's old cronies have been in direct touch with him since his motorcycle accident last summer," *Melody Maker* reported. "Most requests for information get such replies as, 'I don't know, man. As far as I know, he's upstate recuperating.'" The article presented two conflicting possibilities—that Dylan had exaggerated the severity of his injuries or that he was worse off than was publicly known.

Bob was happy to be living beyond the noise. Sara was pregnant again, and the guys in the band, who were being paid through the months that had been set aside for the canceled tour, came up to the Woodstock area for a visit. It wasn't long before they realized, as Bob had, that they no longer needed the city. Garth Hudson,

Richard Manuel, and Rick Danko rented a modest pink house in West Saugerties, and Robbie Robertson took a place even closer to Hi Lo Ha.

In early February, they all went down to a Manhattan nightclub, Steve Paul's the Scene, to meet with the throwback singer and ukulele player Tiny Tim, whom Dylan had gotten to know at the Cafe Wha? early in his Greenwich Village days. With his hair to his shoulders, his lanky six-foot-one frame, and his loud attire, he was a distinctive character of New York show business; he was also an American equivalent to the New Vaudeville Band in his devotion to the music of long ago. But unlike the group behind "Winchester Cathedral," Tiny Tim, born Herbert Khaury in the Washington Heights neighborhood of Manhattan, seemed doomed to living out his days as a local curiosity, an oddball entertainer unable to attract fans beyond his cult. There simply wasn't much of a market for someone hell-bent on bringing back the romantic crooning of the 1920s and '30s, a genre that Tiny Tim had loved since he was five years old, when he had spent hours listening to old 78 rpm discs on the family's windup gramophone.

On this cold night, Dylan saw Tiny Tim take the stage with Robbie, Garth, Richard, and Rick. Barry Feinstein, the photographer who had taken the portraits of Bob in Liverpool, was filming the performance for an experimental movie, *You Are What You Eat*. Bob liked the brief concert so much that he invited Tiny Tim to take part in a film of his own.

On February 13—the day the Beatles released a single with "Penny Lane" on one side and "Strawberry Fields Forever" on the other—a limousine fetched Tiny Tim in Manhattan and took him to Hi Lo Ha in Bearsville. Dylan greeted him at the door around 11 p.m. The two of them sat in the quiet front parlor, where Tiny Tim told Bob that he was as important to today's youth as the crooner Rudy Vallée had been to the young people of 1929. Then he took out his ukulele and sang "Like a Rolling Stone" in the voice of Vallée. He followed that by doing one of Vallée's big hits, "My Time Is Your Time," as Dylan. "He listened to all of this very carefully," Tiny Tim recalled, "and then you know what he said? He said, 'Do you want a banana?' I said, 'No, thanks, I brought my own fruit.' And off he went to bed."

⁂

In March, Dylan started concentrating on making music with Robbie, Garth, Richard, and Rick. They played in a casual and collegial manner, more like a bona fide group than just Bob Dylan with some hired hands. He was also writing songs again. He found he had nothing to say—that is, nothing personal, for the most part—and no point to make; he simply allowed what was in the air to course through him, to make itself felt through his voice and wherever it was that his left hand decided to place itself on the fretboard and however it was that his right hand wanted to pick or strum. Something always came out. Sometimes it was silly, as in "Please, Mrs. Henry," "Quinn the Eskimo (The Mighty Quinn)," and "Bourbon Street," and sometimes it was weighty, as in "This Wheel's on Fire," "I'm Not There," and "I Shall Be Released."

He was always writing, and what he wrote didn't always add up to a song—for instance, the little poem called "John Lennon Hat" that he jotted down in a pocket-size notebook. The title suggests he was inspired by the similar caps they used to wear, and the poem as a whole seems to hint at Dylan's desire to ward off an influence he may not have wanted. Perhaps he partly blamed Lennon for the white-hot fame that had nearly burned him alive.

> *I was bouncing on the seat*
> *with Nothing else to do,*
> *when you came to my window*
> *and stuck your arm thru*
> *I wasn't doing anything to you*

Now that he no longer had to project himself to thousands of people, Bob found himself singing in a clear, nuanced, sometimes crooning voice, the one he had used in those easy after-hours sessions in hotel rooms with Robbie and Joan. His new songs just *were*, untainted by the desire to astound people, or confound them, or even please them. He was writing concisely, too, without expanding on the subject at hand in the manner of "Desolation Row." With Robbie and the other musicians, he recorded a song that would become something of a model for him, "People Get Ready," a recent hit for the Impressions written by the group's leader, the Chicago-born singer and guitarist Curtis Mayfield. It was a song Dylan loved; and Robbie pointed out how Mayfield was able to say so much in so few words. "You're rambling on for an hour," he told Bob bluntly, "and you're losing me."

In the company of these sympathetic players, who had suffered with him through all the booing, Bob played his new stuff along with ancient folk songs, standards, Johnny Cash numbers, and various hits and obscurities from the bank of pop and country songs he had committed to memory. The musicians tucked themselves into a room at Hi Lo Ha called the red room, where Garth captured the sessions on a reel-to-reel tape machine. After a month there, they decamped to a studio in the basement of the West Saugerties house, nicknamed Big Pink.

Their sound had nothing to do with anything on the radio. It was the kind of thing you might have heard coming from a room behind a general store in some frontier outpost of the previous century... but there was nothing precious about it, nothing preservationist... it was alive. Bob was also becoming less of a musical loner, writing "Tears of Rage" with Richard Manuel and "This Wheel's on Fire" with Rick Danko. If there was a thread that held his new songs together, it was some notion of America, its fraught history, its legends, its peculiar characters. "He would pull these songs out of nowhere," Robbie said. "We didn't know if he wrote them or if he remembered them."

Some days they drank beer, smoked pot, and made music with Purna and Lakhsman Das, brothers from Bengal, India, who belonged to the line of freethinking musicians, singers, and dancers known as Bauls. Sally Grossman was an especial admirer of their music, and her husband had brought the Das brothers and their band from Kolkata to the U.S. for a lengthy visit that would include recording sessions for the album *The Bauls of Bengal*. Bob became fast friends with Purna. "One evening, Dylan told me that if I'm a Bengali Baul musician from India, he is an American Baul," Purna said. "We both sing music of the roots. Our objectives, he told me, were the same: To sing for people, tell their tales, and spread love through music."

Dylan was no longer aligned with the Beatles when it came to the sound of his work, given his commitment to making music with an amateur spirit; but like Lennon and McCartney at this time, he was drawing inspiration from his home country and the pre–rock 'n' roll past, weaving himself into the fabric of music history.

So while the Beatles were working place-names such as the Isle of Wight, Lancashire, Bishopsgate, Strawberry Field, and Penny Lane into songs that sounded at once Edwardian and of the moment, he was singing of Santa Fe, Wichita, Jacksonville, Pittsburgh, and Bourbon Street in a style so old it seemed new. Despite their radically different approaches, Dylan and the Beatles were after the same thing in 1967—singing for their people and telling their tales in songs that seemed to exist out of time.

"Penny Lane" had a slow climb to No. 1 on the U.S. charts; "Strawberry Fields Forever" would take even longer to reach its peak of No. 8. In the UK, this so-called "double A-side single" would become the first by the Beatles that failed to reach No. 1 since 1963.

The American TV host Dick Clark aired the promo films (still not called music videos) of the two songs on his pop music program, *American Bandstand*, and interviewed the young people in his audience after each one. "That was *great*," a teenage boy said after watching "Strawberry Fields Forever." The look on his face suggested the ecstasy of a music lover who has just experienced the full force of one of the century's greatest songs—but he would prove the exception. A girl said: "They look like somebody's grandfathers or something." The "Penny Lane" promo film triggered a similar reaction. "I thought it was weird," another girl said.

When that episode aired, the Beatles were still ensconced at EMI Studios, still working on *Sgt. Pepper's Lonely Hearts Club Band*. The *Life* magazine photographer Henry Grossman, who had gotten the shot of Dylan outside the Delmonico Hotel on the night he had met John, Paul, George, and Ringo in 1964, took pictures of the much-changed group for a story that would run in June. The reporter, Thomas Thompson, noted the "droopy French mustaches" and "bizarre clothing" of the Beatles while watching them record. Much to Brian Epstein's chagrin, McCartney told the reporter that he had taken acid. "If the politicians would take LSD, there wouldn't be any more war, or poverty, or famine," Paul said.

The Beatles had gotten deeper into the habit of assembling their songs piecemeal, with overdub after overdub, rather than playing as an ensemble, and George sometimes felt left out, especially after his first offering, the dour "Only a Northern Song," was deemed not up to the *Sgt. Pepper* standard. "I didn't really like making that album much," he said. "I'd just got back from India, and my heart was still out there." His only contribution as a songwriter was "Within You Without You," which he modeled after a Ravi Shankar piece. He was the sole Beatle to appear on the track, which relied on Indian musicians and London orchestral players.

All told, *Sgt. Pepper's Lonely Hearts Club Band* took about seven hundred hours of recording from November to April. The equally ambitious project undertaken by Dylan in the same period, with at least 115 songs recorded, would take about the same number of hours. This encyclopedic labor of love, which would become known as *The Basement Tapes*, wouldn't receive an official release until eight years later, when a portion of it formed a double album credited to Bob Dylan and the Band.

At the time of these homey sessions, no one outside Dylan's camp knew what he was up to—and yet he was arguably more popular than ever. With no new album in the offing, Columbia Records put out a collection of his most accessible songs under the title *Bob Dylan's Greatest Hits*. It would go on to be his bestselling album. More immediately, it made the Top 10 in the U.S. and reached No. 3 in the UK. The album was packaged with a souvenir—a poster created by the New York graphic artist Milton Glaser that would become a dorm-room fixture. It showed Dylan in profile, his face black, his hair a swirl of pink, purple, yellow, green, orange, red, and white, a burst of color meant to suggest the wild fecundity of his brain. That image helped place him within the hippie zeitgeist he had almost nothing to do with, now that he was a family man who spent much of his time making homespun music in a basement.

On a snowy day in May, he opened the front door of Hi Lo Ha to an uninvited visitor. It was Michael Iachetta, a young reporter from the New York *Daily News* who had lately been making phone calls to Dylan's friends and family members and accosting tight-lipped people in Woodstock. He was the first journalist to have found Dylan since he had disappeared from public view nine months earlier. Iachetta reported that he saw before him an "almost emaciated" figure with unkempt hair, a mustache, and a beard. Bob invited him inside. When he talked about the motorcycle accident that had altered the trajectory of his career, he slipped "almost into a trance," Iachetta wrote.

"The back wheel locked, I think," Dylan said. "I lost control, swerving from left to right. Next thing I know I was in some place I never heard of—Middletown, I think—with my face cut up, so I got some scars and my neck busted up pretty good. Just began movin' it around a month ago. New X-rays should be comin' through any day now."

His deal with Columbia Records was about to expire; Albert Grossman, whom Dylan had begun to suspect of taking more money than he deserved, was calling in offers from other labels. In the presence of the reporter, Dylan referred to his business troubles in cryptic terms and made no mention of his recent home recordings, saying only: "But songs are in my head like they always are. And they're not going to get written down until some things are evened up."

This new Dylan spoke softly. He seemed nothing like the person who had charged around the world in a haze of drugs and electricity the year before. And now he had something possessed by Greta Garbo and few other famous entertainers—an aura of mystery. "His royalties have made him a millionaire," Iachetta wrote, "yet he lives like a hermit and hasn't cut a record since his accident."

People these days may look at the cover of *Sgt. Pepper's Lonely Hearts Club Band* and make the assumption that a portrait of the Beatles was superimposed onto a collage of notable personages. That wasn't the case. Early in the spring of 1967, under the direction of the pop artist Peter Blake and the sculptor Jann Haworth, a team of assistants worked for eight days in a studio to create dozens of full-size cutouts of various people and arrange them in jumbled rows, just so. To round out the tableau, they added wax dummies depicting the Beatles as they had appeared in 1963, on loan from Madame Tussauds, as well as a rag doll wearing a sweater stitched with the words "Welcome the Rolling Stones" across the front.

When the painstakingly constructed pantheon was complete, it included representations of fifty-eight people held in high esteem by the Beatles and Blake, the great majority of them selected by John, Paul, George, and Ringo themselves. There were writers (Lewis Carroll, Oscar Wilde, Aldous Huxley), actors (Marlon Brando, Bette Davis, Mae West), comedians (Issy Bonn, Lenny Bruce, W. C. Fields), intellectuals (Albert Einstein, Carl Jung, Karl Marx), and gurus (Sri Mahavatar Babaji, Sri Yukteswar Giri, Sri Paramahansa Yogananda).

On March 30, John, Paul, George, and Ringo arrived for the shoot. They took in the life-size gallery and changed into the custom-made satin garments of their alter egos. The high-band collars, shoulder epaulets, decorative ropes, pleats, spats, and shiny buttons gave them the look of a town band of long ago, but the dazzling hues of green, pink, blue, and orange belonged to the current psychedelic moment.

When it was time for the picture to be taken, John, Paul, George, and Ringo stepped into the center of the frame, posing behind a big bass drum emblazoned with "Sgt Peppers Lonely Hearts Club Band" and a flower bed that included the word "Beatles" rendered in red hyacinths. To their right, the dummies of their former selves seemed to be in mourning. At their backs, their heroes stood watching over them. On the very top row, one person stood slightly taller than all the rest: Bob Dylan.

16 Everybody's Song

Jimi Hendrix, a swaggering Seattle-born musician who had apprenticed under the Isley Brothers and Little Richard, arrived in London and quickly unseated the British sensations Eric Clapton and Jeff Beck to become the new guitar god. On June 4, 1967, shortly after the release of *Sgt. Pepper's Lonely Hearts Club Band*, he signaled his approval of the Beatles' new direction by opening his show at the Saville Theatre with a howling rendition of the title song, much to the surprise of Paul and George, who were in the audience. Praise for the album also arrived from the other end of the musical spectrum, when the classical composer Ned Rorem likened Lennon-McCartney to Mozart and claimed that "She's Leaving Home," a ballad on side one, was "equal to any song that Schubert ever wrote."

Time reported that the Beatles had made pop into "something it has never been before: an art form" and credited them with "absorbing and extending Bob Dylan's folk-rock hybrid and sowing innovations of their own." In the *Partisan Review*, the literary scholar Richard Poirier wrote, "Listening to the *Sgt. Pepper* album, one thinks not simply of the history of popular music but of the history of this century." Like the author of the *Time* story, he included a comparison to the Beatles' American counterpart: "Only Dylan shows something equivalent to the Beatles in his combination of talents as a composer, lyricist, and performer."

A note of dissent was filed by Richard Goldstein, who had written so admiringly of *Blonde on Blonde* and *Revolver*. This much-hyped Beatles LP, he argued in *The New York Times*, was "dazzling but ultimately fraudulent." "Like an over-attended child," he wrote, "'Sergeant Pepper' is spoiled." That view would later gain influential adherents. In a 1979 reassessment, Greil Marcus called the album "a Day-Glo tombstone for its time"; in a 2011 book, the music historian Elijah Wald argued that, with *Sgt. Pepper*, the Beatles had destroyed rock 'n' roll with their pretentiousness and perfectionism.

At the time, though, it was the soundtrack of the so-called Summer of Love. It stayed at No. 1 for twenty-seven weeks in the UK and fifteen weeks in the U.S., and you could hear it everywhere, including Hi Lo Ha. Dylan would describe the album as "very indulgent" in a 1978 interview, but according to his mother, a frequent visitor to his home in the late sixties, he was a fan at the time. "He loves the Beatles, loved *Sgt. Pepper*," Beatty Zimmerman said.

Amid the accolades, John and Paul went right back to work, engaging in a friendly competition to see which one could write something appropriate for a historic program, the first live worldwide satellite telecast. Whatever they came up with would have to be simple and clear, a song for everybody, able to be fully absorbed on first listen.

John beat out Paul's "Hello, Goodbye" with "All You Need Is Love," a sing-along in which he assumed the mantle of spiritual instructor. On June 25, 400 million people around the world saw the Beatles play the song as the representatives of Great Britain. Along with another wide-eyed hit, "San Francisco (Be Sure to Wear Some Flowers in Your Hair)" by the American singer Scott McKenzie, "All You Need Is Love" became a hippie anthem. At the same time, McCartney's statements to *Life* on his use of LSD were making headlines. In follow-up interviews, he doubled down. "God is everything and everywhere and everyone," he said. "It just happened that I've realized all of this through acid, but it could have been through anything."

Amid the spiritual turn, Paul retained his work ethic, whipping his bandmates along their course of fusing past and present, classical and rock, Liverpool grit and London sophistication. He conceived the Beatles' next undertaking, the film *Magical Mystery Tour*, as a psychedelic account of a cheap bus-trip vacation taken by British workers to a surprise destination (typically, a faded seaside resort). There would be more trumpets, more cellos, more costumes.

While writing material for it, John, Paul, and George developed an interest in the teachings of Maharishi Mahesh Yogi, the founder of the Transcendental Meditation movement. Born Mahesh Prasad Varma in the 1910s, near Jabalpur, India, he was called "the giggling guru" thanks to his habit of laughing as he spoke. In late August, the Beatles left London by train to attend his ten-day seminar in Bangor, Wales. Upon their arrival, they delivered a new message to their flock: "LSD isn't a real answer," George told reporters; Paul seconded him, saying, "We were looking for something more natural. This is it."

After the Maharish had given each Beatle a mantra to focus on during meditation, Brian Epstein was found dead at his home in Belgravia, London. The cause was an accidental overdose of sleeping pills, investigators said. Paul was already on a train back to the capital when the others faced the press. "Meditation gives you confidence to withstand something like this, even the short amount we've had," John said. George went further: "There's no such thing as death, anyway. I mean, it's death on a physical level, but life goes on everywhere."

The Beatles kept at their new project, which would include "I Am the Walrus," a track as sonically maximalist as anything else in their catalogue. The inspiration was a fan letter from a student in Liverpool, who wrote that a literature teacher at Quarry Bank High School was playing Beatles songs in class and offering his interpretations of the symbolism contained therein. John was aghast—the same institution where he had been caned was now holding him up as a poet! He started with his own variation on a rude Liverpool schoolyard chant: "Yellow matter custard, green slop pie / All mixed together with a dead dog's eye." From there, with Pete Shotton serving as amanuensis, he strung together one analysis-defying line after another. "Let the fuckers work *that* one out, Pete!" he said.

For inspiration, he once again turned to Dylan—the surrealist Dylan of 1964 to 1966, rather than the reformist Dylan, whose down-home songs had yet to reach the public. "Dylan got away with murder," Lennon said. "I thought, Well, I can write this crap, too. You know, just stick a few images together, thread them together, and you call it poetry." If his goal was to cough up mere gibberish, he failed. "I Am the Walrus" was a peculiar classic with the power to delight children and frighten adults. George Martin got into the spirit of the thing—those eerie cellos, those late-night radio voices—to help render it an aural depiction of alienation.

The lyrics also reflected the Maharishi's teachings, while expanding on a theme at the heart of earlier Lennon compositions—the illusoriness of the world. "Nothing is real," the key phrase of "Strawberry Fields Forever," had given way to the opening statement of his new song: "I am he as you are he." That was a variation of a saying in the collection of Hindu texts known as the Upanishads: "I am That, Thou art That." There was, in other words, no distinction between the personal and the universal. All was one.

John followed this thread to "Across the Universe," a song in which he included the name of the Maharishi's teacher, Guru Dev, and all four Beatles became regular visitors to the Maharishi's large apartment in South Kensington. If they wanted to advance, he told them, they would have to spend a few months at his ashram in India.

■ ■ ■

Dylan was still deep in retirement—or so it seemed to the outside world. He reached a new deal with Columbia Records in the summer of 1967, but had no desire to go into a studio and record cleaned-up versions of the songs he had made in such homey circumstances. Grossman shopped his new material around, hoping for hit versions by the reliable Dylan interpreters Manfred Mann and the Byrds. He also sent it to that new force on the scene, Jimi Hendrix, who had lately been playing "Like a Rolling Stone" in concert.

In November, Nick Jones of *Melody Maker* reported on the existence of "seven secret tapes." "Dylan is sounding beautiful," he wrote. He added that the songs were much different from Dylan's earlier work: "I mean, you hear these tracks and say, 'Wow, they're weird.'"

While recording almost daily with the still-unnamed band, Dylan wrote twelve songs that he kept to himself, among them "All Along the Watchtower" and "John Wesley Harding." These were stately compositions, filled with biblical references and archaic diction. They had no choruses. They had no bridges. Some were as clear as water, bringing to mind Woody Guthrie or Hank Williams. Others were as mysterious as the most head-scratching parables or koans.

On October 3, 1967, Woody Guthrie died at age fifty-five after years of suffering from Huntington's chorea. Dylan called Guthrie's manager, Harold Leventhal, to let him know he would like to take part in any memorial concert that might be planned. Then, with his latest songs fixed in his mind, he went to Nashville. Across three efficient sessions, he spent a mere nine hours recording them in bare-bones fashion. He was backed by two of the musicians who had accompanied him on *Blonde on Blonde*, Kenny Buttrey on drums and Charlie McCoy on bass, with Pete Drake joining on pedal steel guitar for two songs. In contrast with how he had comported himself on his last visit to Studio A, Dylan did not keep anyone waiting. That would have been inconsiderate.

For the album cover, he requested something that looked like a snapshot in a family scrapbook. On a December day, John Berg, a Columbia Records designer, took some pictures with a black-and-white Polaroid in the Grossmans' garden as Dylan posed with his friend Purna Das to his right, Lakhsman Das to his left, and Charlie Joy, a carpenter and stonemason, slightly behind him. A thick old pine with gnarled bark stood in the background.

Mindful of the hullabaloo surrounding *Sgt. Pepper*, Dylan wanted the new record to appear in stores unannounced. "I asked Columbia to release it with no publicity and no hype, because this was the season of hype," he said. He also informed the label that there would be no single and no tour. Because of the lack of fanfare, there is dispute to this day on whether *John Wesley Harding* came out in the last week of 1967 or the first week of 1968. Whichever it was, Dylan made his return to the public sphere at a time when the Beatles were once again inescapable on the radio, thanks to their latest No. 1, the brisk, melodious "Hello, Goodbye."

Despite yet another chart success, the Beatles found themselves on the defensive: *Magical Mystery Tour* had gotten a vicious reception when it was broadcast on BBC Television on Boxing Day. "Rubbish," "boring," and "appalling," were some of the adjectives that popped up in the papers. "Aren't we entitled to have a flop?" McCartney said in a damage-control interview.

The understated *John Wesley Harding* perplexed as many fans and critics as it pleased. It sold well, though—more than 250,000 copies in its first week. Dylan seemed unsure what to make of it. He would say he had tried to capture the pleasurable sound achieved on recent records by the Canadian singer Gordon Lightfoot, only to find he couldn't pull it off. Ralph J. Gleason had a more forgiving view. In *Rolling Stone*, a new magazine dedicated to rock, he described *John Wesley Harding* as a "loving collection of myths, prophecies, allegories, love songs, and good tidings."

Gleason was one of many thoughtful critics who seemed unable to write about Dylan or the Beatles without comparing one to the other: "The point about Dylan's work, and it's a point that really applies only to the Beatles and Dylan, is that the more you listen to the music, the more bits and pieces and thoughts and fragments float up," he wrote. Robert Christgau argued in *Esquire* that *John Wesley Harding* was a reply to *Sgt. Pepper*. Dylan, he wrote, was countering the Beatles' baroqueism by distilling his music to its essence. He called the album "admirable in its straightforwardness" before returning to the Beatles in his conclusion: "This is not a better record than *Sgt. Pepper*, but it should have a better effect."

Rolling Stone continued tying *John Wesley Harding* to *Sgt. Pepper* in a fanciful story headlined "Dylan Record Puts Beatles up a Tree."

Just as the Beatles had put Dylan on their album cover, the article reported, Dylan had sneaked images of John, Paul, George, and Ringo into the bark of the tree that appeared on the front of his. "The faces are very small and almost indistinguishable; however, learned observers say that at least four of them are the Beatles." When the reporter asked John Berg, who had taken the photo, about the faces, he "acknowledged their presence but was reluctant to talk about it." Asked about it many years later, Berg said, "I mean, if you wanted to see it, you saw it. I was just as amazed as anyone else."

Just as he had done with *Sgt. Pepper*, Jimi Hendrix expressed his admiration for *John Wesley Harding* by putting his own spin on one of its tracks. His version of "All Along the Watchtower," vigorous and inventive, brought the song's rage and restlessness to the surface, and Dylan would come to think of it as the definitive interpretation. It became a hit and a standout track on the Jimi Hendrix Experience album *Electric Ladyland*.

Dylan showed the world he still had the old fire when he took the stage for the afternoon and evening shows of the Woody Guthrie tribute at Carnegie Hall on January 20, 1968, as part of a bill that included Joan Baez, Ramblin' Jack Elliott, Richie Havens, Odetta, Tom Paxton, and Pete Seeger. These were Dylan's first public performances since he had faced down the hostile crowds at the Albert Hall nearly two years earlier. He was backed by his usual band, now calling itself the Crackers; Levon Helm, having returned to the fold, was back on drums. Dylan strummed an acoustic guitar as he led the musicians through three lesser-known Guthrie songs, "Grand Coulee Dam," "Dear Mrs. Roosevelt," and "I Ain't Got No Home." A chant of "We want Dylan!" rose from the seats at the end of the night.

Newsweek reported that *John Wesley Harding* had sold more than any previous Dylan album, "eclipsing the Rolling Stones and challenging the front-running Beatles." When Dylan explained his new songwriting mode, he made it sound like the service-minded approach of Guthrie or Purna Das: "I used to think that myself and my songs were the same thing. But I don't believe that anymore. There's myself and there's my song, which I hope is everybody's song."

That certainly applied to "The Mighty Quinn," which appealed to millions of listeners young and old through a version by Manfred Mann. Critics liked it, too. In yet another Dylan-Beatles comparison, *Melody Maker* called it "a pure nonsense song, with much of the cheerful insanity of 'I Am the Walrus.'"

■   ■   ■

On February 14, 1968, the day that "The Mighty Quinn" reached No. 1 in the UK, Mal Evans, weighed down by Lennon's and Harrison's luggage, flew to Delhi. John, Paul, George, and Ringo, along with Cynthia Lennon, Jane Asher, Pattie Harrison, and Maureen Starkey, soon joined him at the Maharishi's ashram in Rishikesh for an extended stay. They arrived with "baggage enough to sink a battleship," according to Cynthia. Among the clothes and toiletries stuffed into their trunks, they had brought along *Blonde on Blonde* and *John Wesley Harding*.

In their own grand and busy fashion, the Beatles were in pursuit of the same peace of mind Dylan was seeking as a simple family man in Bearsville. As the rainy season gave way to sunshine, they found themselves sequestered from the distractions of fame. Other initiates on the fourteen-acre campus included Pattie's sister, Jenny Boyd; the twenty-three-year-old film actress Mia Farrow, who was separated from her fifty-two-year-old husband, Frank Sinatra; her twenty-year-old sister, Prudence Farrow; Mike Love of the Beach Boys; and Donovan. Between lectures and meditation sessions, against a backdrop of chattering monkeys and cawing crows, John, Paul, and George came up with the majority of the thirty songs that would appear on the ambitious double album *The Beatles* (known as the White Album because of its plain white cover), as well as many others that would come out later. In this great outpouring, all three songwriting Beatles wrote songs influenced by Dylan.

For Harrison, it was "Long, Long, Long," the first of his many devotional songs in which "you" may stand for a woman or God. Its chord progression and some of its melody arose from the epic that took up an entire side of *Blonde on Blonde*: "I can't recall much about it except the chords, which I think were coming from 'Sad-Eyed Lady of the Lowlands,'" George said. "D to E minor, A and D—those three chords and the way they moved." The musicologist Walter Everett wrote that "Long, Long, Long" was "as close as the Beatles ever came to plagiarism." "Rocky Raccoon," the tale of a would-be gunslinger in South Dakota, was McCartney's spoof of the Western ballads on *John Wesley Harding*. "Bob Dylan was doing that kind of thing," Paul said, "so I just started imagining the Black Hills in South Dakota."

Lennon's "Yer Blues" contained a shout-out to Dylan in a reference to "Ballad of a Thin Man" at the song's climax: "Feel so suicidal, just like Dylan's Mr. Jones!" It also had the naked candor of certain songs Dylan had written before he started seeing himself as a poet of the people. "The funny thing about the camp was that, although it was very beautiful and I was meditating about eight hours a day, I was writing the most miserable songs on earth," John said. "In 'Yer Blues,' when I wrote, 'I'm so lonely I want to die,' I'm not kidding." In another song he came up with at the ashram, the tender "Julia," he made a connection between Julia, his mother, and Yoko Ono, whom he had seen a few times since meeting her in 1966. Now he couldn't stop his brain from thinking about her, which gave him insomnia and "I'm So Tired."

While John was writing and meditating in Rishikesh, Yoko was hanging out with the experimental jazz musician Ornette Coleman in Paris. At a party there, she sniffed heroin for the first time. Back in London, where she was living with her second husband, the American artist Tony Cox, and their daughter, Kyoko, she joined Coleman on the stage of the Albert Hall. With her moans, yelps, and screeches, Yoko led his band through an improvised show. Coleman respected her musicianship and would perform with her many times in the years to come. In addition to being a creator of installations and performance pieces, Ono was a classically trained pianist who had studied composition at Sarah Lawrence College in Bronxville, New York.

Aside from their shared interest in music, John and Yoko had something elemental in common: They were both idealists. Not in the sense that they had a rosy view of life, but in the literal sense.

Both believed that ideas themselves were greater than reality; or perhaps it's more accurate to say they saw the world as a construct built on our perceptions.

John said in interviews that he had developed the sense that "nothing is real" in the dreamier moments of his childhood; Yoko's idealism was also rooted in her early years, when the war waylaid her privileged existence as the daughter of a Tokyo financier. "I remember, when we were evacuated during the war, my brother was really unhappy and depressed, and really hungry, because we did not have very much food," she said. "So I said, 'OK, let's make a menu together. What kind of dinner would you like?' And he said, 'Ice cream.' So I said, 'Good, let's imagine our ice-cream dinner.' And we did, and he started to look happy. . . . So we had our conceptual dinner, and this is maybe my first piece of art." *Grapefruit*, her 1964 collection of verse, comprised poems written in the same spirit, many beginning with the word "imagine."

In a postcard Yoko sent to John at Rishikesh, she again blurred the lines separating the outer and inner worlds: "I am a cloud. Look for me in the sky." Lennon would carry this notion forward in "Revolution," which he started in Rishikesh. True revolution, he argued, took place in the head, not in the streets; those seeking to overturn the system should "free" their minds, instead of using violence to achieve their aims.

Ringo and Maureen left the ashram after ten days. Paul and Jane stuck it out four weeks. The other two Beatles and their wives stayed on into April, when John turned against the Maharishi, claiming he had made inappropriate advances on at least one young woman, an accusation that would never be substantiated. In a late-night meeting, he roused others against him. Cynthia didn't go along with it. "The Maharishi had been accused and sentenced before he had even a chance to defend himself," she recalled.

With Epstein gone, the Beatles had started Apple Corps, a company that included a record label, an electronics arm, and a clothing store.

It was also meant as a haven for artists looking for their big breaks. In May 1968, a month after the Beatles' Rishikesh adventure had come to a close, Lennon and McCartney went to New York to promote it. "If you come and see me and say, 'I've had such-and-such a dream,' I'll say, 'Here's so much money, go away and do it,'" Paul said.

They stayed at the Upper East Side apartment of Nat Weiss, the lawyer who had been close with Epstein and handled some of the Beatles' business dealings. Weiss's friend the photographer Linda Eastman stopped by in the afternoons. She had met Paul the year before, when she was among the journalists at the *Sgt. Pepper* rollout, and they picked up where they had left off. They would have spent more time together if she didn't have to care for her five-year-old daughter from her first marriage, which had ended in divorce, at her apartment ten blocks away. Although Paul was now engaged to Jane, he felt drawn to Linda—she was attractive, she was a good mom, she knew about rock 'n' roll, and she liked pot as much as he did. And she wasn't after his money, since her father was a wealthy New York lawyer. Paul would soon find himself navigating a series of romantic complications worthy of a French farce.

Nina Tornabene of the Bronx, a sixteen-year-old Beatles fan who was camped outside Weiss's building, made contact with Paul when he stepped out of a limousine. She handed him a copy of a new album she thought he would like. It was *God Bless Tiny Tim*.

Earlier in the year, Tiny Tim had finally started winning fans outside his cult when he appeared on a new sketch comedy show on NBC, *Rowan & Martin's Laugh-In*. That led to a record deal and sessions in Los Angeles with some of the studio pros who had played on the Byrds' cover of "Mr. Tambourine Man." In a review for *Life*, Al Aronowitz, the writer who had introduced Dylan to the Beatles, called *God Bless Tiny Tim* "one of the most dazzling albums of programmed entertainment to come along since the Beatles introduced that new genre with *Sgt. Pepper's Lonely Hearts Club Band*." Paul and John loved it, too. When they got home, Tiny Tim's single, "Tiptoe Through the Tulips," a remake of a 1929 hit, was climbing the charts, and the two Beatles promoted it while appearing on a BBC Radio 1 show.

"Play Tiny Tim!" John said. "He's the greatest ever, man!"

"It's a funny joke at first," Paul said, "but it's not, really. It's real and it's true."

By this time, the Lennons' marriage was wobbling. John had told Cynthia the truth about what life was like for a Beatle on the road, while also confessing to some of his more local affairs, and she had left Kenwood with Julian on a trip to Greece. Alone in the big house, except for the many cats who roamed from room to room, John invited Yoko over.

"I was always shy with her, and she was shy, so instead of making love, we went upstairs and made tapes," he recalled. "I had this room full of different tapes where I would write and make strange loops and things for Beatles stuff. So we made tapes all night. She was doing her funny voices and getting sound effects. And then as the sun rose we made love." In the legend that John and Yoko would build around their romance, this was their first night together.

They were relaxing in the sunroom of Kenwood when Cynthia and Julian returned. "They looked so right together, so naturally self-composed under the circumstances," Cynthia recalled. "I felt totally superfluous." John and Cynthia separated shortly afterward; John and Yoko started attending events together in London.

Feeling sympathy for Cynthia and Julian, Paul decided to pay them a visit. On the drive from London to Weybridge, he felt the first rumblings of a song he would write to console the boy. "I started with the idea 'Hey Jules,' which was Julian," he said.

He brought it to fruition while working on a side project—writing, arranging, and producing an instrumental theme for *Thingumybob*, a comedy show scheduled to make its debut that fall on a regional network, Yorkshire Television. Even after all the trumpets and tubas of *Sgt. Pepper* and *Magical Mystery Tour*, he still craved that brass-band sound, and he wrote the TV theme especially for the Black Dyke Mills Band, a traditional group that would have been right at home on a northern bandstand in 1910.

Serving as conductor, Paul led the band through "Thingumybob" and "Yellow Submarine" before a happy throng in a town square of Bradford, a city in West Yorkshire. From there, he and his small entourage—which included the Beatles aides Tony Bramwell and Derek Taylor, and Paul's sheepdog, Martha—veered off the recently completed M1 motorway and followed narrow roads in search of a proper English pub. They found it in the village of Harrold. Paul didn't need any coaxing to sit at the piano and lead everyone in a sing-along of Beatles hits. He also gave "Hey Jude" its debut. The night ended at the home of the village dentist, who served meat and rice at 3 a.m.

The Beatles selected "Hey Jude" as their next single. Lennon considered it McCartney's finest work, musically and otherwise. "'Hey Jude' is a damn good set of lyrics," he said, "and I made no contribution to that." His opinion was partly rooted in his interpretation of the words: He felt that, while Paul may have started the song with Julian in mind, it was actually his way of expressing his approval of John's relationship with Yoko; Lennon also believed it had something to do with Francie Schwartz, a young American writer whom Paul was seeing as his relationship with Jane Asher was falling apart and he was growing more interested in Linda Eastman. "If you think about it," John said, "Yoko's just come into the picture. He's saying, 'Hey, Jude—Hey, John.' I mean, so I'm sounding like one of those fans that's writing things into it, but you can hear it as a song to me, although it's also a song about him and Frannie Schwartz, at the time, too. . . . And 'go out and get her,' you know, forget everything else. So, subconsciously, I take it he was saying, 'Go ahead.'"

So which was it—a song of consolation for a five-year-old boy, or a song of encouragement for the man who had abandoned him? This was one of McCartney's gifts, the ability to come up with words open-ended enough to justify contradictory interpretations.

Over four days of recording, with the help of a mighty orchestra, the Beatles made "Hey Jude" into a seven-minute, eleven-second epic. The only obstacle to capturing its full power took place early on, when Paul admonished George for tossing in blues licks throughout the first verse. In McCartney's conception, the song had to build gradually to a thunderous finish, an effect that would be spoiled if the accompaniment were busy at the outset. George gave in, though he felt insulted. Was he now nothing but McCartney's sideman?

The finale of "Hey Jude," with its endless chorus of "na, na, na, na-na-na-na," brought together two sides of Paul, his inner rocker and his inner seeker. It echoed "Land of a Thousand Dances," a good-time rhythm and blues record with a "na, na-na-na-na" refrain that had recently been a hit for Cannibal and the Headhunters and Wilson Pickett. But it was just as much informed by Rishikesh. "Na na" was the mantra Paul gave to the world. Those nonsense syllables helped make the song as trance-inducing as the deepest meditation session.

"Hey Jude" would go on to be the Beatles' top-selling single. Like "Over the Rainbow," "This Land Is Your Land," "Blowin' in the Wind," and Paul's own "Yesterday," it was everybody's song.

■ ■ ■

During the making of the "Hey Jude" promo film at Twickenham Studios, the Beatles and three hundred audience members were swept up in the song's rhapsodic spirit. For John, Paul, George, and Ringo, it was a rare moment of happiness in a summer of tension. "They had come back from their trip to India completely different people," Geoff Emerick, the engineer at EMI Studios, recalled. "They had once been fastidious and fashionable; now they were scruffy and unkempt. They had once been witty and full of humor; now they were solemn and prickly. They had once bonded together as life-long friends; now they resented one another's company."

Before settling in at Abbey Road, the Beatles made home recordings, together and separately, of twenty-seven songs they had written in recent months. Of these, nineteen would make it onto the White Album. There were seven by Paul, including the Dylan-inspired "Rocky Raccoon," the Beach Boys takeoff "Back in the U.S.S.R.," and a retro number very much in the Tiny Tim style, "Honey Pie"; two songs in his batch, "Teddy Boy" and "Junk," would never make it onto a Beatles album. John had fifteen, including "Revolution," "Glass Onion," and "Dear Prudence" (written with help from an uncredited George); thirteen of these would find places on the White Album or the group's later LPs. George made demos of five songs; three would be rejected—and he felt his bandmates were iffy on one that would be deemed a keeper, "While My Guitar Gently Weeps."

Emerick and George Martin found the Beatles high-handed and occasionally rude during the White Album sessions, which started at the end of May and went deep into October. They were also put off by the daily presence of John's sidekick, Yoko Ono. "If he went into the toilet," Emerick recalled, "she'd walk him down the hall and wait outside, hunched down on the floor."

Lennon's drug regimen was changing: Heroin replaced LSD. He ingested it with Yoko, always snorting it, never injecting it, or so they would say in interviews, citing a fear of needles. "John was very curious," Yoko said. " . . . I told him that while he was in India with the Maharishi, I had a sniff of it in a party situation. I didn't know what it was. They just gave me something and I said, 'What is *that*?' It was a beautiful feeling. John was talking about heroin one day and he said, 'Did you ever take it?,' and I told him about Paris. . . . So I think maybe because I said it wasn't a bad experience, that had something to do with John taking it."

John and Yoko were now living in a ground-floor flat that Ringo had leased on Montagu Square in Marylebone. Keith Richards, an experienced heroin user at twenty-four, wasn't impressed by Lennon's tolerance. "John would inevitably end up in my john, hugging the porcelain," Richards recalled. "And there'd be Yoko in the background—'He really shouldn't do this.' And I'd go, 'I know, but I didn't force him!'" McCartney, who had tried the drug at the time of *Sgt. Pepper*, only to decide it wasn't for him, felt squeamish when heroin references popped up in Beatles songs: "I need a fix 'cause I'm going down," John sang on "Happiness Is a Warm Gun."

Emerick left EMI Studios two months into the making of the White Album. Martin absented himself from the sessions for much of September. Even Ringo got fed up. He stormed out one day and left the country with Maureen to join the actor Peter Sellers in Sardinia. "From what I heard him telling Sellers on the yacht, Paul wanted a certain drum pattern on a song and Richy was just fed up with his coaching him too much," his wife said. In his absence, the Beatles recorded "Dear Prudence" and "Back in the U.S.S.R.," with Paul on drums.

The album was turning out to be a collection of songs in disparate styles, from the rooty-toot "Honey Pie" to the proto-metal of "Helter Skelter"; from the country-accented "Don't Pass Me By," the first Beatles track written by Ringo, to the avant-garde "Revolution 9," a sound collage credited to Lennon-McCartney that was really the work of Lennon, Ono, and Harrison. Although the Beatles went for a hard sound on many songs, the White Album was by no means a stripped-down rock record. They assembled "Dear Prudence," for instance, from dozens of takes, drawing on the know-how they had gained since "Tomorrow Never Knows." Even the lightweight "Ob-La-Di, Ob-La-Da" required forty-two hours of labor.

For George, the White Album was a trial. He objected to Yoko's presence and felt slighted when the others avoided his songs. He was also disappointed by their handling of "While My Guitar Gently Weeps," though the Beatles recorded forty takes. "I worked on that song with John, Paul, and Ringo one day, and they were not interested in it at all," he said. The group was finally able to get it into shape when George brought in Eric Clapton to play lead guitar. "It helped," he said, "because the others would have to control themselves a bit more. John and Paul, mainly. Because they had to, you know, act more *handsomely*."

George would receive a more welcoming reception a week after the album was released, when he went to Bearsville.

■   ■   ■

Dylan felt distant from the demonstrations rippling across the U.S. in response to the assassination of Martin Luther King Jr. and the military escalation in Vietnam. "Outside of my family, nothing held any real interest for me and I was seeing things through different glasses," he wrote in *Chronicles: Volume One*. He began spending his mornings painting with a neighbor, Bruce Dorfman, an accomplished artist, in his boxlike studio in the trees. Dylan tried to copy

Jan Vermeer's *Girl with a Flute*, but didn't make much progress until he used Marc Chagall as a model. The quiet days with Dorfman were interrupted when he learned his father had died suddenly at age fifty-six. On June 5, Dylan flew to Minnesota for the memorial service. Afterward, his mother joined him at Hi Lo Ha for an extended stay.

Beatty Zimmerman heartily approved of her son's household, which included four children in the summer of 1968. In an interview, she mentioned Bob's "devotion" to his family and his "regulated" routine. He woke at six every morning, read until ten, played with the children, and went to bed at nine each night. "In his house in Woodstock today," she said, "there's a huge Bible open on a stand in the middle of his study. Of all the books that crowd his house, *overflow* his house, that Bible gets the most attention."

Dylan noted his interest in the biblical parables to two friends, the folk musicians John Cohen and Happy Traum, during their interview of him that summer for *Sing Out!* magazine.

"When did you read the Bible parables?" Cohen asked.

"I have always read the Bible," Bob said, "though not necessarily always the parables."

"I don't think you're the kind who goes to the hotel, where the Gideons leave a Bible, and you pick it up," Cohen said.

"Well, you never know."

Asked about the Beatles, Dylan said: "Well, what they do . . . they work much more with the studio equipment, they take advantage of the new sound inventions of the past year or two. Whereas I don't know anything about it. I just do the songs, and sing them, and that's all."

He also mentioned a friend, a painter, whom he described as "all for" U.S. involvement in Vietnam: "He's just about ready to go over there himself. And I can comprehend him."

"My feeling," Traum said, "is that with a person who is for the war and ready to go over there, I don't think it would be possible for you and him to share the same basic values."

"He's a gentleman and I admire him," Bob said. "He's a friend of mine. People just have their views. Anyway, how do you know I'm not, as you say, 'for the war'?"

The musicians who had been playing with Dylan signed a management contract with Grossman and secured a deal with Capitol Records. After having played behind Ronnie Hawkins, Bob Dylan, and Tiny Tim, they started recording under their own steam. Once the sessions were done, they picked a name for themselves as unassuming as their music: the Band.

The debut album, *Music from Big Pink*, was hailed upon its release that summer as a refreshing change from the bombastic rock coming out of London and San Francisco. Its eleven songs, four written by Robbie Robertson and three by Richard Manuel, were at once casual and refined, and about as trendy as a patch of moss. The track chosen as the single, "The Weight," written by Robertson and sung by Levon Helm, would go on to be a classic after stalling out at No. 58 on the *Billboard* chart. The collection otherwise included a new Dylan song, "I Shall Be Released," and the collaborations "Tears of Rage" (Dylan-Manuel) and "This Wheel's on Fire" (Dylan-Danko). Dylan himself didn't play or sing on the album, but one of his paintings, in the Chagall style, was used as its cover.

The pictures on the gatefold sleeve of *Music from Big Pink*, taken by Elliott Landy, a photographer in his mid-twenties who had recently left New York City for Woodstock, suggested a critique of the let-it-all-hang-out youth movement that seemed to be taking over the world. In a black-and-white portrait, there stood the five members of the Band, with their short hair, dark clothing, and sober expressions. That picture appeared next to a color photo in which they posed by a red barn with family members and friends, a group that included little kids and white-haired elders. "It came out looking like we were rebelling against the rebellion," Robbie said.

Music from Big Pink made many musicians and songwriters think twice. Eric Clapton, for one, felt suddenly sheepish about what he was doing and decided to put an end to his trio, Cream, which was known for its exploratory jams. As the cultural winds shifted, Lennon expressed regret for *Sgt. Pepper* and *Magical Mystery Tour*. "We got a bit pretentious," he said toward the end of the White Album sessions. "Like everybody, we had our phase, and now it's a little changeover, trying to be more natural." In the same interview he compared the Beatles' recent evolution to Dylan's embrace of simplicity on *John Wesley Harding*. "Dylan broke his neck, and we went to India," John said. "Everybody did their bit. And now we're all just coming out, coming out of a shell, in a new way, kind of saying: Remember what it was like to play."

In 2025, Paul named *Music from Big Pink* one of his three favorite albums of all time. The Band's debut was also a revelation for George, and its songs were in his head when he made his escape from the White Album sessions in the fall of 1968, flying to California with Pattie and Mal Evans. They took up residence at a rented house in Beverly Hills. George spent the days at a studio on Sunset Boulevard, producing an album for Jackie Lomax, a Liverpool rocker signed to Apple. At night, the place was filled with friends—among them Clapton, Cass Elliot of the Mamas & the Papas, and Robbie Robertson, who invited George to stop by Woodstock on his way back to England.

The White Album came out November 22. Despite some critical carping about its sprawling eclecticism, it was a smash, selling more than any other double album. A few days after it appeared in stores, George, Pattie, and Mal arrived in the Catskills and settled into the Bearsville compound of Albert and Sally Grossman.

Dylan was painting with his friend Bruce Dorfman when a car rolled past. "Bob got himself all excited and said, 'That must be George—he's taken the wrong road,'" the artist recalled. "He was absolutely awestruck." Bob put down his brush and abruptly left the studio.

If he was excited to see George, he didn't show it at first. "Bob was an odd person," Pattie said. "God, it was absolute agony. He just wouldn't talk." George noticed the same thing. "He hardly said a word for a couple of days," he recalled. "Anyway, we finally got the guitars out, and it loosened things up a bit. It was really a nice time, with the kids all around."

Bob sang "I Threw It All Away," a song of heartbreak and regret he had yet to record. It was simple and direct. He was sticking with the aim he had mentioned earlier that year, to write "everybody's song." If that meant risking a cliché along the way—"Love is all there is / It makes the world go 'round" was a couplet in this new one—so be it. George loved what he heard, but sensed it might disappoint those who yearned for the finger-pointing moralist of *The Times They Are A-Changin'* or the tortured romantic of *Blonde on Blonde*. "I know people are going to think, 'Shit, what's Dylan doing?'" he said.

When Bob had written with Manuel and Danko, he had handed over lyrics and asked them to come up with melodies. With George, he engaged in something new, a face-to-face collaboration. It started with Dylan praising Harrison's facility with guitar chords. "Come on," George said, "write me some words." And Bob started "scribbling words down," Harrison recalled.

The most fully formed result of their work was "I'd Have You Anytime." "And it just killed me," George said, "because he'd been doing all these sensational lyrics. And he wrote: 'All I have is yours / All you see is mine / And I'm glad to hold you in my arms / I'd have you anytime.'" They taped themselves singing their song in Everly Brothers–style harmony.

George and Bob also came up with "Maureen," which they didn't manage to complete. It started with Harrison playing the chords to "Thingumybob," the theme Paul had written for the Black Dyke Mills Band, which had recently come out as the first Apple single. The progression was tricky, with a C-sharp seventh and an F-sharp minor. Ringo must have come up in conversation as they played it, given their decision to make the lyrics a tribute to his wife. A finished version of "Maureen" would have been something unique—a McCartney-Harrison-Dylan composition.

George was enjoying making music again and gaining confidence in his own abilities. John and Paul had seemingly looked down on him for so long—and now the man hailed as the world's greatest songwriter was only too happy to write with him. Bob let George in some more by discussing his troubles with his manager and showing him the latest cut of his 1966 tour film, which, long after it had been shelved as a television special, was becoming an avant-garde anti-documentary called *Eat the Document*.

On Thanksgiving at Hi Lo Ha, Sara served turkey with the traditional side dishes to a gathering that included George, Pattie, Mal, the brothers Happy and Artie Traum, and the author Mason Hoffenberg. Bruce Dorfman, the painter, was there, too—until he grew so annoyed with the deference everyone was showing Dylan that he walked out. Tensions eased when there was a knock at the door "and in walked five guys looking like they had just stepped out of a nineteenth-century daguerreotype," Happy Traum recalled. It was the Band. Richard Manuel sat at the piano and led everyone through "I Shall Be Released."

Before his departure, Harrison wrote "All Things Must Pass," an elegy-in-advance for the passing of the Beatles and the sixties. Although it sounded as if it might have been inspired by "I Shall Be Released," George would say he had modeled it after Band's "The Weight." "It had a religious and a country feeling to it," he said, "and I wanted that." "All Things Must Pass" was hugely important for George, a declaration of artistic independence that would mark the end of his reliance on the band he had been with since age fifteen, and it's no coincidence that it came to him while he was in the glow of Dylan's approval.

By the time he left Bearsville, he was a changed person. "Writing and playing with Bob definitely gave him an extra sense of validation," Pattie said. To show his appreciation, George gave Dylan his prize Gibson J-200, an acoustic guitar made of maple, with a sunburst finish and a floral motif on the pickguard.

In the quiet after the visitors were gone, Bob felt bad about having left his friend Bruce Dorfman so abruptly a few days earlier. He asked Sara to convey his apologies and then rejoined him in the boxlike studio, taking up his usual position at his easel in the corner.

George, Pattie, and Mal made their way to Nat Weiss's apartment in Manhattan, where they took care of some Beatle business: making a recording of Tiny Tim doing a song for the group's annual Christmastime flexi disc for Beatles Fan Club members.

Like Lennon, McCartney, and Dylan, Harrison was a big fan of this most unlikely pop sensation of 1968. At a concert at the

Royal Albert Hall in October, Tiny Tim had earned ovations for his falsetto-and-ukulele renditions of Dylan's "Like a Rolling Stone" and the Beatles' "Nowhere Man." At Weiss's apartment, he reprised his bracing version of "Nowhere Man," strumming his uke and pitching his voice an octave higher than Lennon's on the original.

"Thank you, Tiny!" George said. "God bless you."

Back in England, Harrison wrote to Dylan: "Thank you and Sarah and children for being so good to us in Woodstock, it was really beautiful being with you and I hope we shall meet sometime again during this incarnation." Then, thinking of the song they hadn't quite brought to completion, he sent a quick follow-up letter, just in case Bob wanted to return to it.

> Dear Bobbie,
> THINGYMUBOB is Maureen—E to /C#7/F#m Am/to E the middle was E for 4 beats A flat for 4 beats C#m 4 beats to B7
> And I'm glad to hold you in my arms I'd have you anytime
> Love to you all
> George

17   Beatles & Co.

George wasn't the only Beatle seeking his independence in the wake of the White Album sessions. In interviews, Ringo spoke of becoming a real film actor, one who fully inhabits a character. He also started writing a song, "Octopus's Garden," while vacationing in Sardinia with Maureen and their two children.

Paul followed his splits with Jane Asher and Francie Schwartz by inviting Linda Eastman and her five-year-old daughter, Heather, to stay at his house on Cavendish Avenue. He took them to meet the family in Liverpool and then to High Park Farm, his 183-acre property in Kintyre, Scotland. Linda and Heather had a good time, despite the lack of heat in the stone house. Paul was happy to have an instant family and even happier when Linda told him she was pregnant.

John was going through a difficult period. In October, a squadron led by Sergeant Norman Pilcher, an antidrug zealot hell-bent on busting rock stars, raided the Montagu Square flat where he and Yoko were staying. With the aid of two drug-sniffing dogs, the police turned up 219 grains of cannabis resin. They arrested John and Yoko and marched them through a gauntlet of photographers outside a police station. A month later, Yoko suffered a miscarriage; John was at her side during her stay at Queen Charlotte's hospital, sleeping on the floor for much of the night. A week after that, at Marylebone Magistrates' Court, John took the rap, pleading guilty to possession of cannabis. He was fined 150 pounds.

As 1968 drew to a close, with the White Album at No. 1, the Beatles had a hard time settling on what to do next. One thing they agreed on was that they no longer wanted to be thought of as a band that relied on studio production. In November, Apple announced that the Beatles would return to live performance with three shows in December at the Roundhouse, a club in Chalk Farm, London, only to follow up with a statement that the concerts would be postponed to January at a venue to be determined.

John, George, and Ringo went along with an idea hatched by Paul. It was inspired by a film that had made an impression on him, *Le Mystère Picasso*, a 1956 documentary by the French director Henri-Georges Clouzot, which showed Pablo Picasso gradually transforming sketches into fully realized oil paintings and collages. Paul could see it—a cinema verité–style film or TV special that would capture the Beatles as they put themselves through the work of writing new songs and getting them ready for a show and perhaps an album to go with it. If the cameras caught them hitting bum notes, so much the better. The thing now was to be natural.

The project started on Soundstage One at Twickenham Studios on January 2, 1969. Because it was conceived as a series of rehearsals that happened to be documented, a young sound engineer, Glyn Johns—fresh off having worked with the guitarist and producer Jimmy Page on the first album by his new group, Led Zeppelin—took charge of the portable recording unit, leaving George Martin with not much to do. Michael Lindsay-Hogg, an American director who had made the promos for "Rain" and "Hey Jude," signed on to shoot the film.

Lindsay-Hogg and his crew chronicled the Beatles' workdays exhaustively, generating 60 hours of footage and 150 hours of audio recorded by a pair of Nagra reel-to-reel tape machines synched to cameras A and B. Those materials would yield *Let It Be*, an eighty-minute documentary released in 1970, as well as *The Beatles: Get Back*, a 2022 Disney Plus streaming series assembled by the film director Peter Jackson. Complementing those foundational works are the books, articles, and podcasts examining the Nagra reels, many of which were stolen from Apple and leaked. Somewhat lost in the torrent of data and commentary has been the frequent, if ghostly, presence of Bob Dylan in this all but final chapter of the group's story.

During the strained but productive rehearsals, the Beatles, like any other band that finds itself confined to a room for any stretch of time, played songs by other artists when they weren't working on their own stuff. In most cases, they ran through these songs in a tossed-off manner, rather than coming up with fully formed versions, and Dylan was the artist they turned to more than any other. Here's a list of the singers and groups whose music they played more than once in January 1969, along with the number of songs:

> Bob Dylan 15
> Chuck Berry 13
> Elvis Presley 9
> Buddy Holly 8
> Lonnie Donegan . . . 6
> Carl Perkins 6
> Little Richard 6
> Ray Charles 4
> Arthur Alexander . . 3
> Bo Diddley 3
> Duane Eddy 3
> Jerry Lee Lewis 3
> Jackie Lomax 3
> Larry Williams 3
> Louis Armstrong . . . 2
> The Band 2
> Richard Barrett . . . 2
> The Beach Boys 2
> Eddie Cochran 2
> Bobby Darin 2

The Everly Brothers . 2
The Isley Brothers . . 2
The Lovin' Spoonful . 2
The Miracles 2
The Rolling Stones . . 2
Hank Williams 2

On the first morning at the hangar-like soundstage, before Paul's arrival, George led John and Ringo through "I Shall Be Released," the Dylan song that had appeared on the Band's *Music from Big Pink*. Later that day, all four Beatles were working on a new Lennon-McCartney song, "I've Got a Feeling," which put George in mind of Dylan's "The Mighty Quinn," given that both had lines starting with the word "everybody." He began playing it, and the others joined in.

A little more than a month removed from his Thanksgiving sojourn, George seemed intent on trying to import the friendly Bearsville spirit to this cavernous space. On the second day, he broke out "I Want You," the *Blonde on Blonde* track that had also been a hit single, and "Please, Mrs. Henry," which was perhaps the funniest song recorded by Dylan and the Band at Big Pink, with Bob bursting into laughter in the middle of it. Twickenham, however, didn't really lend itself to that kind of bonhomie, given the invasive cameras, oppressive film lights, and overhead microphones that picked up every scrap of conversation. "I had spent the last few months of 1968 producing an album by Jackie Lomax and hanging out with Bob Dylan and the Band in Woodstock, having a great time," George said. "For me, to come back into the winter of discontent with the Beatles in Twickenham was very unhealthy and unhappy."

Later that day, when the Beatles were having a go at George's new one, "All Things Must Pass," Paul seemed stumped while trying to gin up an arrangement. After the song broke down, George idly strummed Dylan's "All Along the Watchtower." That song's opening line, "There must be some way out of here," matched up nicely with what he wanted to say.

Three days later, the Beatles were playing Dylan's "I Want You" a second time, with Harrison picking out a light-fingered variation of Al Kooper's organ part on his guitar and McCartney crying out, "I want you!" Once it had died out, Paul mentioned having seen a "great film" of the 1965 Newport Folk Festival that showed "Dylan coming out amplified for the first time." George chose that moment to unveil "Maureen," the not-quite-complete song he had worked on with Bob at Hi Lo Ha. After telling Ringo that the words were inspired by his wife, he noted that the melody was based on Paul's recent TV theme: "You know, it's 'Thingumybob,'" he said. As George strummed and sang, the others joined in; once Paul got the gist, he sang along.

The mood sank when the Beatles were working on "Two of Us," a new one by Paul that seemed to connect his new relationship with Linda to his old relationship with John. George tossed in guitar licks, which stopped Paul cold. To emphasize the point that he didn't want any fills interrupting the flow, he brought up the moment when he had told George to stop playing responses to his vocal lines in the song that would go on to be the biggest Beatles hit of all: "This one, it's like: 'Should we play guitar through "Hey Jude"?' No, I don't think we should."

"Okay, I don't mind," George replied. Then his voice sharpened: "I'll play, you know, whatever you *want* me to play. Or I won't play at all, if you don't want me to play. Whatever it is that will *please* you, I'll do it."

The next day, as Paul was talking with Lindsay-Hogg about possible venues for the Beatles' return to the stage, George withdrew into a world of Dylan by strumming a song from *Another Side of Bob Dylan*, "My Back Pages." Then, as if wanting to convey the idea that he felt trapped without coming out and saying so, he played one from *Blonde on Blonde*, "Stuck Inside of Mobile with the Memphis Blues Again." A bit later, he mentioned that he had a backlog of new material ("about twenty songs"), but said he didn't feel like presenting it to the group. Paul said he was wrong to take that attitude.

George replied: "We should have a divorce."

"Well, I said that at the last meeting," Paul said. "But it's getting near it."

The rehearsals wore on in mostly dismal fashion. The Beatles were trying to play rock 'n' roll with the bash-it-out enthusiasm that had come so easily to them in the Cavern days, only to find themselves thwarted by the artificiality of the Twickenham setup and the complications that had arisen in their relationships with one another.

More often than not, George was playing his electric guitar through a Leslie speaker, an amplifier built into Hammond organs, or with the aid of a wah-wah pedal. On January 9, he stepped out of the murk when he brought out the Gibson J-200 acoustic he had lately been sharing with John; it was the same model as the guitar he had given Dylan. With John, Paul, and Ringo as his audience, George sang "I Threw It All Away," which Dylan himself still had yet to record. He continued his recital with another unreleased Dylan song, "Mama, You Been on My Mind." If George's heart had been in India during the making of *Sgt. Pepper*, it was now in Bearsville, as he was making abundantly clear.

At the next rehearsal, the Beatles were working on "Get Back," a rocker newly written by McCartney. This kind of thing should have been a cinch—but Paul grew annoyed with George, telling him his chord choices were "passé." George also had a dispute, off camera, with John. The Beatles would deny a report that the two had gotten into a fistfight, but in a later interview, George Martin said: "They actually came to blows. You'd think it would have been with Paul, but it was John. It was all hushed up afterwards." In the wake of the incident, during a rehearsal of "Two of Us," George bristled when Paul told him what to play.

At the end of the workday, George said, "I'll be leaving the band now."

"When?" John asked.

"Now."

He walked out.

In the middle of George's absence, John arrived at Twickenham apparently under the influence of heroin. As he and Yoko were giving an interview to a pair of reporters from the Canadian network

CBC-TV, his face went ashen. "Excuse me," John said, "I feel a bit sick." Mal Evans whisked him away from the camera, and he vomited into a bucket.

Over the next two days, during meetings at Sunny Heights with John, Paul, Ringo, and Yoko, George said he would return to work only if the Beatles left Twickenham and continued the project in the homier environs of the nearly completed studio beneath the Apple building on Savile Row.

When he rejoined the group on January 16, John and Yoko were no-shows. They also missed a scheduled BBC interview to promote their first album, a distillation of the tapes they had made at Kenwood. Released on Apple Records, it was called *Unfinished Music No. 1: Two Virgins*. The cover showed the couple standing naked, like a modern-day Adam and Eve. That portrait had only added to the tensions within the band: When Paul saw it, he "had seven thousand kinds of fits," according to the Beatles associate Tony Bramwell.

The mood improved when Billy Preston entered the Apple basement at George's invitation. Preston, a twenty-two-year-old keyboard player born in Houston, Texas, had been a member of Little Richard's band back when the Beatles were opening for the architect of rock 'n' roll in Hamburg; they had met up with Preston again in California during their U.S. tours. His arrival had the salutary effect of making John, Paul, George, and Ringo less touchy and more civil. And when it came to the music, he was just what they needed.

After two days of jamming with him, the four Beatles were seated close together under the gaze of Lindsay-Hogg's cameras when John proposed making this new lineup official: "I'd just like him in our band, actually. I'd like a fifth Beatle." He added: "At Twickenham, suddenly there were three. Now there's four. Then, there's *five!*"

George nodded along. "If I asked Dylan to join the Beatles—and he would, you know, as well—and we'd get 'em *all* in here," he said.

"Yeah, but they don't need to join the Beatles," Paul put in quickly.

John couldn't be stopped: "We'll call it Beatles & Co.—that'll be our band!"

"I mean, it's Sgt. Pepper's Lonely Hearts Club Band, innit?" George said, citing in lawyerly fashion a precedent for the group's ability to stray from its core identity.

"Yeah," John said.

"We could get 'em *all*," George said.

Paul weighed in once more: "I just don't—because it's just bad enough with *four*."

They all laughed. With that, the idea was struck down.

Although Dylan had been vetoed as a member of Beatles & Co., he was a presence at the final rehearsals. On January 26, as Linda and Heather looked on, George was messing around with the chord progression at the heart of "La Bamba," "Twist and Shout," and "Like a Rolling Stone." In a Dylan-tinged voice, Paul sang: "How does it feel? To be on your own." John came in with: "Shake it up, baby! Twist and shout!" Heather, who had just turned six, joined in, wailing wordlessly into a microphone. During a rehearsal on January 28, the Beatles played "Rainy Day Women" and "Positively 4th Street."

Two days later, at lunchtime, the Beatles, accompanied by Preston and Linsday-Hogg's camera crew, went up on the roof and gave what would be their last public performance. Despite the forty-five-degree chill, despite the recent arguments, despite the fact that they hadn't played in public in more than two years, they recaptured the old spirit as they tore through five Lennon-McCartney songs—"Get Back," "Don't Let Me Down," "I've Got a Feeling," "One After 909," and "Dig a Pony."

Like the Beatles in their rootsy new incarnation, Dylan was no longer all that concerned with putting himself at the forefront of popular music. While the newcomers Sly and the Family Stone and Led Zeppelin were creating the dominant styles of the next decade, the Beatles and Dylan were backing away from innovation, writing and playing songs that had a tight connection to the records they had loved in their teenage years. It was as if they were atoning for having brought the curse of sophistication onto rock 'n' roll. Whatever their motivation, they had once again arrived at the same conclusion at the same time, and much of their work in 1969 reflected their efforts to chase down a lost artistic innocence.

Dylan wrote more songs in the vein of "I Threw It All Away," careful to avoid his old tendencies toward wordiness, abrasiveness, and obscurity. In February, two weeks after the Beatles' rooftop show, he left Bearsville on a work trip to Nashville. The sound he arrived at with the Studio A hotshots was closer to traditional country than anything he had come up with before. He sang in a gentle croon, and nothing in these sturdy songs, including "Lay Lady Lay" and "Tonight I'll Be Staying Here with You," would tempt anyone to call him a prophet.

He titled the collection *Nashville Skyline*. In March, back at home, he played an advance copy for Elliott Landy, who had taken the photos for *Music from Big Pink*. When they stepped into the late-afternoon light, Bob was wearing a small black cowboy hat and carrying the pretty Gibson J-200 given to him by George. Landy squatted low and pointed his lens upward. Dylan, brandishing the guitar, smiled and doffed his hat. They had the cover shot. In addition to conveying a feeling of country contentment, the portrait contained a private message: Dylan told Landy he had tipped his hat as a thank you to George for the gift of the Gibson.

The album sold very well when it came out in April, even as it confused or angered those who wanted Dylan to address the heated sociopolitical climate. He was having none of that, as the cheerful cover portrait suggested. In May, when he appeared on the ABC variety program *The Johnny Cash Show*, he looked nothing like the tortured Orpheus of *Dont Look Back*. The taping took place at the Ryman Auditorium in Nashville, home of the Grand Ole Opry. Bob stood on that stage and delivered "I Threw It All Away" and "Living the Blues." Johnny then joined him for a duet of that Dylan oldie "Girl from the North Country."

While he was in Nashville, his mother was bemoaning the moral decline of America in an interview with Toby Thompson, one of the first writers to put together an accurate account of Dylan's early life. After making the case that the devaluation of the traditional family unit had indirectly led to the recent assassinations, Beatty Zimmerman said: "Probably the main reason Bob hasn't gone back out on the road is just this, the violence. He hasn't said too much about it, but I'm sure he's nervous: assassination isn't so remote a possibility for a figure of Bob's popularity. Also, I think he felt that John Lennon business, with John's wife and him nude, I think Bob felt that silly. Again, he didn't say so, but I could tell."

Although Dylan seemed to be distancing himself from the counterculture, some leftists saw a hidden political message in his embrace of the non-elitist country-pop genre. Carl Oglesby, the first president of the activist organization Students for a Democratic Society, interpreted *Nashville Skyline* as his way of showing he was "becoming interested in the white working class at the same as the movement did." George Harrison, for his part, accepted the album for what it was and sent Dylan a note to tell him so.

> Dear Bobbie,
> Thanks for Nashville Skyline, it is beautiful.
> Love to You All.

Coming in the wake of *John Wesley Harding*, *Music from Big Pink*, and the Byrds' country-flavored *Sweetheart of the Rodeo* (which included two Dylan songs), *Nashville Skyline* conveyed the idea that the rural life was the only life worth living. Communes sprang up around Woodstock. Tie-dyed hippies, equipped with dime bags and acoustic guitars, arrived by the busload to lounge on the village green, and stalkers found their way to Hi Lo Ha. Dylan kept two pistols and a rifle within easy reach for protection against those he would describe as "gatecrashers," "ravens," and "rogue radicals looking for the Prince of Protest."

He moved his family a few miles away, to a remote mansion set on thirty-nine acres along Ohayo Mountain Road. Michael Lang, a budding entrepreneur from Brooklyn who was planning a music festival, stopped by. The event he had in mind, scheduled for mid-August, had a chance to be much bigger than the Monterey Pop Festival in California, a three-day gathering in 1967 with performances by Jimi Hendrix, Otis Redding, the Who, and Ravi Shankar, among others. Displaying a knack for marketing, Lang named his event the Woodstock Music and Art Fair, though it would take place nearly sixty miles southwest of that town. Over lunch, he made Dylan an offer to stand in as the star attraction. The man who had become more or less synonymous with Woodstock, albeit against his will, said no.

Shortly after that, Dylan agreed to be the headliner of a similar festival scheduled to take place at the end of August on the Isle of Wight, an English island in the Solent straight, about ninety miles south of London. He would be paid fifty grand to perform at least one hour. The Band would open for him and serve as his backing group. It would be his first full-length concert in more than three years.

The Beatles came to agree that the January project had been a botch. Instead of a warts-and-all documentary and a rough-and-ready LP to go with it, all they had were reams of unwieldy footage (which Lindsay-Hogg was trying to whip into a film) and a bunch of unsatisfactory tracks (which Glyn Johns was trying to shape into an album). The one thing they deemed worthy of putting out was a single with Paul's "Get Back" on the A-side and John's "Don't Let Me Down" on the B-side. Credited to The Beatles With Billy Preston, it went straight to No. 1.

McCartney was now at odds with his bandmates over their decision to appoint Allen Klein, a sharp-elbowed New Yorker, as the group's manager. Nearly two years after the death of Epstein, the British music papers filled with reports on Beatles business disputes.

In March 1969, Paul and Linda were wed at the Marylebone Register Office in London. Eight days later, John and Yoko were married on the island of Gibraltar. From there, Lennon and Ono embarked on a public honeymoon during which they called for an end to the Vietnam War before an audience of journalists while lying in bed six days straight at the Amsterdam Hilton. In the middle of another weeklong "Bed-in for Peace" at the Queen Elizabeth Hotel in Montreal, they recorded a spontaneous anti-war anthem, "Give Peace a Chance," that referenced "Bobby Dylan" in a litany of names including Timothy Leary and Allen Ginsberg.

There was a moment of rapprochement in April when John showed up at Paul's house on Cavendish Avenue with a nearly completed song, "The Ballad of John and Yoko," that he was hot to record. After Paul helped nail down the final verse, they went around the corner to EMI Studios, despite the fact that George and Ringo were out of town. It proved a happy, efficient session, with George Martin and Geoff Emerick once again in the control room. Paul contributed bass, piano, drums, maracas, and strong vocal harmonies; John sang lead and handled the guitar parts.

The Beatles then decided to put aside their differences long enough to make another album. They would work in their old style, enlisting Martin as producer and embracing state-of-the-art production, complete with overdubs, strings, horns, and something new, a Moog synthesizer. In July, McCartney, Harrison, and Starr got started in earnest, though Lennon was taking a trip through Scotland, where he had spent several idyllic childhood vacations with an aunt and uncle.

In the Highlands on July 1, John was at the wheel of his British Leyland Austin Maxi. Yoko sat beside him, and the two children, Julian and Kyoko, were in the back. While navigating a winding road, he swerved into a ditch. The impact crushed the car. John sustained cuts to his face that required stitches, as did Yoko and Kyoko; Yoko also suffered a back injury; Julian was in a state of mild shock.

After five days in a hospital in Golspie, John and Yoko showed their commitment to making their lives a nonstop art project by transporting the mangled Austin Maxi to their new home, a seventy-two-acre estate near Ascot called Tittenhurst Park, and having it installed on the grounds. To handle their affairs, they hired an assistant, Dan Richter, a friend of Yoko's who last appeared in these pages as an organizer of the International Poetry Incarnation at the Royal Albert Hall in 1965. One of his main tasks was to provide his employers with heroin.

Richter, who had grown up in Connecticut and spent five years at the American Mime Theatre in New York, was a known figure on the London arts scene because of his small but crucial role in the acclaimed 1968 film *2001: A Space Odyssey*. He played the early hominid known as Moon-Watcher in the opening sequence, and he choreographed the movements of the other ape-men. All through the days and nights of working closely with the director Stanley Kubrick in a studio outside London, Richter had been concealing a heroin habit. In the spring of 1969, he went back to his home country with his wife and infant son, hoping to find a quiet place to kick. He stayed clean a few weeks while working as a cook at an Italian restaurant on Cape Cod. Then came a relapse. In July, when he was back in England and working for John and Yoko, he found himself craving the drug more than ever.

Richter made frequent trips to the London flat of an elderly woman who had a heroin prescription under a National Health Service addiction treatment program. He took advantage of the fact that she received more than her share to buy some for his old friend and her new husband. Through July and August, he made deliveries to Abbey Road, where Yoko watched the Beatles record from a double bed that John had arranged to have installed in the studio out of concern for the back injury she had suffered in the car accident.

Before John's arrival at the sessions, the other Beatles had cut the basic tracks for Harrison's "Here Comes the Sun," as well as McCartney's "You Never Give Me Your Money," "Carry That Weight," "Her Majesty," and "Golden Slumbers"—nearly half the album that would be called *Abbey Road*. On his first day back at work, Lennon dragged himself through McCartney's "Maxwell's Silver Hammer," a tuneful novelty number about a gleeful murderer. John didn't get to one of his own songs for more than a week, when the Beatles started "Come Together." "It felt weird to be sitting on the bed talking to Yoko while the Beatles were working across the studio," Richter recalled. "I couldn't help thinking that those guys were making rock 'n' roll history, while I was sitting on this bed in the middle of Abbey Road studio, handing Yoko a small white packet."

August 20 was the last day all four Beatles were together in a recording studio. Not that they realized it at the time. They spent the hours completing "I Want You (She's So Heavy)," which counts as another answer song in the ongoing Dylan-Beatles dialogue.

Like Dylan at the time, Lennon was simplifying his work. The chant-like "Give Peace a Chance," released as an Apple single credited to John's side group, the Plastic Ono Band, was basic enough to become a staple of anti-war demonstrations; similarly, the Beatles single "The Ballad of John and Yoko" was a straightforward first-person story song. John was doing away with all frills in an effort to get at the root of what he needed to say, and "I Want You (She's So Heavy)" was his most radical effort in this regard.

It shared its main title with "I Want You," the Dylan song that the Beatles had played twice during their January rehearsals. Lennon drove the main idea home with repetition:

> *I want you*
> *I want you so bad*
> *I want you*
> *I want you so bad*
> *It's driving me mad*

It goes like that for the whole song, save for the middle eight, when John breaks into "She's so heavy" amid a cascade of guitars.

Dylan's "I Want You" had practically the same refrain:

> *I want you, I want you*
> *I want you so bad*

It differed from Lennon's song in its inclusion of four intricate verses and a bridge filled with enigmatic phrases ("your dancing child in his Chinese suit," for instance). That sort of cryptic poetry, Lennon seemed to be saying in his neo-primitive reply, wasn't worth much. For a songwriter who hoped to capture love or lust, anything other than the bluntest language was an evasion or a lie. In his bare, no-nonsense song, John was also casting himself as an anti-intellectual creature of feeling while placing his friend and rival in the unenviable role of effete intellectual, the kind of guy who would rather poeticize love than make it.

The irony is that, as *Nashville Skyline* had made clear, Dylan had reached much the same conclusion about what a song should be. While both men were paring back their songwriting, however, they were doing so in opposite ways: Lennon sought to chronicle general human experience by documenting the particulars of his own life; Dylan was trying to capture universal truths by doing away with his own individuality to create songs meant to resonate with everybody. In the wake of the *Nashville Skyline* sessions, he followed this idea to its perhaps absurd end point by recording dozens of songs written by others. He was all but erasing himself from his own work.

■　　■　　■

When *Abbey Road* was done, John and Paul couldn't deny that the youngest Beatle had come up with two of its strongest songs, "Here Comes the Sun" and "Something."

"Here Comes the Sun," a tuneful welcome to springtime, would end up the most-streamed Beatles song, with nearly 2 billion listens on Spotify. "Something," a love ballad with an indelible melody, was immediately recognized as a classic, winning the Ivor Novello Award for the best song of 1969 before it became the second-most-covered Beatles song, after "Yesterday," with versions by Elvis Presley, James Brown, Smokey Robinson, Shirley Bassey, Chet Baker, and Frank Sinatra, who called it "the best love song of the twentieth century." John and Paul agreed to make it the first Harrison song released as a Beatles single, part of a so-called double-A-side with "Come Together." At twenty-six, George had arrived.

On August 22, the Beatles convened at Tittenhurst Park, the new seat of John and Yoko, for a photo shoot. It was a momentous day in the group's history: John, Paul, George, and Ringo would never be together again. They spent the hours striking weary poses on the plush grounds. Dan Richter recalled that Lennon and McCartney "were arguing over everything."

After that unhappy gathering, John decided to quit heroin cold turkey. He had himself tied to a chair. He ranted and sweated and screamed. Afterward, weak and shaken, but clean, he wrote a song about the harrowing experience, "Cold Turkey." Although it was a cry of pain, Lennon made sure it was a well-crafted piece of work, with precise lyrics.

> *I wish I was a baby*
> *I wish I was dead*

He was proud of this one and wanted to play it for Dylan, who was about to arrive in England for his comeback show, which the music papers had been hyping for weeks.

Bert Block, an associate of Albert Grossman's, traveled to the Isle of Wight in advance of the festival to make sure the accommodations and stage setup would meet with Dylan's approval. Almost as soon as he arrived, he got some alarming news in a call from New York: The Woodstock Music and Art Fair had attracted more than four hundred thousand people, and it was a mess. Although it would go down as a proud achievement of American baby boomers, and one they would never shut up about, the initial burst of news focused on the abandoned cars clogging the highways, a waste-management nightmare, and the deaths of two young men, one of whom was run over by a tractor. Ray Foulk, a main organizer of the Isle of Wight Festival, assured Block that he had everything well under control.

Foulk, a newcomer to rock promotion who had grown up on the island, was worried his headliner might not show up as he waited on August 25 at Heathrow Airport (as London Airport had been renamed). At 10 p.m., there he was, Bob Dylan, all dressed in white. Sara was at his side, five months pregnant. They were accompanied by Al Aronowitz, now serving as Dylan's road manager. The three of them got into the limousine hired by Foulk and rolled through the darkness for seventy miles. On a cold Southsea promenade, Dylan and his wife sipped hot tea while waiting for the chartered hovercraft to take them across the misty waters.

It was around 2 a.m. when they reached Foreland Farm, a walled compound on the island's easternmost point, about ten miles from the festival grounds. It had a sixteenth-century stone cottage, a pool, a tennis court, and a barn. The staff included a caretaker who made simple meals and a gardener who paid special attention to the flower beds. During the five days leading up to the big night, Dylan spent hours in the barn rehearsing with the Band, whose members were staying at the Halland Hotel in nearby Seaview.

Once Bob and Sara were settled, George and Pattie Harrison pulled up in a blue Ferrari, having crossed the Solent on a car ferry. George had brought along some pot, at Aronowitz's request, as well as an advance copy of *Abbey Road*. He complained that John and Paul had allowed only two Harrison songs on the album before he gave everyone a listen. "I don't remember Bob and the boys lifting George on their shoulders to tell him how much they loved *Abbey Road*," Aronowitz recalled. "In fact, if I detected any sentiment at all, it was envy."

Bob and George spent part of the day poolside. "Look at them," Bert Block said to Ray Foulk. "They're star-struck with each other." Toward evening, they repaired to a sitting room in the cottage. Side by side on a settee, Bob and George strummed guitars and sang in close harmony on the Everly Brothers' "All I Have to Do Is Dream." "What an astonishingly beautiful rendition," Foulk recalled, "and what a tragedy it was not recorded."

Two days before the start of the three-day festival, Dylan reluctantly sat at a table in a public room of the Halland Hotel to give a news conference. The reporters saw before them a stolid figure who bore little resemblance to the angular, wild-haired, vaguely androgynous young man who had once made a game out of flummoxing the press. He was dressed in white, down to his cream-colored shoes, as if he had switched teams from the bad guys to the good guys. He was not wearing sunglasses. His hair was uncombed but tame. When he spoke, he did so in an aw-shucks manner that recalled the taciturn heroes played by Gary Cooper in Hollywood's golden age.

A journalist asked if he was concerned that there might be "some sort of drugs problem" in the crowd on the night of his show.

"I hope there isn't any," Dylan replied.

A BBC correspondent followed up with: "Can you tell us your general views on drug-taking among teenagers and young people these days?"

"I don't have any of those views. I wish I did. I'd be glad to share them with you, but I think everyone should lead their own life."

The BBC man continued: "You used to, I believe, make public pronouncements on your views on things like Vietnam, and it has been noticed in certain quarters you haven't been doing that recently. Is this deliberate policy on your part?"

"No. I think that's more of a rumor than a fact. You check your old newspapers. You won't be able to find too many statements I've made on those issues."

The BBC journalist tried again: "I've heard it said here today by some of your fans that the new Bob Dylan is a bit of a square. Is this true?"

Dylan gave a mild chuckle. "You'll have to ask the fans," he said.

Another reporter asked if he would be seeing the Beatles during his stay.

"George Harrison has come to visit me," he said. "The Beatles have asked me to work with them. I love the Beatles and I think it would be a good idea to do a jam session."

In a nearby village, a BBC camera captured long-haired young people streaming past neat buildings on their way to the fairgrounds. "Here come the hippies, the advance guard of an invasion force expected to number between one and two hundred thousand," the correspondent said. In a field near Woodside Bay, a couple "made love" for all to see, *The Guardian* reported.

The festival was soon underway, with performances by the Nice, Joe Cocker, and the Bonzo Dog Band. A hundred miles north, at Tittenhurst Park, John and Yoko were preparing their journey. They thought they might zoom in on a helicopter and blanket the crowd with anti-war leaflets. When that proved too much trouble, they considered bombarding the festivalgoers with balloons, only to conclude that the stunt wouldn't leave them enough room in the chopper. One thing was certain, though, now that their lives had become an art project: Dan Richter would use something new on the market, a video camera, to create a visual diary of their stay.

On August 30, the day before Dylan's return to the stage, a helicopter touched down on a landing pad a few hundred yards from Foreland Farm. Out stepped Ringo and Maureen. Soon, a second helicopter appeared in the sky. Instead of heading for the landing area, it drew closer and closer to the property. The gardener shouted angrily as the downdraft laid waste to his flower beds. John and Yoko climbed out, trailed by Richter and his wife, Jill. Camera in hand, Richter shot John and Yoko greeting Dylan and a crowd that included George and Pattie, Ringo and Maureen, members of the Band, and Keith Richards and Charlie Watts of the Rolling Stones. Too bad it was all for naught. "The camera just didn't work," Richter said.

The three Beatles stepped away from the others and formed a huddle. "Please pardon us for talking shop," John said, "but we never see each other." Paul probably would have been there, despite his differences with his bandmates, but he was in the middle of what he described at the time as a "new, wonderful experience": Linda had just given birth to a daughter, Mary, at a hospital in St. John's Wood, with her husband at her side.

Ray Foulk, the festival organizer, had the sense that the Beatles and Dylan were in competition with each other. "People talk of the sixties rivalry between the Beatles and the Stones, but this is to miss the point," he wrote. "The significant rivalry was between the world's greatest group and the world's greatest songwriter. The tussle was not for chart positions or numbers of hits. It was for the intellectual or moral high ground."

Twenty-four hours before Dylan was scheduled to take the stage, John, George, and Ringo, along with their wives and the Beatles aide Mal Evans, watched Bob and the Band go through one last rehearsal in the barn. Before bed, George wrote "Behind That Locked Door," a song of encouragement to Dylan.

The next day, Pattie suggested tennis. Bob readily agreed. John said, "I'll play on the condition that nobody really knows how." It started with "about seven people on each side of the net," Pattie recalled. A game of doubles ensued: Bob and John versus George and Ringo. People gathered at the cyclone fence to see the rock stars huffing and puffing. "Tennis was too demanding a sport for a group of cigarette-smoking musicians," Aronowitz recalled.

Late that afternoon, on the festival grounds, Richie Havens, a friend of Dylan's from the folk clubs, won over the crowd with Dylan's "Maggie's Farm," the Beatles' "Strawberry Fields Forever," and a song of his own, "Freedom," which he had improvised onstage at Woodstock sixteen days earlier. On the other side of the island, Bob and the Band were getting ready for their night's work. The music press had been fanning a rumor that Dylan might play for as long as three hours, with members of the Beatles, the Stones, and Blind Faith joining him onstage, but he had enough to worry about without the bother of arranging an all-star jam.

He was jittery as he waited in a trailer near the stage with Sara and Al Aronowitz. George stopped in to lend him the Gibson J-200 he shared with John, the same guitar he had used to record "Here Comes the Sun" and the same model as the one he had given Bob at the end of his Thanksgiving visit.

The Band was supposed to go on at eight thirty, followed by Dylan. At nine, the stage was still empty, and the crowd was restless. Aronowitz left the trailer to see what was happening. When he came back, he said there was a problem with the sound system. Dylan paced. He yawned. Finally, he erupted: "What the fuck's wrong with the fucking sound system?"

He didn't hit the stage till eleven. He was wearing a white suit and strumming the guitar George had lent him. The crowd seemed like a monstrous being to Aronowitz, one that reacted to Dylan's entrance with an "exultant roar." Close to the front, John and Yoko, George and Pattie, and Ringo and Maureen sat wrapped in blankets.

"Great to be here," Dylan said. "Sure is."

He sang seventeen songs, including "I Threw It All Away," "The Mighty Quinn," and "Like a Rolling Stone," to the sea of people at his feet. Absent from his set was anything that smacked of protest. He stayed onstage ten minutes longer than the contractually obligated hour.

George found the concert "marvelous." John described it as "a reasonable, albeit slightly flat, performance." He also regretted the late start time, saying, "We would have jammed, if it had been earlier." During the after-show party at Foreland Farm, with *Abbey Road* blasting from the speakers, Dylan was in high spirits. The next morning, he and Sara joined John and Yoko on the helicopter to Tittenhurst Park.

There's no account of what they talked about, but it seems reasonable to assume that John mentioned an upcoming event of great importance to him and Yoko, a showing of their avant-garde film shorts at the New Cinema Club in London. It included Lennon's boldest act of self-exposure yet, *Self-Portrait*, a fifteen-minute close-up of his penis getting erect. John may have also told Dylan about kicking heroin, given that he wanted him to hear "Cold Turkey."

George arrived at Tittenhurst Park after Bob and Sara had toured the grounds. John set up the reel-to-reel machine in the living room and asked Bob to join in on his new song, but it didn't work out. "I was just trying to get him to record," Lennon said a little more than a year later. "We'd put him on piano for 'Cold Turkey' to make a rough tape, but his wife was pregnant or something and they left." Maybe Dylan felt drained after having played to more than a hundred thousand people the night before. Or maybe he had no interest in contributing to a drug song. He had, after all, gone to great lengths to separate himself from the man John had seen on that limo ride three years earlier.

Back in Bearsville, he shut out the world through the last months of Sara's pregnancy and the first months after the birth of their son Jakob. When he finally returned to a studio, it was to continue the project he had begun after *Nashville Skyline*—steering clear of his own work to record folk ballads, standards, old country hits, and newer songs by Gordon Lightfoot, Joni Mitchell, and Paul Simon. Dylan would assemble his next album from those sessions and give it the same title Lennon had used for his penis film, *Self Portrait*.

18 Serve Yourself

Lennon made a solo demo recording of "Cold Turkey," and it was chilling—too much so for his bandmates. "I went to the other three Beatles and said, 'Hey, lads, I think I've written a single,'" John said. "But they all said, 'Ummm . . . arrrr . . . well.'" Once it was clear to him that the Beatles name would not be attached to a song about the agonies of heroin withdrawal, he decided he had no choice but to record it as a solo single.

Two weeks after Dylan's Isle of Wight show, he put more distance between himself and the Beatles when he said yes to a last-minute offer to play at a festival in Canada, the Toronto Rock 'n' Roll Revival. With Yoko at his side, John led Eric Clapton, his old Hamburg pal Klaus Voormann, and the London session drummer Andy White through a ragged set before a crowd of twenty thousand. During "Cold Turkey," he nearly threw up. "We were full of junk," he said.

Back in London, he met with McCartney, Starr, and the Beatles' new manager, Allen Klein, at the Apple office. The agenda was to sign the new contract allowing for a much-improved royalty rate with EMI. Before putting pen to paper, Paul suggested, as he had before, that the Beatles should go back to playing "little gigs" in clubs. "I think you're daft," John said. "I wasn't going to tell you until after we'd signed the deal, but I'm leaving the group." They agreed not to make any kind of announcement, partly because *Abbey Road* had yet to be released and partly because Paul thought John might change his mind. But on this day—September 20, 1969—the Beatles effectively came to an end.

At the same time, a conspiracy theory was starting to make the rounds: Paul was dead. Not only that, but he had died in 1966 and was replaced by a talented look-alike. Much of the tale was laid out in an article published in the student newspaper at Drake University in Des Moines, Iowa. The story rippled across the Midwest through the fall of 1969 and gained traction when deejays in Detroit and New York talked it up on the air. Didn't it mean *something* that you could hear the phrase "turn me on, dead man" when you played "Revolution 9" backward? And why was Paul (or his replacement) barefoot on the *Abbey Road* cover? And on and on.

Denials from McCartney himself couldn't keep fans from holding vigils outside his house on Cavendish Avenue. He took Linda, Heather, and Mary to the farm in Scotland, only to be accosted by two journalists from *Life* magazine. Paul hurled a slop bucket at the photographer, Terence Spencer, who had distinguished himself as a fighter pilot in World War II. Still cool under fire, Spencer snapped pictures of the tantrum, which further enraged his subject, who punched him on the shoulder.

When Paul calmed down, he offered a deal: In exchange for the damning roll of film, he would give an interview and pose for some pictures. The November 7, 1969, issue of *Life* showed Paul, Linda, and their two children in a gray field. "The Case of the 'Missing' Beatle: Paul Is Still with Us," went the cover line. The rumor of his death was so much in the air that no one, the magazine's editors included, seemed to notice that McCartney had said something truly newsworthy in the interview: "The Beatles thing is over."

It was truly over on April 10, 1970, when the London *Daily Mirror* published an article headlined "Paul Quits the Beatles." The story took its main fact from statements Paul had made about the group's future in a written Q&A he had sent to the press to promote his first solo album, *McCartney*, a modest batch of melodious songs and sonic experiments, many of them recorded at his home studio. John, who had just released the urgent hit single "Instant Karma! (We All Shine On)" under the name John Ono Lennon, was annoyed that Paul had beaten him to making the Beatles breakup public.

While fans around the world were mourning the end of the Beatles, George Harrison was in Manhattan with Al Aronowitz and the suave Beatles associate Derek Taylor. They climbed the front steps of a townhouse on MacDougal Street in Greenwich Village, where Dylan and his family had set up a new home far from Bearsville and its stalkers. Over coffee and cognac, the guests listened to an advance copy of *Self Portrait*, which would soon be released to the harshest reviews of Dylan's career.

The next day, May 1, Bob took George and a few other musicians to CBS Studios on East Fifty-Second Street to record some old songs and a few new ones for an album that would come out in the fall, *New Morning*. Midway through the session, with George on guitar, Dylan played "Yesterday." He brought this McCartney composition right down to earth, stripping away its prettiness and grandeur to make it sound like just another folk song.

When George was back in London, *Let It Be*, the album that had resulted from the Beatles' difficult sessions of January 1969, was on turntables everywhere, having finally been released after some touch-up production work by Phil Spector; and *Let It Be*, the documentary directed by Michael Lindsay-Hogg, was playing in theaters. In the context of the breakup news, even the scenes of the rooftop performance had a melancholy vibe.

At the end of May, George began recording his first major solo release, a triple album that would be acclaimed as a rock masterpiece. He would call it *All Things Must Pass*, after the autumnal song he had written in Bearsville. With Spector in the Abbey Road control room so often occupied by George Martin, Harrison sang and played with sureness as he recorded dozens of songs, including the Harrison-Dylan collaboration "I'd Have You Anytime," which he would select as the album's opening track, and "My Sweet Lord," a lushly produced piece of gospel-rock with choirs harmonizing on "hallelujah" and "Hare Krishna."

Paul had decided to follow his modest first effort with something grander. In October, with Linda and the two girls, he sailed the Atlantic on the SS *France* and checked into the Stanhope Hotel on Manhattan's Upper East Side. At the very same Fifty-Second Street studio where Dylan had recently recorded "Yesterday," he started making the album *Ram*. Between sessions, the McCartney and Dylan families spent a lot of time together. "We used to go round to dinner," Paul said, "and he would come up and see us. So we were really quite intimate." Dylan posed for Linda's camera in the small yard behind the townhouse, with and without baby Jakob.

At one gathering, Paul told Dylan, "Oh, man, I had such strange dreams last night."

"Were you eatin' *cheese* late at night?" Bob asked.

■   ■   ■

Dylan's *New Morning* came out that same month. It pleased most critics—but not A. J. Weberman, a Dylan obsessive who published his musings in a small New York paper, *The East Village Other*. Weberman believed his former hero had lost his way with *Nashville Skyline* and had strayed deeper into the mire since its release. He wasn't alone in holding this opinion, but he was unique in making Dylan the target of a prolonged harassment campaign.

In the fall of 1970, he started giving abstruse lectures in a discipline he called "Dylanology." Then he formed an organization meant to free Dylan from himself, the Dylan Liberation Front. Weberman argued that this supposed voice of a generation was nothing but a fraud, a closet conservative and secret heroin addict who had posed as a man of the people for profit. In search of evidence, he showed up on MacDougal Street to root through Dylan's garbage cans. He would continue his crank crusade for the next fifty-five years, making increasingly unhinged accusations—for instance, that Dylan was a neo-Nazi and Holocaust denier—in a torrent of books, blogs, and online videos.

One of Weberman's first acolytes was David Peel, a New York street singer blessed with more enthusiasm than talent. In January 1971, when the two of them were doing their thing in the presence of a *Rolling Stone* reporter, Peel remarked that Dylan's garbage was the same color as his money—green. Dylan stepped outside just then, and Weberman went into a harangue. "You've got to use your millions to *help* people," he said. He went on to tell Dylan he should send some of his money to aid John Sinclair, a left-wing activist and former manager of the Detroit rock band the MC5 who was serving a ten-year sentence in a Michigan prison for the possession of two joints.

Two days later, in London, John and Yoko were talking politics with a pair of reporters from *Red Mole*, a Marxist newspaper. Flower power had proved soft and ineffectual, Lennon argued. What had to happen now was a proletarian takeover of the British government. "Like Marx said: 'To each according to his need,'" John said. "I think that would work well here. But we'd have to infiltrate the army, too, because they are well trained to kill us all."

He had just released his first solo album, *John Lennon/Plastic Ono Band*, an intensely personal masterwork that included "Mother," which Dylan would single out for praise, and "God," in which John announced that he "didn't believe" in "Beatles" or "Zimmerman." Although it was coproduced by Spector, who was known for the Wall of Sound style that had made "Be My Baby" a sonic treasure in 1963, *John Lennon/Plastic Ono Band* had sparse instrumentation and minimal overdubbing. After having stripped his lyrics to the bone in "I Want You (She's So Heavy)" and "Cold Turkey," Lennon was now giving his music the same treatment. So this was by no means a pop record, and it sold poorly, despite stellar reviews.

Five months after the *Red Mole* interview, John decided to give a sweeter production treatment to one of his new songs, "Imagine," which he recorded at his custom-built studio at Tittenhurst Park. Its lyrics, a utopianist's plea for a better world, drew heavily from the poems starting with the word "imagine" in Yoko's collection *Grapefruit*. Like Dylan's "Blowin' in the Wind," McCartney's "Yesterday," and Harrison's "Something," "Imagine" had a hummable melody and a universal theme. And like those songs, it would spawn hundreds of cover versions. Singers who have taken a crack at it include Joan

Baez, David Bowie, Elton John, Fairuz, King Krule, Nana Mouskouri, Stevie Wonder, Sarah Vaughan, and Eddie Vedder.

During the same sessions, John showed his mercurial nature by writing and recording "How Do You Sleep?," a tirade aimed at Paul. It made the case that his old friend and collaborator was a purveyor of middle-of-the-road schlock for bourgeois squares, a line of attack that many rock critics would parrot, even as the prolific McCartney churned out ingenious songs in a variety of styles, including rock singles ("Hi Hi Hi," "Helen Wheels"), romantic ballads ("Every Night," "My Love"), and multipart pop suites ("Uncle Albert / Admiral Halsey," "Live and Let Die"). Making things all the worse for Paul was the fact that the musicians accompanying John on "How Do You Sleep?" were George and Ringo.

The idealistic "Imagine" and the caustic "How Do You Sleep?" would both appear on the next Lennon album, *Imagine*. In June 1971, John and Yoko left England for New York City, where they planned to add some finishing touches to the tracks at the Record Plant, a studio in Midtown. They had also come to find Yoko's daughter, Kyoko, who had been taken by her father to an unknown location in the U.S. John and Yoko would spend years on the search, an effort that would involve private detectives and court appearances.

They made the Plaza Hotel their home base. As spring bled into summer, they began to feel at home in New York, happy to find they could walk the streets more or less unmolested by the city's blasé residents. One day they bumped into a pair of rabble-rousing activists, Jerry Rubin and Abbie Hoffman, who had recently been acquitted, along with the other members of the Chicago Seven, of trying to incite a riot at the 1968 Democratic National Convention; and they spent five stimulating hours raking over the state of the world at Rubin's apartment in SoHo.

The next day, John and Yoko saw the street singer David Peel performing with his band, the Lower East Side, in Washington Square. As Peel sang "The Pope Smokes Dope," Lennon saw this musical primitivist as a kindred spirit. He decided to sign him to Apple and produce his next album. It wasn't long till John and Yoko met Peel's fellow traveler A. J. Weberman. But before they got in too deep with Dylan's archenemy, they arranged to see Bob at the Plaza.

Incognito in an army jacket and a hat, Dylan found a hidden spot in the ornate lobby and waited until he saw John and Yoko step into an elevator car. He slipped in beside them and said, "Hi." "I had this incredible grass," said Dan Richter, who was reaching the end of his time with John and Yoko. "It was Nigerian or something, and we all smoked it. We spent a couple hours up there, the four of us. Bob and I were on one bed and John and Yoko were on the other."

■ ■ ■

At the time of the little hotel room party, George was in a recording studio in Los Angeles, producing a film soundtrack for Ravi Shankar. The man once known as the Quiet Beatle was now a star in his own right, having announced himself to the world in November 1970 with the grand *All Things Must Pass*, which had won nearly universal praise from critics on its way to sales of more than 7 million. As it made its way up the album charts, "My Sweet Lord" was constantly on the radio, reaching No. 1 in fifteen countries and far outselling the first singles put out by John and Paul.

In Los Angeles, Shankar told George he was distressed by the crisis that had arisen as a result of the war between the provinces of Pakistan then known as West Pakistan and East Pakistan. Millions had fled the conflict to live in squalid conditions along the eastern border of India, and many of them were starving. The war had erupted after the leaders of East Pakistan—formerly East Bengal, an Indian province with a large Hindu minority—announced their intention to form a new nation, Bangladesh. In response, the Muslim ruling body of Pakistan, seated in West Pakistan, launched military attacks. Shankar, a Hindu whose father had been born in East Bengal, wanted to raise money for the displaced people.

George sprang into action. He booked the afternoon and evening slots for the next available date at Madison Square Garden in New York and started making calls. Ringo said yes, as did Clapton, Billy Preston, the Oklahoma-born rocker Leon Russell, and the British band Badfinger. McCartney, who had filed a lawsuit against the other Beatles in his effort to get out of the management deal with Allen Klein, said no. Lennon said yes—if he could go onstage with Ono; George objected to that, and John ended up not participating.

When Harrison got in touch with Dylan . . . well, it *seemed* like Bob gave him a yes . . . but as late as July 31, during a technical rehearsal at Madison Square Garden on the day before the pair of benefit shows, Bob said, "Hey, man, you know, this isn't my scene." George flared with anger, fed up with his friend's refusal to fully commit to the show. "Look," he said, "it's not *my* scene, either." There was another moment of tension later in the rehearsal, when George asked Bob if he would make "Blowin' in the Wind" part of his set. An incredulous Dylan asked Harrison if he planned to play "I Want to Hold Your Hand."

When George took the stage at the sold-out Madison Square Garden the next afternoon, he had a scrap of paper taped to his guitar with his set list scrawled on it, followed by a one-word question: "Bob?" The answer was yes. There he was, in head-to-toe denim, pacing in the backstage darkness. After performances by Shankar, Harrison, Preston, and Ringo, George announced, "I'd like to bring on a friend of us all, Mr. Bob Dylan."

He stepped forward, into the teeming applause. He fiddled with the microphone stands, as he might have done at Gerde's a decade earlier, and then threw himself into a countrified version of "A Hard Rain's A-Gonna Fall," a song he hadn't performed since 1965. George was at his side, playing electric slide guitar; Ringo tapped a tambourine; Leon Russell was on bass. Dylan then led the little band through a set that included "Mr. Tambourine Man," "Just Like a Woman" (with Harrison and Russell singing harmony), and, yes, "Blowin' in the Wind."

The response was tremendous for both the afternoon and evening concerts. At the after-party, Bob told George, "God! If only we'd done *three* shows!" The day's work would yield a bestselling triple album (credited to George Harrison & Friends) and a concert film. It also established the template for Live Aid, Farm Aid, and other large-scale charity efforts to come.

Weberman took credit not only for Dylan's involvement in a worthy cause but for his decision to play his politically engaged songs again. He promised to stop rooting through Dylan's garbage and dissolved the Dylan Liberation Front. From now on, he would channel his energies into a new organization with a wider aim, the Rock Liberation Front. The first target, he decided, would be McCartney. In going after Paul, he was aligned with Lennon, whose "How Do You Sleep?" was creating a stir among Beatles fans, now that *Imagine* was in record stores.

"McCartney's lyrics lack the slightest social commitment and he's quickly becoming the Sinatra of the '70s," Weberman wrote in his announcement of the anti-McCartney action. "He lives like an aristocrat on a huge estate in England, never gives any money to any progressive organizations and hasn't done a benefit in years." Playing on the Paul-is-dead rumor, Weberman and David Peel held a mock funeral on August 26 outside the Eastman family's Park Avenue apartment. Props included a hearse and a coffin containing copies of the albums *McCartney* and *Ram*.

Weberman then went after Capitol Records, which he accused of withholding funds from the war refugees because of its failure to release *The Concert for Bangladesh* album in timely fashion and its plan to keep some of the sales revenue; Harrison had publicly criticized the label for the same reason. At a demonstration outside the company's New York office, Weberman announced that he had two influential people on his side: "John and Yoko are the newest members of the Rock Liberation Front!"

In October, Ono and Lennon hosted a retrospective exhibition of Yoko's artwork, *This Is Not Here*, at the Everson Museum of Art in Syracuse, New York. The couple flew sixty-five journalists to the event on a chartered jet. Their new assistant, May Pang, a twenty-year-old music lover from East Harlem, served as the flight attendant. At the press conference, Yoko's devotion to the mind-over-matter idealism she shared with John was once again front and center. "In this show, I'd like to prove that you don't need talent to be an artist," she said. "'Artist' is just a frame of mind. Anybody can be an artist." In addition to dozens of Yoko pieces, the works on display included contributions from Ringo (a green plastic bag), Harrison (a milk bottle), and Dylan (a copy of his *Nashville Skyline* album, without the sleeve).

On the night of October 9, John's thirty-first birthday, there was a hotel room celebration attended by Ringo and Maureen, Eric Clapton, the drummer Jim Keltner, Klaus Voormann, Neil Aspinall, and Allen Ginsberg. John led them through a few of the songs he had made on his own or with his wife, including "Power to the People," "Oh Yoko!," "Crippled Inside," and "Imagine," which was on its way to No. 3 in the *Billboard* Hot 100. He also sang campfire versions of songs written by Paul ("Yesterday," "Uncle Albert / Admiral Halsey"), George ("My Sweet Lord") and Bob ("Like a Rolling Stone"). Because of the chord progression it shared with so many other songs, "Like a Rolling Stone" inevitably morphed into a medley of "Twist and Shout," "Louie, Louie," and "La Bamba."

Around this time, like a dog going back to its vomit, Weberman returned to the garbage cans on MacDougal Street. Bob got home one afternoon after his stalker's latest foray to find Sara distraught. He marched in the direction of the building where Weberman lived. When he spotted his nemesis on the corner of Bleecker Street and Bowery, Dylan "jumped him, wrestling him to the sidewalk and bouncing his head against the pavement several times," reported Anthony Scaduto, who interviewed both men afterward.

From the summer of 1971 into the first months of 1972, Dylan, Lennon, Harrison, and McCartney were in sync with one another to a remarkable degree when it came to their music. All four wrote and recorded songs meant to raise awareness of political causes.

George struck first, with "Bangladesh," the rare Top 40 entrant to address war and famine. Lennon followed with "John Sinclair," his plea to free the man serving ten years in a Michigan prison cell for the possession of two joints, and "Attica State," a song in support of the inmates who had risen up in protest of their living conditions at Attica state prison in Attica, New York, a rebellion that ended in the deaths of thirty-three prisoners and ten guards. At roughly the same time, Dylan offered up "George Jackson," a tribute to the Black Panther leader who had been slain while trying to escape San Quentin State Prison in California. Lennon liked that one so much that he sang it during an appearance on a French TV show days after Dylan had put it out as a single.

The back-and-forth continued when John and Yoko recorded "Angela," a tribute to George Jackson's wife, the radical activist Angela Davis. McCartney, who had always steered clear of politics in his songs, stepped out of character with the agitprop "Give Ireland Back to the Irish." He drew attention to it by making it the debut single of his newly formed group, Wings. He was inspired by the Bloody Sunday massacre in Derry, Northern Ireland, during which British forces shot twenty-seven unarmed protesters, killing thirteen. Lennon was right there with him, writing a pair of anti-imperialist anthems, "Sunday Bloody Sunday" and "The Luck of the Irish."

On November 1, 1971, John and Yoko committed themselves to New York City when they took up residence in a modest rental apartment on Bank Street, less than a mile from Dylan's townhouse. "Everybody cycles round the Village," Lennon said, soon after moving in. "Dylan goes about on his all the time, chaining it to the railings when he stops, and nobody ever recognizes him. I can't wait to get out on mine."

With their new friends Weberman, Abbie Hoffman, and Jerry Rubin, John and Yoko bandied about the idea of staging rallies meant to thwart President Richard Nixon's reelection bid, a protest campaign that would have its climax at the Republican National Convention in San Diego. The Federal Bureau of Investigation was concerned enough about Lennon's potential to disrupt the election that it placed him under surveillance. In a letter to the White House, the U.S. senator Strom Thurmond, a Republican of South Carolina, proposed that his visa be revoked.

Between recording sessions for their next album, the politically charged *Some Time in New York City*, John and Yoko tried to enlist

Dylan for the anti-Nixon rallies. But there was a sticking point—their close association with his garbage-happy tormentor.

Yoko asked Weberman to issue a mea culpa. He refused. So John and Yoko, with the help of Jerry Rubin and David Peel, went on the attack, collaborating on a letter to *The Village Voice*: "We ask A. J. Weberman to publicly apologize to Bob Dylan for leading a public campaign of lies and malicious slander against Dylan in the past year," they wrote.

They went on to liken Weberman to the nation's most despised figure at the time, the cult leader Charles Manson, who was on trial for having ordered his disciples to go on murderous rampages in Los Angeles County. Those killing sprees had resulted in the deaths of seven people in the summer of 1969. Manson, a frustrated musician with a hippie demeanor, claimed that the Beatles had sent him messages in their lyrics; and his followers painted the words "Healter Skelter," a misspelling of the White Album song title "Helter Skelter," in human blood on the refrigerator of their second murder site.

"Weberman is to Dylan as Manson is to the Beatles—and Weberman uses what he interprets from Dylan's music to try and kill Dylan and build his own fame," Lennon and his confreres wrote in their public letter. "Now A. J. Weberman takes credit for Dylan's 'George Jackson' song. More egocentric bullshit. Dylan wrote it in spite of Weberman and in spite of 'the movement.' Dylan wrote it because he felt it."

On December 9, shortly after the letter was published, John and Yoko traveled to Ann Arbor, Michigan, to perform at the John Sinclair Freedom Rally as the headliners of a bill that included Stevie Wonder, Allen Ginsberg, Phil Ochs, and David Peel. It wasn't the show that many fans were hoping for—John and Yoko didn't take the stage of the Crisler Arena until 3 a.m., and their brief set included "John Sinclair," "Attica State," and "The Luck of the Irish"—but it achieved its aim. Two days later, Sinclair was released.

The quick result suggested that the couple had the power to make an impact with their planned anti-Nixon protests, especially if they could bring Dylan aboard. At the end of December, John invited Bob to the Record Plant, where David Peel was making his album for Apple. But Lennon miscalculated if he thought his friend would be amused by Peel's "The Ballad of Bob Dylan." Perhaps it was the idiotic refrain—"Bob Dylan! Robert Zimmerman!" repeated ad nauseam—that caused Bob to walk out.

The anti-Nixon-rally plan withered and died soon after that, when the U.S. government, citing Lennon's 1968 cannabis conviction, revoked his visa and started deportation proceedings. Dylan was among the writers, artists, and activists who sent a letter of support to the Immigration and Naturalization Service. "Hurray for John & Yoko!" he wrote. "Let them stay and live here and breathe. The country's got plenty of room and space. Let John & Yoko stay!"

On Election Day, John and Yoko were back at the Record Plant, working on an Ono album. As reports came in that Nixon was on his way to a landslide victory, John started swigging from a bottle of tequila. By the time he piled into a Volkswagen with his wife and a few musicians, he was good and drunk. It was around two in the morning, and they were on their way to a party at Rubin's apartment on Prince Street, with the windows down. The man at the wheel was Bob Gruen, a New York–born photographer. "John screamed angrily," Gruen recalled, "cursing wildly at everyone during the car ride—only a Liverpool sailor could have understood some of the language John used that night."

The party was breaking up by the time of their arrival. John announced to the remaining guests that he didn't want to be part of John and Yoko anymore. Then he approached a woman and led her into a bedroom. Yoko was "really upset," according to Gruen, especially when they heard moans coming through the wall. To drown out the noise, Gruen took an album from the stack—*Blonde on Blonde*—and put one of its two discs on the turntable. "I wanted to play something lively," Gruen recalled, "but unfortunately I put on the wrong side of a Bob Dylan album, and the first song that played was 'Sad-Eyed Lady of the Lowlands.'"

Dylan came up with some great songs in the early 1970s, among them "When I Paint My Masterpiece," about the vain pursuit of artistic perfection, and "Watching the River Flow," which pitted the majesty of the natural world against petty human striving. But he couldn't help but notice that his latest work wasn't affecting the world as strongly as his old stuff had.

Self-doubt hit him hard one day in 1972, when he was driving through Arizona and heard "Heart of Gold" on the car radio. It was an enticing song, written and recorded by Neil Young, a distinctive singer and songwriter from Toronto a few years younger than Dylan. It had a melancholy tune, nicely thought-out lyrics, and a harmonica part that sound a lot like one of Dylan's own, minus the piercing notes. "I think it was up at No. 1 for a long time, and I'd say, 'Shit, that's me. If it sounds like me, it should as well be me,'" Dylan recalled. The song was high in the charts when he was playing a small part in a Western movie directed by Sam Peckinpah, *Pat Garrett and Billy the Kid*; Dylan had also agreed to supply the soundtrack.

In addition to Neil Young, the Beatles were on Dylan's mind when he wrote the film's signature song, a hymnlike ballad that said a lot in very few words. In the Tulsa archive, there's a notebook containing an early draft, possibly the first. At the top of a page, Dylan has jotted down a kind of story fragment, or perhaps a dream, involving the Beatles.

> *"You got something for the Beatles?" said a heavy set man with a gun. "Yeah but I gotta deliver it myself" "Give it to [me] and leave." He said, but just then a voice came out of an open door. "What is it, chaps, why the fuss?"*

The ink goes from blue to black. The handwriting goes from cursive to print.

> *Mama, take this badge off me*
> *I can't use it anymore*
> *Mama Mama can you see I'm*
> *Knocking, Knocking on Heaven's door*

He recorded the song at Burbank Studios in Burbank, California, near his family's new oceanside home in Malibu. It reached No. 12 on the *Billboard* chart in the fall of 1973, not a bad showing for a death-haunted ballad at a time when one of the first disco hits, Eddie Kendricks's "Keep on Truckin'," was all the rage. "Knockin' on Heaven's Door" would go on to be one of Dylan's most covered songs, with versions by Guns N' Roses, Ladysmith Black Mambazo, and Antony and the Johnsons, among scores of others.

When it was on the radio, Lennon was in Los Angeles, having split from Yoko in the wake of his election night dalliance, to record some old rock 'n' roll hits under the erratic guidance of Phil Spector. "Maybe I'll take this album on the road, if we ever finish it," John told a reporter. "Maybe I'll just rest and write some songs. There's business things going on, as usual. Hey, when's Dylan going on the road? Maybe I'll go along and play rhythm."

John was at the start of the period he would call his Lost Weekend, though it would last eighteen months and would prove highly productive. Yoko had sent him away from their new home, Apartment 72 on the seventh floor of the grand old Dakota building on the Upper West Side of Manhattan, in the company of the couple's assistant, May Pang. John stayed in touch with his wife, whom he called "Mother," even as his relationship with Pang grew more serious.

Dylan and the four ex-Beatles remained in one another's orbits as they recaptured old glories. It was a time when fans and publicity-seeking promoters were clamoring for a Beatles reunion and music critics kept slapping the tag "new Dylan" onto every new singer-songwriter with half a brain, as if the old one were dead.

The run of success in the mid-seventies included George's second No. 1 single in the U.S., "Give Me Love (Give Me Peace on Earth)"; five Top 10 hits by Ringo, including the chart-topping "Photograph" and "You're Sixteen"; Dylan's sold-out arena tour with the Band and the release of what was arguably his finest LP, *Blood on the Tracks*, which he wrote after splitting with Sara; McCartney's acclaimed *Band on the Run* album and the multiplatinum single of the same title, followed by a tour that packed arenas across the U.S. and Europe; and Lennon's first No. 1 single, "Whatever Gets You Thru the Night," another hit, "#9 Dream," and the No. 1 album *Walls and Bridges*.

In early 1975, weeks after John, Paul, George, and Ringo had signed the papers formally dissolving the Beatles, McCartney returned to the charts with "Junior's Farm," which he said drew lyrical inspiration from two Dylan songs, "Maggie's Farm" and "The Mighty Quinn." John seriously considered joining Paul and his band for a writing and recording session in New Orleans, only to drop the idea when he moved back to the Dakota.

In a sign of their recommitment, John and Yoko posed for a series of portraits taken by Brian Hamill, a younger brother of Pete Hamill, the journalist who had nearly come to blows with Lennon a decade earlier. During the photo shoot, Brian was wearing a cap similar to the one worn by Beatle John in the days of "I Feel Fine." Up on the roof of the Dakota, when it was just the two of them, Brian said, "Sorry about copying your style." Lennon pointed to the young man's cap and said, "Don't worry about copying my style. I copped it from Dylan."

John, at the time, was starting a hiatus that would last nearly five years. Early in this phase, though, he didn't intend to go into semi-retirement, as he made clear in an interview, when he suggested himself as Dylan's next producer. "I think he made a great album in *Blood on the Tracks*," he said, "but I'm still not keen on the backings. I think I could produce him great."

Dylan kicked off his second tour of the seventies, the Rolling Thunder Revue, in the fall of 1975. It was a ragtag circus, with special guests, including Joan Baez, and hastily booked concerts at out-of-the-way venues. Among the new songs he played night after night was "Hurricane," an epic narrative ballad meant to raise awareness of an injustice: The middleweight boxer Rubin "Hurricane" Carter had been wrongfully convicted of murder and was serving a life sentence. Like Lennon's "John Sinclair," this was a song meant to get a man out of prison.

In December, Rolling Thunder pulled into New York for Night of the Hurricane, a benefit at Madison Square Garden. Dylan wanted Lennon to join him onstage, and he tasked a mutual friend, the photographer Bob Gruen, with passing along the invitation. "So I told him about this concert," Gruen recalled, "and John said, 'Well, just tell Bob Dylan that it's *my* turn to watch the river flow.'"

His life had changed: He and Yoko were now parents. Their son, Sean Ono Lennon, had been born October 9, 1975, Lennon's thirty-fifth birthday, and John was determined to be a better father to him than he had been to Julian.

Dylan followed up on his request with a phone call to Apartment 72 at a moment when John was tending to the baby. Gruen was there when Lennon picked up the receiver. "He answered the phone and then he said, 'Oh, hi, Bob, hold on a second,'" Gruen recalled. "And he put the phone down. And I heard him singing a lullaby with an acoustic guitar."

The Rolling Thunder tour clattered to a halt in the spring of 1976, shortly before Paul and Linda hosted a grand party on a seventeen-acre estate in Beverly Hills to celebrate the end of the Wings Over America tour. The celebrity guests included Warren Beatty, Britt Ekland, Michael Jackson, Lorne Michaels, Jack Nicholson, Rod Stewart, and members of the Eagles. Dylan was there, too, but he no longer felt much like partying when a photographer hired by the McCartneys tried to take his picture. "Dylan was hiding in the bushes," Paul recalled. "It was like, 'Bob's here.' I go, 'Oh, great. Where is he?' 'Over there. In those bushes.' So I go into the bushes."

For Dylan and the former Beatles, 1976 marked the peak of their second-act return to cultural relevance. A new one by Wings, "Silly Love Songs," became the year's top-selling single in America. Dylan's latest album, *Desire*, went to No. 1, and he cracked the Top 40 with "Hurricane." In a sign that he would come to be regarded as the artistic conscience of the nation in the manner of Mark Twain or Walt Whitman, Jimmy Carter invoked his name when he accepted the Democratic nomination for president. "We have an America that, in Bob Dylan's phrase, is busy being born, not busy dying," he said in his speech at Madison Square Garden.

The seventies were less kind to the man who had introduced Dylan to the Beatles. Al Aronowitz's plan to leave journalism and make it as a manager or concert promoter hadn't worked out as he had hoped, and he found himself living with his wife, Ann, and their three children in what he described as "a cockroach-infested Manhattan tenement." When Ann was diagnosed with cancer, which would prove fatal, the lack of steady income became even more worrisome, and he turned to Harrison for help: "George enabled her to live out her life in rented suburban comfort by giving me a loan of $50,000 that he knew I could never possibly repay," Aronowitz wrote in his memoir. "To me, George's $50,000 'loan' was an exhibition of saintliness unequalled by *any* rock superstar I knew."

Lennon would characterize his Dakota years as a time of tranquil domesticity, but it wasn't all bread-baking and bedtime stories. Yoko sometimes sent him on solo trips around the world based on the counsel of numerologists and astrologers. On her advice, he also refrained from speaking for weeks at a time. Heroin still had a hold on him, and he dabbled now and then. One day he took off on a whim to spend some wild nights in Honolulu with the guitarist Jesse Ed Davis, who had been one of his Lost Weekend running buddies.

John wrote heartfelt songs at the piano, many of which showed great promise, but he didn't have the need or the will to bring them to completion. When he took out his guitar, his thoughts often went to Dylan. He taped himself playing a medley of Dylan's "Subterranean Homesick Blues" and the song that had inspired it, Chuck Berry's "Too Much Monkey Business." While watching television news on November 27, 1978, he broke out his Dylan voice to sing the words of the Reuters international news feed crawling across the screen, an impromptu satire that ended with a reference to "Stuck Inside of Mobile with the Memphis Blues Again": "I'm stuck inside of Lexicon," John sang, "with the *Roget's Thesaurus* blues again." He used the same voice in a spoof of "Knockin' on Heaven's Door."

In the spring of 1977, Lennon became a regular viewer of TV shows hosted by evangelist preachers and told friends he was a born-again Christian. He wrote two religious songs, "Talking with Jesus" and

"Amen," and he took Yoko and Sean to Easter services at a church near the Dakota. During a trip that summer to see his wife's family in Japan, he stopped in at a church in Karuizawa, where he spoke with parishioners, telling them he had made a mistake when he had claimed the Beatles were bigger than Jesus.

Dylan was often alone in the big house in Malibu after his divorce from Sara in 1977. "I wasn't a very good husband," he said. He assembled a band, with eight musicians and a trio of female backing vocalists, and embarked on a world tour. On October 5, 1978, during a sound check in Nashville, he played something new, "Slow Train Coming." It had strong biblical overtones and made use of the same train imagery that had figured in one of his favorite religious songs, Curtis Mayfield's "People Get Ready."

During a show in San Diego, a fan threw a silver cross onto the stage. Dylan picked it up. A night or two later, in a hotel room in Arizona, he felt a presence. "Jesus put his hand on me," he said. He went on to attend three months of Bible study classes at the Los Angeles chapter of the Vineyard Christian Fellowship, a fundamentalist organization.

Evangelical songs poured out of him. He asked Jerry Wexler, who had produced Ray Charles and Aretha Franklin, to help him record the album *Slow Train Coming* at Muscle Shoals Sound Studio in Sheffield, Alabama. Wexler was precise with the arrangements, insisting that Dylan give up his improvisational style and take special care with his singing. The result was a record with a bright clean sound that fit in nicely with the pop music of 1979. With "Gotta Serve Somebody," the single from the album, Dylan not so subtly informed all those who had not accepted Christ as their savior that they were following Satan. It would be his last Top 40 hit on the *Billboard* Hot 100, reaching No. 24; it would also win a Grammy.

Like many critics and Dylan fans, Lennon was flabbergasted when he heard "Gotta Serve Somebody" on its release in August 1979. By this time, he was long past his own brief born-again phase. On September 5, while recording an audio diary, he referred to McCartney, Jagger, and Dylan as "company men." "Well," he continued, "I was listening to the radio and Dylan's new single or album, whatever the hell it was, came on.... The singing was really pathetic, and the words were just embarrassing. So here we sit, watching the mighty Dylan and the mighty McCartney and the mighty Jagger slide down the mountain, blood and mud in their nails."

A month later, on his birthday, he spoke once more into a tape recorder: "Here we are, aged thirty-nine, looking out of my hotel window, wondering whether to jump out or get back in bed. So, got back in bed." He was alluding to a terrifying Yoko song about suicidal ideation, "Looking Over from My Hotel Window." "My body's full of smack," John continued, "but not enough of it, and I'm thinking, 'What the hell am I doing this for? I thought I would have quit it all by now.'"

A few weeks later, Dylan performed "Gotta Serve Somebody" when he appeared as the musical guest on *Saturday Night Live*, a show Lennon was known to watch. Soon after that episode aired, John replied to "Gotta Serve Somebody" with a new composition of his own, "Serve Yourself." It was vicious, profane, full of life, and it stands as his last great work.

The title suggests that it's an anthem of self-empowerment, and it does have that element to it, instructing listeners to save themselves, rather than wait to be delivered from suffering by Jesus, Muhammad, Buddha, or Krishna; but the song also makes the case that mothers should be revered more than any religious figure.

Lennon received a second jolt on a spring day in 1980 when he was listening to the car radio while running errands with Fred Seaman, the latest assistant to John and Yoko, near a house they owned on Long Island. "Fuck a pig!" John cried. "It's Paul!" The song blasting out of the speakers was "Coming Up," a catchy but experimental single from *McCartney II*, an album Paul had recorded at his home studios, playing all the instruments himself, including an array of synthesizers. The next morning, John told his assistant he couldn't get "Coming Up" out of his head. "It's driving me crackers!" he said.

Lennon threw himself into a new hobby, sailing. He spent several weeks in the summer of 1980 learning the basics. Then he arranged to go on a voyage from Newport, Rhode Island, to Hamilton, Bermuda, aboard a forty-three-foot sloop with a crew of four. In the middle of the Atlantic, the winds began to whistle through the rigging as waves rocked and pounded the boat. As the storm intensified, three crew members were incapacitated with seasickness, leaving John and the captain, Hank Halsted, alone on deck. Halsted held firm at the wheel through thirty hours of gales and towering seas . . . and then he was too tired to go on.

"Come on up here, big boy," he told Lennon. "You've got to drive this little buggy."

John protested at first, saying his piddly rock star muscles weren't up to the job, but there was no other choice. From down in the hold, the captain heard him shouting at the elements and singing sea shanties at the top of his lungs. "I heard rapture," Halsted said. "He was acting like a very sane madman." John stood at the wheel for six hours straight. When the storm broke, the boat was seventy miles off course. He helped mend the sails.

In Bermuda, he was joined by Fred Seaman and the four-year-old Sean at a house overlooking a bay. He performed lively versions of his latest songs, including "Serve Yourself." "It was a wicked parody, sung over a galloping guitar riff, that left no doubt that John had begun to reclaim his muse," Seaman recalled. Lennon decided, with Yoko, to book time at the Hit Factory in Manhattan.

From August to October, they recorded the album *Double Fantasy*. John considered making "Serve Yourself" one of its tracks, only to decide against it, perhaps because it was in the vein of the cruelly truthful songs he had written nearly a decade earlier for *John Lennon/Plastic Ono Band* and seemed out of place among "Beautiful Boy," a lullaby to Sean, and "(Just Like) Starting Over," a fifties-style rocker with remarriage as its theme.

Like "Strawberry Fields Forever," "Serve Yourself" had an especially lengthy gestation period. All told, Lennon worked on it for more than a year, recording twelve known versions on cassette. Each was different from the last. On November 14, 1980, he made the final version—a raw, energetic take—as part of his last-known home-recording session. John's work tapes would eventually escape the Dakota and fall into the hands of bootleggers. "Serve Yourself" would reacquaint listeners with the furious Lennon who seemed at odds with the peacenik of "Imagine."

In 1992, Dylan was asked if he had ever heard "Serve Yourself" and if it bothered him. He mentioned that someone in his touring band had come across a bootleg tape of the song and shared it with him. "It didn't bother me," Dylan said. "It intrigued me." Referring to "Gotta Serve Somebody," the song that had given rise to Lennon's response, he added: "Why would it affect him in such a way? Who cares? It was just a song."

19 Rolling On

Around 11 p.m. on December 8, 1980, after four hours of working with Yoko on her song "Walking on Thin Ice" at the Hit Factory, John stepped out of a limousine near the Dakota and walked slightly ahead of his wife toward the archway entrance. It was an unseasonably warm night, about sixty degrees. A man was standing in the shadows. "Mr. Lennon?" he said. He fired his .38-caliber revolver five times. Four bullets hit the target.

A call went out over the police radio: "Man shot, One West Seventy-Second Street." The first cops on the scene put the gunman up against the building and handcuffed him. The second team carried Lennon out of the Dakota courtyard. He was still alive, with blood coming out of his mouth.

They took him to the third squad car to pull up outside the building and put him in the back seat. The man at the wheel, Jim Moran, had been among the officers on patrol outside the Plaza Hotel sixteen years earlier. His job back then was to keep screaming fans from storming the lobby. Now he was driving the man who had started the Beatles to Roosevelt Hospital.

Later that night, as the *Daily News* columnist Jimmy Breslin wrote, Moran and his partner "stood in the emergency room as John Lennon, whose music they knew, whose music was known everywhere on earth, became just another person who died after being shot with a gun on the streets of New York."

The weather in the city went cold, dropping into the low twenties, with sharp gusts. More than one hundred thousand people held vigils in Central Park, which lay across Central Park West from the eastern facade of the Dakota. Flags in New York State were flown at half-mast on the order of Governor Hugh Carey. Reporters across the U.S. compared the general outpouring of grief to the reactions that had come in the wake of the assassinations of John F. Kennedy and Martin Luther King. More than four thousand people sang "Give Peace a Chance" at the Red Rocks Amphitheater in Colorado, where the Beatles had once braved the stage after a lunatic had threatened to throw a hand grenade at them. Thousands gathered in the streets of Liverpool.

Al Aronowitz called George Harrison and found him "disconsolate." "It's like a bad Hollywood script-writer wrote it," George said. "It's hard to believe anyone would do that to John." The killer was Mark David Chapman, a twenty-five-year-old Lennon fan and amateur musician who had been treated for psychiatric disabilities. Born in Fort Worth, Texas, and raised in Georgia, he had been living in Honolulu before he set out for New York to commit the deed that the police would describe as a "premeditated execution."

George was the first person close to Lennon to react to the murder in song, with "All Those Years Ago," a bouncy single that referenced "All You Need Is Love" and "Imagine" in its portrayal of him as someone who had been ridiculed for preaching a message of love. He recorded it in the spring of 1981, with Paul and Linda singing harmonies and Ringo on drums, and it went on to be a hit on both sides of the Atlantic that summer.

Although George viewed death as the soul's transition from its earthly incarnation to its next stage, he began taking greater security precautions. "That's when George became quite paranoid," said his friend Michael Palin of the comedy troupe Monty Python. He had a barbed-wire fence installed around Friar Park, his thirty-acre estate in Henley-on-Thames, and started spending more time at his isolated properties in Hawaii and Tasmania. "He was always worried that somebody would try to kill him," said Colin Davis, the Friar Park gardener.

McCartney wrote the poignant "Here Today" in tribute to Lennon in the summer of 1981. He recorded it, with George Martin producing, for his thoughtful 1982 album *Tug of War*. The song describes John as someone whose combative, contrarian surface camouflaged a soft heart.

Dylan would also commemorate John in song—but not till many decades had gone by. More immediately, while Harrison was on the radio with "All Those Years Ago" and McCartney was working on "Here Today," he was preparing a tour of Europe. Before the first show, in Toulouse, France, on June 21, 1981, Dylan gave something to Tim Drummond, the bass player in his band. "I thought, 'Bob Dylan's given me a present—maybe a box full of diamonds?'" Drummond said. "It was a bulletproof vest."

The guitarist Fred Tackett remembered the same thing. "John Lennon was shot in the winter of 1980, and that concerned everyone, because you thought, My God, if someone went after John, why wouldn't they go after Bob?" he said. "So we were much more concerned. When we started the European tour, everyone had bulletproof vests, and all this kind of stuff, special security guys checking out all the apartment buildings around the venues. That lasted for a little bit. Maybe one concert we wore those bulletproof vests, and then someone said, 'This sucks, enough of that.' But there was a feeling of danger."

Less than a week after the show in Toulouse, Dylan called Harrison and asked him if he'd like to sit in with the band during his six-night residency at Earl's Court in London. "Oh, no, I don't really want to do that," replied George, who hadn't performed in public since he had appeared on *Saturday Night Live* five years earlier. On the final night of the residency, with George in the audience, Dylan made a valiant, if unrehearsed, attempt at "Here Comes the Sun." Even that most optimistic of songs couldn't quell the potential for violence that seems to lie dormant in any crowd. Later that night, during one of his Christian songs, a fan close to the stage threw a bottle. It hit Bob's guitar.

"You're gonna have to go out a long way to hurt me!" Dylan shouted.

The tour reached the U.S. in the fall. At the Music Hall in Cincinnati, Dylan didn't want to risk walking from the dressing room to the stage, according to Mary Judge, the theater's chief librarian. "It was very shortly after John Lennon was killed," Judge recalled, "and Bob was convinced that someone was out to kill him, too. Even though he had eight bodyguards and his dressing room was one hundred feet from the stage, he refused to walk. At curtain time, I heard a loud back-firing sound, and then Bob Dylan came roaring down the hallway on a huge motorcycle. He jumped off the bike just feet from the stage and rushed onstage. The stagehand who caught the bike turned it around and, when the first half was almost over, revved it up . . . and, sure enough, Bob jumped back on and roared back to his dressing room, filling the backstage with exhaust and gas fumes."

■　　　■　　　■

A number of people who had survived the sixties seemed lost in the new cultural atmosphere of Ronald Reagan, Margaret Thatcher, and MTV. Al Aronowitz, for one, was in worse shape than ever. "They used to say that marijuana, although it is a comparatively harmless substance, leads to harder drugs, and I suppose that was true in my case," he wrote. "I eventually joined many others of the sixties in smoking cocaine freebase, now more commonly known as crack, which drove me crazy enough to alienate myself from just about everybody I ever knew."

The mid-1980s also represented a low point for Dylan and the surviving Beatles. Two generations of pop and rock stars had come along since they had gotten their starts, and as they approached their mid-forties they didn't look quite right in the clothes that were in style at the time. George and Ringo stepped back from public life, while Paul and Bob continued taking their wares to a marketplace dominated by Michael Jackson, Madonna, Prince, AC/DC, Whitney Houston, Van Halen, and Run-DMC.

Several seasoned musicians—Bruce Springsteen, Peter Gabriel, Phil Collins, Billy Joel, Lionel Richie—made impressive showings in the charts after having adapted to the increasingly digital production techniques. But Dylan just sounded odd on *Empire Burlesque*, an album coproduced by the remix specialist Arthur Baker, who had worked with Madonna; and it was the same for McCartney when he recorded *Press to Play* under the guidance of Hugh Padgham, who had made his name with the Human League and the Police.

Strangely enough, Harrison was the one who broke through. After a five-year break, he found a sympathetic producer in Jeff Lynne, the onetime leader of the Electric Light Orchestra, or ELO, a British band that Lennon had once called (accurately) "son of Beatles" during its run of hits in the 1970s. When Harrison and Lynne started working together at Friar Park, they found a happy midpoint between sixties-style rock and the drum-first sound then in vogue. This was a surprising development for George, who had begun to sound like an old crank when he spoke in interviews about the latest artists.

With a mad scientist's glee, Lynne worked the control board at George's home studio to arrive at sounds that were of-the-moment in 1987. Whenever a bum note or tech glitch marred a track, George would say, "We'll bury it in the mix." "We'll bury" became "Wilbury," which turned into a running joke. And when George floated the notion of forming a band, he said its name should be the Trembling Wilburys. Lynne wasn't so sure about the "Trembling" part. What about "Traveling"?

In the middle of the sessions, George took a trip to Los Angeles. Dylan tracked him down and invited him to go see Taj Mahal, a blues, rock, and folk artist, at the Palomino, a down-home club in North Hollywood. "So we went there and had a few of these Mexican beers, and had a few more," George recalled. "And Jesse Ed Davis, who played guitar on 'Watching the River Flow,' is in the audience, and Bob says, 'Hey, why don't we all get up and play? We've had a few beers, right? And *you* can sing!'" They mounted the stage and found themselves playing fifties rockers and Dylan's "Watching the River Flow" with Mahal and his band. George was the frontman. As he sang, an exuberant Bob moved in close and shouted nonsense phrases in his ear to throw him off.

On another L.A. evening around this time, George and Bob attended a garden party thrown by Elton John. Bistro lights were twinkling by the swimming pool, and Elton's longtime assistant, Bob Halley, was working the grill. Everything might have gone smoothly if Elton hadn't gotten into the cocaine. "By the middle of the evening, I was flying, absolutely out of my mind," he recalled in his memoir, "when a scruffy-looking guy I didn't recognize wandered into the party. Who the hell was he? He must be one of the staff, a gardener. I loudly demanded to know what the gardener was doing helping himself to a drink. There was a moment's shocked silence, broken by the sound of Bob Halley's voice: 'Elton, that's not the fucking gardener, it's *Bob Dylan*.'" Undeterred, the host decided that Bob needed a new outfit. "We can't have you in those terrible clothes, darling," Elton said. As he led Dylan toward the house, George stepped in. "Elton," he said, "I really think you need to go steady on the old marching powder."

Those nights were enjoyable enough, but they came in the middle of a period that Dylan would describe as his personal and professional nadir.

He had thrown in his lot with Tom Petty and the Heartbreakers, a sturdy, disciplined band that managed to put out a string of hits while playing a brand of rock that owed a lot to Dylan, the Beatles, the Stones, and the Byrds. As Dylan performed at stadiums and arenas with Petty on a tour that stretched across eighteen months, he worried that the ticket buyers weren't really there for him, that he was just another oldies act, the latest in the long line of entertainers who had entered "the bottomless pit of cultural oblivion," as he put it in his memoir. "Tom was at the top of his game and I was at the bottom of mine," he wrote. "I couldn't overcome the odds. Everything was smashed. My own songs had become strangers to me, I didn't have the skill to touch their raw nerves, couldn't penetrate the surfaces. It wasn't my moment of history anymore. There was a hollow singing in my heart and I couldn't wait to retire and fold up the tent. One more big payday with Petty and that would be it for me. I was what they called over the hill."

It was bad enough to have those thoughts. It was worse when the outside world confirmed them. The morning after a show with Petty in Helsinki, Finland, in 1987, Bob was out walking when he noticed a woman reading a newspaper with the word "Dylan" in a headline. "What's it say there in that paper?" he asked. The woman shook her head. He persuaded her to read the headline. Translated from Finnish to English, it was this: "The God Arrived! The Man Performed." That made Dylan laugh. But he was silent when the woman summed up the rest of the review: "It says you would have been better off if you'd have died young like other legends—like Elvis and Marilyn or James Dean."

The next month, Harrison attended two of the three Petty-Dylan concerts in Birmingham, England. He was in the crowd once again when the show came to Wembley Stadium in London for a four-night engagement. At the final Wembley show, George stood onstage with Bob to sing "Rainy Day Women." Although he could quote Dylan at will, the words somehow slipped his mind that night, and he found himself shouting out a bunch of gibberish. Afterward, in a reference to that night at the Palomino, Bob said, "So you got even with me!"

By this time, *Cloud Nine*, the album Harrison had been making with Jeff Lynne, was just about ready for release. And as he had done with *All Things Must Pass* seventeen years earlier, George surprised everybody by having a hit record. Even more unlikely, given the fact that he was the Beatle most irked by the trials and tribulations of Beatlemania, a standout track on the album, "When We Was Fab," was a mostly fond portrait of the group's heyday. It played up the Dylan-Beatles connection by quoting the title of one of Bob's best-known songs in the chorus.

> *Fab! Long time ago when we was fab*
> *Fab! But it's all over now, baby blue*

The hit single from the album was "Got My Mind Set on You," a cover of an obscure 1962 song by the American rhythm and blues singer James Ray. George's version was supercharged for the late eighties, with an in-your-face snare drum. It shot to No. 1 in the U.S. and No. 2 in the UK, its popularity helped along by a music video that made heavy rotation on MTV and its sibling channel for baby boomers, VH1. George got around the fact that he had aged out of the youth market by making the video funny, following a strategy that had worked the year before for the thirty-six-year-old Peter Gabriel and his megahit "Sledgehammer."

"Got My Mind Set on You" was at the top of the charts when George showed up at the Grand Ballroom of the Waldorf-Astoria Hotel in New York on January 20, 1988, for a black-tie event, the third annual Rock & Roll Hall of Fame ceremony. He accepted the Beatles' induction into the hall with Ringo; Paul had decided to skip it after a recent flare-up of intra-band feuding over business matters. Dylan was there, too, to accept his own induction. At the end of the night, George and Bob stood at the front of the oversize band, with Ringo on drums, for a performance of "All Along the Watchtower" based on the Jimi Hendrix version. Dylan looked ill at ease on that stage of superstars, which included his early heroes Little Richard and Clyde McPhatter, so George stepped forward to sing the opening lines.

A few weeks later, a reporter spotted an unusual gathering at Mr. Chow, a Chinese restaurant in Beverly Hills: Dylan, Harrison, Petty, Lynne, and Roy Orbison, the Texas-born singer of "Oh, Pretty Woman," were seated at a table in a private room.

In promotion mode for *Cloud Nine*, George and Jeff then stopped in at the Los Angeles station KLOS to be interviewed for the nationally syndicated radio show *Rockline*. They had their guitars with them. George sang "Something" only half-seriously, but when he played "Every Grain of Sand," a great but comparatively obscure Dylan song from 1981, he gave it his all. Asked about his plans, he said, "What I'd really like to do next is to do an album with me and some of my mates. It's this new group I got, it's called the Traveling Wilburys."

On April 3, Dylan hosted Harrison, Lynne, Petty, and Orbison at the garage studio next to his Malibu mansion. They planned to record the B-side of a Harrison single earmarked for the European market. All they had to work with was a riff, some chords, and the outline of a vocal melody. Once they had gotten a solid recording of themselves strumming away at their acoustic guitars in back-porch style, George asked Bob to come up with some words, just as he had done in Bearsville twenty years earlier.

"Well, what's it about?" Bob asked. "What's it called?"

George noticed a cardboard box with "Handle with Care" stamped on the side.

"It's called 'Handle with Care.'"

"Oh, yeah, that's good, I like that," Bob said.

The song had a loose, casual sound, but the lyrics were a heartfelt depiction of the ravages of fame and the damages of daily life. Orbison lent his pure tenor to the bridge, singing, "I'm so tired of being lonely," and when Dylan followed him, rough-voiced, it sounded like a punch line. They completed the song quickly and delivered it Mo Ostin, the top executive at Warner Bros., the label that had put out *Cloud Nine*. Ostin asked for a whole album of this kind of thing, and the musicians gathered again at the home studio of Dave Stewart, of the British synth-pop duo the Eurythmics, in the Toluca Lake neighborhood of Los Angeles. His place was not quite so homey as Big Pink, but the songs the Wilburys came up with had the old basement spirit. Without the pressure of having to make a grand statement, Bob sang conversationally on "Margarita":

> *It was in Pittsburgh late one night*
> *I lost my head, got into a fight*

His voice was deep and sure and expressive, captured more clearly by the microphones than it had been on the last few Bob Dylan albums. The Wilburys also had a go at parody, summoning Prince for "Dirty World" and Springsteen for "Tweeter and the Monkey Man." The role-playing freed Dylan up, and the words rolled forth, funny and exact. Once the basic tracks were recorded, Lynne gave this summer camp–style musical enterprise a sheen that would make it seem not so out of place in the 1988 pop marketplace.

Dylan made a big decision when George brought him into the Wilburys. He was going to stop going through the motions. He was going to reconnect with his old songs. He was going to rid himself of the fans who had come to gawk at the legend and replace them with people who wanted to hear the music. It would mean a lot of hard touring, and he might get kicked around, playing pavilions, fairs, hockey rinks, small theaters, clubs, didn't matter—the main thing was to get out there, on his own, with his name the only name on the marquee.

He shared his plan with his tour manager, who was skeptical. A few weeks after the last Wilburys session, he was on a stage with a simple, hard-hitting trio at his back. From June through October, he played seventy-one dates. The next year he played one hundred. And so on until the present day of what has become known as the Never Ending Tour.

Traveling Wilburys Vol. 1 came out in the fall of 1988. It was so charming that critics couldn't help but like it, though they didn't really want to give their blessing to a bunch of wealthy superstars on a lark. It also sold more than 3 million copies, reaching No. 3 on the *Billboard* album chart. It was a nice change for Dylan, whose last three albums had made it to No. 61 (*Down in the Groove*), No. 53 (*Knocked Out Loaded*), and No. 33 (*Empire Burlesque*). Thanks in large part to George, he had climbed out of "the bottomless pit of cultural oblivion."

Bob had once given George the confidence he needed to become the writer of "All Things Must Pass" and "Here Comes the Sun." Twenty years on, George kept putting himself at Dylan's doorstep until he had returned the favor. Once that work was done, he took out some cream-colored stationery and wrote Bob a thank you note, being sure to include the hint of an apology for having pulled him back into the fray.

Dear Bob,
    I hope you are O.K. after the last 6 months, maybe you can have a rest. I personally am a nervous wreck but would like to think I can recover myself again eventually!

Anyway I want you to know that it was great being in the band with you—and you were very generous in being a Wilbury! Thanks, for doing the record and video and I hope it was not too embarrassing for you; who knows— maybe we will meet again someday on the avenue. . . .
    love from
    George

A few months later, Dylan walked with some trepidation into a house in New Orleans to meet with the producer Daniel Lanois, who'd had a strong hand in Peter Gabriel's "Sledgehammer," and he started work on one of his finest albums, *Oh Mercy*. Like Jeff Lynne and Dave Stewart, Lanois was able to capture Dylan's mature voice, which contained everything he had been through, good and bad. With songs like "Man in the Long Black Coat" and "Disease of Conceit," Dylan also created the persona, a wizened stranger familiar with rivers and roads, that would serve him well into the twenty-first century. Unlike the many rock stars who lost their creativity after hitting forty, he still had something to stay. In finding this new manner, this new gear, at an advanced age, he was like Leo Tolstoy or Henry James or Picasso.

■   ■   ■

After the release of the second Traveling Wilburys album in 1990 and a brief tour of Japan with Eric Clapton the next year, Harrison found he was more or less done with being a public figure. He had proved his artistic mettle as a Beatle and proved it again as a solo artist before his surprise encore in middle age. He no longer needed the applause, or at least the bother that went with it.

Ringo stepped away from the party circuit that had occupied more and more of his time as the years went by to make an album in Nashville with Chips Moman, who had produced Elvis Presley's 1969 comeback album, *From Elvis in Memphis*. But these were unhappy sessions, even when Ringo recorded a duet with Dylan, "I Wish I Knew Now What I Knew Then," a country waltz written by Charlie

Craig and Vince Gill. Ringo successfully sued to keep the album from reaching the public, saying he had been too much under the influence to make good music at the time. Not long afterward, he quit drinking and drugs. He became a slender, healthful vegetarian, rededicated himself to the meditation practice he had learned at Rishikesh, and began touring at regular intervals with a revolving crew of famous rock musicians who weren't too proud to satisfy an audience's appetite for nostalgia.

He and Dylan kept up with each other when they were out on the road. On December 17, 1997, Ringo stopped into the dressing room before Bob played the El Rey Theatre in Los Angeles. Dylan's opening act, the singer Jewel Kilcher, looked on as the two legends talked about their efforts to quit smoking. From the stage that night, Bob gave a rare shout-out: "One of the great drummers of this kind of music is in the house tonight—Ringo Starr. Ringo! Stand up and take a bow, wherever you are. Everybody loves you." In a 2021 interview, Ringo showed he had been keeping up with his old friend's work when he named "When the Deal Goes Down," a ballad from the 2006 album *Modern Times*, as one of his favorite Dylan songs.

McCartney regained the confidence he had seemingly lost and returned to touring in 1989, after a decade-long break from the road, happily serving up Beatles songs and his own greatest hits to stadium crowds around the world. He also made some adventuresome music, including a classical work, *Paul McCartney's Liverpool Oratorio*, and three electronic albums under the name the Fireman with the musician and producer Youth. The second of these, *Rushes*, was an unusually confessional work made in the wake of Linda's death to cancer in 1998.

Harrison spent some quiet years tending the grounds of Friar Park and occasionally recording new songs at his home studio until he was diagnosed with throat cancer in 1997. In the wake of surgery and radiation treatments, he was told it was in remission. Then, on the last day of 1999, a man broke into his home and stabbed George forty times. The attacker was Michael Abram, a thirty-four-year-old paranoid schizophrenic from Liverpool. His mother told reporters that he believed the Beatles were "witches." While recovering in the hospital, George was asked if the intruder had meant to kill him or just rob his house. "Well, he certainly wasn't auditioning for the Traveling Wilburys," he replied.

The cancer returned the next year. Ringo visited him while he was undergoing treatment in Switzerland. As his condition worsened, George was moved to a hospital on Staten Island in New York. Paul spent time with him there toward the end. They held hands. "We joked about things—just amusing, nutty stuff," Paul said. "It was like we were dreaming. He was my little baby brother, almost, because I'd known him that long." After Harrison died, Dylan called him "a giant—a great, great soul," and said, "The world is a profoundly emptier place without him."

■   ■   ■

Life is wonderful and horrible. The hours may pass sweetly, but we know from an early age that we're under a death sentence. Those in positions of power can try to avoid the inevitable by redrawing maps, building empires, creating moral panics, waging wars. They can move groups of people from place to place, amass fortunes they will never spend, build palaces they will visit only rarely. The rest of us try to stay sane, try to keep some money in the bank, try to find love and solace. There are happy days, blank days, and days so bad you want to bury yourself in the ground. An artist records it all from deep inside experience and thought.

The Beatles' "A Day in the Life" begins with the news of a death, and then comes the phrase "I'd love to turn you on," with the melody veering off into an eerie realm, as if to suggest a connection between death and desire. Dylan's "Tomorrow Is a Long Time" captures in words and melody the dearest moments of romantic love, but every line is shot through with sadness. An artist provides an account of such contrarieties and gives expression to the dreamlike logic of our private worlds. An artist does not impose order on things that make no sense in the manner of a propagandist, who wants to get you to believe something for a certain practical purpose. An artist tells the awful truth simply to tell it and to make a genuine connection with other people.

An artist is Lennon finding sustenance and inspiration in a variety of experiences, from lying in bed for six days straight to steering a sloop through a storm. An artist is McCartney in his Hunt Hanson disguise, watching the café patrons and imagining what their lives are like. An artist is Harrison hearing heavenly choirs in his head and forever lamenting in "My Sweet Lord" that he may never know God. An artist is Ringo, the ultimate songwriter's drummer, going out of his mind on "Rain" and holding back to build the subtle groove of "Come Together." An artist is Dylan walking phantomlike through city streets only to find himself landing somewhere between amusement and amazement when someone stops him to ask if he is registered to vote, as he describes in the 1997 song "Highlands." An artist is Little Richard singing, "A-wop-bop-a-loo-mop, a-lop-bam-boom!"

An artist is protecting something precious that has no inherent monetary value. An artist is different from even the journalist or historian who tries to chronicle and make sense of the who-what-where-when-why-and-how of endless events. An artist tries to get at the core of what it means to be a human being—that is, a being who necessarily loves and suffers. An artist tries to capture life and share it. We feel relief to learn we're not the only ones who feel a certain way, who have endured a hard or happy experience.

In addition to being the ultimate show business hoofers, Dylan and McCartney have maintained their dedication to art into their eighties. They know it is a struggle. They know they will probably fail more than they succeed. They can never be sure if they have lost the thing that makes them great, but they go on anyway.

In 2006, Dylan started sharing his idea of art with the wider world when he began hosting *Theme Time Radio Hour*. Deep in the first season, he did an episode with the theme Friends and Neighbors, playing everything from "Let's Invite Them Over," a rather twisted country duet from 1963 by George Jones and Melba Montgomery about a couple who find themselves besotted with another couple, to "Why Can't We Be Friends?," a rollicking hit for the soul band War in 1975. McCartney sent Dylan a note after he heard this episode.

> Dear Bob,
>   Just had the pleasure of listening to your Theme Time radio show, "Friends and Neighbors," and enjoyed it so much that I had to write and tell you. The music you played was fabulous and the chat in between was both edifying and amusing. Thanks for an hour of listening pleasure.
>   Hope all is well with you.
>   All the best you lovely boy,
>   Cheers, Paul

Perhaps only Paul had the stature to get away with calling Dylan "lovely boy." The feeling was mutual. In 2007, when an interviewer was pushing Dylan to talk about Lennon, he turned the subject to McCartney, saying, "I mean, I'm in awe of McCartney. He's about the only one that I am in awe of. But I'm in awe of him. He can do it all and he's never let up, you know. He's got the gift for melody, he's got the rhythm, he can play any instrument. He can scream and shout as good as anybody and he can sing the ballad as good as anybody, you know, so . . . And his melodies are, you know, effortless. . . . I'm in awe of him maybe just because he's so damn effortless. I mean, I just wish he'd quit, you know."

In 2009, on that chilly springtime afternoon in Liverpool, he made his visit to Mendips, Lennon's childhood home, and stepped up to the door of 20 Forthlin Road, the former McCartney residence. Hours later, he took the stage of the Liverpool Echo Arena before a crowd of eleven thousand. Midway through the show, he paid tribute to George by performing "Something."

Perhaps inspired by his visit to Mendips, he thought seriously about Lennon and what he had meant to the world. In 2011, he started playing a newly written song, "Roll On John," with his band during the sound checks before his concerts.

The song makes reference to Liverpool, Hamburg, and the Quarry Men. It includes allusions to "A Day in the Life," "Come Together," and "The Ballad of John and Yoko." It is suffused with nautical imagery, and the third verse describes its hero sailing "through the trade winds," which are particularly strong near Bermuda, suggesting that Dylan knew about the nine-day voyage that gave John the final push he needed to make music again.

In its treatment of the murder, "Roll On John" strips the killer of his individuality, making him an anonymous "they."

They shot him in the back and down he went

Dylan had, after all, faced death threats of his own; had seen the footage of the fans leaving his Manchester concert who said, "Dylan was shit" and "He needs shooting"; knew all too well that malevolence was the flip side of adulation; knew it could have been almost anyone.

The John Lennon of "Roll On John" is akin to the enduring folksong character John Henry—an emblematic person, someone who stands for something larger than himself. Dylan's song tells us that this person was forever on a quest, sailing through storms and perhaps never reaching the destination, like any one of us.

After he released the song as the closing track of the 2012 album *Tempest*, Dylan was asked why he had written about Lennon. "John came from the northern regions of Britain," he said. "The hinterlands. Just like I did in America, so we had some kind of environmental things in common. Both places were pretty isolated. Though mine was more landlocked than his. But everything is stacked against you when you come from that. You have to have the talent to overcome everything. That was something I had in common with him. We were all about the same age and heard the same exact things growing up. Our paths crossed at a certain time, and we both had faced a lot of adversity. We even had that in common. I wish that he was still here because we could talk about a lot of things now."

He has performed "Roll On John" only twice in concert, both times in 2013—first at the Opera House in Blackpool, England, a venue the Beatles had often played, and then at the Royal Albert Hall, where, so many years earlier, Dylan had been waiting nervously backstage when he heard someone say, "Hey, the Beatles are here."

> *Shine your light*
> *Move it on*
> *You burned so bright*
> *Roll on, John*

Coda: McCartney on Dylan

On August 28, 2025, Paul McCartney took a break from rehearsals for a concert tour to speak with the author about his relationship with Bob Dylan.

In *The Lyrics*, you write that you and John Lennon first wrote songs like Buddy Holly. Then it was Motown, and then Bob Dylan. Would you mind expanding on that a little?
That's just a timeline of the kind of people we were listening to and being inspired by, and there was a moment when it was Bob. I think his attitude was admirable, and his lyrics, you know, were great. Bob was inspirational. I always just think: "The vandals took the handles." Just that little phrase out of everything. It's so sort of corny but brilliant.

At the 2016 music festival Desert Trip, in California, you were on the bill with Dylan, the Rolling Stones, and the Who. Dylan played the night before you did. Did you get a chance to see his show?
I did see him play, because I'm a fan. That was a great show. He's a presence. If you've liked his work and his—what would you call it? *Personality* is an okay word for it, but it doesn't quite sum it up. His *thing*, the Dylan *thing* that he just has. It's fascinating. So I saw his show and really enjoyed it. And I was walking around backstage, and this really nice lady, Shelley Lazar, who was our ticket lady, came

in. She was networking with all the acts. She said, "Bob wants to see you. He doesn't want to see Mick or Keith or anyone else. He's asked to see *you*." So I said, "Well, where is he? Show me where."

So she showed me into his tent. His backstage [area] was a great big tent. And he's just sitting there, with his shirt unbuttoned to the navel. And he says, "Hey, Paul. How ya doin'?" And we just started talking. I was talking to him about how much I'd enjoyed his standards album that he'd just done about a year before that. 'Cause I like all those old songs. I also like hearing his voice. Because in a lot of his live performances—[*imitates Dylan singing in gibberish*]— What the fuck's he saying? What song *is* this? You just don't know. And then you'll hear: "A rollin' stone!" Oh, it's *that* one. But on the standards album, he's very clear and very beautiful. You can see he loves those songs like I do.

Those songs come from a deep place. So I was tellin' him *that*, and he was tellin' me *this*. And the striking comment—he said, "Hey, Paul, you know, you're a *star*." Pointing at me. I go, "Huh? Wow!" Hearing Dylan say, "You're a star." And just using that word, rather than, you know, "You're a good musician." So I sort of heard that he *liked* me.

Did you stay a while?

I wasn't aware of how long we were going on, but somebody later said, "You were in there for forty-five minutes." We had quite a little bunch of stuff to talk about. I told Bob I really liked his book *Chronicles*. He's a really good writer. I shouldn't sound surprised, but writing songs is different from writing novels or whatever you'd call that.

I'm kind of, I wouldn't call it *shy*, but I'm reluctant to approach him too much. It's silly, I know. And particularly silly because, in the early days, when he used to live down in Greenwich Village with Sara, when Jakob was a baby, we used to go round to dinner, and he would come up and see us. We were staying at the Stanhope Hotel. And he would come up and have dinner with us; we'd go down there. So we were really quite intimate. We knew each other quite well. But I have a sort of strange thing in my personality. I'm not very good at following those things up. My wife, Nancy, is good at encouraging me to do that.

In Linda's book *A Life in Photographs*, there's a photo she took of Dylan in 1971 at his townhouse in Greenwich Village. The kids were there, your kids and his kids, and I was wondering if you played music together after dinner.

It's quite possible, but I don't have a recollection—"Hey, Bob! Have you heard *this* one? [sings:] *Ob-la-di, ob-la-da!*" But I remember telling him at one point, "Oh, man, I had such strange dreams last night." And he said: "Were you eatin' *cheese* late at night?" [Laughs.] I thought that was a very practical comment. I said, "I don't know, I don't think so."

Last year I went to your old house at Forthlin Road in Liverpool on the National Trust tour. The guide said Dylan had been there. I was wondering if you'd heard that.

I didn't know that, but that's gotta be true. I don't think the tour guide would be making it up.

That's what I thought, but I called the National Trust, and they wouldn't confirm it, maybe out of regard for Dylan's privacy. It's known that Dylan went to John Lennon's house, but people say he also went to yours, which didn't get into the press.

I guess if he's up in Liverpool, what are you going to do in your spare hours? Go and see the Beatles' houses. I like the thought that he saw that, because that was a very big part of my youth.

Do you remember your television theme from 1968, the song "Thingumybob"?

Yeah!

In Dylan's archive, there's a letter from George Harrison to Dylan about a song they wrote together called "Maureen." It uses the melody of "Thingumybob." And George writes to Bob: "Here are the chords to 'Thingumybob,'" in case he wanted to finish the lyrics, it seems. And in the "Get Back" sessions on YouTube, there's a moment when George is playing this song, and you sing along. The song was never completed, but to me it's interesting, because it's a McCartney-Harrison-Dylan composition.

Wow. [Laughs.] I remember writing it. But I had no idea that George was even *remotely* interested, and even less idea that he'd turned Dylan on to it and they were going to write something.

Do you remember seeing Dylan at the Albert Hall? He played there solo in 1965 and with the Band in 1966.

I remember particularly the one with the Band. It was really good. We didn't agree with the folkies who were complaining that he was playing with an electric band. We just liked him. We were big fans. When Bob came along, he was something new. [In Dylan voice:] *The Dylan styyyle. So rec-og-niz-able.* For a little while, everyone started singing like that. John was particularly smitten: *Hey! You've got to hide your love a-way.* That was really his Dylan moment.

We went to the Albert Hall as fans. I remember particularly him doing "Mr. Tambourine Man," which, if I go and see him in concert, I'm always hoping he'll do that bloody song, because I like it, you know? And he never does! And I think, Oh, he *might* have done. Maybe I didn't recognize it. [Another impression of Dylan singing gibberish.] Anyway. So we saw that. The first half was just him acoustic. And then the Band, which we thought was great. Great idea for a show.

I was trying to pin down the moment you first heard Dylan. Your brother Michael said in an interview that he brought Dylan's first album home to Forthlin Road in 1962. He was dating a girl named Celia Mortimer at the time. She was a Dylan fan and gave him the record. When you heard it, your first impression was: "That's folk crap."

I'd forgotten that Mike brought it. And Celia Mortimer—that's true. I think she was also my girlfriend at some point. I did like that album. That's when I first heard him. I hadn't realized I'd said "folk crap." But it's possible. I was probably deep into rock 'n' roll.

You and Dylan have something interesting in common in that you've both written songs about John Lennon. You wrote "Here Today" and he wrote "Roll On John," which came out about ten years ago. Have you heard it?

I did hear that. It was very nice. John was sort of a big personality that when he was killed it was a worldwide shock. And those of us who knew him, and were writers, you had to put it somewhere. So, yeah, that was where Bob put it, and I thought it was nice. It was a good sentiment. Mine, I think, was a bit sadder, and it was sort of reminiscing. Most of it's accurate, in my song, but there's one line that isn't. I can't remember what it is now. I think I said that John would say something about me that was a bit disparaging.

Yes.
But I don't know, I left it in.

To me, it makes the song feel real, that line. I like that line.
Yeah.

Did you return to John in the song "Vanity Fair"? I've always wondered if that's about him.
Uhhhhhh—*no*.

Do you know the Dylan song "Fourth Time Around," which has just about the same melody as the Beatles song "Norwegian Wood"?
No. But I'm suing him.

When the Beatles played Shea Stadium, there were a few evenings at the Warwick Hotel with Dylan, along with the Rolling Stones, the Supremes, and the music journalist Al Aronowitz. Do you remember those parties?
Yeah. Particularly him and Al Aronowitz. They were a good little team. But you know what they say about the sixties: If you remember it, you weren't there. But I remember the Supremes came to our hotel, and Bob, and Al Aronowitz. There was a steady flow of people coming through. And we loved it. We loved having people to hang out with.

And, you know, about Bob: One of the things that struck me recently, and why I say how stupid it is to feel awkward about contacting him—what's amazing is, I've read stuff that he's written about me. And he actually says that he's "in awe" of me. And I'm reading this. Well, come on, it's nice to get a good review, but to get one from Bob Dylan? Such a glowing review? I love the way he finishes: "I wish he'd fucking stop."

Yes, "I wish he'd quit." In a more recent interview, he praised the lyrics of "Paperback Writer." And in 2014, he recorded a Beatles song you wrote, "Things We Said Today."
I just heard that the other day. I was in the office in New York and I saw this album, *The Art of McCartney*. I'd kind of half forgotten it. It's like every cool person on earth is on there, singing my songs. And then I noticed Bob. I said, "Fuck, I'd forgotten this." And he does a great version of "Things We Said Today." I'd thought: Which song of mine will he be able to do easily? Which one will translate into Dylan-esque? And it was that one. I was very happy to listen to that, very proud that he did it.

In his *Bootleg Series*, he recently put out his recording of "Yesterday," which he did in 1970.
Wow.

George Harrison was on the session, too.
So Bob recorded it? And you say George is playing on it?

George is playing guitar. In 1970, when he was hanging around a lot with Dylan.
As a fan, this is great stuff to hear about Bob. I love that. The thing about "Yesterday" is, they used to say, "Oh, three thousand people have recorded it." So one day I said to one of my guys, "Look, I'm never going to listen to the three thousand, but get me the top ten. Let me listen to the top ten ones." But I don't think they knew that Bob had done it. So he is certainly added to that list. It was Elvis, Ray Charles, Marvin Gaye. I love the fact that he's done it.

Have you ever run into Bob in an airport? I figure you're both touring all the time.
I did, yeah. I was going through an airport and this kind of homeless guy comes shuffling up to me in a gray hoodie. And I'm going, "Yeah? Can I help you?" [Dylan voice:] "Hey, Paul. It's Bob." I must say, you know, he was very incognito. I would not have recognized him at all.

I've run into him quite a few times through my life. And people have said, "If you were ever going to write with someone, whom would you choose?" And I say, "Well, I think Bob would be great." And the minute I say it, I think, "Ah, God, I don't know. Would it be too difficult? Would our styles *match*?" And I begin to get nervous about the idea. Which, again, it's stupid, because George was perfectly at home with the Wilburys, and that was great. I think George just knew him more intimately and was a little less apt to be awkward.

I reached out vaguely through people: "Hey, Bob, would you like to write something?" And it gets to be: "Maybe you could meet up. And maybe you could meet up *there*. Oh, no, he can't make *that*." So it all gets a bit mysterious, and that's when I tend to go, "Oh, well, it's not meant to be," and I don't pursue it heavily. But it's still an interesting idea. It might be a good thing, to try to write together, but *don't tell anyone*. So if it doesn't work out, we'll just say, "Okay, great, see you, man, it didn't work out, that's okay."

Around the time of the Wings Over America tour in the mid-1970s, you and Linda hosted a party aboard the *Queen Mary* and another one at a Beverly Hills estate. Dylan went to both parties. Do you remember seeing him on those nights?
The Harold Lloyd estate. That was a big party, a blow-out. We blew every bit of profit we'd made on the tour on that one. It was great. Dylan was hiding in the bushes. It was like, "Bob's here." I go, "Oh, great. Where is he?" "Over there. In those bushes." So I go into the bushes. And, you know, meet him.

Was he was hiding from a photographer?
He could have been. I don't blame him. I don't know, we might have even hired a photographer to take pictures for us. The *Queen Mary* was another good party. There's no bushes to go to on the *Queen Mary*. He could have hidden in a cabin.

So many singers and songwriters lose their creative force after they make it big, but you and Dylan have kept going. Not only that, but you try to do new things. What is it about the two of you that drives you to keep exploring?
I just love making music. I love making up songs. I would say that if I didn't do it as a living, I'd do it as a hobby. It's so fascinating. That's what keeps moving me forward.

Do you feel like you're searching for truth? Or trying to make sense of the world? Or is it just like a bird who just sings because it sings?

I started off just doing it kind of to see if I could do it. But then, as it went on, it became more fascinating, and it kind of drew me forward. You started to develop a little bit and then you started to think, "Wow, this is kind of magic." You'll often hear composers saying that they don't know where it comes from. It just kind of comes down and you're like a conduit.

You were writing "Yesterday" at the very same time Dylan was writing "Like a Rolling Stone," and both songs took a long time to complete. Dylan said he felt like a ghost was writing "Like a Rolling Stone," and you've said the melody of "Yesterday" came to you in a dream. And you both said, "Gee, do I really deserve credit for this song?"

Yeah, it's crazy. There's the magic I'm talking about.

Acknowledgments

This book benefited greatly from my visits to the Bob Dylan Center at the University of Tulsa in Oklahoma. Mark Davidson, the archives director, and Stephanie Stewart, the archives manager, patiently guided me through the more than one hundred thousand items in the collection to help me find the materials pertaining to Dylan's interactions with the Beatles.

I wish I could have met the music journalist Alfred G. Aronowitz, who died in 2005. He spent a lot of time with the heroes of this book and wrote insightful stories about them for *The Saturday Evening Post,* the *New York Post,* and his own website, which he expanded for his self-published memoir. Al's son Myles Aronowitz kindly shared with me the papers left behind by his father before they were packed off to Stanford University, where librarians are organizing them into a collection sure to be of great value to scholars.

Thanks to the staff at the Rare Books Room of the New York Public Library, where I viewed some of Aronowitz's private correspondence. I'm also grateful to James Kaplan and Kenneth Womack for sharing some of their research with me, and to Nick Windolf for digging up materials at the New York Public Library for the Performing Arts and the Paley Center for Media.

320 ACKNOWLEDGMENTS

Dylan and the Beatles remain a big part of cultural life six decades after their breakthroughs, but they are little by little passing into history, and the number of people who were present on the nights when they got together is sadly dwindling. I would like to thank those who are still around and generously shared their stories with me: Richard Alderson, Deborah Brandstatter Marks, Dana Gillespie, Dan Richter, and Gloria Steinem. And my heartfelt thanks to Sir Paul McCartney for taking the time to talk with me.

This book would have been a curio on my hard drive if not for the literary agent Michael Signorelli of Aevitas. Thank you, Michael. I would also like to thank my editors for their encouragement and criticism: Rick Horgan, Sophie Guimaraes, and Rob Sternitzky at Scribner in the U.S.; Lee Brackstone and Lily McIlwain at White Rabbit in the UK. Thanks also to Tanner Curtis for photo research.

I have the deepest gratitude to the biographers, journalists, memoirists, podcasters, and critics who have shaped my understanding of Dylan and the Beatles: Andy Babiuk, Joan Baez, Stephen Bard, Derek Barker, Joe Boyd, Allison Bumsted, Robert Christgau, Maureen Cleave, Ray Coleman, Ray Connelly, Hunter Davies, Peter Doggett, Tom Doyle, Howie Edelson, Diana Erickson, Walter Everett, Bill Flanagan, Mikal Gilmore, Jonathan Gould, Clinton Heylin, Andrew Hickey, Barney Hoskyns, Tudor Jones, Norman Jopling, Allan Kozinn, Mark Lewisohn, Greil Marcus, James A. Mitchell, Ray Padgett, May Pang, Robbie Robertson, Robert Rodriguez, Suze Rotolo, Daryl Sanders, Anthony Scaduto, Fred Seaman, Ray Schweighardt, Chris Shaw, Robert Shelton, Adrian Sinclair, Howard Sounes, Bob Spitz, Doug Sulpy, Graeme Thomson, Toby Thompson, Dave Van Ronk, Elijah Wald, Scott Warmuth, Jann Wenner, Jon Wiener, Paul Williams, and Kenneth Womack.

For the last eleven years, I've been fortunate to be employed as an editor at *The New York Times*, which day after day demonstrates the importance of disinterested reporting to civic life, while also making plain that the world would be a dreary place without the arts. Thanks to Stella Bugbee, Joe Kahn, Carolyn Ryan, and Sam

Sifton for generously allowing me to take time away from my duties to work on this book.

I wouldn't have been able to keep up the effort necessary to write these pages without the help of those who read my chapters-in-progress and told me what was working and what wasn't. My deepest gratitude to George Gurley and Steven Kurutz. Thanks also to: Lori Crispo, Andrew S. Curran, Joe Ehrlich, Connor Ennis, John Fotiadis, Jay Greene, Hillary Johnston, James Kaplan, Katherine Rosman, Charlie Windolf, and Nick Windolf. Special thanks to the friends who have patiently read and critiqued my various writings over the years: David Bailey, William Berlind, Deirdre Dolan, Stuart Emmrich, Alexandra Jacobs, John Koblin, and Peter Stevenson. And I owe Nick Paumgarten a dinner at Sevilla for helping me reach McCartney.

I have special appreciation for my mentors in journalism and the teachers who taught me how to read and write: Rick Bass, Lynn Benediktsson, Bill Bullard, Graydon Carter, Nate Fuller, Bill Hammond, Peter Kaplan, Peter La Salle, Susan Morrison, Ellen Pollock, William Rosenfeld, Penny Sharp, and Fred Wagner.

My parents, Jack and Muriel Windolf, have always encouraged me, even when I was writing poems or blasting music in my room, rather than preparing for a career in the family business. It's great to have them in my corner.

This book is dedicated to my wife, Susan Rushing. About forty years ago, in a rented Renault during a long traffic jam in the middle of France, she was at the wheel, singing her very own extended version of Dylan's "Country Pie." It's still stuck in my head.

Notes

With rolling bibliography.

Introduction

xi *"What about Bob Dylan?"*: Dennis Elsas, producer, *The Beatles Arrive in America*, a radio documentary first broadcast February 6, 2014.

xi *"Paul got them off whoever"*: Ray Coleman, "Beatles Say—Dylan Shows the Way," *Melody Maker*, January 6, 1965.

xiv *"don't want to be cute"*: Paul Du Noyer, *Conversations with McCartney* (Abrams, 2015), 61.

xv *"took all the music"*: Neil Hickey, "Bob Dylan Today," *TV Guide*, September 11, 1976.

xv *"If I'd had him"*: Jeff Slate, "Bob Dylan on Music's Golden Era," *Wall Street Journal*, December 19, 2022.

xv *"never been to Strawberry Fields . . ."*: Audience recording, April 7, 2004, Boone, North Carolina.

xv *"George quoted Bob like people quote scripture"*: Mim Udovitch and David Wild, "Remembering George," *Rolling Stone*, January 17, 2002.

xvi *"We used to go round"*: Author interview with McCartney, August 28, 2025.

xvii *"They offered intimacy"*: Bob Dylan, *Chronicles: Volume One* (Simon & Schuster, 2004), 204.

xvii *minds in dialogue*: I took this phrase, not to mention general guidance, from George Steiner, *Tolstoy or Dostoevsky* (Yale University Press, second ed., 1996), 11.

CHAPTER 1 Pilgrimage

1 *On a chilly spring afternoon*: My account of Dylan's experience on the Beatles Childhood Homes Tour is based on: BBC News, "Dylan Unnoticed on Beatles Tour," May

12, 2009; Stephanie Power and Alexei Sayle, "The Lennon Visitors," BBC Radio 4, October 7, 2010; Robert Chalmers, "Dylan Was, As, and Always Will Be Rock 'n' Roll," British *GQ*, May 24, 2020; Jesse Molyneaux, "Life Living in the Back Bedroom of John Lennon's Childhood Home," *Liverpool Echo*, September 24, 2023; Colin Hall, September 2025 Facebook comment; James Kaplan, unpublished interview of Hall, 2011; statements made in May 2009 by the knowledgeable Gloi of the Beatles message board Abbeyrd; David Kinney, *The Dylanologists* (Simon & Schuster, 2014), 30–32. When I went on the Beatles Childhood Homes Tour in 2024, a National Trust tour guide told me Dylan had paid a visit to the McCartney home and made it as far as the front door. Asked for clarification, a National Trust spokesman told me Dylan "did not enter" the McCartney home, which was consistent with what I had gathered from other sources. Hall declined requests to be interviewed.

1 *spent his childhood days*: For the account of Lennon's early years and family life, I relied on: Julia Baird, *Imagine This: Growing Up with My Brother John Lennon* (Hodder & Stoughton, 2007); Mark Lewisohn, *All These Years: Tune In*, extended special ed. (Little, Brown, 2013); The Beatles, *The Beatles Anthology* (Chronicle Books, 2000), 7–14; Ray Coleman, *Lennon: The Definitive Biography*, revised and updated ed. (Pan Books, 1995); Hunter Davies, *The Beatles*, updated ed. (W. W. Norton, 2009; originally published 1968).

3 *cited by Dylan*: Elliot Mintz, host and producer, *The Beatle Years*, Westwood Radio One, originally broadcast January 18, 1993.

5 *"Don't keep writing poetry"*: Robert Shelton, *No Direction Home: The Life and Music of Bob Dylan* (Ballantine Books, 1986), 35.

6 *the McCartney home*: Sources for my account of McCartney's early years and family life include: Mike McCartney, *Thank U Very Much: Mike McCartney's Family Album* (Granada, 1982); Barry Miles, *Paul McCartney: Many Years from Now* (Henry Holt, 1997); Lewisohn, *Tune In*; *The Beatles Anthology*, 17–23; Howard Sounes, *Fab: The Intimate Life of Paul McCartney* (Da Capo Press, 2010); and Davies, *The Beatles*.

6 *"hiding of our lives"*: This paragraph draws from Mike McCartney, "My Brother Paul," *Woman* magazine, August 21, 1965.

7 *"just sort of slap me"*: Paul McCartney on *The Howard Stern Show*, October 18, 2001.

7 *"bloke called Bob Dylan"*: Mike McCartney, *Thank U Very Much*, 94–95.

CHAPTER 2 Disciples of Little Richard

8 *Dylan's hometown*: For the history of Hibbing, Minnesota, and Dylan's early years, I relied on: Louie Kemp, *Dylan & Me: 50 Years of Adventures* (WestRose Press, 2019); Dylan, *Chronicles: Volume One*; Jeff Taylor and Chad Israelson, *The Political World of Bob Dylan* (Palgrave MacMillan, 2015); Shelton, *No Direction Home*; Howard Sounes, *Down the Highway: The Life of Bob Dylan* (Grove Press, 2021); Toby Thompson, *Positively Main Street: Bob Dylan's Minnesota* (University of Minnesota Press, 2009); Bob Spitz, *Dylan: A Biography* (W. W. Norton, 1991); and hibbingmn.gov.

9 *"Bobby's so sentimental"*: Thompson, *Positively Main Street*, 158.

10 *"hated the Jews"*: Shelton, *No Direction Home*, 27.

10 *"pretty smart remarks"*: Spitz, *Dylan*, 61.

11 *four thousand slaving voyages*: Hugh Thomas, *The Slave Trade: The Story of the Atlantic Slave Trade, 1440–1870* (Simon & Schuster, 1997), 72.
12 *"Elvis Presley's voice"*: Dylan in *US Weekly*, August 24, 1987.
12 *the architect of rock 'n' roll*: Little Richard frequently used this descriptor for himself, including at the Grammy Awards ceremony on March 2, 1988.
12 *"used to get so upset"*: Thompson, *Positively Main Street*, 68.
13 *"What's the best kind"*: From the 1958 recording known as the Bucklen Tape.
13 *"To join 'Little Richard'"*: *Hematite*, the 1959 Hibbing High yearbook, 76.
14 *"My whole life changed"*: Lewisohn, *Tune In*, 257.
14 *"His reaction that day"*: Lewisohn interviewed Hill for *Tune In*, 259.
14 *"When I heard it"*: Lewisohn, *Tune In*, 259.
14 *"Little Richard was this voice"*: Ibid., 291.
15 *"The first song I ever sang"*: McCartney in Charles White, *The Life and Times of Little Richard: The Authorized Biography*, rev. ed. (Omnibus Press, 2003), 114.
15 *On the last day*: Miles, *Many Years from Now*, 200.
15 *"If you want to live"*: This quotation appeared in newspapers around the world, including in the un-bylined article "Little Richard Gives Up 'Rock' for Religion," *Coventry Evening Telegraph*, October 12, 1957, 3.
15 *Tower Ballroom stage*: See Lewisohn, *Tune In*, 1411–12; and White, *The Life and Times of Little Richard*, 114–15.
15 *"How do you describe"*: Chris Hutchins, *New Musical Express*, October 12, 1962, as quoted in Bill Wyman, "Little Richard Put Wild Sex into the Top 40 for Good," *Vulture*, May 9, 2020.
15 *For John*: Lewisohn, *Tune In*, 1413.
16 *"When Pat Boone covered"*: Little Richard in the documentary *Hail! Hail! Rock 'n' Roll*, directed by Taylor Hackford (Universal Pictures, 1987).
17 *"flash shirt"*: White, *The Life and Times of Little Richard*, 116.
18 *"Thank you very much"*: Video clip at the Rock & Roll Hall of Fame website.
18 *"Cherry Red"*: The Dylan sleuth Scott Warmuth told me about the lyrical similarities between Little Richard's version of "Cherry Red" and Dylan's "Lay Lady Lay."
18 *"sat by my bed"*: John Waters, "Little Richard, Happy at Last?," *Playboy*, July 1987.
18 *"I owe a lot"*: @PaulMcCartney, Twitter, May 10, 2020.
18 *"He was my shining star"*: @bobdylan, Twitter, May 9, 2020.

CHAPTER 3 The Names

19 *"going to call myself"*: Shelton, *No Direction Home*, 44.
20 *Now that "the Beatles"*: See Davies, *The Beatles*, 64; and Lewisohn, *Tune In*, 602–4.
20 *group masturbation sessions*: Miles, *Many Years from Now*, 28; Pete Shotton and Nicholas Schaffner, *John Lennon: In My Life* (Stein and Day, 1983), 43–44; and Chris Heath, "The Untold Stories of Paul McCartney," *GQ*, September 11, 2018.
20 *"He was accustomed"*: Shotton and Schaffner, *In My Life*, 52.
20 *July 6, 1957*: The Beatles story would have a big hole in it if not for Mark Lewisohn, who nailed down the correct date of the first meeting of Lennon and McCartney when he was working as a researcher for Philip Norman, *Shout! The True Story of*

the Beatles (Elm Tree Books, 1983). My brief retelling of this much-told tale is based on the accounts in *The Beatles Anthology*; Lewisohn, *Tune In*; Norman, *Shout!*; Davies, *The Beatles*; Miles, *Many Years from Now*; and Shotten and Schaffner, *In My Life*.

21 *"All day long, silhouetted"*: Kemp, *Dylan & Me*, 8.
23 *"may have rolled my eyes"*: Dave Van Ronk with Elijah Wald, *The Mayor of MacDougal Street* (Da Capo Press, 2006), 158.
23 *"We were sitting around"*: Van Ronk, *The Mayor of MacDougal Street*, 162.
23 *antisemitic insults*: See Shotten and Schaffner, *In My Life*, 61.
23 *"Dylan is bullshit"*: Wenner's interview of Lennon was first published in *Rolling Stone*, in two parts, January 21, 1971, and February 4, 1971. See Jann S. Wenner, *Lennon Remembers*, new ed. (Verso, 2000), 11.
25 *"When he started out"*: Suze Rotolo, *A Freewheelin' Time: A Memoir of Greenwich Village in the Sixties* (Broadway Books, 2008), 155.
26 *"would get all of these"*: Van Ronk, *The Mayor of MacDougal Street*, 161.
26 *"There was a vice president"*: Hammond interviewed by Peter Gzowski on the Canadian Broadcasting Corporation program *90 Minutes Live*, February 6, 1978.
26 *"They were more than"*: Lewisohn, *Tune In*, 1021.
27 *"they had enormous talent"*: Kenneth Womack, *Maximum Volume: The Life of Beatles Producer George Martin, The Early Years, 1926–1966* (Chicago Review Press, 2017), 95.
27 *"Quietly Bob said"*: Rotolo, *A Freewheelin' Time*, 158.
27 *"biggest bastards on earth"*: Wenner, *Lennon Remembers*, 87.
27 *"best fucking group"*: Sheff, *All We Are Saying*, 72.
27 *British radio airplay*: Lewisohn first noted the October 1962 BBC broadcasts of Dylan and the Beatles in *Tune In*, 1450.
27 *stepped into Tony Pastor's*: Caspar Llewellyn Smith, "Flash-Back: Bob Dylan," *The Guardian*, September 18, 2005.
28 *he was Sweet William*: See Rotolo, *A Freewheelin' Time*, 197; and Derek Barker, *The Songs He Didn't Write: Bob Dylan Under the Influence* (Chrome Books, 2008), 32.
28 *receive a hefty cut*: Sounes, *Down the Highway*, 130.
29 *Dylan flew to London*: For my account of Dylan's first London trip, I relied on: Tudor Jones, *Bob Dylan and the British Sixties: A Cultural History* (Routledge, 2019); Derek Barker, "One Time in London," from *Isis: A Bob Dylan Anthology* (Helter Skelter, 2001); Elizabeth Thomson and David Gutman, "Bob Dylan in the Madhouse," from *The Dylan Companion* (Dell, 1990); Peggy Seeger, "Ewan MacColl Controversy," an essay I found on Seeger's personal website, which has since disappeared from the internet; Clinton Heylin, *The Double Life of Bob Dylan: A Restless, Hungry Feeling, 1941–1966,* (Little, Brown, 2021); Ben Harker, *Class Act: The Cultural and Political Life of Ewan MacColl* (Pluto Press, 2007); Andrew Whitehead, *Curious Kings Cross* (Five Leaves, 2018); Llewellyn Smith, "Flash-Back: Bob Dylan"; and Jim Farber, "Ewan MacColl, Dogmatist of British Folk, Gets a Tribute Album," *The New York Times*, October 28, 2015.
29 *courtesy of the BBC*: Details of the financial arrangement appear in Heylin, *The Double Life of Bob Dylan*, 191.

29 *He showed himself*: See Thomson and Gutman, "Bob Dylan in the Madhouse"; Heylin, *The Double Life of Bob Dylan*, 186; and Llewellyn Smith, "Flash-Back: Bob Dylan."
29 *"I don't know what"*: Llewellyn Smith, "Flash-Back: Bob Dylan."
29 *"uncommunicative American"*: Thomson and Gutman, *The Dylan Companion*, 68.
29 *"There he was at the top"*: Llewellyn Smith, "Flash-Back: Bob Dylan."
30 *Carthy spotted him*: David Brazier, "A Conversation with Martin Carthy," *The Telegraph*, vol. 42, 1992.
30 *"first time I heard Dylan"*: David Hajdu, *Positively 4th Street: The Lives and Times of Joan Baez, Bob Dylan, Mimi Baez Fariña, and Richard Fariña* (Farrar, Straus and Giroux, 2001), 127.
31 *"Our problem was"*: Jones, *Bob Dylan and the British Sixties*, 12.
31 *"completely non-critical audience"*: Ewan MacColl, et. al., in "A Symposium/Topical Songs and Folksinging 1965," *Sing Out!: The Folk Song Magazine*, September 1965.
31 *aspects of show business*: In *Chronicles: Volume One*, Dylan recounts seeing Gorgeous George (43), and "one of the last blackface minstrel shows" (234).
32 *"folk police"*: Dylan, *Chronicles: Volume One*, 248.
32 *drunken New Year's Eve*: Lewisohn, *Tune In*, 1529–30.
32 *into the Royal Court*: Daffyd Rees, *The Beatles 1963: A Year in the Life* (Omnibus Press, 2022), 9.
32 *new pal Martin Carthy*: Hajdu, *Positively 4th Street*, 127.
32 *"What's all this"*: Llewellyn Smith, "Flash-Back: Bob Dylan."
33 *at the Invicta Ballroom*: Rees, *The Beatles 1963*, 23.
33 *"To be brutally honest"*: Alan Cackett, "Beatle Country," at alancackett.com.
34 *"seemed so wasted"*: Von Schmidt, interviewed for Anthony Scaduto, *Dylan: An Intimate Biography* (New American Library, 1971). The complete version of the interview, which I have drawn from here, appears in Anthony Scaduto, *The Dylan Tapes: Friends, Players & Lovers Talkin' Bob Dylan*, ed. by Stephanie Trudeau (University of Minnesota Press, 2022).

CHAPTER 4 **Picture Imperfect**

36 *Martin's initial idea*: Mark Lewisohn, *The Beatles Recording Sessions: The Official Abbey Road Studio Session Notes, 1962–1970* (Harmony Books, 1998), 32.
36 *"went into the door"*: See Piet Schreuders, Mark Lewisohn, and Adam Smith, *The Beatles' London: A Guide to 467 Beatles Sites* (Interlink Books, 2009), 44–45.
37 *its superpower status*: See Randall Stevenson, *The Oxford English Literary History, Volume 12, 1960–2000: The Last of England?* (Oxford University Press, 2004), 14.
38 *"rumpled clothes"*: Rotolo, *A Freewheelin' Time*, 214.
38 *"an 'image' choice"*: Ibid., 215.
38 *"Well, I can't tell you"*: John Bauldie, "Positively 4th Street Revisited," *Q*, May 1995, 57.
38 *Moses, who did more*: This sketch draws from Robert A. Caro, *The Power Broker: Robert Moses and the Fall of New York* (Alfred A. Knopf, 1974).
38 *Mayor's Committee on Slum Clearance*: "Villagers Attack Proposed Housing," *The New York Times*, October 15, 1953, 35. This un-bylined article was one of hundreds of news reports on the yearslong battle over the city's plans for Greenwich Village.

39 *prime gathering spot*: See Jane Jacobs, *The Death and Life of Great American Cities* (Vintage Books, 1992), 127.
39 *"Listen, Robert Moses"*: Ben Yakas, "Confirmed: Bob Dylan Did Co-Write Protest Song about Robert Moses with Jane Jacobs," *Gothamist*, May 1, 2016.
39 *also Dylan's teacher*: See Shelton, *No Direction Home*, 152; Rotolo, *A Freewheelin' Time*, 135; Dylan, *Chronicles: Volume One*, 268–70; Scaduto, *Dylan*, 132.
40 *"most erotic thing"*: Dylan, *Chronicles: Volume One*, 265.
40 *"We got along"*: Rotolo, *A Freewheelin' Time*, 10.
40 *confessed he had been born*: Ibid., 105–6.
40 *wealthy Chicago industrialist*: Spitz, *Dylan*, 154.
41 *"most important part"*: Scaduto, *Dylan*, 157.
42 *"lying shit of a guy"*: Rotolo, *A Freewheelin' Time*, 286.
42 *its enchanting melody*: Details of the composition of "Lay Down Your Weary Tune" are from Cameron Crowe's interview of Dylan for the liner notes of Dylan's *Biograph* (Columbia Records, 1985).
42 *"feeling confined"*: Rotolo, *A Freewheelin' Time*, 280.
42 Newsweek *poked holes*: "I Am My Words," *Newsweek*, November 4, 1963.
43 *"proud that I'm young"*: A transcript of Dylan's Tom Paine Award speech appears in Shelton, *No Direction Home*, 222–24.
44 *"I was in a sort of blind rage"*: Davies, *The Beatles*, 53.
44 *"under his spell"*: Cynthia Lennon, *A Twist of Lennon* (W. H. Allen, 1978), 25.
44 *"more like a funeral"*: Ibid., 75.
44 *"almost inseparable"*: Shotton and Schaffner, *In My Life*, 73.
44 *"let him toss me off"*: Ibid., 73.
45 *"almost a love affair"*: David Sheff, *All We Are Saying: The Last Major Interview with John Lennon and Yoko Ono* (St. Martin's Griffin, 2000), 170.
45 *"insinuated that me and Brian"*: Lennon interviewed in 1971 by Peter McCabe and Robert D. Schonfeld for *Apple to the Core: The Unmaking of the Beatles* (Pocket Books, 1972). The interview, conducted on background, wasn't used for the book and ended up appearing in *Penthouse*, September 1984.
45 *"loud beyond reason"*: "Beatlemania," *Newsweek*, October 18, 1963.
46 *"nice to know"*: From the January 3, 1964, episode of *The Jack Paar Program*.

CHAPTER 5 It'll Never Happen

47 *"Hair-do wigs"*: Bruce Spizer, *The Beatles Are Coming! The Birth of Beatlemania in America* (498 Productions, 2003), 73.
48 *called them "bubblegum"*: Al Aronowitz, *Bob Dylan and the Beatles: Volume One of the Best of the Blacklisted Journalist* (1st Books, 2003), 7.
48 *"Bob seemed to be"*: Ibid., 8.
48 *"I felt that his message"*: Ibid., 7.
49 *received a call*: As reported in Michael Braun, *Love Me Do!: The Beatles' Progress* (Graymalkin Media, 2019; originally published by Penguin, 1964).
49 *McCartney was the one*: Coleman, "Beatles Say—Dylan Shows the Way."

50 *"from that moment"*: Harrison in Derek Taylor, *It Was Twenty Years Ago Today* (Bantam Books, 1987).
51 *"Paul bought a Bob Dylan record"*: Braun, *Love Me Do!*, 106.
51 *immediately teased Paul*: See Jason Barnard's interview of Mike McCartney on the episode "Mike McCartney's Early Liverpool" of the podcast *The Strange Brew*, August 12, 2021.
51 *a texture that may have arrived*: I ran this notion past Paul McCartney, who said, "Could have been," before adding: "I think that's a bit of a slim connection."
51 *"Assigned by The Saturday Evening Post"*: Aronowitz, *Bob Dylan and the Beatles*, 6–7.
51 *3,500 words*: Ibid., 27.
52 *the CBC program* Quest: Dylan episode of *Quest* has surfaced on YouTube.
52 *"Chimes of Freedom"*: A draft manuscript of this song is reproduced in Mark Davidson and Parker Fishel, *Mixing Up the Medicine* (Callaway, 2023), 110–11.
52 *planned cross-country trip*: My account of the trip draws from: Victor Maymudes and Jacob Maymudes, *Another Side of Bob Dylan: A Personal History on the Road and off the Tracks* (St. Martin's Press, 2014); Bob Coleman, *Paul Clayton and the Folksong Revival* (Scarecrow Press, 2008); Shelton, *No Direction Home*; Rotolo, *A Freewheelin' Time*; Scaduto, *Dylan*; and the interview of Peter Karman in Scaduto's *The Dylan Tapes*.
54 *"America has always had"*: Bill Harry, *The British Invasion: How the Beatles and Other U.K. Bands Conquered America* (Chrome Books, 2004), 27.
55 *"the commanding officer"*: Aronowitz, *Bob Dylan and the Beatles*, 17.
56 *"to see this instrument"*: Andy Babiuk, *Beatles Gear*, rev. ed. (Backbeat Books, 2015), 194.
57 *"wasn't what it used to be"*: Rotolo, *A Freewheelin' Time*, 302.
57 *"snaking through the dark"*: Greil Marcus, "The Beatles," a chapter in *The Rolling Stone Illustrated History of Rock and Roll*, ed., Anthony DeCurtis et al. (Random House, 1979), 213.
57 *folk-style arrangements*: Andrew Daly, "Roger McGuinn: The Story Behind 'She Said, She Said,'" *Guitar Player*, May 8, 2025.
57 *a debate with Dylan*: See Scaduto, *Dylan*, 197; and Maymudes, *Another Side of Bob Dylan*, 75.
58 *"sing that very well"*: Maymudes, *Another Side of Bob Dylan*, 77.
58 *"all just stops"*: Ibid., 79.
59 *"Never mind the music"*: The Beatles' train journey was filmed by Albert and David Maysles for the 1964 documentary originally titled *What's Happening!: The Beatles in the U.S.A.* and later released as *The Beatles: The First U.S. Visit*.
59 *"potentially dangerous"*: NBC News report, February 12, 1964.
59 *students, who carried signs*: Spizer, *The Beatles Are Coming!*, 188.
59 *Girls charged them*: "Wild-Eyed Mobs Pursue Beatles," *The New York Times*, February 13, 1964, 26.
59 *"wasn't a rock show"*: Lennon interviewed by Howard Smith on WPLJ-FM, January 23, 1972. A transcript appears in Jeff Burger, *Lennon on Lennon: Conversations with John Lennon* (Chicago Review Press, 2017), 290.

NOTES

- 60 *"How about fixing me a drink"*: Jill Haworth, "Beatle Paul and Me: Jill Haworth's Own Story," *Photoplay*, July 1964, 18.
- 60 *took a swing at him*: This and other details of the Beatles' night out in New York are from Steve Brandt, "7 Days and 7 Nights with the Beatles," *Photoplay*, June 1964, 36.
- 61 *"Did you hear that?"*: Hajdu, *Positively 4th Street*, 197.
- 61 *"had heard the Beatles"*: Scaduto, *Dylan*, 203–4. Dylan's claim here, that the Beatles had eight songs in the Top 10, is not quite accurate. They had three songs in the *Billboard* Top 10 in February 1964; in April, they would occupy the top five slots.
- 62 *"for the teenyboppers"*: Ibid., 204.
- 62 *quarters into a jukebox*: Catherine James, *Dandelion: Memoir of a Free Spirit* (St. Martin's Press, 2007), 54.
- 62 Muldaur's recollection of the Santa Monica show appears in Sounes, *Down the Highway*, 156.

CHAPTER 6 Ego Equals

- 63 *"stricken by the photograph"*: Al Aronowitz, "The Beatles: Music's Gold Bugs," *The Saturday Evening Post*, March 21, 1964, 32.
- 64 *interest in the written word*: Shelton documents Dylan's teenage reading habits in *No Direction Home*.
- 64 *classical authors*: See Richard F. Thomas, *Why Bob Dylan Matters* (Dey Street Books, 2017).
- 65 *"the outstanding composers"*: William Mann, "What Songs the Beatles Sang . . . ," London *Times*, December 23, 1963.
- 65 *"The Menace of Beatlism"*: Johnson's piece ran in *The New Statesman*, February 28, 1964.
- 66 *"a separate songwriting John Lennon"*: Wenner, *Lennon Remembers*, 83–84.
- 67 *Al Aronowitz considered*: See Aronowitz, *Bob Dylan and the Beatles*, 9.
- 67 *"Totally ignorant"*: C. Lennon, *A Twist of Lennon*, 100.
- 68 *"silence was deafening"*: Ibid., 101.
- 68 *"Uh, thank you all"*: ITN footage of the Foyle's luncheon is available on YouTube.
- 68 *"A shameful affair"*: Brian Epstein, *A Cellarful of Noise* (Souvenir Press, 2021; originally published 1964), 86.
- 68 *"had a lot of fun"*: Spitz, *Dylan: A Biography*, 274.
- 68 *"wrote several pages"*: Maymudes, *Another Side of Bob Dylan*, 97.
- 68 *"LSD is medicine"*: Dylan, interviewed by Studs Terkel for *Playboy*. The interview took place in the fall of 1965 and was published in the February 1966 issue, after Dylan had edited his own words heavily. The published version is used here.
- 68 *a letter to Lawrence Ferlinghetti*: The April 28, 1964, letter was published in *The Telegraph*, Summer 1990 issue (#36).
- 69 *"Things That Go Wham"*: British *Vogue*, August 1964 issue.
- 69 *"future nostalgia"*: Miles, *Many Years from Now*, 122.
- 70 *Dylan started with*: Jones's *Bob Dylan and the British Sixties* is a reliable guide to Dylan's borrowings from British folk songs. See especially p. 16.

71 *"that's pretty neat"*: Sounes, *Down the Highway*, 160.
71 *a man weeping*: Sounes, *Down the Highway*, 160.
71 *"Mind your own damn business!"*: Ibid., 161.
72 *"I was a mess"*: Rotolo, *A Freewheelin' Time*, 281.
72 *shoved each other*: Sounes, *Down the Highway*, 158.
72 *"two of us were really"*: Spitz, *Dylan: A Biography*, 264.
72 *"knew how to maul me"*: Rotolo, *A Freewheelin' Time*, 288.
72 *"That one, I look back"*: Bill Flanagan, *Written in My Soul: Candid Interviews with Rock's Great Songwriters* (Omnibus Press, 1990), 97.
73 *"amount of Beatle screwing"*: Bob Rogers, a radio host who accompanied the Beatles on the Australian tour, quoted in Glenn A. Baker with Roger Dilernia, *The Beatles Down Under: The 1964 Australia & New Zealand Tour* (Pierian Press, 1985).
74 *"hell with Dylan"*: Pete Hamill, "The Death and Life of John Lennon," *New York Magazine*, December 20, 1980. Hamill recounts the conversation in that piece.
74 *"a fear each one had"*: Aronowitz, *Bob Dylan and the Beatles*, 116.
75 *"John kept saying"*: Ibid., 9.
75 *"no longer looks like"*: Elijah Wald, *Dylan Goes Electric!: Newport, Seeger, Dylan, and the Night That Split the Sixties* (Dey Street Books, 2015), 171.
76 *"my version!"*: Hank Reineke, *Ramblin' Jack Elliott: The Never-Ending Highway* (Scarecrow Press, 2010), 158.
76 *"these four boys from Liverpool"*: Al Aronowitz, "The Return of the Beatles," *The Saturday Evening Post*, August 8, 1964, 27.
76 *"Most of the month"*: Joan Baez, *And a Voice to Sing With* (Summit Books, 1987), 86.
77 *"grating singing"*: "Joan Baez Sings at Forest Hills," *The New York Times*, August 10, 1964, 21.
77 *first lengthy tour*: For details on the crowd sizes, venues, and Beatles' lodgings, I have relied on Chuck Gunderson, *Some Fun Tonight!: The Backstage Story of How the Beatles Rocked America: The Historic Tours of 1964–1966, Volume 1: 1964* (Backbeat Books, 2013).
77 *"Hollywood Bowl was marvelous"*: *The Beatles Anthology*, 150.
77 *"Things We Said Today"*: Description based on the version recorded August 23, 1964, for *The Beatles at the Hollywood Bowl* (Capitol and Parlophone, 1977).
78 *"We understand"*: The letter appears in Baez, *And a Voice to Sing With*, 87.
78 *signed himself "Beatle Hater"*: Sam Tabachnik, "Inside the Violent Threat against the Beatles' Only Colorado Concert," *Denver Post*, November 25, 2023.
79 *"We looked down"*: *The Beatles Anthology*, 153.
79 *"All she could talk about"*: Harry Tuft interviewed by G. Brown, *Colorado Music Experience* podcast, July 24, 2018.
79 *carrying a rifle*: During the press conference at the Delmonico Hotel on August 28, 1964, a reporter told the Beatles that the police had confiscated a rifle from a man in the airport crowd. There was no mention of any charges filed, and the Beatles laughed it off.
79 *the Brandstatter sisters*: Details of the Brandstatters' hotel stay appeared in Mike Pearl, "They're Wonderful, I Love 'em All," *New York Journal-American*, August 29, 1964.

NOTES

79 *to breach the sixth floor*: Author interview of Deborah Brandstatter Marks, October 7, 2022.
80 *"Where is he?"*: Aronowitz, *Bob Dylan and the Beatles*, 13.

CHAPTER 7 Beatlemania Here

81 *Dylan sat next to him*: This chapter draws from: Maymudes, *Another Side of Bob Dylan*, 99–113; Aronowitz, *Bob Dylan and the Beatles*, 1–24; Rotolo, *A Freewheelin' Time*, 321–22; Miles, *Many Years from Now*, 184–90; *The Beatles Anthology*, 158; Peter Brown and Steven Gaines, *The Love You Make: An Insider's Story of the Beatles* (New American Library, 2002; originally published 1983), 142–45; and Barry Miles, *The Beatles Diary: Volume 1, The Beatles Years* (Omnibus Press, 1998), 165.
83 *chain-link fence*: The fencing didn't surround the stage, as it would in later Beatles shows, and some online commenters have questioned whether or not there was such a barrier at this concert. But in his August 31, 1964, dispatch for the London *Daily Express*, Ivor Davis reported on overzealous fans slipping under "barbed-wire fences."
83 *"not sure George saw me"*: Gunderson, *Some Fun Tonight!*, vol. 1, 130.
83 *"Good evening, Mr. Starr"*: See Pearl, "They're Wonderful." Pearl interviewed Brandstatter shortly after she met the Beatles.
85 *until forty years later*: See Henry Grossman, *Places I Remember: My Time with the Beatles* (Curvebender, 2012).
85 *came to his rescue*: Maymudes recalled in his memoir that his rescuer was the Beatles aide Derek Taylor. But the photograph taken outside the hotel by Henry Grossman (a picture not discovered until after Maymudes's death) points to Aspinall.
91 *Dylan stood on a chair*: Aronowitz, *Bob Dylan and the Beatles*, 472.
92 *"I knew nothing"*: Author interview of Gloria Steinem, December 23, 2021.
93 *"It's gear"*: Steve Turner, *The Complete Beatles Songs: The Stories Behind Every Track Written by the Fab Four* (Dey Street Books, 1994), 87.
93 *"i am outside"*: Dylan's letter to Tony Glover (born Dave Glover) went public when it was listed by RR Auction in 2020. The sale price, including fees, was $36,188.

CHAPTER 8 Hide Your Love

94 *"An Open Letter"*: Irwin Silber, *Sing Out!*, November 1964, 22–23.
94 *"another current idol"*: Eileen Strong's letter appears on p. 101 of the same issue.
95 *postage-stamp-size photos*: I viewed a PDF of a clipping of Gleason's November 16, 1964, column for the *San Francisco Chronicle* in the Northwestern University Libraries' Digital Collections.
95 *"John, is it true"*: Beatles press conference, Toronto, August 17, 1965. Published in the online resource Beatles Interview Database, Jay Spangler, proprietor.
96 *"Rather different from what"*: Derek Johnson, "Beatles Next Album," *New Musical Express*, November 13, 1964.

97 *"One might hope"*: Maureen Cleave, "Beautiful Beatles," *Evening Standard*, November 28, 1964.
97 *"Beatles Say—Dylan Shows the Way"*: Headline of article by Ray Coleman in *Melody Maker*, January 9, 1965, 3.
97 *Seven movies made in the UK*: This fact is noted in Barry Miles, *The British Invasion: The Music, the Times, the Era* (Sterling, 2009), 174.
98 *"The Byrds took the best"*: Derek Taylor, on-camera interview for *The Beatles Anthology* (produced by Neil Aspinall, ITV and ABC, 1995).
99 *"'That's it!'"*: Richie Unterberger, *Turn! Turn! Turn!: The '60s Folk-Rock Revolution* (Backbeat Books, 2002), 81. My account of the Byrds' origins draws from Unterberger's book; the episodes on the Byrds on the podcast *A History of Rock Music in 500 Songs* by Andrew Hickey; and *The Byrds Under Review* (Prism Films, 2012).
100 *"Wow," Dylan said*: Roger McGuinn interview, Creative Commons, 2005. McGuinn has consistently quoted Dylan as saying, "Wow, you can dance to it" in interviews going back decades.
101 *"I thought folk"*: Michael Watts, "Tom Wilson: The Man Who Put Electricity into Dylan," *Melody Maker*, January 31, 1976.
101 *"I said to Albert Grossman"*: Ibid.
104 *"voice was so deep"*: Cher, as told to Jeff Coplon, *The First Time* (Simon & Schuster, 1998), 92.
105 *"I couldn't escape"*: Cynthia Lennon, *John* (Hodder & Stoughton, 2005), 162.
105 *"bit of a song buff"*: Miles, *Many Years from Now*, 203.
106 *a 2006 interview*: Sandra Cogan was interviewed for the 2007 BBC Four documentary *Alma Cogan: Fabulous*, directed by Merryn Threadgould, part of the Legends series.
106 *"the women I suspected"*: C. Lennon, *John*, 161.
107 *après ski evening*: See C. Lennon, *A Twist of Lennon*, 123; and Kenneth Womack, *Maximum Volume, vol. 1*, 246.
107 *"unique and memorable"*: Ned Rorem, "The Music of the Beatles," *New York Review of Books*, January 18, 1968.
107 *"an affair I was having"*: Sheff, *All We Are Saying*, 178.
108 *"liked it straightaway"*: Womack, *Maximum Volume*, vol. 1, 246.
108 *asserted himself in the studio*: This is the first Beatles track on which McCartney played lead guitar; see Babiuk, *Beatles Gear*, 284. In Sheff, *All We Are Saying*, 196, Lennon gives credit to McCartney for Starr's drum part. In Miles, *Many Years from Now*, 193, McCartney stops just shy of taking full credit for the coda.
109 *allowing for more overdubs*: Walter Everett, *The Beatles as Musicians: The Quarry Men through Rubber Soul* (Oxford University Press, 2001), 282.
109 *not bothering to conceal*: Everett notes the lyrical similarities between "You've Got to Hide Your Love Away" and earlier Dylan songs in *The Beatles as Musicians*, 288.
110 *the classical player John Scott*: Mark Lewisohn, *The Complete Beatles Chronicle* (Harmony Books, 1992), 184.
110 *"I asked him not to"*: Womack, *Maximum Volume*, vol. 1, 250.
110 *"It was as if John felt"*: Miles, *Many Years from Now*, 195.
110 *"Dylan's initial impact"*: Shotton and Schaffner, *In My Life*, 110.

CHAPTER 9 The Savoy

112 *a mock Q&A:* J. R. Goddard, "Bob Dylan Meets the Press," *Village Voice*, March 25, 1965.

113 *on the back cover:* See the Columbia Records release numbered 4-43242. Parlophone played up the Beatles' connection to Dylan in its near-simultaneous (April 6, 1965) release of a four-track *Beatles for Sale* EP. On the back cover, Tony Barrow, a publicist for the group, described each of the collection's songs. Concerning the lead track, "I'm a Loser," he wrote: "It demonstrates the powerful influence which Bob Dylan's style has had on John Lennon, whose collection of Dylania—albums and sets of lyrics—swells week by week."

113 *"country folk blueser":* "Best Bets," *Cash Box*, March 20, 1965, 12.

113 *"I'd rather listen to Jimmy Reed":* Paul Jay Robbins, "Bob Dylan as Bob Dylan: All I Can Do Is Be Me," *Los Angles Free Press*, September 17, 1965, 1. Robbins's in-depth interview was conducted in March 1965 and published, in three parts, in September.

113 *"Great—very Chuck Berry-ish":* Ray Coleman, "Life with the Lennons," *Melody Maker*, April 10, 1965, 11.

115 *After the meal:* I've drawn from the firsthand accounts in: Wenner, *Lennon Remembers*, 49–50; C. Lennon, *A Twist of Lennon*, 131–32; Pattie Boyd with Penny Junor, *Wonderful Tonight* (Three Rivers Press, 2007), 100–103; the interview of George Harrison on *The Dick Cavett Show*, ABC, November 23, 1971; *The Beatles Anthology*, 177–78; as well as the well-researched accounts in Joe Goodden, *Riding So High: The Beatles and Drugs* (Pepper & Pearl, 2017), 77–84, and Graeme Thomson, *George Harrison: Behind That Locked Door* (Ombibus Press, 2016), 110–12.

116 *"George was still the little kid":* Shotton and Schaffner, *In My Life*, 105.

116 *"I meant it":* Lennon in Barry Miles, *Beatles in Their Own Words* (Omnibus Press, 1978), 80.

117 *Suitcases "went flying":* Max Jones and Ray Coleman, "Screams for Dylan," *Melody Maker*, May 1, 1965, 3.

118 *"What's the lightbulb for?":* D. A. Pennebaker, *Bob Dylan, Dont Look Back: A Film and Book* (New Video Group, 2006 ed.), 21.

118 *"Dylan and I became involved":* Bill Harry, "Down at the Blue," published in the *Mersey Beat* section of the Triumph PC website.

118 *a sheet of paper:* This sheet is in the collection at the Bob Dylan Center archives.

119 *"some sort of spark":* Dana Gillespie, *Weren't Born a Man* (Hawksmoor, 2020), 67. For details of Gillespie's life, I relied on her book and our interview on April 2, 2025.

119 *"I can't remember now":* Gillespie, *Weren't Born a Man*, 70. Note: In the mid-sixties, the age of sexual consent in Britain was sixteen, as it still is. I asked Gillespie if it seemed strange to anyone that a twenty-three-year-old man was in a relationship with a sixteen-year-old girl. "Nobody cared about things like age in those days," she said. "I don't even remember him being twenty-three—it didn't come into anything—and he didn't care about me being sixteen. We've now become so woke that you can't do anything, and I'm so pleased that I'm not a teenager now, with those dreadful, stupid attitudes."

119 *"Beatles are a little confused"*: Baez letter quoted in Hajdu, *Positively 4th Street*, 252.
119 *a* Record Mirror *reporter noted*: Norman Jopling, "How the Beatles Spend an Evening," *Record Mirror*, May 15, 1965. After visiting Dylan, the Beatles ordered porridge, pea sandwiches, and owls' legs at the Savoy's famously high-end restaurant, Jopling reported.
119 *"played a few records"*: Lennon quoted in Shelton, *No Direction Home*, 338.
119 *"don't remember what it was"*: Cameron Crowe, *Biograph* liner notes.
120 *"I dig John"*: Ray Coleman, "Dylan in Depth," *Melody Maker*, May 22, 1965.
120 *"They were great then"*: I viewed the *Dont Look Back* outtake footage of the Sheffield conversation at the Bob Dylan Center archive.
121 *"'What would you like'"*: Bill Harry, "Down at the Blue."
121 *not-quite-on-pitch version*: Mike McCartney, *Thank You Very Much*, 119. He expanded on the story in his interview with Jason Barnard on *The Strange Brew* podcast.
122 *sang the first line*: The scene of Donovan singing his "tangerine eyes" song was apparently not filmed. But D. A. Pennebaker described what happened in the room on the commentary track to the *Dont Look Back* DVD. His remarks match up with the description in Marianne Faithfull (with David Dalton), *Faithfull: An Autobiography* (Cooper Square Press, 2000), 50.
122 *"Dylan was, at that moment"*: Faithfull, *Faithfull*, 40.
123 *"swallow-tailed waiters"*: Ibid., 41.
123 *"completely overwhelmed"*: Ibid., 42.
123 *took out her guitar*: As seen in *Dont Look Back*, directed by D. A. Pennebaker, 1967.
123 *"Yonder stands your orphan"*: Ibid.
123 *"leaving Bobby's entourage"*: Baez letter quoted in Hajdu, *Positively 4th Street*, 251–52.
125 *Lesberg wanted details*: Interview of May 9, 1965, in Spangler, *Beatles Interview Database*.
125 *That same afternoon*: Descriptions here come from my viewings of scenes and outtakes of Pennebaker, *Dont Look Back*.
126 *"had to have an escort"*: Faithfull, *Faithfull*, 53.
126 *"Beatles are here"*: Pennebaker, *Dont Look Back*.
126 *flipping through a program*: Photos of the program's pages are posted online at Come Writers and Critics: The Bob Dylan Paper Site, https://www.bobdylan-comewritersandcritics.com.
127 *"quietly took over"*: Max Jones, "Different Dylan," *Melody Maker*, May 15, 1965
127 *In the postshow crush*: The scene immediately after the concert, as well as the party at the Savoy, are described in: Keith Altham, "Dylan's Not a Singer At All—Says His Friend Dana," *New Musical Express*, July 9, 1965; and Faithfull, *Faithfull*, 53–55.
128 *Levy's Sound Studios*: See Shelton, *No Direction Home*, 339–40; and Heylin, *The Double Life of Bob Dylan*, vol. 1, 330. A recording of the session circulates online.
128 *laid low by bad acid*: Heylin, *The Double Life of Bob Dylan*, vol. 1, 334.
128 *"I went unannounced"*: Baez, *And a Voice to Sing With*, 98.
129 *to persuade Dylan*: This scene and the next one draw from Donovan Leitch, *The Autobiography of Donovan: The Hurdy Gurdy Man* (St. Martin's Press, 2005), 85–90.

CHAPTER 10 How Does It Feel

130 *"long, hot, dusty drive"*: Miles, *Many Years from Now*, 204.
130 *"Scrambled eggs"*: Ibid., 202.
131 *bards from around the world*: Stevenson, *The Last of England?*, 183.
131 *Richter was amazed*: Dan Richter, *The Dream Is Over: London in the 60s, Heroin, and John & Yoko* (Quarter Books Limited, 2012), 46.
131 *half-drunk on wine*: Peter Watts, "Allen Ginsberg, LSD Poetry and Sacrificing Chickens: The Birth of the '60s Hippie Underground, Revealed," *Uncut*, May 29, 2015.
131 *raving and gesticulating*: As seen in *Wholly Communion*, a thirty-three-minute documentary of the event directed by Peter Whitehead.
131 *"I set the alarm"*: The website Beatles Bible has a partial transcript posted under the headline "Press conference about the MBE announcement."
132 *"taken aback"*: Shotton and Schaffner, *In My Life*, 99.
132 *"the difference is"*: McCartney in an interview with Rick Rubin for the 2021 Hulu documentary series *McCartney, 3, 2, 1*.
132 *"I wrote it when"*: Miles, *Many Years from Now*, 21.
133 *"'Are you kidding?'"*: McCartney, as quoted in Dave Rybczewski, Beatles Music History!, an online resource.
133 *"That's Paul's song"*: Sheff, *All We Are Saying*, 177.
133 *"Take these sorts"*: Everett, *The Beatles as Musicians*, 302.
133 *"That would have been"*: Miles, *Many Years from Now*, 208.
134 *"vomitific in its structure"*: Shelton, *No Direction Home*, 319.
134 *"ten pages long"*: Jules Siegel, "Bob Dylan, Rebel King of Rock 'n' Roll," *Saturday Evening Post*, July 30, 1966.
134 *"like a ghost is writing"*: Robert Hilburn, "Rock's Enigmatic Poet Opens a Long-Private Door," *Los Angeles Times*, April 4, 2004.
134 *"just a riff"*: Dylan interviewed by Bob Coburn, *Rockline*, KLOS-FM, June 17, 1985. The interview is published in Jeff Burger, *Dylan on Dylan*.
135 *"B.B. King shit"*: Larry "Ratso" Sloman, *On the Road with Bob Dylan* (Three Rivers Press, 2002), 288.
135 *When Dylan attempted*: My account of this session draws from Al Kooper, *Backstage Passes & Backstabbing Bastards: Memoirs of a Rock 'n' Roll Survivor* (Backbeat Books, updated ed., 2008), 34–37.
137 *"People jumped to their feet"*: Shaun Considine, "The Hit We Almost Missed," *The New York Times*, December 3, 2004.
138 *Dylan waved friends*: Barney Hoskyns, *Small Town Talk: Bob Dylan, the Band, Van Morrison, Janis Joplin, Jimi Hendrix & Friends in the Wild Years of Woodstock* (Da Capo Press, 2016), 60.
138 *"dug his situation"*: Shelton, *No Direction Home*, 338.
139 *"back to the Sullivan show"*: Scaduto, *Dylan*, 246.
139 *"After it was over"*: Mike Bloomfield, "Dylan Goes Electric," in Lynda Rosen Obst, *The Sixties* (Rolling Stone, 1977).
139 *"birth of Rock"*: Joe Boyd, *White Bicycles: Making Music in the 1960s* (Serpent's Tail, 2006), 105.

- 141 *side-by-side pictures*: Dylan's appearances in teen magazines are noted in Allison Bumsted, *TeenSet: Teen Fan Magazines and Rock Journalism* (University of Mississippi Press, 2024).
- 141 *"meaningful rock 'n' roll lyrics"*: Robert Shelton, "The Beatles Will Make the Scene Here Again, but the Scene Has Changed," *The New York Times*, August 11, 1965, 40.
- 141 *"absolute rubbish"*: McCartney in "John Lennon & Paul McCartney Speak Up! Speak Out!," *Flip* magazine, May 1966, 8.
- 141 *"bridged the gap"*: "Dylan Pop Idol: Folk King Now Hottest Thing in Rock Field," *KRLA Beat*, August 7, 1965, 2.
- 142 *"exemplified by the Beatles and Bob Dylan"*: Quoted from "The Jazz Liverpool of the West," a 1965 *San Francisco Chronicle* column by Ralph J. Gleason, in Don Armstrong, *The Life and Writings of Ralph J. Gleason: Dispatches from the Front* (Bloomsbury Academic, 2024).
- 142 *"see how easy"*: Daryl Sanders, *That Thin Wild Mercury Sound: Dylan, Nashville, and the Making of Blonde on Blonde* (Chicago Review Press, 2019), 17.
- 142 *"Paul's arrangement of John's song"*: Spencer Leigh, "Mike Ramsden," *The Independent*, February 7, 2004. This obituary includes quotations from Leigh's 1998 interview of Ramsden.
- 143 *"Americans still like us"*: Harrison quoted in Tony Barrow, *John, Paul, George, Ringo & Me: The Real Beatles Story* (André Deutsch, 2005), 152.
- 144 *Aronowitz had been charged*: The descriptions of Dylan's visits to the Warwick in this chapter draw from Aronowitz's *Bob Dylan and the Beatles*, 189–239; a Mal Evans diary entry shared with me by Evans's biographer, Kenneth Womack; and my interview with McCartney.
- 144 *had been losing confidence*: See Ken Emerson, *Always Magic in the Air: The Bomp and Brilliance of the Brill Bulding Era* (Penguin Books, 2005), 197–98. Goffin said he felt "like a dwarf" in comparison with Dylan, adding, "I had a desire . . . to be a poet—but I wasn't able to."
- 148 *"the famous Stones"*: Lennon in Chris Hutchins, "Prisoners on Floor 33," *New Musical Express*, August 20, 1965. Hutchins had close access to the Beatles that weekend.
- 148 *"You couldn't hear"*: Kenneth Womack, *Living the Beatles Legend: The Untold Story of Mal Evans* (Dey Street Books, 2023), 140.
- 148 *one hundred thousand people*: George Dugan, "100,000 Fill Yankee Stadium to Hear Graham," *The New York Times*, July 21, 1957.

CHAPTER 11 Number One

- 151 *Beatles earned $160,000*: Gunderson, *Some Fun Tonight!*, vol. 2, 40.
- 151 *faux-live versions*: See Mark Lewisohn, *The Complete Beatles Chronicle*, 215, for details on the January 5, 1966, session meant to "sweeten" *The Beatles at Shea Stadium*.
- 152 *one of six acts*: See "Support Acts, 1965 Tour," in Gunderson, *Some Fun Tonight!*, vol. 2.
- 152 *hundreds of Beatlemaniacs*: This account of the Houston airport scene draws from: Larry Kane, *Ticket to Ride* (Running Press, 2003), 225–26; Alf Bicknell, *Alf Bicknell's Beatles Diary* (Jack Edwards Productions, 1996), 76; Mark Lewisohn, *The Beatles*

Live!: The Ultimate Reference Book (Henry Holt, 1986), 184; and Gunderson, *Some Fun Tonight!*, vol. 2, 64–66.

154 *"These poor girls"*: Kurt Loder, *Joan Baez: The Rolling Stone Interview*, April 14, 1983. I have condensed some quotations from this interview, which is worth reading in full.

154 *two Beatles looked on*: Unterberger, *Turn! Turn! Turn!*, 180.

155 *had gotten their start*: See Barney Hoskyns, *Across the Great Divide: The Band and America* (Rowman & Littlefield, 2006 ed.).

155 *"booed their former culture hero"*: Jack Newfield, "Mods, Rockers Fight Over New Thing Called 'Dylan,'" *The Village Voice*, September 2, 1965, 1.

155 *"Where's Ringo?"*: In the September 8, 1965, edition of his column for the *San Francisco Chronicle,* headlined "Bob Dylan Does as He Pleases," Ralph J. Gleason noted this detail from *Newsday*'s report.

155 *"the childishness of the audience's reaction"*: Robert Shelton, "Folk Singer Offers Works in 'New Mood' at Forest Hills," *The New York Times*, August 30, 1965.

156 *"on my ass"*: Kooper, *Backstage Passes and Backstabbing Bastards*, 44.

156 *"A real carnival"*: Ibid., 45.

156 *"in an extraordinary way"*: Kane, *Ticket to Ride*, 257.

157 *"kind of Florence Nightingale"*: Ibid., 257.

157 *"the monumental difference"*: Charles Champlin, "Dylan: Hottest Folk Singer," *The Los Angeles Times,* September 3, 1965.

157 *Dylan quickly realized*: Hoskyns, *Across the Great Divide*, 99–100.

158 *"could become Elvis Presley"*: Ochs's statements here and in the pages to come are from Scaduto, *Dylan*, 257.

159 *"a collector's item"*: Tony Hall, "George Harrison's Fab Forty," *Record Mirror*, January 1, 1966.

159 *"haven't influenced the songs"*: From the transcript of Dylan's Austin press conference put together by the archivist Artur Jarosinski for the collection *Every Mind Polluting Word*.

160 *gave way to boos*: Robbie Robertson, *Testimony* (Windmill Books, 2016), 187.

160 *working in that tradition*: Dylan went way back with it: In 1954, at age thirteen, he performed one of the biggest answer-song hits, Hank Ballard and the Midnighters' "Annie Had a Baby," at summer camp. That song was a sequel to Ballard's "Work with Me, Annie."

161 *"never made it onto an album"*: Crowe, *Biograph* liner notes.

161 *"could have pulled it off"*: Scaduto, *Dylan*, 257.

161 *"Bobby wanted to be a superstar"*: Ibid., 262.

162 *"Everywhere we went"*: Sounes, *Down the Highway*, 194.

162 *"It's a hell of a sound"*: Ibid., 194.

162 *"backed up by celli"*: *Sing Out!*, January 1966, 117.

CHAPTER 12 Northern Songs

163 *"childish, tribal" phase*: From an interview Lennon gave to Maurice Hindle and Daniel Wiles of *Unit*, a student magazine, December 2, 1968. See Burger, *Lennon on Lennon*, 49.

NOTES 339

163 *"spent five hours"*: Sheff, *All We Are Saying*, 193.
165 *"Salvation Army song"*: Francis Wyndham, "Close-Up: Paul McCartney as Songwriter," *London Life*, December 4, 1965.
165 *"Wait till you hear it"*: Cleave, "Have You Heard What They're Singing These Days?", *Evening Standard*, October 19, 1965.
166 *"fantastic composer"*: McCartney in *Flip*, May 1966.
168 *"tried to do too much"*: Cleave, "The Beatles: Rubber Soul," *Evening Standard*, December 4, 1965.
168 *"I tried to Work It Out"*: *Beatles Book Monthly*, February 1966.
169 *lines wouldn't make it*: Daryl Sanders details the evolution of "Leopard-Skin Pill-Box Hat" in *That Thin, Wild Mercury Sound*, 55–58; as well as its relationship to "Drive My Car," 66.
170 *"It's a war"*: From my transcription of the *Radio Unnameable* episode posted on YouTube by "nightly moth."
170 *a squat building*: The researcher Bob Egan published his findings about the *Blonde on Blonde* cover shoot at www.PopSpotsNYC.com.
171 *"Johnston came to us"*: Sanders, *That Thin, Wild Mercury Sound*, 94.
172 *"Dylan was quite blatant"*: Derek Barker, "From You to Me," *Isis*, 96.
172 *"very ballsy"*: Kooper quoted in Andy Gill, *Bob Dylan: The Stories Behind the Songs, 1962–1969* (Carlton Books, 2011 ed.), 150.
172 *"a funny thing"*: Vic Garbarini, "George Harrison Looks Back," *Guitar World*, January 2001 (interview conducted in 1992), 70.
174 *"the kind of insensitivity"*: Sheff, *All We Are Saying*, 139.
175 *"It actually describes"*: Ibid., 181.
175 *Bible close at hand*: My mentions of Dylan's specific uses of biblical imagery in *Blonde on Blonde* are indebted to Sanders, *That Thin, Wild Mercury Sound*.
176 *"a lot of medicine"*: Shelton, *No Direction Home*, 395.
176 *leaving that detail out*: The complete audio of the airborne interview surfaced in 2011, some sixteen years after Shelton's death. See Andy Greene, "Questions about Dylan's Claim That He Was Once a Heroin Addict," *Rolling Stone*, May 23, 2011.
176 *"like to be accepted"*: Shelton, *No Direction Home*, 398.
177 *"it's the thing to do"*: Ibid., 398.
177 *"What do you think"*: Robert Westfield and Jim Monaghan interview of Dylan, April 18, 1966. Transcript by Jarosinski, *Every Mind Polluting Word*.
177 *"Australia's war"*: Perth press conference, April 23, 1966.
178 *"What's your opinion"*: Stockholm press conference, April 26, 1966.
178 *$100,000 for the rights*: Scaduto, *Dylan*, 282.
178 *"Dylan Month"*: Neil Aspinall, "Neil's Column," *Beatles Book Monthly*, June 1966, 25.
178 *"the term 'folk rock'"*: May Fair Hotel press conference, May 3, 1966. See Carl Benson, *The Bob Dylan Companion: Four Decades of Commentary* (Schirmer Books, 1998), 77.
179 *"quite jealous"*: The jacket was sold at auction in 2015 for $5,000. Bramwell's description of Lennon's envy of this garment was noted in the Heritage Auctions listing.
179 *"It was a bit like"*: McCartney quoted in Johnny Black, "Dylan! Thirty Days That Electrified the World," *Mojo*, November 1998.

340 ■ NOTES

179 *"until all this blows over"*: Robertson, *Testimony*, 238.
179 *"listening to music"*: Author interview.
180 *"What caught my ear"*: Robertson, *Testimony*, 238.
180 like *"the Dalai Lama singing"*: George Martin in Lewisohn, *The Beatles Recording Sessions*, 72.
180 *"very far ahead"*: Faithfull, *Faithfull*, 55.
180 *"Oh, I get it"*: Du Noyer, *Conversations with McCartney*, 61.
180 *"The expression on Paul's face"*: Faithfull, *Faithfull*, 55.
180 *"Something new, Bobby"*: Robertson, *Testimony*, 239.
181 *"That ought to be"*: Lennon, as quoted by Dylan in an outtake from the documentary *Eat the Document* (directed by Dylan, released, briefly, in 1972).
181 *"I don't like it"*: Lennon recalled the exchange in Jonathan Cott, "John Lennon: The Rolling Stone Interview," *Rolling Stone*, November 23, 1968.
181 *"I didn't like it"*: Ibid.
182 *"want to go home"*: Dylan in *No Direction Home: Bob Dylan* (directed by Martin Scorsese, 2005).

CHAPTER 13 Costars

183 vast swimming pools: See Colum Giles and Bob Hawkins, *Storehouses of Empire: Liverpool's Historice Warehouses* (English Heritage, 2004). This chapter is also informed by my visit to Liverpool's Maritime Museum and the Clarence Warehouse.
184 *"He was notorious"*: Lewisohn, *Tune In*, 1319.
184 Beatles didn't know: Ibid., 1353.
184 *"We'd send him out"*: Alderson quoted in Heylin, *The Double Life of Bob Dylan*, vol. 1, 435. Alderson made a similar statement in an interview with me.
185 with, Dennis Peter Flynn: The photo of Dylan with George Harrison's likely fight opponent is posted at the apparently anonymously written blog *Liverpool Miscellany* in the story "Bob Dylan: Friday the 13th [1966/05/13]."
185 Dylan was accompanied: I viewed the film footage of the Liverpool photo shoot at the Bob Dylan Center archive. The dialogue here comes from my transcription.
185 *"Bob felt great"*: Barry Feinstein, *Real Moments: Bob Dylan by Barry Feinstein* (Vision On, 2008), 52.
186 *"loved those kids"*: Ibid., 52.
186 *"Really stoned"*: Spencer Leigh in a story for Neil Cossar, *Bob Dylan: The Day I Was There* (This Day in Music Books, 2017), 190.
187 *"don't mind being shot"*: Dylan in Scorsese, *No Direction Home*.
187 *"Dylan was shit"*: Footage at the Bob Dylan Center.
188 *"came right up"*: Heylin, *The Double Life of Bob Dylan*, vol. 1, 444.
188 *"pulls a knife"*: Keylock in David McLean, "Recalling the Legendary Night in Glasgow When Dylan Went Electric," *The Scotsman*, May 24, 2021.
188 *"I wanna get out of here"*: Bob Dylan, *The 1966 Live Recordings* (Columbia, 2016), Disc 26.

188 *"spewed toward the stage"*: Robertson, *Testimony*, 240.
189 *rocking harder*: Gillespie described her impression in Norrie Drummond, "Dylan Shocked by British Fans," *New Musical Express*, June 17, 1966.
189 *earliest versions*: As heard on the box set *Revolver: Special Edition* (Apple, 2022).
189 *"going to put me down!"*: Wenner, *Lennon Remembers*, 149.
190 *At the start of the scene*: I viewed a newly restored version of this footage at the Bob Dylan Center. The dialogue in this chapter is from my transcription.
195 *"kept looking at me"*: Pennebaker quotes here are from: Daniel Mark Epstein, *The Ballad of Bob Dylan: A Portrait* (Harper, 2011), 178; and Hajdu, *Positively 4th Street*, 291.
195 *"You got one more"*: Robertson, *Testimony*, 241.
196 *"no fit state"*: Tyler quoted in Heylin, *The Double Life of Bob Dylan*, vol. 1, 451.
196 *"any of the Beatles"*: Norman Jopling, "With a Mixture of Folk, Rock & Comedy, Dylan Shows He Can Take Every Insult but Not a Compliment," *Record Mirror*, June 11, 1966.
196 *"tempo and attitude"*: Robertson, *Testimony*, 241.
196 *"Shut up! Leave him alone!"*: Shelton, *No Direction Home*, 416.
196 *"The people who walked out"*: Ibid., 416.
196 *"We didn't agree"*: Author interview.
196 *after the concert*: The postshow scenes here draw from Robertson's account in *Testimony*.

CHAPTER 14 Retreat

198 *Schonfield was born*: Details on Schonfield's background and religious views are from Owen Power, *Hugh Schonfield: A Case Study of Complex Jewish Identities* (Wipf & Stock, 2013).
199 *"Christianity will go"*: Maureen Cleave, "John Lennon: How Does a Beatle Live?," *Evening Standard*, March 4, 1966.
199 *"loyal in their own way"*: Hugh J. Schonfield, *The Passover Plot*, 40th anniversary ed. (Disinformation Company, 2005), 99.
200 *"I think you might be"*: Barrow's letter is quoted in Turner, *Beatles '66*, 277.
200 *"won't live beyond"*: *The Beatles Anthology*, 216.
201 *kept secret from*: Barrow, *John, Paul, George, Ringo & Me*, 179.
201 *"Well, we think about it"*: Tokyo press conference, June 30, 1966.
201 *"thugs in short-sleeved shirts"*: *The Beatles Anthology*, 217.
202 *"Alas, they performed"*: Review quoted in Turner, *Beatles '66*, 247.
202 *"Imelda Stood Up"*: Headline cited in *John, Paul, George, Ringo & Me*, 198.
203 *"I was petrified"*: *The Beatles Anthology*, 220.
203 *"more than they could earn"*: George Harrison, *I Me Mine* (Chronicle Books, 1980), 53.
203 *"No more for me"*: Turner, *Beatles '66*, 254.
203 *"beaten up by the Americans"*: Barrow, *John, Paul, George, Ringo & Me*, 198.
203 *found Dylan "comatose"*: Hoskyns, *Small Town Talk*, 74.
204 *"high on speed"*: Ibid., 74.

NOTES

204 *"a major step"*: Richard Goldstein review, *Village Voice*, June 1966.
204 *"the king of rock 'n' roll"*: Jules Siegel, "Bob Dylan: Rebel King of Rock 'n' Roll," *Saturday Evening Post*, July 30, 1966.
205 *concert in Moscow*: Ian Woodward, "Interview with Mickey Jones," in Barker, *Isis*, 124.
205 *top of the page*: Dylan's notes on editing his film are at the Bob Dylan Center archives.
206 *"Hold on"*: Howard Sounes fleshed out the story of the accident, or incident, with his interviews of Grossman and Thaler for *Down the Highway*.
207 *"Dylan Hurt"*: *The New York Times*, August 2, 1966, 25.
207 *"That is it for me"*: Turner, *Beatles '66*, 266.
209 *"This is getting"*: Ibid., 268.
209 *"a brilliant album"*: *Melody Maker*, July 30, 1966 (uncredited writer).
209 *"a load of rubbish"*: "Ray Davies Reviews the Beatles LP," *Disc and Music Echo*, July 30, 1966, 16 (uncredited writer).
210 *"a revolutionary record"*: Richard Goldstein, "The Beatles: *Revolver*," *The Village Voice*, August 25, 1966.
210 *"most outstanding pop album"*: Ralph J. Gleason. "The Beatles' Hot 'Revolver,'" *This World* (Sunday magazine), *The San Francisco Examiner*, September 25, 1966, 35.
210 *the North American tour*: My account of the 1966 tour draws from: Barrow, *John, Paul, George, Ringo & Me*; Gunderson, *Some Fun Tonight!, Volume 2: 1965–1966*; *The Beatles Anthology*; Turner, *Beatles '66*; and Womack, *Living the Beatles Legend*.
213 *"As a spectacle"*: Ralph J. Gleason, "A Puppet Show for the Beatles," *San Francisco Chronicle*, August 31, 1966.
213 *"not a Beatle anymore"*: Barrow, *John, Paul, George, Ringo & Me*, 208.

CHAPTER 15 Penny Lane and Bourbon Street

214 *"reminiscent of his childhood"*: Sounes, *Down the Highway*, 223.
214 *"Something's gotta change"*: Ben Fong-Torres, *Knockin' on Dylan's Door* (Pocket Books, 1974), 107.
215 *"Now John loved"*: C. Lennon, *A Twist of Lennon*, 139.
215 *"a little like Bob Dylan"*: Fred Robbins interview, October 29, 1966, included in Burger, *Lennon on Lennon*, 14.
215 *didn't ask for star treatment*: Leonard Gross, "John Lennon: Beatle on His Own," *Look*, December 13, 1966, 62.
215 *"going down the road"*: *The Beatles Anthology*, 231.
216 *"highly reminiscent"*: Everett, *The Beatles as Musicians*, 76.
216 *"He met Yoko"*: C. Lennon interviewed in Lesley Ann Jones, "Yes, I Lost John to Another Woman . . . But It Wasn't Yoko," *Daily Mail*, April 4, 2015.
217 *called himself Hunt Hanson*: Womack, *Living the Beatles Legend*, 194.
217 *In Lydd, Kent*: McCartney's travels are described in Miles, *Many Years from Now*, and Womack, *Living the Beatles Legend*.
217 *"Dear Ringo"*: Ringo Starr, *Postcards from the Boys* (Chronicle Books, 2004), 8.
218 *"in terrible pain"*: Harrison, *I Me Mine*, 55.
219 *He read* Raja-Yoga: Thomson, *Behind the Locked Door*, 120.

219 *"deepest sleep I ever had"*: Harrison, *I Me Mine*, 296.
219 *"I'm just having a good time"*: "Ringo Says," *New Musical Express*, November 11, 1966 (uncredited author), 10.
219 *Twenty-five takes*: Details of Beatles recording sessions from Lewisohn, *The Complete Beatles Chronicle*; Lewisohn, *The Beatles Recording Sessions*; and *The Beatles Anthology*.
221 *"Dylan's old cronies"*: Ren Grevatt, "He's Upstate Recuperating—the Dylan Mystery Grows," *Melody Maker*, November 26, 1966, 7.
222 *"listened to all of this"*: Harry Stein, *Tiny Tim: An Unauthorized Biography* (Playboy Press, 1976), 96.
223 *"I was bouncing"*: The manuscript of "John Lennon Hat" appears in Davidson and Fishel, *Mixing Up the Medicine*, 224.
224 *"You're rambling on"*: Robertson quoted in Hoskyns, *Across the Great Divide*, 136.
224 *"would pull these songs"*: Robertson quoted in Greil Marcus, *The Old, Weird America: The World of Bob Dylan's Basement Tapes* (Picador, 1997), xxii.
224 *"One evening, Dylan told me"*: Shamik Bag, "Bob Dylan and the Bauls, an Indian Story," *Hindustan Times*, May 21, 2021.
225 *"That was great"*: *American Bandstand*, March 11, 1967.
226 *"French mustaches"*: Thomas Thompson, "The New Far-Out Beatles," *Life*, June 16, 1967.
226 *"didn't really like"*: *The Beatles Anthology*, 242.
227 *"back wheel locked"*: Michael Iachetta, "Scarred Dylan Is Comin' Back," *Daily News*, May 8, 1967.

CHAPTER 16 Everybody's Song

229 *"equal to any song"*: Rorem quoted in "The Messengers," *Time*, September 22, 1967, (uncredited author), 60.
229 *"something it has never been"*: Ibid., 60.
229 *"Listening to the* Sgt. Pepper *album"*: Richard Poirier, "Learning from the Beatles," *Partisan Review*, Fall 1967.
230 *"dazzling but ultimately fraudulent"*: Richard Goldstein, "We Still Need the Beatles, but . . . ," *The New York Times*, June 18, 1967, 104.
230 *"a Day-Glo tombstone for its time"*: Greil Marcus, *Stranded: Rock and Roll for a Desert Island* (Knopf, 1979), 258.
230 *destroyed rock 'n' roll*: See Elijah Wald, *How the Beatles Destroyed Rock 'n' Roll* (Oxford University Press, 2009).
230 *"very indulgent"*: Dylan interview with Matt Damsker, September 15, 1978.
230 *"He loves the Beatles"*: Thompson, *Positively Main Street*, 162.
230 *"God is everything"*: Celia Simpson, "Paul McCartney," *Queen*, July 19, 1967.
231 *"LSD isn't a real answer"*: Statements here by Harrison and McCartney are from the Beatles' press conference on August 26, 1967, in Bangor, Wales.
231 *"Meditation gives you confidence"*: Lennon and Harrison spoke with television reporters in Bangor on August 27, 1967. Footage available on YouTube.
231 *"Yellow matter custard, green slop pie"*: Shotton and Schaffner, *In My Life*, 124.

232 *"Let the fuckers"*: Ibid., 124.
232 *"Dylan got away with murder"*: Sheff, *All We Are Saying*, 184.
233 *"Dylan is sounding beautiful"*: Nick Jones, "Bob Dylan Today," *Melody Maker*, November 4, 1967, 5.
233 *"I asked Columbia"*: Cameron Crowe, *Biograph* liner notes.
234 *"Aren't we entitled to have a flop?"*: Norrie Drummond, "I Still Say Beatles' 'Tour' Was Entertaining," *New Musical Express*, January 6, 1968, 5.
234 *"loving collection of myths"*: Ralph J. Gleason, "Dylan Has Returned with 'John Wesley Harding,'" *Rolling Stone*, February 11, 1968.
234 *"admirable in its straightforwardness"*: Robert Christgau, "Secular Music," *Esquire*, May 1968, 22.
235 *"if you wanted to see it"*: Rob MacBeath, "Looking Up Dylan's Sleeves," *The Telegraph*, issue 51, Spring 1995.
235 *"We want Dylan!"*: Sue C. Clark, "Bob Dylan Turns Up for Woody Guthrie Memorial," *Rolling Stone*, February 24, 1968.
235 *"used to think"*: Hubert Saal, "Dylan Is Back," *Newsweek*, February 26, 1968.
236 *"pure nonsense song"*: Chris Welch, "Manfred Beats Up Dylan's Eskimo," *Melody Maker*, January 13, 1968.
236 *"baggage enough to sink a battleship"*: C. Lennon, *A Twist of Lennon*, 153.
236 *"can't recall much"*: Harrison, *I Me Mine*, 132.
237 *"as close as the Beatles"*: Everett, *The Beatles as Musicians*, 204.
237 *"Dylan was doing"*: Paul McCartney, *The Lyrics* (Liveright, 2021), 423.
237 *"when I wrote"*: *The Beatles Anthology*, 283.
237 she sniffed heroin: Yoko Ono in an interview with Steven Gaines published in Peter Brown and Steven Gaines, *All You Need Is Love: The Beatles in Their Own Words* (St. Martin's Press, 2024), 215.
238 *"we were evacuated"*: Sean O'Hagan, "Yoko Ono at 80," *The Guardian*, May 25, 2013.
238 *"I am a cloud"*: Betty Rollin, "'I Have Always Dreamed of This One Woman Coming into My Life," *Daily Express*, March 12, 1969. Interviewed alongside Ono, Lennon mentioned receiving this postcard during his Rishikesh stay.
238 *"Maharishi had been accused"*: C. Lennon, *A Twist of Lennon*, 160.
239 *"'If you come and see me'"*: Apple press conference, New York, May 14, 1968.
239 Nina Tornabene of the Bronx: Jennifer H. Cunningham, "Bronx Beatles Fans Reminisce on Brush with Fab Four," *Daily News*, February 6, 2014.
239 *"one of the most dazzling albums"*: Aronowitz, "It's High Time Fame Came to Tiny Tim," *Life*, June 14, 1968, 10.
240 *"Play Tiny Tim!"*: Lennon and McCartney were interviewed by Kenny Everett on June 6, 1968. Audio available on YouTube.
240 *"I was always shy"*: Sheff, *All We Are Saying*, 208.
240 *"looked so right together"*: C. Lennon, *A Twist of Lennon*, 167.
240 *"started with the idea"*: Miles, *Many Years from Now*, 465.
240 Paul led the band: See Alan Smith, "A Beatle in Bradford and a Big Brass Band," *New Musical Express*, July 6, 1968.
241 *"damn good set of lyrics"*: Lennon's remarks on "Hey Jude" in Sheff, *All We Are Saying*, 139.

242 *"They had come back"*: Geoff Emerick and Howard Massey, *Here, There and Everywhere: My Life Recording the Music of the Beatles* (Gotham Books, 2007), 224.
243 *"went into the toilet"*: Ibid., 234.
243 *"John was very curious"*: Brown and Gaines, *All You Need Is Love*, 215.
243 *"John would inevitably"*: Keith Richards, *Life* (Little, Brown, 2010), 261.
243 *"just fed up"*: Maurice Devereux, "Interview with Maureen Cox," *Le Chroniqueur*, July 1988.
244 *"worked on that song"*: Dan Forte, "George Harrison, Guitarist," *Guitar Player*, November 1987.
244 *"Outside of my family"*: Dylan, *Chronicles: Volume One*, 114.
244 *painting with a neighbor*: Sounes, *Down the Highway*, 232–33.
245 *"In his house in Woodstock"*: Thompson, *Positively Main Street*, 161.
245 *"When did you read the Bible parables?"*: John Cohen and Happy Traum, "Conversations with Bob Dylan," *Sing Out!*, October/November 1968, 6.
246 *"rebelling against the rebellion"*: Simon Harper, citing his 2005 interview with Robertson, in "Remembering Robbie Robertson," *Louder*, August 8, 2024.
246 *"got a bit pretentious"*: Jonathan Cott, "John Lennon: The Rolling Stone Interview," *Rolling Stone*, November 23, 1968.
247 *three favorite albums*: McCartney in a Facebook chat with the Paul McCartney Official Fan Group, June 25, 2025. The other two were the Beach Boys' *Pet Sounds* and Neil Young's *Harvest*.
247 *"'must be George'"*: Hoskyns, *Small Town Talk*, 100.
247 *"Bob was an odd person"*: Thomson, *Behind That Locked Door*, 159.
247 *"hardly said a word"*: Mitchell Glazer, "The George Harrison Interview," *Crawdaddy*, February 1977. The next two Harrison quotations are from the same interview.
249 *"in walked five guys"*: Elliott Landy, *The Band Photographs, 1968–1969*, vol. 2 (Weldon Owen, 2025). This book includes a piece by Traum on his memories of Thanksgiving 1968.
249 *"religious and a country feeling"*: Timothy White, "George Harrison Reconsidered," *Musician*, November 1987.
249 *"Writing and playing with Bob"*: Thomson, *Behind That Locked Door*, 160.
249 *to convey his apologies*: Sounes, *Down the Highway*, 239.
250 *"Thank you, Tiny!"*: As heard on *The Beatles 1968 Christmas Record* (Lyntone Recordings).
250 *"Thank you and Sarah and children"*: The letter is housed at the Bob Dylan Center archive. Harrison gave an 'h' to Sara's name.
250 *"Dear Bobbie"*: Also at the Bob Dylan Center archive.

CHAPTER 17 Beatles & Co.

253 *Here's a list*: List compiled with the help of: Joe Goodden, "Get Back / Let It Be Sessions: Complete Song List," Beatles Bible website; and Doug Sulpy and Ray Schweighardt, *Drugs, Divorce and a Slipping Image: The Unauthorized Story of the Beatles' "Get Back" Sessions* (The 910, 1994).
254 *"hanging out with Bob Dylan"*: *The Beatles Anthology*, 316.

NOTES

255 *"Dylan coming out amplified"*: Dialogue from the sessions comes from *Let It Be* (directed by Michael Lindsay-Hogg, Apple Films, ABKCO, 1970); *The Beatles: Get Back* (directed by Peter Jackson, Disney, 2022); the podcast *Winter of Our Discontent* by Nick Anthony; and the many video and audio clips that have surfaced online.

256 *"They actually came to blows"*: Philip Norman, *John Lennon: The Life* (Doubleday, 2008), 583.

257 *"seven thousand kinds of fits"*: Tony Bramwell, *Magical Mystery Tours: My Life with the Beatles* (Thomas Dunne Books, 2005), 288.

259 *a private message*: Babiuk, *Beatles Gear*, 439.

259 *"Probably the main reason"*: Thompson, *Positively Main Street*, 162.

260 *"white working class"*: Scaduto, *Dylan*, 299.

260 *"Dear Bobbie"*: Harrison letter housed at Bob Dylan Center archive.

260 *those he would describe*: Dylan, *Chronicles: Volume One*, phrases from the "New Morning" chapter.

263 *concealing a heroin habit*: Details from Richter, *The Dream Is Over*, and our interview on April 28, 2024.

263 *"It felt weird"*: Richter, *The Dream Is Over*, 85.

265 *"were arguing over everything"*: Ibid., 89.

266 *there he was*: Details of Dylan's Isle of Wight visit from: Ray Foulk, with Caroline Foulk, *Stealing Dylan from Woodstock* (Medina, 2015); Bill Bradshaw, *Bob Dylan at the Isle of Wight Festival 1969* (Medina, 2019); Aronowitz, *Bob Dylan and the Beatles*; Boyd, *Wonderful Tonight*; and Thomson, *Behind That Locked Door*.

267 *"it was envy"*: Aronowitz, *Bob Dylan and the Beatles*, 308.

267 *"Look at them"*: Foulk, *Stealing Dylan from Woodstock*, 134.

267 *"astonishingly beautiful rendition"*: Ibid., 144.

267 *"some sort of drugs problem"*: From my transcription of the BBC South Archive footage of the Isle of Wight news conference, which appeared on YouTube.

268 *"Here come the hippies"*: From BBC News footage posted on YouTube.

268 *a couple "made love"*: "Dylan Finally Happens at Isle of Wight," *The Guardian*, September 1, 1969.

269 *"just didn't work"*: Author interview.

269 *"we never see each other"*: Aronowitz, *Bob Dylan and the Beatles*, 310.

269 *"the sixties rivalry"*: Foulk, *Stealing Dylan from Woodstock*, 97.

269 *Pattie suggested tennis*: Boyd, *Wonderful Tonight*, 169.

269 *"I'll play on the condition"*: Aronowitz, *Bob Dylan and the Beatles*, 310.

269 *"seven people on each side"*: Boyd, *Wonderful Tonight*, 169.

270 *"too demanding a sport"*: Aronowitz, *Bob Dylan and the Beatles*, 310.

270 *"What the fuck's wrong"*: Ibid., 324.

270 *"exultant roar"*: Ibid., 317

270 *"Great to be here"*: *The Bootleg Series Vol. 10: Another Self Portrait (1969-1971)*, deluxe edition, Disc 3: *Live at the Isle of Wight Festival*.

271 *George found the concert "marvelous"*: Foulk, *Stealing Dylan from Woodstock*, 244.

271 *"albeit slightly flat"*: Ibid., 244

271 *"would have jammed"*: Chip Madinger and Scott Raile, *Lennonology: Strange Days Indeed* (Open Your Books, 2015), 142.

271 *"trying to get him to record"*: Lennon made this statement in December 1970 in an interview with Jann Wenner for *Rolling Stone*. The version that appeared in the magazine in 1971 differs from the version in the book *Lennon Remembers*. I've gone to the audio of the interview, available on YouTube, and made my own transcription.

CHAPTER 18 Serve Yourself

272 *"'written a single'"*: Richard Williams, "John and Yoko," *Melody Maker*, December 6, 1969.
272 *"full of junk"*: Wenner, *Lennon Remembers*, 17.
272 *"think you're daft"*: *The Beatles Anthology*, 347.
275 *"eatin' cheese late at night"*: Author interview.
276 *"use your millions"*: Claudia Dreifus, "The Alan J. Weberman Story," *Rolling Stone*, March 4, 1971, 43.
276 *"Like Marx said"*: Lennon was interviewed by Tariq Ali and Robin Blackburn for Red Mole on January 21, 1971, for an article published in its March 8, 1971, issue.
276 *drew heavily from*: In his last interview, on December 6, 1980, with Andy Peebles of BBC 1, Lennon said of "Imagine": "Actually, that should be credited as a Lennon-Ono song, because a lot of it, the lyric and the concept, came from Yoko. But in those days I was a bit more selfish, a bit more macho, and I *omitted* to mention her contribution. But it was right out of *Grapefruit*, her book." On June 14, 2017, the National Music Publishers Association announced that the credit had been formally changed to include Ono.
278 *"It was Nigerian"*: Author interview.
279 *"this isn't my scene"*: This exchange was recalled by Harrison in a 1987 interview with *Rolling Stone*. It was republished in the Editors of *Rolling Stone*, *Harrison* (Simon & Schuster, 2002), 146.
279 *"a friend of us all"*: As heard on George Harrison and Friends, *The Concert for Bangladesh* (Apple, 1971).
279 *"If only we'd done three shows!"*: Editors of *Rolling Stone*, *Harrison*, 146.
280 *"McCartney's lyrics lack"*: An image of the flier appears on the website of the New York archive Boo-Hooray.
280 *"the newest members"*: Jon Wiener, *Come Together: John Lennon in His Time* (University of Illinois Press, 1991), 181.
280 *"you don't need talent"*: Ono news conference, Syracuse, New York, October 8, 1971. Transcribed footage available on Vimeo.
281 *"bouncing his head"*: Scaduto, *Dylan*, 319.
282 *"Dylan goes about"*: Richard Williams, "So This Is Christmas," *Uncut*, January 1998. Williams interviewed John and Yoko in New York in 1971.
283 *"We ask A. J. Weberman"*: Letter in December 2, 1971, edition of *The Village Voice*.
284 *caused Bob to walk out*: Clinton Heylin, *The Double Life of Bob Dylan, Vol. 2 1966–2021, Far Away From Myself* (The Bodley Head, London, 2023), 157.
284 *"Let them stay"*: Wiener, *Come Together*, 237–38.
284 *"John screamed angrily"*: Bob Gruen, *John Lennon: The New York Years* (Abrams, 2005), 61.

NOTES

285 *"'Shit, that's me'"*: Scott Cohen, "Bob Dylan: Not Like a Rolling Stone Interview," *Spin*, December 1985.
285 *"something for the Beatles"*: Notebook at Bob Dylan Center archive.
286 *"when's Dylan going"*: Steve Peacock, "Lennon, Exile on the Strip," *Sounds*, November 17, 1973.
287 *"copped it from Dylan"*: Sam Gillette, "Brian Hamill Remembers Photographing John Lennon," *People*, December 8, 2020.
287 *"not keen on the backings"*: Pete Hamill, "Long Night's Journey into Day," *Rolling Stone*, June 5, 1975.
288 *"watch the river flow"*: Madinger and Raile, *Lennonology*, 463.
288 *"Dylan was hiding"*: Author interview.
288 *"We have an America"*: "Transcript of Carter Address," *The New York Times*, July 16, 1976.
289 *"George enabled her"*: Aronowitz, *Bob Dylan and the Beatles*, 486.
289 *November 27, 1978*: Date identified by Madinger and Raile, *Lennonology*, 499.
289 *"stuck inside of Lexicon"*: This home-recorded Dylan parody was officially released as "Satire 2" on the 1998 compilation *John Lennon Anthology*.
290 *a church in Karuizawa*: See Carol Fleenor, "I Saw Him Standing There," *Guideposts*, September 2008.
290 *"wasn't a very good husband"*: Shelton, *No Direction Home*, 550.
290 *"Jesus put his hand"*: Karen Hughes, *The Dominion*, August 2, 1980. The article is reprinted in Jonathan Cott, ed., *Bob Dylan: The Essential Interviews* (Simon & Schuster, 2006), 292.
290 *"company men"*: See Madinger and Raile, *Lennonology*, 506. Lennon's audio diaries have surfaced online.
291 *"full of smack"*: Ibid., 507.
291 *a new composition*: A version of "Serve Yourself" and other Dylan parodies appear on the box set *John Lennon Anthology* (Capitol, 1998).
291 *"It's Paul!"*: Frederic Seaman, *The Last Days of John Lennon* (Birch Lane Press, 1991), 122.
292 *"Come on up here"*: Wayne Kaminski, *Yesterday and Today*, episode 136: '80, pt. 3. This podcast episode includes audio of an interview with Captain Hank. My description of the voyage relies on it as well as: Madinger and Raile, *Lennonology*, 515; Scott Neil, *Lennon Bermuda* (Brimstone Media, 2012); and Sheff, *All We Are Saying*.
292 *"a wicked parody"*: Seaman, *The Last Days of John Lennon*, 151–52.
292 *On November 14, 1980*: Kenneth Womack, *John Lennon 1980* (Omnibus Press, 2020), 204.
293 *"It didn't bother me"*: Elliot Mintz, *The Beatle Years*, Westwood One Radio, January 1, 1993.

CHAPTER 19 Rolling On

294 *"Mr. Lennon?"*: Chapman's statement is noted in Les Ledbetter, "John Lennon of Beatles Is Killed; Suspect Held in Shooting at Dakota," *The New York Times*, December 9, 1980.

294 *Four bullets*: In a statement on the day after the murder, the medical examiner Dr. Elliot Gross said that four bullets entered the body. See Joyce Wadler and Mike Sager, "'I Just Shot John Lennon,' He Said Coolly," *Washington Post*, December 9, 1980.
294 *A call went out*: This detail and others in this paragraph are from Jimmy Breslin, "A Part of Cop's Past Lies Dead," *Daily News*, December 9, 1980.
295 *"a bad Hollywood script-writer"*: Aronowitz, *Bob Dylan and the Beatles*, 447.
295 *"became quite paranoid"*: Thomson, *Behind That Locked Door*, 330.
296 *"try to kill him"*: Ibid.
296 *"bulletproof vest"*: Drummond in Sounes, *Down the Highway*, 338.
296 *"Lennon was shot"*: Tackett was interviewed by Tim Cumming. The full text appears on the blog *Tim Cumming: Art Music Poetry* under the headline "Gospel Bob: Guitarist Fred Tackett on Playing with Dylan, 1979–1981."
296 *"I don't really want to do that"*: Thomson, *Behind That Locked Door*, 331.
297 *"gonna have to go"*: Audience recording, Earl's Court, London, July 1, 1981.
297 *"very shortly after John Lennon was killed"*: Mary Judge is quoted in "I Remember When . . . ," *Music Hall Marks* (a publication of the Music Hall in Cincinnati), Summer 2016.
297 *"They used to say"*: Aronowitz, *Bob Dylan and the Beatles*, 22.
298 *"We'll bury" became "Wilbury"*: John Van der Kriste, *Jeff Lynne: Electric Light Orchestra: Before and After* (Fonthill, 2015), 112.
298 *"a few of these Mexican beers"*: Mark Ellen, "George Harrison: The Q Interview," *Q*, January 1988, 55.
299 *"I was flying"*: Elton John, *Me* (Henry Holt, 2019), 223.
299 *"Tom was at the top"*: Dylan, *Chronicles: Volume One*, 148.
300 *"What's it say there"*: Britta Lee Shain, *Seeing the Real You at Last: Life and Love on the Road with Bob Dylan* (Jawbone, 2016), 176–77.
300 *"So you got even with me!"*: Ellen, "George Harrison: The Q Interview," *Q*, 56.
301 *"What I'd really like to do"*: *Rockline*, February 10, 1988. Available on YouTube.
302 *"Well, what's it about?"*: Harrison in an episode of the radio show *Classic Albums*, February 10, 1990. Audio available on YouTube.
303 *"I hope you are O.K."*: Letter housed at the Bob Dylan Center archive.
305 *efforts to quit smoking*: From Jewel's interview with Simon Barber and Brian O'Connor, *Sodajerker on Songwriting* podcast, episode 228, May 2022.
305 *"One of the great drummers"*: From *Still on the Road*, the online resource established by the Dylan researcher Olof Björner. See the "bobtalk" section of "The 1997 Winter Club Tour."
306 *"certainly wasn't auditioning"*: Thomson, *Behind That Locked Door*, 388.
306 *"We joked about things"*: "Paul McCartney Reveals His Last Moments with George Harrison," *Uncut*, July 1, 2008.
306 *"profoundly emptier"*: Dylan in Udovitch and Wild, "Remembering George."
308 *"Dear Bob"*: Letter from McCartney at Bob Dylan Center archive.
308 *"in awe of McCartney"*: Wenner, "Bob Dylan Hits the Big Themes," *Rolling Stone*, May 3–17, 2007.
309 *"northern regions of Britain"*: Mikal Gilmore, "Dylan Unleashed," *Rolling Stone*, September 27, 2012.

Index

1962–1966 (Beatles compilation album), 36
1967–1970 (Beatles compilation album), xii, 37

Abbey Road (Beatles), 263, 265, 267, 271, 273
Abram, Michael, 305–6
AC/DC, 297
"Across the Universe" (Beatles), 232
Adams, Derroll, 122
Alderson, Richard, 177, 184–85
Alexander, Arthur, 33, 253
Alk, Howard, 117, 178, 185, 189–90, 205
Alk, Jones, 117, 178, 185
"All Along the Watchtower" (Dylan), 137, 233, 235, 254, 301
"All I Have to Do Is Dream" (Everly Brothers), 267
"All I Really Want to Do" (Dylan), 75, 103, 104, 140
"All My Loving" (Beatles), 56
Allsop, Kenneth, 66, 74
"All Things Must Pass" (Harrison), 249, 254, 303
All Things Must Pass (Harrison album, 1970), 274, 278, 300
"All Those Years Ago" (Harrison), 295

"All You Need Is Love" (Beatles), xvii, 230, 295
Alpert, Richard, 89, 175
"Amen" (Lennon), 290
American Bandstand (TV program), 225
American Top 40 (syndicated radio show), xiii
"Angela" (Lennon and Ono), 282
Angry Young Men, 66
Animals, the, 76, 100
Another Side of Bob Dylan (Dylan), 72, 73, 76, 96, 99, 100, 109, 255
  making of, 128
  position on British album chart, 117
answer songs, 160–61, 171–73, 190, 263, 291
Anthology of American Folk Music, 138
Antony and the Johnsons, 280
Apple Corps company, 238–39
Apple Records, 257
Armstrong, Louis, 253
Arnold, Jerome, 138
Aronowitz, Al, 63, 67, 72, 73–75, 80, 144, 205
  Beatles' American tour and, 54–55
  crack cocaine use in 1980s, 297
  Dylan's meeting with the Beatles and, 84–85

352 ■ INDEX

Aronowitz, Al (*cont.*)
   family background, 48
   Harrison's financial aid in 1970s, 288–89
   at Isle of Wight Festival, 266
   Lennon's murder and, 295
   marijuana supplied by, 82–83, 87
   second feature on the Beatles, 76
   at the Warwick Hotel meeting, 315
   won over by Dylan, 51
Art of McCartney, The (various artists), 316
Asher, Jane, 45, 60, 69, 105, 130, 241
   difficulty in relationship with Paul McCartney, 167–68
   engagement to Paul, 239
   in India, 236
   Paul's split with, 251
"Asolutely Sweet Marie" (Dylan), 173
Aspinall, Neil, 54, 55, 85, 145, 147, 281
   on the Beatles' reception in Manila, 201
   Beatles' turn away from live performance and, 203
   contribution to "Eleanor Rigby," 174
   on "Dylan Month" (May 1966), 178
   as road manager for the Beatles, 215
"As Tears Go By" (Jagger and Richards), 122, 123
Atkins, Chet, 177
"Atlantic Ocean" (McCartney, 1987), xvi
Atlantic Records, 137
"Attica State" (Lennon), 281–82, 283
"Automobile Blues" (Lightnin' Hopkins, 1961), 167, 170
Avalon, Frankie, 61

Babbs, Rev. Thurman H., 211–12
"Baby Blue" (Vincent), 102
"Baby Love" (Supremes), 98
"Baby's in Black" (Beatles), 96, 97, 151
"Back in the U.S.S.R." (Beatles), 242, 244
"Bad Boy" (Williams), 126
Badfinger, 279

Baez, Joan, 42, 83, 89, 111, 119, 123, 136, 213
   courage in helping injured children, 156–57
   on Dylan's habits at Bearsville, 76–77
   Dylan's published thoughts on, 176
   Dylan's UK tour and, 123–24, 128–29
   "Imagine" sung by, 276–77
   meeting with the Beatles, 78–79
   on near-sexual encounter with Lennon, 154
   Rolling Thunder Revue and, 287
   Royal Albert Hall debut, 128
   tour with Dylan, 113, 117
   at Woody Guthrie tribute, 235
Baez, Mimi, 119, 123, 213
Baker, Arthur, 298
Baker, Chet, 99, 265
"Ballad in Plain D" (Dylan), 72, 88, 96, 172
"Ballad of a Thin Man" (Dylan), 138, 164, 173
"Ballad of Bob Dylan, The" (Peel), 284
"Ballad of Hollis Brown" (Dylan), 31, 71
"Ballad of John and Yoko, The" (Beatles), 262, 264, 309
"Ballad of the Green Berets, The" (Sadler, 1966), 170–71, 193
"Bamba, La" (Valens), 134–35, 258, 281
Band, the, xii, xv, 226, 246, 247, 253, 254, 267, 286, 314
Band on the Run (McCartney), xiii, 286
"Bangladesh" (Harrison), 281
Bardot, Brigitte, 5, 20
Barrett, Richard, 253
Barrow, Tony, 157, 200
Basement Tapes, The (Dylan and the Band), 226
Bassey, Shirley, 265
Bauls of Bengal, The (Das brothers), 224–25
Bay City Rollers, 201
Beach Boys, 157, 236, 242, 253
"Bear Cat" (Thomas, 1953), 160, 172

INDEX 353

Beatlemania, 6, 45, 59, 73, 90, 105, 145, 300
   deafening sound of screaming fans, 148
   early days of, xi
   fans swarming airplane, 152–53
   height of, xiv
   press reviews and, 168
   as religious phenomenon, 199
Beatles, the
   AABA format of songs, 103
   album cover photos and art, 35–38, 45, 168, 228
   albums burned in the Deep South, 208, 210, 211
   American tour (1964), xi, 54–61, 91–92
   in Australia, 72–73
   at Cavern Club in Liverpool, 25, 26–27
   compared to classical music greats, 229
   country squire life and, 115
   cracks in public image of, 43–46
   disenchantment with live performances, 200
   Dylan songs played by, xv
   end of, 273–74
   Fab Four nickname, 102
   first meeting of Lennon and McCartney, 20–21
   in Hamburg, 16–17, 32, 33, 88, 96
   at the Hollywood Bowl, 77, 156
   in India, 203, 236–38
   inducted into Rock & Roll Hall of Fame, 17–18
   in Japan, 200–201
   LSD experiences, 115–16, 153–54, 175, 226, 230
   marijuana use by, 86, 87, 111
   as Members of the Order of the British Empire, 130
   new identities for, 217–19
   at Olympia Theatre (Paris), 49
   origin of band name, 19–20
   in the Philippines, 200, 201–3
   recording studio used as compositional tool, 171
   rooftop show (last public appearance), 258, 259
   sartorial incarnations of, 24
   second North American tour, 143–47
   Shea Stadium concerts, 148–49, 151, 212–13, 315
   songs by other artists played by, 253–54
   threats against, 77, 78–79, 200, 201, 211, 214
   Twickenham documented rehearsals, 256–58
Beatles, The: Get Back (Jackson, streaming series, 2022), 252–53
Beatles at Shea Stadium, The (TV special), 151
Beatles Book Monthly (fan magazine), 168, 178, 179
Beatles for Sale (Beatles, 1964), 95–96, 97, 108, 114, 117
Beatles VI (Beatles), 143
Beatty, Warren, 288
"Beautiful Boy" (Lennon), 292
"Be-Bop a-Lula" (Vincent, 1956), 12
Before the Flood (Dylan live album), xii
"Behind That Locked Door" (Harrison), 269
Belafonte, Harry, 177
"Be My Baby" (Ronettes), 55, 109, 276
Benn, Al, 207, 208
Bentley Boys, 138
Berg, John, 233
Berlin, Irving, 160
Berry, Chuck, 12, 13, 74, 76, 101, 253, 289
Best, Pete, 15, 21, 24, 64
Bhagavad Gita, 219
Bicknell, Alf, 153, 203
Big Mama Thornton, 160, 167
Big Pink house (West Saugerties, NY), 222, 224, 302
Billboard chart, 52, 141, 157, 281, 286, 290, 303
Bill Haley and His Comets, 20
Black, Cilla, 50

Black American music, 11, 16, 29, 32, 65
Black Dyke Mills Band, 240, 248
blackface minstrels, 31
Blaine, Hal, 103, 109
Blake, Peter, 228
Blake, William, 124, 127
Blind Faith, 270
"Blind Willie McTell" (Dylan), 32, 41
Block, Bert, 266, 267
Blonde on Blonde (Dylan), 173, 175–76, 179, 192, 230, 233, 255, 284
   Dylan's name absent from cover of, 170
   reviews of, 204, 210
   tortured romanticism of, 248
Blood on the Tracks (Dylan), 286, 287
Bloomfield, Mike, 135, 138, 139
Blow, Kurtis, xvi
"Blowin' in the Wind" (Dylan), 28–29, 242, 276, 279
Bluesbreakers, the, 120, 123
Bob Dylan (Dylan debut album), 27
Bob Dylan Center archives (Tulsa, Oklahoma), 190, 205, 285
"Bob Dylan's 115th Dream" (Dylan), 102
"Bob Dylan's Dream" (Dylan), 70–71
Bob Dylan's Greatest Hits, 226–27
Bo Diddley, 41, 180, 253
Bono, Sonny, 104, 141
Bonzo Dog Band, 268
Booker T. & the MG's, 177
Boone, Pat, 16, 31
Bootleg Series, The (Dylan), 316
"Boots of Spanish Leather" (Dylan), 33, 51, 96, 216
Bound for Glory (Guthrie), 64
"Bourbon Street" (Dylan & The Band), 223
Bowie, David, xiii, 119, 277
Boyd, Jenny, 236
Boyd, Joe, 139
Boyd, Pattie, 70, 115, 219, 236, 247, 249
   at Isle of Wight Festival, 267, 269–70
Brambell, Wilfrid, 67
Bramwell, Tony, 179, 181, 241, 257

Brandstatter sisters (Lynn, Penny, and Debbie), 79, 83
Braun, Michael, 51, 63
Breslin, Jimmy, 294–95
Bringing It All Back Home (Dylan), 102, 117, 139, 147, 206
British Invasion, 102
Brooks, Harvey, 154, 155
Brown, James, 265
Browne, Tara, 221
Bucklen, John, 12, 13, 16, 70–71
Bury, Cyndy, 115
Buttrey, Kenny, 233
Byrds, the, 57, 100, 102–4, 113, 137, 141, 157, 232
   Dylan and the Beatles synthesized by, 98
   origins of, 98–99
   See also "Mr. Tambourine Man"

Cackett, Alan, 33
Cannibal and the Headhunters, 242
"Can't Buy Me Love" (Beatles), 51, 93, 152, 166
"Can't Get Enough of Your Love, Babe" (White), xiii
"Can You Please Crawl Out Your Window?" (Dylan), 159, 161
Capitol Records, 47, 56, 57, 156, 246, 280
Carroll, Lewis, 2, 5, 64, 65, 228
"Carry That Weight" (McCartney), 263
Carter, Bo, 50
Carter, Jimmy, 288
Carter, Rubin "Hurricane," xii–xiii, 287
Carthy, Martin, 29–30, 32
Cash, Johnny, 140, 156, 191, 224
Cash Box (music industry publication), 49, 158
Castro, Fidel, 89
"Catch the Wind" (Donovan), 113
Cavern Club (Liverpool), 25, 26, 35, 69, 83, 121, 184, 220
   closure of, 185
   enthusiasm of Beatles' early days at, 256

Cedar Tavern (Greenwich Village), 111
"Chains" (Goffin and King), 144
Champlin, Charles, 157
Charles, Ray, 33, 63, 121, 137, 253, 290
    music as fusion of various genres, 61
    "Yesterday" sung by, 316
Charles, Tommy, 207, 208, 209, 210
Chaucer, Geoffrey, 65, 80
Chelsea Hotel (New York), 203
Cher, 104, 140
"Cherry Red" (Little Richard), 18
Chiffons, the, 63
"Chimes of Freedom" (Dylan), 52, 57, 60, 75, 103
CHOBA B CCCP (McCartney, 1987), 17
Christgau, Robert, 234
Chronicles: Volume One (Dylan, 2004), xvii, 244, 312
Chubby Checker, 55
City Lights publishing company, 64, 68
Civil Rights Act (1964), 170
civil rights movement, 208
Clapton, Eric, 128, 229, 244, 246, 272, 278, 304
Clark, Dick, 225
Clark, Gene, 99
Clayton, Paul, 52, 53, 61
Cleave, Maureen, 70, 97, 108, 116, 122, 165, 208
    profile of Lennon in *Evening Standard*, 199–200, 208
    profile of McCartney, 208
Cliff Richard and the Shadows, 20
Cloud Nine (Harrison), 300, 301, 302
Clouzot, Henri-Georges, 252
Cochran, Eddie, 14, 21, 253
Cocker, Joe, 268
Cogan, Alma, 105, 106, 216
Cohen, John, 245
"Cold Turkey" (Lennon), xiii, 266, 271, 272, 276
Cold War, 8, 28
Coleman, Ray, 97, 120, 196
Collins, Phil, 298

Columbia Records, 26, 100, 102, 108, 137, 232
    Recording Studios on Sunset Boulevard, 154
    Studio A (New York), 72, 101
"Come All Ye Bold Highwaymen" (Scottish-Irish ballad), 70
"Come All Ye Tender-Hearted Maidens" (Scottish-Irish ballad), 70
"Come Go with Me" (Del-Vikings), 21
"Come Together" (Beatles), 263, 265, 307, 309
"Coming Up" (McCartney), 291
Concert for Bangladesh, The (1971), 280
Considine, Shaun, 137
Cookies, the, 33
"Corrina, Corrina" (country blues song), 50, 100
Count Basie, 177
country blues, 50
country music, 18, 31, 33, 61, 123, 128, 260
Cox, Kyoko, 237, 262, 277
Cox, Tony (second husband of Yoko Ono), 237
"Crackerbox Palace" (Harrison), xiii
Crackers, the, 295
Crawford, Michael, 216
Cream, 246
Crickets, the, 19
"Crippled Inside" (Lennon), 281
Crompton, Richmal, 5, 108
Crosby, David, 99, 100, 153
Cuban Missile Crisis (1962), 88
Cut Piece (Ono), 112, 216
cutting contests, 161

Dallas, Karl, 30
D'Amato, Maria, 62
Danko, Rick, 157, 169, 196, 222
Darin, Bobby, 253
Das, Lakhsman, 224–25
Das, Purna, 224–25, 233, 235
Das, Shambhu, 218
Datebook (teen magazine), 200, 208, 209

Dave Clark Five, 98
Davies, Ray, 209–10
Davis, Angela, 282
Davis, Colin, 296
Davis, Jesse Ed, 289, 298
Davis, Miles, 38, 82
Davis, Sammy, Jr., 105
"Day in the Life, A" (Beatles), 221, 306, 309
"Day Tripper" (Beatles), 211
"Dear Mrs. Roosevelt" (Guthrie), 235
"Dear Prudence" (Beatles), 242, 244
Del-Vikings, 21
Denver, Nigel, 30, 32
Desire (Dylan, 1976), 288
"Desolation Row" (Dylan), 142, 147, 224
Dickson, Jim, 99, 100
"Dirty Old Town" (MacColl), 30–31
"Dirty World" (Traveling Wilburys), 302
"Disease of Conceit" (Dylan), 304
"Dizzy Miss Lizzy" (Williams), 126
Donegan, Lonnie, 253
Donovan, 113–14, 118, 129, 236
"Don't Bother Me" (Beatles), 114
"Don't Let Me Down" (Beatles), 261
Dont Look Back (film, dir. Pennebaker), 112, 119, 124, 178, 189–95, 259
"Don't Pass Me By" (Beatles), 244
"Don't Think Twice It's All Right" (Dylan), 28, 53, 58, 71
Dorfman, Bruce, 244–45, 247, 249
Double Fantasy (Lennon and Ono), 292
Down in the Groove (Dylan), 303
"Down on Penny's Farm" (Bentley Boys, 1929), 138
Drake, Pete, 233
Drifters, the, 13
"Drive My Car" (Beatles), 165–67, 169
Drummond, Tim, 296
Dunbar, John, 122
Dunn, Donald "Duck," 166
Dylan, Bob, xvii, 21–22, 69, 253
    acting role in *Pat Garrett and Billy the Kid*, 285
    adoption of "Bob Dylan" name, 19, 22, 23
    album cover photos and art, 38–41, 51, 170, 226–27
    amphetamine use, 176
    artwork of, 244–45, 246
    Bangladesh benefit concert and, 279–80
    Beatles songs played by, xv
    biblical inspirations, 175–76
    birth name, 10, 40, 42, 284
    breakup with Sara, 286
    Christian religious conversion of, 290–91
    on cover of *Sgt. Pepper* album, xii, 228
    distancing from counterculture, 260
    electric turn of, xi, 100, 255
    Fender Stratocaster guitar of, 135
    folk-rock hybrid of, 229
    fondness for Beaujolais, 72, 121, 128, 146
    in Glasgow, 187–88
    Greenwich Village days of, 25, 27–28
    heckled and booed by audiences, 159, 187, 188, 196
    heroin and, 176, 190, 275
    Hi Lo Ha mansion, 138, 204, 205, 214, 222, 227
    holes in public image of, 42–43
    hometown (Hibbing, Minnesota), 3, 5, 8–10, 31
    as individualist, xvii
    at Isle of Wight Festival, 266–71
    Jewish identity and, 22–23
    in Liverpool, 183–87
    in London, 29–32, 33–34, 69–70, 188–89
    McCartney interviewed about (2025), 311–18
    mentioned in Carter's Democratic nomination speech (1976), 288
    motorcycle accident of, 205–7, 221, 227

public image as tragic romantic figure, 204
reaction to Lennon's murder, 296–97, 314–15
retreat from forefront of popular music, 258
road trip with friends, 52–54, 57, 58
as rock star and family man, 169
Rolling Thunder Revue tour (1975), 287–88
as Saturday Night Live guest, 291
at Shea Stadium, 197
songs written with Harrison, xv
as target of stalkers and cranks, 260, 275–76, 281
threats against, 187, 188, 214
toll of touring on, 203–4
tour with Baez, 113, 117
Traveling Wilburys and, 301–4
turn away from folkdom, 52, 94, 95, 128, 138–39
views on Vietnam War, 118, 129, 170, 177–78, 201, 245, 267
Dylan, Jakob (son of Bob), 271, 275, 312
Dylan, Sara Lownds (first wife of Bob Dylan), 112, 128, 138, 175, 206, 214, 221, 248
at Isle of Wight Festival, 266, 267
split with Bob, 286
Dylan–Beatles relationship, 62, 66, 71
answer songs, 160–61, 171–73, 190, 263
Beatles known as Dylan fans, 156
in *Dont Look Back*, 190–95
Dylan's Albert Hall concert and, 178–82
Dylan's initial dismissal of the Beatles, 48
Dylan's pilgrimage to Beatles' childhood homes in Liverpool, 1–7, 308, 313
Dylan's UK tour (1965) and, 125–27
first contacts, xiv, 70, 82, 85–91
hangout at the Warwick Hotel, 143–48, 315

Harrison on, 97, 98
Lennon and Dylan's shared literary ambitions, 64
mutual admiration of Dylan and McCartney, 308
Dylan Liberation Front, 275, 280

Eagles, the, 288
Eastman, Linda
See McCartney, Linda Eastman
Eat the Document (anti-documentary), 248
Eddy, Duane, 140, 253
Ed Sullivan Show, The (CBS TV variety program), 41, 49, 55, 56–57, 60
Eight Arms to Hold You [Beatles Production 2] (film), 108
"Eight Days a Week" (Beatles), 105
Ekland, Britt, 288
"Eleanor Rigby" (Beatles), xv, 174, 210, 212, 217
Electric Ladyland (Jimi Hendrix Experience), 235
Electric Light Orchestra (ELO), 298
Elektra Records, 99
Elliot, Cass, 247
Emerick, Geoff, 180, 220, 242, 243, 262
EMI Studios, 27, 92, 131, 143, 162, 175, 262
Abbey Road recording studios, 36, 108, 126, 189, 219
Beatles' contract with, 272
Capitol Records owned by, 47
EMI House, 36, 37
Parlophone record label and, 26
studio logs, 109
Empire Burlesque (Dylan), 298, 303
Epstein, Brian, xii, 49, 50, 68, 79, 104, 145, 239
on Beatles' American tour (1964), 54, 56
death of, 231
as department store magnate, 24
Dylan's meeting with the Beatles and, 86

Epstein, Brian (*cont.*)
   homosexuality of, 44–45
   Jewish identity and, 44, 90
   marijuana use by, 87–88
   Northern Songs company and, 181
   refusal to meet Marcos in Philippines, 201–3
Estes, Sleepy John, 191
Eurythmics, 302
Evans, Mal, 54, 88, 90, 92, 145, 179, 189
   Beatles' exit from Philippines and, 203
   contribution to "Eleanor Rigby," 174
   on deafening sound of screaming fans, 148
   in India, 236
   at Isle of Wight Festival, 269
   shocked by electrical equipment, 212
   travel with McCartney, 217–18
   at Twickenham rehearsals, 257
   in Woodstock, NY, 247
"Eve of Destruction" (McGuire), 193
Everett, Walter, 133, 216, 237
Everly Brothers, xv, 14, 96, 120, 254
"Every Grain of Sand" (Dylan), 301
"Every Little Thing" (Beatles), 91
"Every Night" (McCartney), 277

Fabian, 61
Fabulous 208 (fan magazine), 140–41
Fairuz, 277
Faithfull, Marianne, 122, 123, 126, 127, 180
"Fame" (Bowie), xiii
Family Way, The (film), 217
Farrow, Mia, 236
Farrow, Prudence, 236
Fass, Bob, 170
Fats Domino, 4, 14
Feinstein, Barry, 185, 186, 222
feminism, 91
Ferlinghetti, Lawrence, 64, 68
Fleetwood Mac, 128
Flint, Hughie, 128
Flynn, Dennis Peter, 184, 185

folk music, xi, 41, 54, 57, 101
   Dylan's turn away from, 52, 94, 95, 128
   urban revival of, 48
"folk rock," 98, 99, 212, 229
Fonda, Peter, 153
"For No One" (Beatles), 174
Foulk, Ray, 266, 267, 269
Four Seasons, the, 140
"Fourth Time Around" (Dylan), 171–73, 180–81, 186, 190, 192, 196, 315
Frankie Lymon and the Teenagers, 20
Franklin, Aretha, 26, 290
"Freedom" (Havens), 270
Freeman, Robert, 104, 105, 143, 168
Freeman, Sonny, 104, 105, 107
Freewheelin' Bob Dylan, The (Dylan), 38, 39, 40–41, 49, 88, 109
   romantic vision of bohemian life and, 136
   at top of British album chart, 117
"Freight Train Blues" (Dylan), 27
From Elvis in Memphis (Presley, 1969), 304

Gabor, Zsa Zsa, 153
Gabriel, Peter, 298, 301, 304
Garland of Scots Folksong, A (Miller and MacColl), 30
"Gates of Eden" (Dylan), 131
Gaye, Marvin, 61, 63, 316
"George Jackson" (Dylan), 282, 283
Gerde's Folk City (New York), 25, 279
"Get Back" (Beatles), 256, 261
"Get Back" sessions (Beatles, 1969), xv
Gillespie, Dana, 118–19, 126, 127, 179, 188–89
Gillespie, Dizzy, 65
Ginsberg, Allen, 48, 64, 82, 102, 112, 126, 261, 281
   admiration for Dylan, 124
   at John Sinclair Freedom Rally, 283
   Lennon's meeting with, 127–28
   at Royal Albert Hall, 131
"Girl" (Beatles), 167

"Girl from the North Country" (Dylan), 32–33, 70, 259
"Give Ireland Back to the Irish" (McCartney), 282
"Give Me Love (Give Me Peace on Earth)" (Harrison), 286
"Give Peace a Chance" (Lennon, 1969), xvi, 261, 264, 295
Glaser, Milton, 226
"Glass Onion" (Lennon), 242
Gleason, Ralph J., 95, 142, 210, 213, 234
Glover, Tony, 93
"God Bless America" (Berlin), 160
God Bless Tiny Tim (Tiny Tim), 239–40
Goddard, J. R., 112
Goffin, Gerry, 144
Goldberg, Barry, 138
"Golden Slumbers" (Beatles), 263
Gold Star Studios (Hollywood), 104
Goldstein, Richard, 204, 210, 230
"Go Now" (Moody Blues), 123
"Good Day, Sunshine" (McCartney), 174
"Good Golly, Miss Molly" (Little Richard), 16
Goon Show, The (BBC radio comedy program), 64, 73, 98
gospel music, 15, 16, 31, 33, 56, 61, 121
"Got My Mind Set on You" (Ray, 1962), 300–301
"Gotta Serve Somebody" (Dylan), 290, 291, 293
"Got to Get You into My Life" (Beatles), 174–75
Graham, Billy, 148
"Grand Coulee Dam" (Guthrie), 235
Grapefruit (Ono), 276
Grapes of Wrath, The (Steinbeck), 64
Grossman, Albert, 32, 52, 91, 101, 117, 157, 187
    Bearsville farmhouse of, 42, 68, 76, 102, 247
    Dylan as star client of, 203–4
    Dylan's suspicions of, 227
    Dylan's UK tour and, 120, 125
    rights for *Dont Look Back* and, 178

Grossman, Henry, 84–85, 225–26
Grossman, Sally, 102, 206, 224, 247
Gruen, Bob, 284, 288
Guevara, Che, 89
Guns N' Roses, 286
Guru Dev, 232
Guthrie, Woody, 22, 23, 25, 31, 41, 52
    answer song subgenre and, 160
    autobiography of, 64
    Dylan's response to death of, 233, 235

Haley, Bill, 50, 121
Hall, Colin, 3, 5
Hall, Francis, 56
Halsted, Hank, 292
Hamill, Brian, 287
Hamill, Pete, 74, 287
Hammond, John, II, 26, 27
"Handle with Care" (Traveling Wilburys), 302
"Hang On Sloopy" (McCoys), 139
Hank Ballard and the Midnighters, 55
"Happiness Is a Warm Gun" (Beatles), 243
Hard Day's Night, A (Beatles album), 66, 80
"Hard Day's Night, A" (Beatles song), 81–82, 83, 97, 172
Hard Day's Night, A (film, 1964), 67, 69, 99, 111, 137, 152
    Goon Show sensibility of, 73
    reviews of, 80, 219
"Hard Rain's A-Gonna Fall, A" (Dylan), 30, 71, 279
Harrison, George, xi, xii, xvii, 56, 172, 174, 260
    Bangladesh benefit concert (1971), 278–80
    on Beatles' American tour (1964), 54–56
    collaboration with Dylan, 248, 249
    death of (2001), 306
    Dylan quoted by, xv
    Dylan's relationship with, 8

Harrison, George (*cont.*)
    on first impression of Dylan, 50
    Gibson J-200 guitar of, 256, 270
    in *A Hard Day's Night* film, 137
    Indian instruments owned/played by, 114, 165, 180, 203, 218
    interest in Indian music and religion, 114, 218
    Irish ancestry of, 11
    at Isle of Wight Festival, 267, 270
    Kinfauns house, 115, 116, 132
    murder attempt against (1999), 305–6
    post-Beatles work, xiii
    reaction to Lennon's murder, 295–96
    Rickenbacker guitar of, 56, 82, 99
    songs written with Dylan, xv, 248, 274
    as songwriter, 114, 175
    Transcendental Meditation and, 231
    Traveling Wilburys and, 298–304, 317
    work with Lynne, 298
Harry, Bill, 118, 185
Harry, Virginia, 185
Havens, Richie, 235, 270
Hawkins, Ronnie, 155, 246
Hawks, the, 154–55, 157, 159–60, 161, 162
Haworth, Jann, 228
Haworth, Jill, 60
"Heartbreak Hotel" (Presley), 14
"Heart of Gold" (Young), 285
"Helen Wheels" (McCartney), 277
"Hello, Goodbye" (Beatles), 230, 234
Helm, Levon, 154, 155, 157, 162, 235, 246
Help! (film, 1965), 116, 120, 124–25
    premiere of, 141
"Help!" (Beatles song), 116, 141, 151, 162, 166
    at top of *Billboard* chart, 158
Helstrom, Echo, 12, 16, 19
"Helter Skelter" (Beatles), 244, 283
Hendrix, Jimi, 229, 260, 301
Herbert, Sir Alan, 68

"Here, There and Everywhere" (Beatles), 174
"Here Comes the Night" (Them), 123
"Here Comes the Sun" (Beatles), 263, 265, 270, 296, 303
"Here Today" (McCartney), 296, 314–15
"Her Majesty" (Beatles), 263
heroin, 185, 237, 263
    Dylan and, 176, 190, 275
    Lennon's use of, 190, 243, 256–57, 265–66, 289
"Hey, Little Richard" (Dylan), 12
"Hey Jude" (Beatles), 241–42, 255
Heylin, Clinton, 128
"Highlands" (Dylan, 1997), 307
Highway 61 Revisited (Dylan), xiv, 142, 146, 154
"Hi Hi Hi" (McCartney), 277
Hill, Michael, 14
Hillman, Chris, 99
hippies, 82, 220, 260
Hoffman, Abbie, 282
Holiday, Billie, 38
Holly, Buddy, 4, 13–14, 19, 253, 311
Hollywood Bowl, 77, 156, 157
Holzman, Jac, 99
"Honey, Just Allow Me One More Chance" (Dylan), 109
"Honey Pie" (Beatles), 242, 244
Hooker, John Lee, 179
"Hound Dog" (Leiber and Stoller), 160, 172
"House of the Rising Sun, The" (folk song), 75–76, 100, 101
Houston, Whitney, 297
"How Do You Sleep?" (Lennon), 277, 280
How I Won the War (film, dir. Lester, 1967), 215–16, 217
Howl and Other Poems (Ginsberg, 1958), 64
Hudson, Garth, 157, 196, 221–22, 224
Hunstein, Don, 36, 38
"Hurricane" (Dylan, 1975), xii–xiii, 287, 288
Huxley, Aldous, 198, 228

Iachetta, Michael, 227
"I Ain't Got No Home" (Guthrie), 235
"I Am the Walrus" (Beatles), 231, 232
"(I Can't Get No) Satisfaction" (Rolling Stones), 141
"I Can't Leave Her Behind" (Dylan), 187
"I'd Have You Anytime" (Harrison and Dylan), 248, 274
"I Don't Believe You (She Acts Like We Never Have Met)" (Dylan), 109
"I Don't Want to Spoil the Party" (Beatles), 97
"I Feel Fine" (Beatles), 92, 95, 139, 151, 166, 287
"If I Fell" (Beatles), 95
"If I Needed Someone" (Beatles), 211
"If You Gotta Go, Go Now (Or Else You Got to Stay All Night)" (Dylan), 128, 140
"I Got You Babe" (Sonny and Cher), 141
"I'll Cry Instead" (Beatles), 66–67
"I'll Follow the Sun" (Beatles), 114
"I Lost My Little Girl" (McCartney), 132–33
Imagine (Lennon album, 1971), 277
"Imagine" (Lennon song), xiii, 276, 277, 281, 295, 347
"I'm a Loser" (Beatles), 96, 97, 172
"I'm Down" (Beatles), 132
"I'm Looking Through You" (Beatles), 167
"I'm Not There" (Dylan & The Band), 223
"I'm Only Sleeping" (Beatles), 175
Impressions, the, 224
"I'm So Tired" (Beatles), 237
"I Need You" (Beatles), 114
In His Own Write (Beatles), 64, 66, 68, 69, 80, 81
   Lennon's reputation as intellectual and, 134
   reviews of, 92
"Instant Karma! (We All Shine On)" (Lennon), 274
International Poetry Incarnation, 131, 262

"I Once Loved a Lass" (traditional song), 77
"I Saw Her Standing There" (Beatles), 33, 56
"I Shall Be Released" (Dylan), 223, 246, 249, 254
Isle of Wight festival (1969), xiv, 261, 266
Isley Brothers, 135, 229, 254
"It Ain't Me, Babe" (Dylan), 75, 103, 140
"I Threw It All Away" (Dylan), 247, 256, 259, 270
"It's All Over, Baby Blue" (Dylan), 102, 123
"It's All Over Now" (Rolling Stones), 74
"It's Alright, Ma (I'm Only Bleeding)" (Dylan), 102
"It's Not Unusual" (Tom Jones), 152
"It Takes a Lot to Laugh, It Takes a Train to Cry" (Dylan), 139
"I've Got a Feeling" (Beatles), 254
"I've Just Seen a Face" (Beatles), 132
"I Wanna Be Your Lover" (Dylan), 160–61
"I Wanna Be Your Man" (Beatles), 50, 160
"I Want to Hold Your Hand" (Beatles), 56, 61, 62, 66, 95, 279
   Beatles' popularity in America and, xi–xii, 47
   at top of U.S. charts, 49, 52
"I Want to Tell You" (Beatles), 175
"I Want You" (Dylan), 173, 204, 254, 255, 264
"I Want You (She's So Heavy)" (Beatles), 263, 264, 276
"I Wish I Knew Now What I Knew Then" (Craig and Gill), 304–5

Jack Paar Program, The (NBC TV show), 46
Jackson, George, 282
Jackson, Michael, 288, 297
Jackson, Peter, 252
Jacobs, Jane, 39

Jagger, Mick, 122, 141, 148, 149, 193
James, Dick, 181, 192
jazz, 48, 61, 65, 100, 161, 171
    experimental, 237
    West Coast, 99
Jefferson Airplane, 167
"Jenny, Jenny" (Little Richard), 12
Jimi Hendrix Experience, 235
Jim Mac's Jazz Band, 6
Joaquin, Nick, 202
Joel, Billy, 298
John, Elton, 277, 299
"John Lennon Hat" (Dylan poem), 223
John Lennon/Plastic Ono Band (Lennon, first solo album), 276, 292
Johnny Cash Show, The (ABC variety program), 259
Johns, Glyn, 252, 261
"John Sinclair" (Lennon), 281, 283, 287
John Sinclair Freedom Rally, 283
Johnson, Lyndon B., 148
Johnson, Paul, 65
Johnson, Pete, 18
Johnson, Robert, 191
Johnston, Bob, 142, 170
"John Wesley Harding" (Dylan), 233
John Wesley Harding (Dylan), 233–35, 247, 260
Jones, Brian, 74, 179
Jones, Evan, 29
Jones, George, 307–8
Jones, Max, 127
Jones, Mickey, 177, 196
Jones, Nick, 233
Jones, Tom (Thomas Woodward), 23–24, 152
Jopling, Norman, 196
Joyce, James, 65, 80, 92
Judge, Mary, 297
Judson, Horace, 126
"Julia" (Beatles), 237
"Junior's Farm" (McCartney), 287
"Junk" (McCartney), 242
"Just Like a Woman" (Dylan), 173, 279

"(Just Like) Starting Over" (Lennon), 292
Just William series (Crompton), 5, 105, 108

Karman, Peter, 52, 53, 57, 58, 61
"Keep on Truckin'" (Kendricks), 286
Keltner, Jim, 281
Kendricks, Eddie, 286
Kennedy, John F., assassination of, xv, 43, 57, 60, 157, 295
Kerouac, Jack, 52, 57, 64, 82
Kettle of Fish (Greenwich Village tavern), 146
Keylock, Tom, 184–85, 188, 190
Khaury, Herbert
    See Tiny Tim
Kilcher, Jewel, 305
King, Carole, 144
King, Martin Luther, Jr., 41, 244, 295
King Curtis, 152
King Krule, 277
Kingston Trio, 85, 87
Kinks, the, 98, 118, 209
Kirchherr, Astrid, 96–97
Kiss, 201
Klein, Allen, 261, 272, 279
Knechtel, Larry, 103
Knocked Out Loaded (Dylan), 303
"Knockin' on Heaven's Door" (Dylan), 285–86, 289
Kooper, Al, 135, 138, 154, 155, 159, 169, 255
    on being assaulted by audience member, 156
    on cultural backlash in Nashville, 170
    on Dylan's "Fourth Time Around," 172
Kramer, Billy J., 50
Kramer, Daniel, 112
Kubrick, Stanley, 263
Ku Klux Klan, 210, 211

Ladysmith Black Mambazo, 286
"Land of a Thousand Dances" (Kenner, 1962), 242

Landy, Elliott, 246
Lang, Michael, 260–61
Lanois, Daniel, 304
Lay, Sam, 138
"Lay Down Your Weary Tune" (Dylan), 42, 52
Layton, Doug, 207, 208
Lazar, Shelley, 311–12
Lear, Edward, 65
Leary, Timothy, 89, 175, 261
Led Zeppelin, 201, 252, 258
Leiber, Jerry, 160
Leigh, Spencer, 186–87
Lennon, Alfred (father of John), 2
Lennon, Cynthia Powell (John's first wife), 44, 54, 59, 67–68, 69, 104, 114, 119
  in India, 236, 238
  John's affairs during marriage to, 105, 106, 216
  on John's eyeglasses, 215
  on John's first meeting with Yoko Ono, 216
  LSD experience (1965), 115, 116
Lennon, John, xi, xii, xvi, xvii
  acting role in *How I Won the War*, 215–16, 217
  Aronowitz piece on, 63–64
  arrested in drug bust, 251–52, 284
  backlash against comments about Christianity, 207–10
  Bangladesh benefit concert and, 279
  on Beatles' American tour (1964), 54–57, 59–60
  Beatles' breakup and, 273–74
  brief born-again Christian phase, 289–90
  critics on similarity to Dylan, 94–97
  in *Eat the Document*, 190–95
  early dismissal of Dylan, 74
  on Elvis Presley and Little Richard, 14
  heroin use by, 190, 243, 256–57, 265–66, 289
  Irish ancestry of, 11, 184
  at Isle of Wight festival, 268, 270–71
  Kenwood mansion, 105–6, 113, 115–16, 118–20, 131, 132, 163, 174
  literary work of, 66–67
  Lost Weekend period, 17, 286, 289
  Melody Maker interview, 101–2
  Mendips (childhood home in Liverpool), 1–5, 308
  murder of (1980), 294–97, 309
  post-Beatles work, xiii
  relocation to New York City, 277, 282
  Rolling Thunder Revue and, 287–88
  sailing adventure of, 291–92, 309
  songs influenced by Dylan, 171–73
  Transcendental Meditation and, 231
  U.S. government campaign against, 282, 284
Lennon, John, first marriage (Cynthia Powell), 44, 54, 59, 67–68, 104
  John's affairs during, 105, 106, 107, 216
  separation, 240
  ski trip and lessons, 106–7
Lennon, John, second marriage (Yoko Ono)
  as creative partnership, 257
  Dakota Hotel years, 289
  legend of first night together, 240
  life as nonstop art project, 262
  marriage ceremony in Gibraltar, 261
Lennon, Julian (son of John and Cynthia), 44, 240, 262, 288
Lennon, Julia Stanley (mother of John), 2–3, 44
Lennon, Sean Ono (son of John and Yoko), 288
"Leopard-Skin Pill-Box Hat" (Dylan), 169–70
Lesberg, Sandy, 125
Lester, Richard, 215
Let It Be (Beatles, final album, 1970), 274
Let It Be (documentary, 1970), 252
"Let's Invite Them Over" (Jones and Montgomery, 1963), 307–8
Leventhal, Harold, 233

364 ■ INDEX

Levy's Sount Studios (London), 128
Lewis, Jerry Lee, 253
Lewisohn, Mark, 14
Life in Photographs, A (L. McCartney), 313
Lightfoot, Gordon, 234, 271
Lightnin' Hopkins, 167, 170
"Like a Rolling Stone" (Dylan), 134–38, 139, 146, 216, 258, 270
   chart position of, 145, 158, 166
   composition process of, 318
   Jimi Hendrix rendition of, 233
   Lennon's performance of, 281
   radio airplay of, 141
   Tiny Tim rendition of, 222, 250
Lindsay-Hogg, Michael, 252, 255, 257, 274
"Listen, Robert Moses" (Dylan and Jacobs), 39
Little Richard, xv, 17, 74, 83, 132, 198, 257, 307
   Beatles' admiration for, 14–16, 18, 66
   Dylan's admiration for, 12–13, 18, 301
   Jimi Hendrix as apprentice of, 229
   near-fatal car crash, 18
   Presley's debt to, 13, 32
   songs played by the Beatles, 21, 213, 253
   turn to religion and gospel music, 15, 16, 61
Little Richard Is Back (Little Richard, 1964), 18
"Live and Let Die" (McCartney), 277
Liverpool
   Clarence Dock, 183–84, 185
   Echo Arena, 1
   history of, 10–11, 183
   Mendips (Lennon childhood home), 1–5, 308
   Odeon Theater, 184, 186
   Penny Lane, xv, 2
   See also Cavern Club; Strawberry Field
"Living the Blues" (Dylan), 259

Lockhart-Smith, Judy, 106
Lomax, Jackie, 247, 253, 254
"Lonesome Death of Hattie Carroll, The" (Dylan), 69–70
"Long, Long, Long" (Beatles), 236, 237
"Long Tall Sally" (Little Richard), 14, 15, 16, 17, 83, 213
"Looking Over from My Hotel Window" (Ono), 291
Lopez, Trini, 49
"Lord Randall" (Anglo-Scottish folk ballad), 28, 30
"Lost Highway" (Payne), 123, 134
Love, Mike, 236
Love and Theft (Dylan), 32
"Love Me Do" (Beatles), 27
Love Me Do: The Beatles' Progress, 51
Lovin' Spoonful, the, 254
Lownds, Hans, 112
Lownds, Sara
   See Dylan, Sara Lownds (first wife of Bob Dylan)
LSD (lysergic acid diethylamide), 89, 115, 153, 175, 226, 230
   Beatles' discounting of, 231
   Dylan on LSD as medicine, 68
   replaced by heroin for Lennon, 243
"Lucille" (Little Richard), 17
"Luck of the Irish, The" (Lennon), 282, 283
Lynne, Jeff, 298, 300, 301, 302, 304
Lyrics, The (McCartney, 2021), xiv, 311

MacColl, Ewan, 30–31
MacGregor, Rolbert Roy, 193
Madhouse on Castle Street (BBC TV play), 29
Madonna, 297, 298
"Maggie Mae" (folk song), 4
"Maggie's Farm" (Dylan), 138–39, 270, 287
Magical Mystery Tour (film), 231, 234, 240, 246
Maharishi Mahesh Yogi (Mahesh Prasad Varma), 231, 232, 236, 243

Maher, Albert, 89
"Mama, You Been on My Mind" (Dylan), 256
Mamas & the Papas, the, 247
Manfred Mann, 118, 140, 232, 236
"Man in the Long Black Coat" (Dylan), 304
Mann, William, 65
Manson, Charles, 283
Manuel, Richard, xv, 157, 196, 222, 224, 246
Marcos, Ferdinand, 200, 201, 202
Marcus, Greil, 57, 139, 230
Marden, Brice, 203
Margaret, Princess, 105
"Margarita" (Traveling Wilburys), 302
marijuana/pot/cannabis/grass, 53, 82–83, 175, 220, 224, 239, 278, 297
    Beatles' use of, 75, 88, 90, 91, 111, 239, 267
    Dylan's use of, 3, 25, 29, 34, 90
    John and Yoko arrested for possession of, 251–52, 284
    Maymudes as supplier of, 83, 85, 86, 87, 90
    as "wonder drug," 82
Martin, George, 36, 100, 108, 133, 165, 232, 262, 296
    ballet dancing of, 107
    on Beatles' American tour (1964), 54, 56
    concern for safety of the Beatles, 79
    enhancement of "Strawberry Fields Forever," 219–20
    as expert assistant to the Beatles, 135
    as the fifth Beatle, xii
    on first meeting with the Beatles, 26–27
    Lennon's voice recorded through rotating speaker, 180
    overdubs and, 109, 110, 151
    on the Twickenham rehearsals, 256
    White Album sessions and, 243
Martin, Mary, 154–55
Marvelettes, the, 33, 63
"Maureen" (Harrison and Dylan), 248, 313
"Maxwell's Silver Hammer" (Beatles), 263
Mayall, John, 123, 128
Mayfield, Curtis, 224, 290
Maymudes, Victor, 52–53, 54, 57, 58, 61, 62, 80, 91
    as a Dylan lieutenant, 100
    on Dylan's meeting with the Beatles, 84, 85–86, 91
    marijuana supplied by, 83, 85, 86, 87, 90
Maysles, Albert, 55, 59, 111, 112
Maysles, David, 55, 111, 112
MC5 (band), 276
McBean, Angus, 36–37, 38
McCartney (Paul's first solo album), 273
McCartney, Heather (adopted daughter of Paul), 251, 258, 273
McCartney, Jim (father of Paul), 6
McCartney, Linda Eastman (first wife of Paul), 239, 241, 255, 273, 275
    death of (1998), 305
    A Life in Photographs, 313
    marriage ceremony, 261
McCartney, Mary Mohin (mother of Paul), 6
McCartney, Michael (brother of Paul), 6–7, 51, 121, 314
McCartney, Nancy Shevell (third wife of Paul), 312
McCartney, Paul, xi, xii, xvii, 27
    on Beatles' American tour (1964), 54–56, 59–60
    childhood home of, 1, 6, 308
    conspiracy theory about death of, 273, 280
    Dylan's relationship with, xvi
    early friendship with Lennon, 4
    heroin use rejected by, 243
    High Park Farm property of, 251
    house near Abbey Road, 132

McCartney, Paul (*cont.*)
  "Hunt Hanson" persona, 217, 307
  interviewed about Dylan (2025), 311–18
  Irish ancestry of, 11
  on Little Richard's death, 18
  music composed for *The Family Way* film, 217
  poor first impression of Dylan, 27, 49–50, 314
  reaction to Lennon's murder, 296, 314–15
  relationship with Jane Asher, 45
  return to touring (1989), 305
  splits with Asher and Schwartz, 251
  Transcendental Meditation and, 231
  Wings band of, xiii, 288
  Wings Over America tour, 317
McCartney II (McCartney), 291
McCoy, Charlie, 142, 171, 176, 233
McCoys, the, 139
McGough, Roger, 121
McGuinn, Roger, 57, 98–99, 100, 103, 139, 153
McGuire, Barry, 141, 193
McKenzie, Scott, 230
McPhatter, Clyde, 13, 301
McVie, John, 128
"Me and My Chauffeur Blues" (Memphis Minnie, 1941), 166–67, 170
Meet the Beatles (Beatles), 57
Melcher, Terry, 103
Melody Maker, 97, 101–2, 117, 127, 172, 209, 221, 236
Memphis Minnie, 167, 170
"Menace of Beatlism, The" (Johnson), 65
Merman, Ethel, 22
Mersey Beat publication, 25, 27, 121, 185
Metzner, Ralph, 175
Michaels, Lorne, 288
"Michelle" (Beatles), 177
"Midnight at the Oasis" (Muldaur), 62
Miller, Betsy, 30
Miller, Geri, 55
Milligan, Spike, 64

Miracles, the, 198, 254
Mississippi Sheiks, the, 50
"Mr. Tambourine Man" (Dylan), 55, 71, 75, 279, 314
  Byrds' version of, 99–100, 102–3, 113, 135, 137, 140, 141, 239
  folk-rock treatment of, 154
  solo acoustic guitar rendition of, 155
  UK chart position of, 141
  U.S chart position of, 140
Mitchell, Joni, 271
Modern Times (Dylan, 2006), 305
Moman, Chips, 304
"Money (That's What I Want)" (Beatles), 37
Monterey Pop Festival (1967), 260
Montgomery, Melba, 307–8
Moody Blues, the, 123
Moore, Dudley, 115
Moran, Jim, 294
Morrison, Van, 123
Mortimer, Celia, 314
Moses, Robert, 38–39
"Mother" (Lennon), 3
Motown, 98, 311
Mouskouri, Nana, 277
Muldaur, Maria, 62
Mulligan, Gerry, 99, 140
"Murder Most Foul" (Dylan), xv
Murray the K (Murray Kaufman), xi, xii, 47, 85, 155, 170
Music from Big Pink (The Band), 246–47, 254, 260
"My Back Pages" (Dylan), 255
Myddle Class, the, 144, 145
"My Guy" (Wells), 98
"My Love" (McCartney), 277
Mystère Picasso, Le (film, dir. Clouzot, 1956), 252
"My Sweet Lord" (Harrison), 274, 278, 281, 307

Nashville Skyline (Dylan), 260, 265, 271, 275, 281

Nelson, Ricky, 13
Neuwirth, Bob, 62, 111, 117, 126, 127, 185, 205
    barbed wisecracks of, 144–45, 147
    Clapton criticized by, 128
    Donovan and, 122, 129
    as Dylan's lieutenant, 100
    as "Miss Lonely," 136
New Morning (Dylan, 1970), 274, 275
New Musical Express, 15, 96, 195
Newport Folk Festival, 41, 43, 56, 75, 100, 138–39, 255
New Vaudeville Band, 220, 222
Nice, the, 268
Nicholson, Jack, 288
Nixon, Richard, 282, 284
"No More Auction Block" (spiritual), 29
Northern Songs company, 181, 192–93
"Norwegian Wood" (Beatles), 107–8, 109, 169, 315
    Dylan's "Fourth Time Around" as answer to, 171–73, 190
    George's sitar playing in, 165, 203
"Not a Second Time" (Beatles), 110
"Nowhere Man" (Beatles), xv, 163–64, 172, 173, 250
Noznisky, Shirley
    See Dylan, Sara Lownds
"#9 Dream" (Lennon), 287

"Ob-La-Di, Ob-La-Da" (Beatles), 244
Ochs, Phil, 89, 158–59, 161, 283
"Octopus's Garden" (Beatles), 251
Odetta, 31, 32, 206, 235
Oglesby, Carl, 260
"Oh, Pretty Woman" (Orbison), 98, 301
Oh Mercy (Dylan), 304
"Oh Yoko!" (Lennon, 1971), 281
Oldham, Andrew Loog, 50, 147, 149
"On a Rainy Afternoon" (Dylan), 187
"One and One Is Two" (Lennon-McCartney), 50
"One of Us Must Know (Sooner or Later)" (Dylan), 173
"One Too Many Mornings" (Dylan), 51

"Only a Northern Song" (Beatles), 226
Ono, Yoko, xvi, 112, 131, 263
    arrested in drug bust, 251
    Bangladesh benefit concert and, 279
    idealism shared with John Lennon, 237–38
    at Isle of Wight festival, 268, 270–71
    John Lennon's first meeting with, 216
    miscarriage of, 251
    New York City as new home, 277, 282
    presence at White Album sessions, 243, 244
    work with Ornette Coleman, 237
    See also Lennon, John, second marriage (Yoko Ono)
On the Road (Kerouac), 52, 64
"Ooh! My Soul" (Little Richard), 198
"Open Letter to Bob Dylan, An" (Silber, 1964), 94
Orbison, Roy, 67, 98, 301, 302
Orlando, Benny, 10

Paddy, Klaus & Gibson, 115
Padgham, Hugh, 298
Page, Jimmy, 252
Palin, Michael, 295
Pang, May, 280, 286
"Paperback Writer" (Beatles), xv, 174, 316
Parker, Bobby, 92, 139
Passover Plot, The (Schonfield), 198–99
Pat Garrett and Billy the Kid (film, dir. Peckinpah, 1973), 285
Pathé Marconi Studios (Paris), 51
Paul Butterfield Blues Band, 68, 135
Paul McCartney's Liverpool Oratorio (McCartney), 305
Paxton, Tom, 235
Payne, Leon, 123
Peckinpah, Sam, 285
Peel, David, 275–76, 277–78, 280, 283, 284

368 ■ INDEX

Pennebaker, D. A., 111–12, 117, 178, 189–91, 195, 205
Penniman, Richard
   See Little Richard
"Penny Lane" (Beatles), 220–21, 222, 225
"People Get Ready" (Mayfield), 224, 290
Peppermint Lounge (New York), 55
Perkins, Carl, 253
Perry, Fred, 125
Peter, Paul and Mary, 40, 41
Peterson, Ray, 50
Petty, Tom, xv, 299–300, 301
Phillips, Sam, 160
"Photograph" (Starr), 286
Picasso, Pablo, 252
Pickett, Wilson, 242
Pilcher, Sergeant Norman, 251
"Pilgrim of Sorrow" (traditional song), 77
Pink Floyd, 220
Pitt, Kenneth, 71
Plastic Ono Band, 264
"Please, Mrs. Henry" (Dylan & The Band), 223, 254
Please Please Me (Beatles album), 36, 37–38, 41, 44
"Please Please Me" (Beatles song), 33, 35, 66
"pop folk," 98
"Positively 4th Street" (Dylan), 158–59, 198, 258
Powell, Cynthia
   See Lennon, Cynthia Powell
"Power to the People" (Lennon), 281
Presley, Elvis, xvii, 4, 5, 12, 101, 110, 160, 267
   Black artists' influence on, 13, 32
   comeback album (1969), 304
   Dylan compared to, 158
   Ed Sullivan Show and, 41
   inducted into the army, 61
   influence on the Beatles, 4, 14
   songs played by the Beatles, 253
   "Yesterday" sung by, 265, 316

Press to Play (McCartney), 298
Preston, Billy, 257, 261, 278
"Pretty Polly" (folk song), 31
Pretty Things, the, 175
Price, Alan, 120
"Price of Love, The" (Everly Brothers), 120
Prince, 297, 302
Prince, Viv, 175
Psychedelic Experience, The (Leary, Alpert, and Metzner, 1964), 175

Quarry Men, the, xvi, 19, 20, 21, 24
Queen, 201
"Quinn the Eskimo (The Mighty Quinn)" (Dylan), 223, 236, 254, 270, 287

radio stations, 31, 47
Radio Unnameable (WBAI show), 170
ragas, Indian, 180
"Rain" (Beatles), 175, 252, 307
"Rainy Day Women #12 & 35" (Dylan), 175–76, 188, 189, 204, 258, 300
Ram (McCartney), xvi, 275
Rambling Boys, The (Adams and Ramblin' Jack Elliott, 1958), 122
Ramblin' Jack Elliott (Elliott Adnopoz), 23, 72, 75, 76, 99, 122, 235
Ramsden, Mike, 142
"Ready Teddy" (Little Richard), 14
Reagan, Ronald, 297
Reagon, Bernice Johnson, 56
Record Mirror, 196
Record Plant (Manhattan studio), 277, 284
Redding, Otis, 165, 260
Red Mole (Marxist newspaper), 276
"Respect" (Redding), 165
"Revolution" (Beatles), 242
"Revolution 9" (Beatles), 244, 273
Revolver (Beatles), xiv, 174–76, 179, 189, 192, 198, 230
   chart position of, 212
   reviews of, 209–10
rhythm and blues, 13, 16, 31, 33, 55, 92, 160

songwriters' turn away from, 133
    white singers and Black originators, 101
Richard, Cliff, 49
Richards, Keith, 74, 122, 141, 148, 149, 179, 243
Richie, Lionel, 298
Richter, Dan, 131, 262–63, 265, 269, 278
Rickles, Don, 60
"Riding to Vanity Fair" (McCartney), 315
"Rikki Don't Lose That Number" (Steely Dan), xiii
Riley, John, 115
"Ringo, I Love You (Yeah, Yeah, Yeah)" (Cher/"Bonnie Jo Mason"), 104
"Rip It Up" (Little Richard), 14
Robertson, Robbie, 157, 169, 170, 177, 179, 197, 222
    in Dylan's band, 154, 169
    as member of the Hawks, 154–55
    Music from Big Pink and, 246, 247
Robinson, Smokey, 61, 110, 265
Rock & Roll Hall of Fame, 301
"Rock Around the Clock" (Bill Haley and His Comets), 121
Rock Liberation Front, 280
rock 'n' roll, 11, 15, 16, 72, 139, 212, 258
    4/4 meter of, 100
    Beatles as destroyers of, 230
    beat music as alternative name for, 20
    birthplace of, 49
    diluted for British hit parade, 32
    resurgence of, 46
Rock 'n' Roll (Lennon), 17
"Rocky Raccoon" (Beatles), 237, 242
Rolling Stone magazine, 234, 276
Rolling Stones, the, 74, 120, 122, 141, 145, 184, 311
    Dylan's dislike of, 177
    manager's marketing strategy, 147
    songs played by the Beatles, 254
    at the Warwick Hotel meeting, 315
"Roll On John" (Dylan), xvi, 308–10, 314–15

Ronettes, the, 33, 61, 109, 145
Rorem, Ned, 229
Rory Storm and the Hurricanes, 20
Ross, Diana, 201
Ross, Scott, 145, 147
Rothchild, Paul, 68
Rotolo, Carla, 48, 72
Rotolo, Suze, 25–26, 35, 51, 53, 139, 176
    on Dylan's friends and companions, 53
    Dylan's meeting with the Beatles and, 88, 89
    early admiration for the Beatles, 48
    final breakup with Dylan, 72
    on *Freewheelin' Bob Dylan* cover, 38–39, 40, 50
    on impact of Beatles in America, 57
    political activism of, 88–89
    relationship with Dylan, 39–40, 42, 47
Royal Albert Hall (London), xiv, 124, 125, 128, 178, 188, 310
    Dylan's performance at, 195–97, 314
    International Poetry Incarnation, 131, 262
    mentioned in "A Day in the Life," 221
    Tiny Tim at, 250
Royal Festival Hall (London), 70
Rubber Soul (Beatles, 1965), 168–69, 170, 177
Rubin, Jerry, 282
Run-DMC, 297
Rushes (The Fireman [McCartney]), 305
Russell, Leon, 278, 279

"Sad-Eyed Lady of the Lowlands" (Dylan), 175, 237, 284
Sadler, Barry, 171, 193
Sam the Sham and the Pharaohs, 139
Sandburg, Carl, 54
"San Francisco (Be Sure to Wear Some Flowers in Your Hair)" (McKenzie), 230
Saturday Night Live, 291, 296

Saville, Philip, 27–28, 29
Savoy Hotel (London), 118–19, 122, 129
Scaduto, Anthony, 61, 281
Schonfield, Hugh J., 198
Schwartz, Francie, 241, 251
"Scrambled Eggs" (McCartney), 105, 106
Seaman, Fred, 291, 292
Secombe, Harry, 64
Sedgwick, Edie, 136
Seeger, Peggy, 30, 31
Seeger, Pete, 30, 235
Self Portrait (Dylan album, 1970), 274
Self-Portrait (Lennon's penis film), 271
Sellers, Peter, 64, 98, 243
Sgt. Pepper's Lonely Hearts Club Band (Beatles), xii, 220–21, 225–26, 239, 256
   album cover art, 228
   John Wesley Harding compared to, 234–35
   Lennon's regret for, 246
   reviews of, 229–30
"Serve Yourself" (Lennon), 291, 292–93
Shankar, Ravi, 99, 203, 218, 219, 260, 278, 279
Shaved Fish (Lennon), xiii
"She Belongs to Me" (Dylan), 186, 196
"She Loves You" (Beatles), 45, 47, 56, 61, 62, 65, 66, 141
Shelton, Robert, 25, 53, 75, 141, 155, 176–78
"She Said She Said" (Beatles), 175
"She's Leaving Home" (Beatles), 229
"Shop Around" (Miracles), 198
Shotton, Pete, 20, 21, 23, 44, 108, 110, 132, 232
   contribution to "Eleanor Rigby," 174
   on relationship of George and John, 116
Siegel, Jules, 204
Silber, Irwin, 94
Silkie, the, 142, 194

Silkie Sing the Songs of Bob Dylan, The (The Silkie), 143, 194
"Silly Love Songs" (Wings), xiii, 288
Simon, Carly, 204
Simon, Paul, 271
Simon and Garfunkel, 140
Simone, Nina, 177
Sinatra, Frank, xvii, 201, 236, 265
Sinclair, John, 276
Singers Club, 30–31
Sing Out! (folk music magazine), 29, 94–95, 100, 162, 245
"Sledgehammer" (Gabriel), 301, 304
"Slippin' and Slidin'" (Little Richard), 14
Sloan, P. F., 141
"Slow Down" (Williams), 126
Slow Train Coming (Dylan album), 290
"Slow Train Coming" (Dylan song), 290
Sly and the Family Stone, 258
Smith, George, 2, 3
Smith, Mary Stanley (Mimi), 2–3, 4–5
"Something" (Beatles), 265, 276, 301
Some Time in New York City (Lennon and Ono), 282
Sonny and Cher, 141, 157
Sonny Boy Williamson, 190
"Sounds of Silence, The" (Simon and Garfunkel), 140
Sounes, Howard, 206
Spain, Dave, 184
Spaniard in the Works, A (Lennon), 134
"Spanish Harlem Incident" (Dylan), 103
Spector, Phil, 54, 55, 104, 109, 274, 276, 286
Springsteen, Bruce, 298, 302
Star-Club (Hamburg, Germany), 16, 17
Starkey, Maureen Cox (first wife of Ringo), 69, 127, 217, 220, 243
   at ashram in India, 236, 238
   at Isle of Wight Festival, 269, 270
Starr, Ringo (Richard Starkey), xi, xii, xv, xvii, 11, 33, 110

at ashram in India, 236, 238
Bangladesh benefit concert and,
    278, 279
on Beatles' American tour (1964),
    54–57
collaboration with Dylan, 304–5
drinking and drugs given up by, 305
drum playing of, 78, 307
family of, 217
interaction with young fans, 83–84
at Isle of Wight Festival, 269, 270
as replacement for Pete Best, 184
as singer, 50
Sunny Heights home, 219, 257
Top 10 hits after the Beatles, 286
White Album sessions and, 243
Steely Dan, xiii
Steinbeck, John, 64
Steinem, Gloria, 91–92
Stewart, Dave, 302, 304
Stewart, Rod, 288
Stoller, Mike, 160
Strawberry Field (Liverpool), 1, 6, 20,
    215–16, 218
"Strawberry Fields Forever" (Lennon),
    216–17, 219–20, 221, 222, 270, 292
    chart position of, 225
    Upanishads influence in, 232
"Street Rock" (Dylan and Blow, 1986), xvi
Strong, Eileen, 94, 95
Stroud, Rev. Jimmy, 211
"Stuck Inside of Mobile with the
    Memphis Blues Again" (Dylan),
    255, 289
"Subterranean Homesick Blues"
    (Dylan), 102, 113, 128, 135, 136,
    142, 289
    in *Don't Look Back* film, 124
    "Too Much Monkey Business" as
        influence on, 101
Sullivan, Ed, 56, 148
"Sunday Bloody Sunday" (Lennon), 282
Sunday Night at the London Palladium
    (ITV program), 45, 105
Sun Ra, 100

Sun Records, 101, 160
Supremes, the, 98, 177, 315
Sutcliffe, Stuart, 15, 19–20, 21, 96
Sweetheart of the Rodeo (Byrds), 260
Sweet Honey in the Rock, 56
Swinging London fashions, 37

Tackett, Fred, 296
Taj Mahal, 298
"Take Good Care of My Baby" (Goffin
    and King), 144
"Talking with Jesus" (Lennon), 289
"Talkin' John Birch Paranoid Blues"
    (Dylan), 41
"Talkin' New York" (Dylan), 50
Talley, Nedra, 145
Tarantula (Dylan, 1971), 69, 176, 197, 204,
    207
"Taxman" (Beatles), 175
Taylor, Cecil, 100
Taylor, Derek, 76, 92, 98, 241, 274
"Tears of Rage" (Dylan and Manuel), xv,
    224, 246
"Teddy Boy" (McCartney), 242
"Tell Me, Momma" (Dylan), 187, 196
Tempest (Dylan, 2012), 309
Thaler, Edward, 206
Thaler, Selma, 214
Thatcher, Margaret, 297
"That'll Be the Day" (Holly), 4
Them, 123
Theme Time Radio Hour series (Dylan),
    307–8
"There's a Place" (Beatles), 66, 175
"Things We Said Today" (Beatles), 69,
    77, 316
"Thingumybob" (McCartney), 240, 248,
    255, 313
Thirty-Three & ⅓ (Harrison), xiii
This Is Not Here (Ono, art exhibition),
    280–81
"This Land Is Your Land" (Guthrie,
    1940), 160, 242
"This Wheel's on Fire" (Dylan and
    Danko), 223, 246

Thomas, Rufus, 160
Thompson, Toby, 259
Thorne, Ken, 143
Thurmond, Strom, 282
"Ticket to Ride" (Beatles), 108, 109, 147
"Till There Was You" (Willson), 56
Times They Are A-Changin,' The (Dylan album), 48–49, 51, 53, 75, 85, 100
    moralism of, 248
    position on British album chart, 117
"Times They Are A-Changin,' The" (Dylan song), xvii, 52, 70, 117, 127, 165
Tin Pan Alley, 177
Tiny Tim, 222–23, 239–40, 246, 249–50
"Tiptoe Through the Tulips" (Tiny Tim remake of 1929 song), 239
"Tomorrow Is a Long Time" (Dylan), 39, 306
"Tomorrow Never Knows" (Beatles), 175, 180, 244
Tom Petty and the Heartbreakers, 299
Tony Pastor's Downtown (New York), 27–28
"Too Much Monkey Business" (Berry), 101, 289
"To Ramona" (Dylan), 75
Tornabene, Nina, 239
Toronto Rock 'n' Roll Revival (1969), 272
Transcendental Meditation movement, 231
Traum, Artie, 249
Traum, Happy, 245, 249
Traveling Wilburys, xv, 298, 301, 302, 317
Traveling Wilburys Vol. 1 (1988), 303
Troubadour club (London), 33, 35, 119
Tuft, Harry, 79
Tug of War (McCartney, 1982), 296
Turner, Big Joe, 18, 50
Turtles, the, 140
"Tutti Frutti" (Little Richard), 15, 16, 17
"Tweeter and the Monkey Man" (Traveling Wilburys), 302
"Twenty Flight Rock" (Cochran), 21
Twickenham Film Studios, 113, 114, 131, 252, 254
    Beatles documentaries filmed at, 252–53
    Help! filmed at, 120
    "Hey Jude" film made at, 242
"Twist, The" (Hank Ballard and the Midnighters), 55
Twist and Shout (Beatles), 36
"Twist and Shout" (Medley and Berns), 135, 148, 258, 281
"Two of Us" (Beatles), 255, 256
2001: A Space Odyssey (film, dir. Kubrick, 1968), 262–63
Tyler, Tony, 195–96

UFO club (London), 220
"Uncle Albert/Admiral Halsey" (McCartney), 277, 281
"Under the Red Sky" (Dylan, 1990), 8
Unfinished Music No. 1: Two Virgins (Ono and Lennon), 257
Unfinished Paintings (Ono), 216
Unger, Arthur, 200, 208, 209
United Artists, 108

Valens, Ritchie, 134
Vallée, Rudy, 222
Van Halen, 297
Van Ronk, Dave, 23, 26, 161
vaudeville, 33, 152
Vaughn, Sarah, 277
Vedder, Eddie, 277
Vietnam War, 118, 148, 170, 178, 208
    Beatles' opposition to, 201
    "Bed-in for Peace" to protest, 261
    escalation of, 129, 244
    Gulf of Tonkin resolution, 89
Village Voice, The, 113, 155, 204, 283
Vincent, Gene, 14, 102
Vincent Gene, 12
Vivekananda, Swami, 219
Von Schmidt, Eric, 33–34
Voormann, Klaus, 115, 272, 281

Wald, Elijah, 23, 75, 230
"Walking on Thin Ice" (Ono), 294
Waller, Fats, 65
Walls and Bridges (Lennon), 287
Ward, Gollins Melvin, 37
Warhol, Andy, 136
"Watching the River Flow" (Dylan), 285, 298
"Watch Your Step" (Parker, 1961), 92, 139
Weberman, A. J., 275–76, 278, 280, 281, 283
"We Can Work It Out" (Beatles), 167
Wednesday Morning, 3 AM (Simon and Garfunkel), 140
"Weight, The" (Robertson), 246, 249
Weiss, Nat, 212, 239, 249
Wells, Mary, 98
Wexler, Jerry, 290
"What'd I Say" (Charles), 33, 137
"Whatever Gets You Thru the Night" (Lennon), 17, 287
"What Kind of Friend Is This" (Dylan), 187
"What You're Doing" (Beatles), 91
Wheatstraw, Peetie, 191
"When I'm Sixty-Four" (McCartney), 26, 220, 221
"When I Paint My Masterpiece" (Dylan), 285
"When the Deal Goes Down" (Dylan), 305
"When We Was Fab" (Harrison), 300
"Where Did Our Love Go" (Supremes), 98
"While My Guitar Gently Weeps" (Harrison), 242, 244
White, Andy, 272
White, Barry, xiii
White, Kristin, 162
White Album [*The Beatles*] (Beatles, 1968), 236, 242–44, 246, 247, 251, 252, 283
Who, the, 260, 311

"Who's Gonna Buy Your Ribbons (When I'm Gone)" (Clayton), 53
"Why Can't We Be Friends?" (War, 1975), 308
Wilde, Oscar, 106, 228
Wilentz, Sean, 40–41
Williams, Hank, 123, 233, 254
Williams, Larry, 14, 126, 253
Willson, Meredith, 56
Wilson, Tom, 100–101, 117, 120–21, 128, 135, 136
"Winchester Cathedral" (New Vaudeville Band, 1966), 220, 222
"With God on Our Side" (Dylan), 71, 129
"Within You Without You" (Harrison), 226
With the Beatles (Beatles, 1963), 160
Wonder, Stevie, 17, 277, 283
Woodstock Music and Art Fair (1969), 261, 266
Wooler, Bob, 25, 45
"Wooly Bully" (Sam the Sham and the Pharaohs), 139
"Word, The" (Beatles), 164–65, 173
World Pacific Studios (Los Angeles), 99, 103

Yarrow, Peter, 40
Yarrow, Vera, 40
"Yellow Submarine" (Beatles), 189, 240
"Yer Blues" (Beatles), xvi, 237
"Yesterday" (Beatles), 130–35, 162, 174, 216, 265, 276
  composition process of, 318
  as a contemporary standard, 177
  Dylan's performance of, 274, 275, 316
  as everybody's song, 242
  Lennon's performance of, 281
You Are What You Eat (film), 222
"You Like Me Too Much" (Beatles), 114
"You Never Give Me Your Money" (Beatles), 263

Young, Neil, 285
"Young But Daily Growing" (Scottish folk song), 123
"You Really Got Me" (Kinks), 98, 108
"You're Sixteen" (Starr), 286
"You've Got to Hide Your Love Away" (Beatles), 109–10, 114, 133, 141
"You Won't See Me" (Beatles), 167

Zanzinger, William, 70, 71
Zimmerman, Abraham (father of Bob Dylan), 9–10, 42–43, 147, 245
Zimmerman, Beatrice Stone [Beatty] (mother of Bob Dylan), 9–10, 230, 245, 259–60
Zimmerman, Robert Allen
See Dylan, Bob

About the Author

Jim Windolf is a features editor at *The New York Times*. He has published articles, reviews, essays, and humor pieces in *Vanity Fair*, *The New Yorker*, *New York* magazine, *Rolling Stone*, and other publications. Additionally, his short fiction has appeared in *Ontario Review*, *3:AM Magazine*, *Puerto del Sol*, and other literary journals. He lives in New York City.